T0198166

Get the eBook FREE!

(PDF, ePub, Kindle, and liveBook all included)

We believe that once you buy a book from us, you should be able to read it in any format we have available. To get electronic versions of this book at no additional cost to you, purchase and then register this book at the Manning website.

Go to https://www.manning.com/freebook and follow the instructions to complete your pBook registration.

That's it!
Thanks from Manning!

Redis in Action

JOSIAH L. CARLSON

MANNING
Shelter Island

For online information and ordering of this and other Manning books, please visit
www.manning.com. The publisher offers discounts on this book when ordered in quantity.
For more information, please contact

    Special Sales Department
    Manning Publications Co.
    20 Baldwin Road
    PO Box 261
    Shelter Island, NY 11964
    Email: orders@manning.com

Manning Publications Co.
20 Baldwin Road
PO Box 261
Shelter Island, NY 11964

Development editor:	Elizabeth Lexleigh
Technical proofreaders:	James Philips, Kevin Chang, and Nicholas Lindgren
Java translator:	Eric Van Dewoestine
Copyeditor:	Benjamin Berg
Proofreader:	Katie Tennant
Typesetter:	Gordan Salinovic
Cover designer:	Marija Tudor

ISBN 9781617290855

Printed in the United States of America

To my dear wife, See Luan,
and to our baby girl, Mikela

brief contents

contents

foreword

Redis was created about three years ago for practical reasons: basically, I was trying to do the impossible with an on-disk SQL database. I was handling a large write-heavy load with the only hardware I was able to afford—a little virtualized instance.

My problem was conceptually simple: my server was receiving a stream of page views from multiple websites using a small JavaScript tracker. I needed to store the latest *n* page views for every site and show them in real time to users connected to a web interface, while maintaining a small history.

With a peak load of a few thousand page views per second, whatever my database schema was, and whatever trade-offs I was willing to pick, there was no way for my SQL store to handle the load with such poor hardware. My inability to upgrade the hardware for cost concerns coupled with the feeling that to handle a capped list of values shouldn't have been so hard, after all, gave me the idea of creating a throw-away prototype of an in-memory data store that could handle lists as a native data type, with constant-time pop and push operations on both sides of the lists. To make a long story short, the concept worked, I rewrote the first prototype using the C language, added a fork-based persistence feature, and Redis was born.

Fast-forward to the present. After three years, the project has evolved in significant ways. We have a more robust system now, and with Redis 2.6 just released and the major work in progress being cluster and HA features, Redis is entering its maturity period. One of the most remarkable advancements in the Redis ecosystem, in my opinion, is its community of users and contributors, from the redis.io website to the Redis Google Group. Stemming from the GitHub issues system, there are thousands of people involved in the project, writing client libraries, contributing fixes, and helping other users.

Redis is still a community project: it's BSD licensed. There are no closed source add-ons or enhanced versions you need to pay for. The reference documentation is as accurate as possible, and it's extremely easy to get help and get in touch with Redis developers or experts.

Redis started in a pragmatic way, with a programmer who needed to get things done and couldn't find the right tool for the tasks at hand. This is why I think a theoretical book wouldn't serve Redis well, and why I like *Redis in Action:* it's a book for people that want to get things done. It doesn't limit itself to a sterile description of the API; Redis features and data types are explored in depth using compelling examples.

At the same time, *Redis in Action* comes from the Redis community, and more specifically from someone who, before publishing this book, has already helped hundreds of Redis users in many different ways—from schema designs to hardware latency issues. The Redis Group is full of Josiah's advice and contributions.

The fact that system operation topics are also covered is a big plus. The reality is that most people need to both develop the application software and handle the deployment of the server. And I'd say that you need to understand system operations and the fundamental limits of the hardware and the system software you're using in order to write an application that makes the best use of both.

The result of these efforts is a book that will get you into Redis in a direct way, pointing your attention in the right directions to avoid common pitfalls. I think *Redis in Action* is a great addition to the Redis ecosystem and will be welcomed by the community of Redis users.

SALVATORE SANFILIPPO
CREATOR OF REDIS

preface

In March of 2010 I began working in Beverly Hills with Chris Testa, a friend I'd met while at Google in Santa Monica. He had hired me to be the architect of a small startup that he was team lead/director for; I was to be the research branch.

While talking one afternoon about how to solve an unrelated problem, Chris mentioned Redis as a database that I might find interesting (given my education in theoretical computer science). Several weeks later, after using and patching Redis for our purposes, I started participating on the mailing list, offering advice and a patch or two.

As time went on, I used Redis for a wider variety of projects at our startup: searching, an ad targeting engine, a Twitter analytics engine, and many pieces to connect the different parts of our infrastructure. Each project forced me to learn more about Redis. And as I saw others on the mailing list using Redis, asking questions, I couldn't help but offer more and more advice (my all-time favorite was actually a job-search problem, which became section 7.4), becoming one of the most prolific posters on the Redis mailing list.

In late September 2011, while on my honeymoon in Paris, I received a call from a Manning Publications acquisitions editor named Michael Stephens. I didn't receive the call immediately, because my phone doesn't work outside the United States. And due to bugs in my phone's firmware, I didn't even receive the message until the second week of October.

When I finally got the message and spoke to Michael, I learned that someone at Manning had decided that it was about time to publish *Redis in Action*. After reading the relevant mailing lists and asking around for suggestions as to who should write the book, my name came up. Luckily, Manning was still taking book proposals when I called.

After a few weeks of discussions and a few book proposal revisions (primarily resulting from farming several dozen of my past Redis mailing list advice posts), Manning accepted my proposal, and I started writing. It's now around 17 months since I first spoke with Michael, and *Redis in Action* is essentially complete, missing only a few details that I'm finishing up now. I've spent a full year of evenings and weekends producing a book to help others understand and utilize one of the most interesting technologies I've come across—more interesting than almost anything I've run into since the day I sat down at my family's first computer, 20 years ago this past Christmas.

My only regret in all of this is not having had the foresight to invent Redis in the first place. But at least I had the opportunity to write the book on it!

acknowledgments

I thank my editor at Manning, Beth Lexleigh, for her help throughout the writing process: your patience and gentle pushes have kept me on track.

I also thank my development editor Bert Bates: thank you for pointing out that my writing style needed to change for a book audience. Your influence on my writing early on continued during my work on the entire book, which I hope is reasonably accessible to readers with a wide range of expertise.

Thank you, Salvatore Sanfilippo: without you, there would be no Redis, and no one would be reading this. And a huge thank you for writing the foreword on such short notice.

Thank you, Pieter Noordhuis: in addition to working on Redis, you shared several drinks with me during RedisConf 2012 while listening to my ideas on Redis data structure layouts. Even if none of them happen (which is likely), it was great getting a chance to meet and talk about Redis internals.

A huge thank you goes to my technical proofreading team (in alphabetical order by first name): James Phillips, Kevin Chang, and Nicholas Lindgren. You helped when I needed help, and through your collective efforts, *Redis in Action* has been polished even further.

Thank you, my friend and colleague Eric Van Dewoestine: you took the time to write Java versions of examples from the book, which are available at GitHub: https://github.com/josiahcarlson/redis-in-action.

Thank you, all of my reviewers, for the first, second, and third reviews of my manuscript during development, and to my final QA reviewer. I tried to take all of your advice into consideration whenever I could. Thanks to Amit Nandi, Bennett Andrews, Bobby Abraham, Brian Forester, Brian Gyss, Brian McNamara, Daniel Sundman, David Miller, Felipe Gutierrez, Filippo Pacini, Gerard O' Sullivan, JC Pretorius, Jonathan Crawley, Joshua White, Leo Cassarani, Mark Wigmans, Richard Clayton, Scott Lyons, Thomas O'Rourke, and Todd Fiala

Thank you, those who offered feedback in the Manning *Redis in Action* Author Online forum; your eyes caught some errors that were hiding from us.

And most of all, I want to say thank you to my wife, See Luan, who graciously allowed me to spend countless evenings and weekends over the last year and a half writing the manuscript that you're now reading—evenings and weekends when she suffered through the discomfort and hard work of pregnancy and, more recently, of caring for our newborn daughter as I worked on final edits.

And one final thank you goes to my family and friends, who have been patient with me when I've been far too busy working on this book.

about this book

This book covers the use of Redis, an in-memory database/data structure server, originally written by Salvatore Sanfilippo, but recently patched through the open source process. Though you don't necessarily need to know anything about Redis, to get the most out of this book you should have at least a modest familiarity with the Python programming language, since almost all of the examples use Python to interact with Redis.

You can learn enough about Python by going through the Python language tutorial for Python 2.7.x and reading the Python documentation for certain syntactical constructs when I mention them. Though source code listings will be translated to Java, JavaScript, and Ruby in time, they may not be as clear or concise as the code already listed. And they may not even be available in time for the print edition of *Redis in Action*.

If you don't already have experience with Redis, you should at least read chapters 1 and 2 before reading any other chapter (except for appendix A, which includes the basic installation instructions). The first couple chapters will give you an idea of what Redis is, what it does, and why you might want to use it. From there, chapter 3 is an introduction to what each structure can do and the general concepts around them, and chapter 4 is about Redis administration and making choices about data persistence.

If you already have experience with Redis, you can go ahead and skip chapters 1 and 3—they're primarily introduction-level topics for people who don't know what Redis is or what it does. Though chapter 2 is at the same level, it introduces a style used throughout the rest of the book: show a problem, solve the problem, revisit the problem later to improve it, and point out that there are even better solutions if you keep thinking about it.

When we revisit a topic, I mention where we first discussed the topic or problem. Not all of the topics require that you've read the earlier section to understand what's going on, but trust me when I say that you'll get much more out of the section talking about improving a solution X from a previous section Y if you read and remember the content from Y. This will help you to recognize examples in your own code where you can make similar improvements. But this recognition gets a lot harder if you don't understand the earlier example.

If while reading a topic you think to yourself, "There's a (better/faster/simpler) method to solve this problem," great! Few of the solutions listed in this book are necessarily the "best" solution to a particular problem in Redis (or otherwise). The examples chosen are meant to get you thinking about solving a class of problems, and building solutions to problems in both intuitive and non-intuitive ways.

Remember that if you have difficulty understanding an example or how it works, the source code for each chapter includes a test runner, which offers example uses of almost every function and method defined in that chapter (including solutions to most of the exercises).

Roadmap

This book is divided into three parts. Part 1 introduces the basics of what Redis is and some examples of its use. Part 2 begins with documentation about many of the commands available in Redis, and then grows to encompass Redis administration and ever more expansive application components that Redis can support. Part 3 completes the content with methods to help you scale Redis using memory-saving techniques, horizontal sharding, and Lua scripting.

Chapter 1 is a basic introduction to what Redis is. It introduces the five data structures that are available in Redis, compares Redis to other databases, and implements a simple article aggregation site that allows voting on submitted articles.

Chapter 2 picks up the pace a little bit, where we use Redis to improve application performance and offer some basic web analytics. If you have little-to-no background with Redis, you may want to start with chapter 2 to understand why Redis has become so popular in recent years (simplicity and performance).

Chapter 3 is mostly a command reference with examples of almost all of the commonly used commands, including basic transactions, sorting, and expiring keys.

Chapter 4 combines the concepts of data persistence, performance, failure recovery, and data loss protection. While some sections are primarily geared toward the systems administration side of things, sections 4.4 and 4.5 discuss Redis transactions and pipelined command performance in depth, which is a must-read for beginner and intermediate Redis users, as we revisit the problem introduced in 4.4 later in the book.

Chapter 5 is where we discuss Redis as a database for supporting logging, counters, IP-address-to-location lookup, and other service configuration.

In chapter 6, I introduce components that are very useful when dealing with growing applications, including autocomplete, locking, task queues, messaging, and even file distribution.

Through chapter 7, I introduce and deeply examine a class of search-based problems and solutions that can change the way you think about data querying and filtering.

Chapter 8 goes in depth into the construction of a full Twitter-like social network, and includes implementations for the entire back end, including a streaming API.

Chapter 9 discusses the major techniques for reducing memory use when using Redis at scale, including structure sharding and the use of short structures.

Chapter 10 discusses the horizontal sharding and slaving of Redis to offer greater performance and access to more memory when a single Redis server can't sustain your needs.

Chapter 11 discusses the use of Lua scripting as a server-side method of extending Redis functionality, and in some cases as a way of improving performance.

Appendix A primarily discusses basic installation of Redis, Python, and the Redis client library for Python in Linux, OS X, and Windows.

Appendix B is a reference to various other resources that might be useful when using Redis. It includes documentation references to some Python language constructs that we use, references to other examples of Redis being used, third-party libraries for using Redis for a variety of tasks, and more.

Code conventions and downloads

All source code in listings or in text is in a `fixed-width font like this` to separate it from ordinary text. Code annotations accompany many of the listings, highlighting important concepts. In some cases, numbered bullets link to explanations that follow the listing.

You can download the source code for all listings from the Manning website, www.manning.com/RedisinAction. If you would like to see translations into other programming languages or would like to browse the Python source code online, you can find the source code in the GitHub repository, https://github.com/josiahcarlson/redis-in-action.

Author Online

The purchase of *Redis in Action* includes free access to a private web forum run by Manning Publications, where you can make comments about the book, ask technical questions, and receive help from the author and from other users. To access the forum and subscribe to it, point your web browser to www.manning.com/RedisinAction. This page provides information on how to get on the forum once you are registered, what kind of help is available, and the rules of conduct on the forum.

Manning's commitment to our readers is to provide a venue where a meaningful dialogue between individual readers and between readers and the author can take place. It is not a commitment to any specific amount of participation on the part of the author, whose contribution to the forum remains voluntary (and unpaid). We suggest you try asking the author some challenging questions lest his interest stray!

The author online forum and the archives of previous discussions will be accessible from the publisher's website as long as the book is in print.

About the author

After graduating college, Dr. Josiah Carlson continued his education at UC Irvine, where he studied theoretical computer science. While applying theory in his spare time, he worked on and off as a teaching assistant, taking up occasional contract programming positions. Near the end of his graduate school career, Josiah found academic positions rare, so he started his professional career at Networks in Motion, where he worked on real-time GPS navigation software and a traffic incident notification system.

Since leaving Networks in Motion, Josiah has worked for Google, and then later for Adly, where he first learned about and began using Redis for content-targeting advertising and Twitter analytics platforms. Several months later, Josiah was a regular participant on the Redis mailing list, where he answered hundreds of questions about using and configuring Redis. Shortly after leaving Adly for ChowNow, where Josiah acts as Chief Architect and cofounder, he began working on *Redis in Action*, which you are now reading.

about the cover illustration

The figure on the cover of *Redis in Action* is captioned "A Man of the People." The illustration is taken from a nineteenth-century edition of Sylvain Maréchal's four-volume compendium of regional dress customs published in France. Each illustration is finely drawn and colored by hand. The rich variety of Maréchal's collection reminds us vividly of how culturally apart the world's towns and regions were just 200 years ago. Isolated from each other, people spoke different dialects and languages. On the streets or in the countryside, it was easy to identify where they lived and what their trade or station in life was just by their dress.

Dress codes have changed since then and the diversity by region, so rich at the time, has faded away. It is now hard to tell apart the inhabitants of different continents, let alone different towns or regions. Perhaps we have traded cultural diversity for a more varied personal life—certainly for a more varied and fast-paced technological life.

At a time when it is hard to tell one computer book from another, Manning celebrates the inventiveness and initiative of the computer business with book covers based on the rich diversity of regional life of two centuries ago, brought back to life by Maréchal's pictures.

Part 1

Getting started

These first two chapters are an introduction to Redis and offer some basic use cases for Redis. After reading these chapters, you should start to get a sense for some low-hanging optimizations that Redis might be well suited for in your current projects.

Getting to know Redis

This chapter covers

- How Redis is like and unlike other software you've used
- How to use Redis
- Simple interactions with Redis using example Python code
- Solving real problems with Redis

Redis is an in-memory remote database that offers high performance, replication, and a unique data model to produce a platform for solving problems. By supporting five different types of data structures, Redis accommodates a wide variety of problems that can be naturally mapped into what Redis offers, allowing you to solve your problems without having to perform the conceptual gymnastics required by other databases. Additional features like replication, persistence, and client-side sharding allow Redis to scale from a convenient way to prototype a system, all the way up to hundreds of gigabytes of data and millions of requests per second.

My first experience with Redis was at a company that needed to search a database of client contacts. The search needed to find contacts by name, email address, location, and phone number. The system was written to use a SQL database that performed a series of queries that would take 10–15 seconds to find matches among 60,000 clients. After spending a week learning the basics of what was available in Redis, I built a search engine that could filter and sort on all of those fields and more, returning responses within 50 milliseconds. In just a few weeks of effort involving testing and making the system production-worthy, performance improved 200 times. By reading this book, you can learn about many of the tips, tricks, and well-known problems that have been solved using Redis.

This chapter will help you to understand where Redis fits within the world of databases, and how Redis is useful for solving problems in multiple contexts (communicating between different components and languages, and more). Remaining chapters will show a variety of problems and their solutions using Redis.

Now that you know a bit about how I started using Redis and what we'll cover, let's talk more about what Redis is, and how it's probably something you've always needed, even though you didn't realize it.

INSTALLING REDIS AND PYTHON   Look in appendix A for quick and dirty installation instructions for both Redis and Python.

USING REDIS FROM OTHER LANGUAGES   Though not included in this book, source code for all examples possible will be provided in Ruby, Java, and JavaScript (Node.js) shortly after all chapters have been completed. For users of the Spring framework, the author of Spring Data's Redis interface, Costin Leau, has teamed up with Redis author Salvatore Sanfilippo to produce a one-hour introduction for using Spring with Redis available at http://www.springsource.org/spring-data/redis.

1.1   What is Redis?

When I say that Redis is a database, I'm only telling a partial truth. Redis is a very fast non-relational database that stores a mapping of keys to five different types of values. Redis supports in-memory persistent storage on disk, replication to scale read performance, and client-side sharding[1] to scale write performance. That was a mouthful, but I'll break it down by parts.

1.1.1   Redis compared to other databases and software

If you're familiar with relational databases, you'll no doubt have written SQL queries to relate data between tables. Redis is a type of database that's commonly referred to as *NoSQL* or *non-relational*. In Redis, there are no tables, and there's no database-defined or -enforced way of relating data in Redis with other data in Redis.

It's not uncommon to hear Redis compared to memcached, which is a very high-performance, key-value cache server. Like memcached, Redis can also store a mapping

---

[1] Sharding is a method by which you partition your data into different pieces. In this case, you partition your data based on IDs embedded in the keys, based on the hash of keys, or some combination of the two. Through partitioning your data, you can store and fetch the data from multiple machines, which can allow a linear scaling in performance for certain problem domains.

of keys to values and can even achieve similar performance levels as memcached. But the similarities end quickly—Redis supports the writing of its data to disk automatically in two different ways, and can store data in four structures in addition to plain string keys as memcached does. These and other differences allow Redis to solve a wider range of problems, and allow Redis to be used either as a primary database or as an auxiliary database with other storage systems.

In later chapters, we'll cover examples that show Redis being used for both a primary and a secondary storage medium for data, supporting a variety of use cases and query patterns. Generally speaking, many Redis users will choose to store data in Redis only when the performance or functionality of Redis is necessary, using other relational or non-relational data storage for data where slower performance is acceptable, or where data is too large to fit in memory economically. In practice, you'll use your judgment as to where you want your data to be stored (primarily in Redis, or primarily somewhere else with a copy in Redis), how to ensure data integrity (replication, durability, and transactions), and whether Redis will fit your needs.

To get an idea of how Redis fits among the variety of database and cache software available, you can see an incomplete listing of a few different types of cache or database servers that Redis's functionality overlaps in table 1.1.

Table 1.1 Features and functionality of some databases and cache servers

Name	Type	Data storage options	Query types	Additional features
Redis	In-memory non-relational database	Strings, lists, sets, hashes, sorted sets	Commands for each data type for common access patterns, with bulk operations, and partial transaction support	Publish/Subscribe, master/slave replication, disk persistence, scripting (stored procedures)
memcached	In-memory key-value cache	Mapping of keys to values	Commands for create, read, update, delete, and a few others	Multithreaded server for additional performance
MySQL	Relational database	Databases of tables of rows, views over tables, spatial and third-party extensions	`SELECT, INSERT, UPDATE, DELETE,` functions, stored procedures	ACID compliant (with InnoDB), master/slave and master/master replication
PostgreSQL	Relational database	Databases of tables of rows, views over tables, spatial and third-party extensions, customizable types	`SELECT, INSERT, UPDATE, DELETE,` built-in functions, custom stored procedures	ACID compliant, master/slave replication, multi-master replication (third party)
MongoDB	On-disk non-relational document store	Databases of tables of schema-less BSON documents	Commands for create, read, update, delete, conditional queries, and more	Supports map-reduce operations, master/slave replication, sharding, spatial indexes

1.1.2   *Other features*

When using an in-memory database like Redis, one of the first questions that's asked is "What happens when my server gets turned off?" Redis has two different forms of persistence available for writing in-memory data to disk in a compact format. The first method is a point-in-time dump either when certain conditions are met (a number of writes in a given period) or when one of the two dump-to-disk commands is called. The other method uses an append-only file that writes every command that alters data in Redis to disk as it happens. Depending on how careful you want to be with your data, append-only writing can be configured to never sync, sync once per second, or sync at the completion of every operation. We'll discuss these persistence options in more depth in chapter 4.

Even though Redis is able to perform well, due to its in-memory design there are situations where you may need Redis to process more read queries than a single Redis server can handle. To support higher rates of read performance (along with handling failover if the server that Redis is running on crashes), Redis supports master/slave replication where slaves connect to the master and receive an initial copy of the full database. As writes are performed on the master, they're sent to all connected slaves for updating the slave datasets in real time. With continuously updated data on the slaves, clients can then connect to any slave for reads instead of making requests to the master. We'll discuss Redis slaves more thoroughly in chapter 4.

1.1.3   *Why Redis?*

If you've used memcached before, you probably know that you can add data to the end of an existing string with APPEND. The documentation for memcached states that APPEND can be used for managing lists of items. Great! You add items to the end of the string you're treating as a list. But then how do you remove items? The memcached answer is to use a blacklist to hide items, in order to avoid read/update/write (or a database query and memcached write). In Redis, you'd either use a LIST or a SET and then add and remove items directly.

By using Redis instead of memcached for this and other problems, not only can your code be shorter, easier to understand, and easier to maintain, but it's faster (because you don't need to read a database to update your data). You'll see that there are also many other cases where Redis is more efficient and/or easier to use than relational databases.

One common use of databases is to store long-term reporting data as aggregates over fixed time ranges. To collect these aggregates, it's not uncommon to insert rows into a reporting table and then later to scan over those rows to collect the aggregates, which then update existing rows in an aggregation table. Rows are inserted because, for most databases, inserting rows is a very fast operation (inserts write to the end of an on-disk file, not unlike Redis's append-only log). But updating an existing row in a table is fairly slow (it can cause a random read and may cause a random write). In Redis, you'd calculate the aggregates directly using one of the atomic INCR commands—random writes to Redis data are always fast, because data is always in memory,[2] and queries to Redis don't need to go through a typical query parser/optimizer.

By using Redis instead of a relational or other primarily on-disk database, you can avoid writing unnecessary temporary data, avoid needing to scan over and delete this temporary data, and ultimately improve performance. These are both simple examples, but they demonstrate how your choice of tool can greatly affect the way you solve your problems.

As you continue to read about Redis, try to remember that almost everything that we do is an attempt to solve a problem in real time (except for task queues in chapter 6). I show techniques and provide working code for helping you remove bottlenecks, simplify your code, collect data, distribute data, build utilities, and, overall, to make your task of building software easier. When done right, your software can even scale to levels that would make other users of so-called web-scale technologies blush.

We could keep talking about what Redis has, what it can do, or even why. Or I could show you. In the next section, we'll discuss the structures available in Redis, what they can do, and some of the commands used to access them.

1.2   *What Redis data structures look like*

As shown in table 1.1, Redis allows us to store keys that map to any one of five different data structure types; STRINGs, LISTs, SETs, HASHes, and ZSETs. Each of the five different structures have some shared commands (DEL, TYPE, RENAME, and others), as well as some commands that can only be used by one or two of the structures. We'll dig more deeply into the available commands in chapter 3.

Among the five structures available in Redis, STRINGs, LISTs, and HASHes should be familiar to most programmers. Their implementation and semantics are similar to those same structures built in a variety of other languages. Some programming languages also have a set data structure, comparable to Redis SETs in implementation and semantics. ZSETs are somewhat unique to Redis, but are handy when we get around to using them. A comparison of the five structures available in Redis, what they contain, and a brief description of their semantics can be seen in table 1.2.

> **COMMAND LISTING**   As we discuss each data type in this section, you'll find small tables of commands. A more complete (but partial) listing of commands for each type can be found in chapter 3. If you need a complete command listing with documentation, you can visit http://redis.io/commands.

Throughout this section, you'll see how to represent all five of these structures, and you'll get a chance to start using Redis commands in preparation for later chapters. In this book, all of the examples are provided in Python. If you've installed Redis as

---

[2]   To be fair, memcached could also be used in this simple scenario, but with Redis, your aggregates can be placed in structures that keep associated aggregates together for easy access; the aggregates can be a part of a sorted sequence of aggregates for keeping a toplist in real time; and the aggregates can be integer or floating point.

Table 1.2 The five structures available in Redis

Structure type	What it contains	Structure read/write ability
STRING	Strings, integers, or floating-point values	Operate on the whole string, parts, increment/decrement the integers and floats
LIST	Linked list of strings	Push or pop items from both ends, trim based on offsets, read individual or multiple items, find or remove items by value
SET	Unordered collection of unique strings	Add, fetch, or remove individual items, check membership, intersect, union, difference, fetch random items
HASH	Unordered hash table of keys to values	Add, fetch, or remove individual items, fetch the whole hash
ZSET (sorted set)	Ordered mapping of string members to floating-point scores, ordered by score	Add, fetch, or remove individual values, fetch items based on score ranges or member value

described in appendix A, you should also have installed Python and the necessary libraries to use Redis from Python as part of that process. If possible, you should have a computer with Redis, Python, and the redis-py library installed so that you can try everything out while reading.

> **REMINDER ABOUT INSTALLING REDIS AND PYTHON** Before you continue, you'll want to install Redis and Python. Again, quick and dirty installation instructions for both Redis and Python can be found in appendix A. Even quicker and dirtier instructions for Debian-based Linux distributions are as follows: download Redis from http://redis.io/download, extract, run make && sudo make install, and then run sudo python -m easy_install redis hiredis (*hiredis* is an optional performance-improving C library).

If you're familiar with procedural or object-oriented programming languages, Python should be understandable, even if you haven't used it before. If you're using another language with Redis, you should be able to translate everything we're doing with Python to your language, though method names for Redis commands and the arguments they take may be spelled (or ordered) differently.

> **REDIS WITH OTHER LANGUAGES** Though not included in this book, all code listings that can be converted have translations to Ruby, JavaScript, and Java available for download from the Manning website or linked from this book's Manning forum. This translated code also includes similar descriptive annotations so that you can follow along in your language of choice.

As a matter of style, I attempt to keep the use of more advanced features of Python to a minimum, writing functions to perform operations against Redis instead of constructing classes or otherwise. I do this to keep the syntax of Python from interfering with the focal point of this book, which is solving problems with Redis, and not "look at this cool stuff we can do with Python." For this section, we'll use a redis-cli console to interact with Redis. Let's get started with the first and simplest structure available in Redis: STRINGs.

1.2.1 Strings in Redis

In Redis, STRINGs are similar to strings that we see in other languages or other key-value stores. Generally, when I show diagrams that represent keys and values, the diagrams have the key name and the type of the value along the top of a box, with the value inside the box. I've labeled which part is which as an example in figure 1.1, which shows a STRING with key hello and value world.

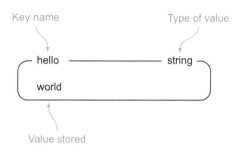

Figure 1.1 An example of a STRING, world, stored under a key, hello

The operations available to STRINGs start with what's available in other key-value stores. We can GET values, SET values, and DEL values. After you have installed and tested Redis as described in appendix A, within redis-cli you can try to SET, GET, and DEL values in Redis, as shown in listing 1.1, with the basic meanings of the functions described in table 1.3.

Table 1.3 Commands used on STRING values

Command	What it does
GET	Fetches the data stored at the given key
SET	Sets the value stored at the given key
DEL	Deletes the value stored at the given key (works for all types)

Listing 1.1 An example showing the SET, GET, and DEL commands in Redis

USING REDIS-CLI   In this first chapter, I introduce Redis and some commands using the *redis-cli* interactive client that comes with Redis. This allows you to get started interacting with Redis quickly and easily.

In addition to being able to GET, SET, and DEL STRING values, there are a handful of other commands for reading and writing parts of STRINGs, and commands that allow us to treat strings as numbers to increment/decrement them. We'll talk about many of those commands in chapter 3. But we still have a lot of ground to cover, so let's move on to take a peek at LISTs and what we can do with them.

1.2.2   Lists in Redis

In the world of key-value stores, Redis is unique in that it supports a linked-list structure. LISTs in Redis store an ordered sequence of strings, and like STRINGs, I represent figures of LISTs as a labeled box with list items inside. An example of a LIST can be seen in figure 1.2.

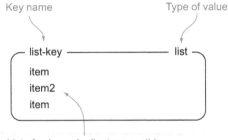

The operations that can be performed on LISTs are typical of what we find in almost any programming language. We can push items to the front and the back of the LIST with LPUSH/RPUSH; we can pop items from the front and back of the list

Figure 1.2   An example of a LIST with three items under the key, list-key. Note that item can be in the list more than once.

with LPOP/RPOP; we can fetch an item at a given position with LINDEX; and we can fetch a range of items with LRANGE. Let's continue our Redis client interactions by following along with interactions on LISTs, as shown in listing 1.2. Table 1.4 gives a brief description of the commands we can use on lists.

Table 1.4   Commands used on LIST values

Command	What it does
RPUSH	Pushes the value onto the right end of the list
LRANGE	Fetches a range of values from the list
LINDEX	Fetches an item at a given position in the list
LPOP	Pops the value from the left end of the list and returns it

Listing 1.2   The RPUSH, LRANGE, LINDEX, and LPOP commands in Redis

```
redis 127.0.0.1:6379> rpush list-key item
(integer) 1
redis 127.0.0.1:6379> rpush list-key item2
(integer) 2
```

When we push items onto a LIST, the command returns the current length of the list.

```
redis 127.0.0.1:6379> rpush list-key item
(integer) 3
redis 127.0.0.1:6379> lrange list-key 0 -1
1) "item"
2) "item2"
3) "item"
redis 127.0.0.1:6379> lindex list-key 1
"item2"
redis 127.0.0.1:6379> lpop list-key
"item"
redis 127.0.0.1:6379> lrange list-key 0 -1
1) "item2"
2) "item"
redis 127.0.0.1:6379>
```

We can fetch the entire list by passing a range of 0 for the start index and -1 for the last index.

When we push items onto a LIST, the command returns the current length of the list.

We can fetch individual items from the list with LINDEX.

Popping an item from the list makes it no longer available.

Even if that was all that we could do with LISTs, Redis would already be a useful platform for solving a variety of problems. But we can also remove items, insert items in the middle, trim the list to be a particular size (discarding items from one or both ends), and more. We'll talk about many of those commands in chapter 3, but for now let's keep going to see what SETs can offer us.

1.2.3 *Sets in Redis*

In Redis, SETs are similar to LISTs in that they're a sequence of strings, but unlike LISTs, Redis SETs use a hash table to keep all strings unique (though there are no associated values). My visual representation of SETs will be similar to LISTs, and figure 1.3 shows an example SET with three items.

Because Redis SETs are unordered, we can't push and pop items from the ends like we did with LISTs. Instead, we

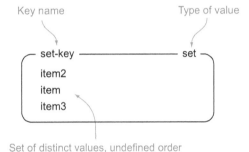

Figure 1.3 **An example of a SET with three items under the key, set-key**

add and remove items by value with the SADD and SREM commands. We can also find out whether an item is in the SET quickly with SISMEMBER, or fetch the entire set with SMEMBERS (this can be slow for large SETs, so be careful). You can follow along with listing 1.3 in your Redis client console to get a feel for how SETs work, and table 1.5 describes the commands used here.

Table 1.5 **Commands used on SET values**

Command	What it does
SADD	Adds the item to the set
SMEMBERS	Returns the entire set of items
SISMEMBER	Checks if an item is in the set
SREM	Removes the item from the set, if it exists

Listing 1.3 The SADD, SMEMBERS, SISMEMBER, and SREM commands in Redis

```
redis 127.0.0.1:6379> sadd set-key item
(integer) 1
redis 127.0.0.1:6379> sadd set-key item2
(integer) 1
redis 127.0.0.1:6379> sadd set-key item3
(integer) 1
redis 127.0.0.1:6379> sadd set-key item
(integer) 0
redis 127.0.0.1:6379> smembers set-key
1) "item"
2) "item2"
3) "item3"
redis 127.0.0.1:6379> sismember set-key item4
(integer) 0
redis 127.0.0.1:6379> sismember set-key item
(integer) 1
redis 127.0.0.1:6379> srem set-key item2
(integer) 1
redis 127.0.0.1:6379> srem set-key item2
(integer) 0
redis 127.0.0.1:6379>  smembers set-key
1) "item"
2) "item3"
redis 127.0.0.1:6379>
```

When adding an item to a SET, Redis will return a I if the item is new to the set and 0 if it was already in the SET.

We can fetch all of the items in the SET, which returns them as a sequence of items, which is turned into a Python set from Python.

We can also ask Redis whether an item is in the SET, which turns into a Boolean in Python.

When we attempt to remove items, our commands return the number of items that were removed.

As you can probably guess based on the STRING and LIST sections, SETs have many other uses beyond adding and removing items. Three commonly used operations with SETs include intersection, union, and difference (SINTER, SUNION, and SDIFF, respectively). We'll get into more detail about SET commands in chapter 3, and over half of chapter 7 involves problems that can be solved almost entirely with Redis SETs. But let's not get ahead of ourselves; we've still got two more structures to go. Keep reading to learn about Redis HASHes.

1.2.4 *Hashes in Redis*

Whereas LISTs and SETs in Redis hold sequences of items, Redis HASHes store a mapping of keys to values. The values that can be stored in HASHes are the same as what can be stored as normal STRINGs: strings themselves, or if a value can be interpreted as a number, that value can be incremented or decremented. Figure 1.4 shows a diagram of a hash with two values.

In a lot of ways, we can think of HASHes in Redis as miniature versions of Redis itself. Some of the same commands that we can perform on STRINGs, we can perform

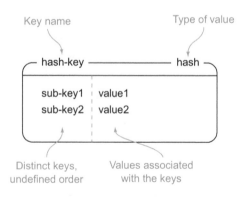

Figure 1.4 An example of a HASH with two keys/values under the key hash-key

on the values inside HASHes with slightly different commands. Try to follow listing 1.4 to see some commands that we can use to insert, fetch, and remove items from HASHes. Table 1.6 describes the commands.

Table 1.6 Commands used on HASH values

Command	What it does
HSET	Stores the value at the key in the hash
HGET	Fetches the value at the given hash key
HGETALL	Fetches the entire hash
HDEL	Removes a key from the hash, if it exists

Listing 1.4 The HSET, HGET, HGETALL, and HDEL commands in Redis

```
redis 127.0.0.1:6379> hset hash-key sub-key1 value1
(integer) 1
redis 127.0.0.1:6379> hset hash-key sub-key2 value2
(integer) 1
redis 127.0.0.1:6379> hset hash-key sub-key1 value1
(integer) 0
redis 127.0.0.1:6379> hgetall hash-key
1) "sub-key1"
2) "value1"
3) "sub-key2"
4) "value2"
redis 127.0.0.1:6379> hdel hash-key sub-key2
(integer) 1
redis 127.0.0.1:6379> hdel hash-key sub-key2
(integer) 0
redis 127.0.0.1:6379> hget hash-key sub-key1
"value1"
redis 127.0.0.1:6379> hgetall hash-key
1) "sub-key1"
2) "value1"
```

When we add items to a hash, again we get a return value that tells whether the item is new in the hash.

We can fetch all of the items in the HASH, which gets translated into a dictionary on the Python side of things.

When we delete items from the hash, the command returns whether the item was there before we tried to remove it.

We can also fetch individual fields from hashes.

For those who are familiar with document stores or relational databases, we can consider a Redis HASH as being similar to a *document* in a document store, or a *row* in a relational database, in that we can access or change individual or multiple fields at a time. We're now one structure from having seen all of the structures available in Redis. Keep reading to learn what ZSETs are and a few things that we can do with them.

1.2.5 *Sorted sets in Redis*

Like Redis HASHes, ZSETs also hold a type of key and value. The keys (called *members*) are unique, and the values (called *scores*) are limited to floating-point numbers. ZSETs have the unique property in Redis of being able to be accessed by member (like a HASH), but items can also be accessed by the sorted order and values of the scores. Figure 1.5 shows an example ZSET with two items.

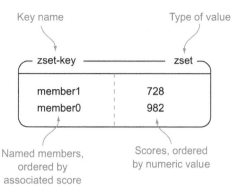

Figure 1.5   **An example of a ZSET with two members/scores under the key zset-key**

As is the case with all of the other structures, we need to be able to add, remove, and fetch items from ZSETs. Listing 1.5 offers add, remove, and fetching commands for ZSETs similar to those for the other structures, and table 1.7 describes the commands that we'll use.

Table 1.7   **Commands used on ZSET values**

Command	What it does
ZADD	Adds member with the given score to the ZSET
ZRANGE	Fetches the items in the ZSET from their positions in sorted order
ZRANGEBYSCORE	Fetches items in the ZSET based on a range of scores
ZREM	Removes the item from the ZSET, if it exists

Listing 1.5   **The ZADD, ZRANGE, ZRANGEBYSCORE, and ZREM commands in Redis**

```
redis 127.0.0.1:6379> zadd zset-key 728 member1
(integer) 1
redis 127.0.0.1:6379> zadd zset-key 982 member0
(integer) 1
redis 127.0.0.1:6379> zadd zset-key 982 member0
(integer) 0
redis 127.0.0.1:6379> zrange zset-key 0 -1 withscores
1) "member1"
2) "728"
3) "member0"
4) "982"
redis 127.0.0.1:6379> zrangebyscore zset-key 0 800 withscores
1) "member1"
2) "728"
redis 127.0.0.1:6379> zrem zset-key member1
(integer) 1
redis 127.0.0.1:6379> zrem zset-key member1
(integer) 0
redis 127.0.0.1:6379> zrange zset-key 0 -1 withscores
1) "member0"
2) "982"
```

When we add items to a ZSET, the command returns the number of new items.

We can fetch all of the items in the ZSET, which are ordered by the scores, and scores are turned into floats in Python.

We can also fetch a subsequence of items based on their scores.

When we remove items, we again find the number of items that were removed.

Now that you've seen ZSETs and a little of what they can do, you've learned the basics of what structures are available in Redis. In the next section, we'll combine the data storage ability of HASHes with the built-in sorting ability of ZSETs to solve a common problem.

1.3 Hello Redis

Now that you're more familiar with the structures that Redis offers, it's time to use Redis on a real problem. In recent years, a growing number of sites have offered the ability to vote on web page links, articles, or questions, including sites such as reddit and Stack Overflow, as shown in figures 1.6 and 1.7. By taking into consideration the votes that were cast, posts are ranked and displayed based on a score relating those votes and when the link was submitted. In this section, we'll build a Redis-based back end for a simple version of this kind of site.

1.3.1 Voting on articles

First, let's start with some numbers and limitations on our problem, so we can solve the problem without losing sight of what we're trying to do. Let's say that 1,000 articles are submitted each day. Of those 1,000 articles, about 50 of them are interesting enough that we want them to be in the top-100 articles for at least one day. All of those 50 articles will receive at least 200 up votes. We won't worry about down votes for this version.

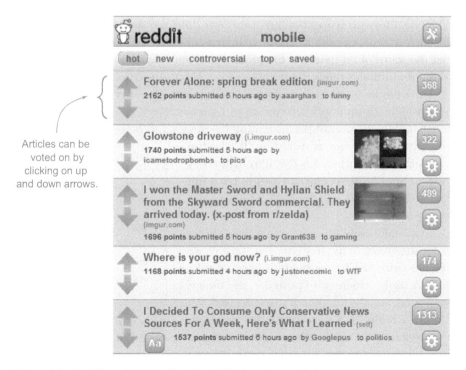

Articles can be voted on by clicking on up and down arrows.

Figure 1.6   Reddit, a site that offers the ability to vote on articles

Voting occurs
after you have
clicked through
to read a question
and any existing
answers.

Figure 1.7   Stack Overflow, a site that offers the ability to vote on questions

When dealing with scores that go down over time, we need to make the posting time, the current time, or both relevant to the overall score. To keep things simple, we'll say that the score of an item is a function of the time that the article was posted, plus a constant multiplier times the number of votes that the article has received.

The time we'll use the number of seconds since January 1, 1970, in the UTC time zone, which is commonly referred to as *Unix time*. We'll use Unix time because it can be fetched easily in most programming languages and on every platform that we may use Redis on. For our constant, we'll take the number of seconds in a day (86,400) divided by the number of votes required (200) to last a full day, which gives us 432 "points" added to the score per vote.

To actually build this, we need to start thinking of structures to use in Redis. For starters, we need to store article information like the title, the link to the article, who posted it, the time it was posted, and the number of votes received. We can use a Redis HASH to store this information, and an example article can be seen in figure 1.8.

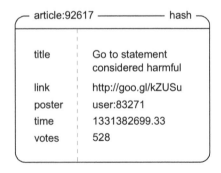

Figure 1.8   An example article stored as a HASH for our article voting system

USING THE COLON CHARACTER AS A SEPARATOR Throughout this and other chapters, you'll find that we use the colon character (:) as a separator between parts of names; for example, in figure 1.8, we used it to separate *article* from the ID of the article, creating a sort of namespace. The choice of : is subjective, but common among Redis users. Other common choices include a period (.), forward slash (/), and even occasionally the pipe character (|). Regardless of what you choose, be consistent, and note how we use colons to define nested namespaces throughout the examples in the book.

To store a sorted set of articles themselves, we'll use a ZSET, which keeps items ordered by the item scores. We can use our article ID as the member, with the ZSET score being the article score itself. While we're at it, we'll create another ZSET with the score being just the times that the articles were posted, which gives us an option of browsing articles based on article score or time. We can see a small example of time- and score-ordered article ZSETs in figure 1.9.

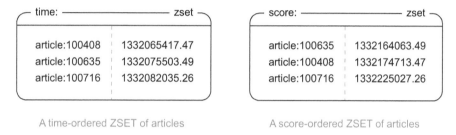

A time-ordered ZSET of articles   A score-ordered ZSET of articles

Figure 1.9   Two sorted sets representing time-ordered and score-ordered article indexes

In order to prevent users from voting for the same article more than once, we need to store a unique listing of users who have voted for each article. For this, we'll use a SET for each article, and store the member IDs of all users who have voted on the given article. An example SET of users who have voted on an article is shown in figure 1.10.

For the sake of memory use over time, we'll say that after a week users can no longer vote on an article and its score is fixed. After that week has passed, we'll delete the SET of users who have voted on the article.

Before we build this, let's take a look at what would happen if user 115423 were to vote for article 100408 in figure 1.11.

Now that you know what we're going to build, let's build it! First, let's handle voting. When someone tries to vote on an article, we first verify that the article was posted within the last week by checking the article's post time with ZSCORE. If we still have time, we then try to add the user to the article's voted SET

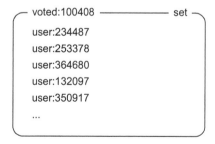

Figure 1.10   Some users who have voted for article 100408

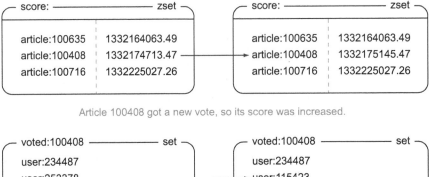

Article 100408 got a new vote, so its score was increased.

Since user 115423 voted on the article, they are added to the voted SET.

Figure 1.11   What happens to our structures when user 115423 votes for article 100408

with SADD. Finally, if the user didn't previously vote on that article, we increment the score of the article by 432 (which we calculated earlier) with ZINCRBY (a command that increments the score of a member), and update the vote count in the HASH with HINCRBY (a command that increments a value in a hash). The voting code is shown in listing 1.6.

Listing 1.6   The `article_vote()` function

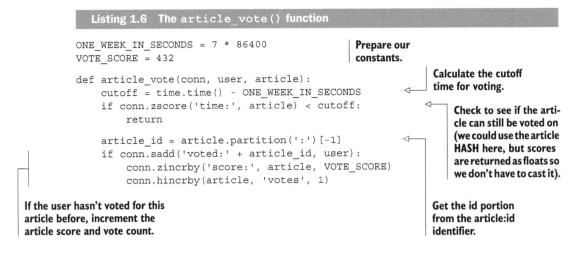

```
ONE_WEEK_IN_SECONDS = 7 * 86400          │ Prepare our
VOTE_SCORE = 432                         │ constants.

def article_vote(conn, user, article):
    cutoff = time.time() - ONE_WEEK_IN_SECONDS       ←── Calculate the cutoff time for voting.
    if conn.zscore('time:', article) < cutoff:       ←── Check to see if the article can still be voted on
        return                                           (we could use the article HASH here, but scores
                                                         are returned as floats so we don't have to cast it).
    article_id = article.partition(':')[-1]          ←── Get the id portion from the article:id identifier.
    if conn.sadd('voted:' + article_id, user):
        conn.zincrby('score:', article, VOTE_SCORE)
        conn.hincrby(article, 'votes', 1)
```

If the user hasn't voted for this article before, increment the article score and vote count.

REDIS TRANSACTIONS   In order to be correct, technically our SADD, ZINCRBY, and HINCRBY calls should be in a transaction. But since we don't cover transactions until chapter 4, we won't worry about them for now.

Voting isn't so bad, is it? But what about posting an article?

1.3.2 Posting and fetching articles

To post an article, we first create an article ID by incrementing a counter with INCR. We then create the voted SET by adding the poster's ID to the SET with SADD. To ensure that the SET is removed after one week, we'll give it an expiration time with the EXPIRE command, which lets Redis automatically delete it. We then store the article information with HMSET. Finally, we add the initial score and posting time to the relevant ZSETs with ZADD. We can see the code for posting an article in listing 1.7.

Listing 1.7 The post_article() function

```
def post_article(conn, user, title, link):
    article_id = str(conn.incr('article:'))          ⟵—— Generate a new article id.

    voted = 'voted:' + article_id
    conn.sadd(voted, user)                                Start with the posting user having
    conn.expire(voted, ONE_WEEK_IN_SECONDS)               voted for the article, and set the
                                                          article voting information to
    now = time.time()                                     automatically expire in a week (we
    article = 'article:' + article_id                     discuss expiration in chapter 3).
    conn.hmset(article, {
        'title': title,
        'link': link,
        'poster': user,                                   Create the
        'time': now,                                      article hash.
        'votes': 1,
    })

    conn.zadd('score:', article, now + VOTE_SCORE)        Add the article to the time
    conn.zadd('time:', article, now)                      and score ordered ZSETs.

    return article_id
```

Okay, so we can vote, and we can post articles. But what about fetching the current top-scoring or most recent articles? For that, we can use ZRANGE to fetch the article IDs, and then we can make calls to HGETALL to fetch information about each article. The only tricky part is that we must remember that ZSETs are sorted in ascending order by their score. But we can fetch items based on the reverse order with ZREVRANGEBYSCORE. The function to fetch a page of articles is shown in listing 1.8.

Listing 1.8 The get_articles() function

```
ARTICLES_PER_PAGE = 25

def get_articles(conn, page, order='score:'):
    start = (page-1) * ARTICLES_PER_PAGE              Set up the start and end indexes
    end = start + ARTICLES_PER_PAGE - 1               for fetching the articles.

    ids = conn.zrevrange(order, start, end)       ⟵—— Fetch the article ids.
    articles = []
    for id in ids:                                    Get the article information
        article_data = conn.hgetall(id)               from the list of article ids.
```

```
      article_data['id'] = id                          ⤒ Get the article information
      articles.append(article_data)                    | from the list of article ids.

   return articles
```

DEFAULT ARGUMENTS AND KEYWORD ARGUMENTS   Inside listing 1.8, we used an argument named order, and we gave it a default value of score:. Some of the details of default arguments and passing arguments as names (instead of by position) can be strange to newcomers to the Python language. If you're having difficulty understanding what's going on with function definition or argument passing, the Python language tutorial offers a good introduction to what's going on, and you can jump right to the particular section by visiting this shortened URL: http://mng.bz/KM5x.

We can now get the top-scoring articles across the entire site. But many of these article voting sites have groups that only deal with articles of a particular topic like cute animals, politics, programming in Java, and even the use of Redis. How could we add or alter our code to offer these topical groups?

1.3.3 *Grouping articles*

To offer groups requires two steps. The first step is to add information about which articles are in which groups, and the second is to actually fetch articles from a group. We'll use a SET for each group, which stores the article IDs of all articles in that group. In listing 1.9, we see a function that allows us to add and remove articles from groups.

> **Listing 1.9   The add_remove_groups() function**

```
def add_remove_groups(conn, article_id, to_add=[], to_remove=[]):
    article = 'article:' + article_id                       ◁──┐ Construct the article
    for group in to_add:                                        | information like we
        conn.sadd('group:' + group, article)        ◁──────────┘ did in post_article.
    for group in to_remove:
        conn.srem('group:' + group, article)     ◁──┐

            Remove the article from                 |    Add the article
            groups that it should be                |    to groups that it
            removed from.                           |    should be a part of.
```

At first glance, these SETs with article information may not seem that useful. So far, you've only seen the ability to check whether a SET has an item. But Redis has the capability to perform operations involving multiple SETs, and in some cases, Redis can perform operations between SETs and ZSETs.

When we're browsing a specific group, we want to be able to see the scores of all of the articles in that group. Or, really, we want them to be in a ZSET so that we can have the scores already sorted and ready for paging over. Redis has a command called ZINTERSTORE, which, when provided with SETs and ZSETs, will find those entries that are in all of the SETs and ZSETs, combining their scores in a few different ways (items in SETs are considered to have scores equal to 1). In our case, we want the maximum score from each item (which will be either the article score or when the article was posted, depending on the sorting option chosen).

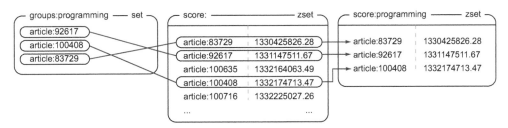

Figure 1.12 The newly created `ZSET`, `score:programming`, is an intersection of the `SET` and `ZSET`. Intersection will only keep members from `SET`s/`ZSET`s when the members exist in all of the input `SET`s/`ZSET`s. When intersecting `SET`s and `ZSET`s, `SET`s act as though they have a score of 1, so when intersecting with an aggregate of `MAX`, we're only using the scores from the `score:` input `ZSET`, because they're all greater than 1.

To visualize what is going on, let's look at figure 1.12. This figure shows an example `ZINTERSTORE` operation on a small group of articles stored as a `SET` with the much larger (but not completely shown) `ZSET` of scored articles. Notice how only those articles that are in both the `SET` and the `ZSET` make it into the result `ZSET`?

To calculate the scores of all of the items in a group, we only need to make a `ZINTERSTORE` call with the group and the scored or recent `ZSET`s. Because a group may be large, it may take some time to calculate, so we'll keep the `ZSET` around for 60 seconds to reduce the amount of work that Redis is doing. If we're careful (and we are), we can even use our existing `get_articles()` function to handle pagination and article data fetching so we don't need to rewrite it. We can see the function for fetching a page of articles from a group in listing 1.10.

Listing 1.10   The `get_group_articles()` function

```
def get_group_articles(conn, group, page, order='score:'):        Create a key for
    key = order + group                                           each group and
    if not conn.exists(key):                                      each sort order.
        conn.zinterstore(key,              If we haven't sorted these articles
            ['group:' + group, order],     recently, we should sort them.
            aggregate='max',
        )                                  Tell Redis to automatically
        conn.expire(key, 60)               expire the ZSET in 60 seconds.
    return get_articles(conn, page, key)
                                           Call our earlier get_articles()
                                           function to handle pagination
                                           and article data fetching.
```

Actually sort the articles in the group based on score or recency.

On some sites, articles are typically only in one or two groups at most ("all articles" and whatever group best matches the article). In that situation, it would make more sense to keep the group that the article is in as part of the article's `HASH`, and add one more `ZINCRBY` call to the end of our `article_vote()` function. But in our case, we chose to allow articles to be a part of multiple groups at the same time (maybe a picture can be both cute and funny), so to update scores for articles in multiple groups, we'd need to increment all of those groups at the same time. For an article in many groups, that could be expensive, so we instead occasionally perform an intersection. How we choose to offer flexibility or limitations can change how we store and update our data in any database, and Redis is no exception.

Exercise: Down-voting

In our example, we only counted people who voted positively for an article. But on many sites, negative votes can offer useful feedback to everyone. Can you think of a way of adding down-voting support to `article_vote()` and `post_article()`? If possible, try to allow users to switch their votes. Hint: if you're stuck on vote switching, check out `SMOVE`, which I introduce briefly in chapter 3.

Now that we can get articles, post articles, vote on articles, and even have the ability to group articles, we've built a back end for surfacing popular links or articles. Congratulations on getting this far! If you had any difficulty in following along, understanding the examples, or getting the solutions to work, keep reading to find out where you can get help.

1.4   *Getting help*

If you're having problems with Redis, don't be afraid to look for or ask for help. Many others will probably have had a similar issue. First try searching with your favorite search engine for the particular error message you're seeing.

If you can't find a solution to your problem and are having problems with an example in this book, go ahead and ask your question on the Manning forums: http://www.manning-sandbox.com/forum.jspa?forumID=809. Either I or someone else who's familiar with the book should be able to help.

If you're having issues with Redis or solving a problem with Redis that isn't in this book, please join and post your question to the Redis mailing list at https://groups.google.com/d/forum/redis-db/. Again, either I or someone who's familiar with Redis should be able to help.

And finally, if you're having difficulties with a particular language or library, you can also try the Redis mailing list, but you may have better luck searching the mailing list or forum for the library you're using.

1.5   *Summary*

In this chapter, we covered the basics of what Redis is, and how it's both similar to and different from other databases. We also talked about a few reasons why you'll want to use Redis in your next project. When reading through the upcoming chapters, try to remember that we aren't building toward a single ultimate application or tool; we're looking at a variety of problems that Redis can help you to solve.

If there's one concept that you should take away from this chapter, it's that Redis is another tool that you can use to solve problems. Redis has structures that no other database offers, and because Redis is in-memory (making it fast), remote (making it accessible to multiple clients/servers), persistent (giving you the opportunity to keep data between reboots), and scalable (via slaving and sharding) you can build solutions to a variety of problems in ways that you're already used to.

As you read the rest of the book, try to pay attention to how your approach to solving problems changes. You may find that your way of thinking about data-driven problems moves from "How can I bend my idea to fit into the world of tables and rows?" to "Which structures in Redis will result in an easier-to-maintain solution?"

In chapter 2, we'll use Redis to solve problems that come up in the world of web applications, so keep reading to get an even bigger sense of what Redis can help you do.

Anatomy of a Redis web application

In the first chapter, I introduced you to what Redis is about and what it's capable of. In this chapter, I'll continue on that path, starting to dig into several examples that come up in the context of some types of web applications. Though I've simplified the problems quite a bit compared to what happens in the real world, each of these pieces can actually be used with little modification directly in your applications. This chapter is primarily meant as a practical guide to what you can do with Redis, and chapter 3 is more of a command reference.

To start out, let's look at what we mean by a web application from the high level. Generally, we mean a server or service that responds over the HTTP protocol to requests made by web browsers. Here are the typical steps that a web server goes through to respond to a request:

1 The server parses the request.
2 The request is forwarded to a predefined handler.
3 The handler may make requests to fetch data from a database.
4 With the retrieved data, the handler then renders a template as a response.
5 The handler returns the rendered response, which gets passed back to the client.

This list is a high-level overview of what happens in a typical web server. Web requests in this type of situation are considered to be *stateless* in that the web servers themselves don't hold information about past requests, in an attempt to allow for easy replacement of failed servers. Books have been written about how to optimize every step in that process, and this book does similarly. How this book differs is that it explains how to replace some queries against a typical relational database with faster queries against Redis, and how to use Redis with access patterns that would've been too costly using a relational database.

Through this chapter, we'll look at and solve problems that come up in the context of Fake Web Retailer, a fairly large (fake) web store that gets about 100 million hits per day from roughly 5 million unique users who buy more than 100,000 items per day. These numbers are big, but if we can solve big problems easily, then small and medium problems should be even easier. And though these solutions target a large web retailer, all but one of them can be handled by a Redis server with no more than a few gigabytes of memory, and are intended to improve performance of a system responding to requests in real time.

Each of the solutions presented (or some variant of them) has been used to solve real problems in production environments. More specifically, by reducing traditional database load by offloading some processing and storage to Redis, web pages were loaded faster with fewer resources.

Our first problem is to use Redis to help with managing user login sessions.

2.1 Login and cookie caching

Whenever we sign in to services on the internet, such as bank accounts or web mail, these services remember who we are using *cookies*. Cookies are small pieces of data that websites ask our web browsers to store and resend on every request to that service. For login cookies, there are two common methods of storing login information in cookies: a signed cookie or a token cookie.

Signed cookies typically store the user's name, maybe their user ID, when they last logged in, and whatever else the service may find useful. Along with this user-specific information, the cookie also includes a signature that allows the server to verify that the information that the browser sent hasn't been altered (like replacing the login name of one user with another).

Token cookies use a series of random bytes as the data in the cookie. On the server, the token is used as a key to look up the user who owns that token by querying a database of some kind. Over time, old tokens can be deleted to make room for new tokens. Some pros and cons for both signed cookies and token cookies for referencing information are shown in table 2.1.

Table 2.1   Pros and cons of signed cookies and token cookies

Cookie type	Pros	Cons
Signed cookie	Everything needed to verify the cookie is in the cookie Additional information can be included and signed easily	Correctly handling signatures is hard It's easy to forget to sign and/or verify data, allowing security vulnerabilities
Token cookie	Adding information is easy Very small cookie, so mobile and slow clients can send requests faster	More information to store on the server If using a relational database, cookie loading/storing can be expensive

For the sake of not needing to implement signed cookies, Fake Web Retailer chose to use a token cookie to reference an entry in a relational database table, which stores user login information. By storing this information in the database, Fake Web Retailer can also store information like how long the user has been browsing, or how many items they've looked at, and later analyze that information to try to learn how to better market to its users.

As is expected, people will generally look through many different items before choosing one (or a few) to buy, and recording information about all of the different items seen, when the user last visited a page, and so forth, can result in substantial database writes. In the long term, that data is useful, but even with database tuning, most relational databases are limited to inserting, updating, or deleting roughly 200–2,000 individual rows every second per database server. Though bulk inserts/updates/deletes can be performed faster, a customer will only be updating a small handful of rows for each web page view, so higher-speed bulk insertion doesn't help here.

At present, due to the relatively large load through the day (averaging roughly 1,200 writes per second, close to 6,000 writes per second at peak), Fake Web Retailer has had to set up 10 relational database servers to deal with the load during peak hours. It's our job to take the relational databases out of the picture for login cookies and replace them with Redis.

To get started, we'll use a HASH to store our mapping from login cookie tokens to the user that's logged in. To check the login, we need to fetch the user based on the token and return it, if it's available. The following listing shows how we check login cookies.

Listing 2.1   The check_token() function

```
def check_token(conn, token):
    return conn.hget('login:', token)
```

> Fetch and return the given user, if available.

Checking the token isn't very exciting, because all of the interesting stuff happens when we're updating the token itself. For the visit, we'll update the login HASH for the user and record the current timestamp for the token in the ZSET of recent users. If the user was viewing an item, we also add the item to the user's recently viewed ZSET and trim that ZSET if it grows past 25 items. The function that does all of this can be seen next.

Listing 2.2 The `update_token()` function

```
def update_token(conn, token, user, item=None):
    timestamp = time.time()                              ⟵— Get the timestamp.
    conn.hset('login:', token, user)                     ⟵
    conn.zadd('recent:', token, timestamp)               ⟵
    if item:                                                    Keep a mapping
        conn.zadd('viewed:' + token, item, timestamp)           from the token to
        conn.zremrangebyrank('viewed:' + token, 0, -26)         the logged-in user.
```

Record that the user viewed the item. ⟶

Remove old items, keeping the most recent 25.

Record when the token was last seen.

And you know what? That's it. We've now recorded when a user with the given session last viewed an item and what item that user most recently looked at. On a server made in the last few years, you can record this information for at least 20,000 item views every second, which is more than three times what we needed to perform against the database. This can be made even faster, which we'll talk about later. But even for this version, we've improved performance by 10–100 times over a typical relational database in this context.

Over time, memory use will grow, and we'll want to clean out old data. As a way of limiting our data, we'll only keep the most recent 10 million sessions.[1] For our cleanup, we'll fetch the size of the ZSET in a loop. If the ZSET is too large, we'll fetch the oldest items up to 100 at a time (because we're using timestamps, this is just the first 100 items in the ZSET), remove them from the recent ZSET, delete the login tokens from the login HASH, and delete the relevant viewed ZSETs. If the ZSET isn't too large, we'll sleep for one second and try again later. The code for cleaning out old sessions is shown next.

Listing 2.3 The `clean_sessions()` function

```
QUIT = False
LIMIT = 10000000

def clean_sessions(conn):                        Find out how many
    while not QUIT:                               tokens are known.
        size = conn.zcard('recent:')          ⟵
        if size <= LIMIT:                        We're still under our limit;
            time.sleep(1)                        sleep and try again.
```

---

[1] Remember that these sorts of limits are meant as examples that you could use in a large-scale production situation. Feel free to reduce these to a much smaller number in your testing and development to see that they work.

```
        continue

    end_index = min(size - LIMIT, 100)                    Fetch the token IDs that
    tokens = conn.zrange('recent:', 0, end_index-1)       should be removed.

    session_keys = []                                     Prepare the key names
    for token in tokens:                                  for the tokens to delete.
        session_keys.append('viewed:' + token)

    conn.delete(*session_keys)                            Remove the
    conn.hdel('login:', *tokens)                          oldest tokens.
    conn.zrem('recent:', *tokens)
```

How could something so simple scale to handle five million users daily? Let's check the numbers. If we expect five million unique users per day, then in two days (if we always get new users every day), we'll run out of space and will need to start deleting tokens. In one day there are 24 x 3600 = 86,400 seconds, so there are 5 million / 86,400 < 58 new sessions every second on average. If we ran our cleanup function every second (as our code implements), we'd clean up just under 60 tokens every second. But this code can actually clean up more than 10,000 tokens per second across a network, and over 60,000 tokens per second locally, which is 150–1,000 times faster than we need.

WHERE TO RUN CLEANUP FUNCTIONS   This and other examples in this book will sometimes include cleanup functions like listing 2.3. Depending on the cleanup function, it may be written to be run as a daemon process (like listing 2.3), to be run periodically via a cron job, or even to be run during every execution (section 6.3 actually includes the cleanup operation as part of an "acquire" operation). As a general rule, if the function includes a while not QUIT: line, it's supposed to be run as a daemon, though it could probably be modified to be run periodically, depending on its purpose.

PYTHON SYNTAX FOR PASSING AND RECEIVING A VARIABLE NUMBER OF ARGUMENTS   Inside listing 2.3, you'll notice that we called three functions with a syntax similar to conn.delete(*vtokens). Basically, we're passing a sequence of arguments to the underlying function without previously unpacking the arguments. For further details on the semantics of how this works, you can visit the Python language tutorial website by visiting this short url: http://mng.bz/8I7W.

EXPIRING DATA IN REDIS   As you learn more about Redis, you'll likely discover that some of the solutions we present aren't the only ways to solve the problem. In this case, we could omit the recent ZSET, store login tokens as plain key-value pairs, and use Redis EXPIRE to set a future date or time to clean out both sessions and our recently viewed ZSETs. But using EXPIRE prevents us from explicitly limiting our session information to 10 million users, and prevents us from performing abandoned shopping cart analysis during session expiration, if necessary in the future.

Those familiar with threaded or concurrent programming may have seen that the preceding cleanup function has a race condition where it's technically possible for a user to manage to visit the site in the same fraction of a second when we were deleting their information. We're not going to worry about that here because it's unlikely, and because it won't cause a significant change in the data we're recording (aside from requiring that the user log in again). We'll talk about guarding against race conditions and about how we can even speed up the deletion operation in chapters 3 and 4.

We've reduced how much we'll be writing to the database by millions of rows every day. This is great, but it's just the first step toward using Redis in our web application. In the next section, we'll use Redis for handling another kind of cookie.

2.2 Shopping carts in Redis

One of the first uses of cookies on the web was pioneered by Netscape way back in the mid '90s, and ultimately resulted in the login session cookies we just talked about. Originally, cookies were intended to offer a way for a web retailer to keep a sort of shopping cart for the user, in order to track what items they wanted to buy. Prior to cookies, there were a few different solutions for keeping track of shopping carts, but none were particularly easy to use.

The use of shopping cart cookies is common, as is the storage of the entire cart itself in the cookie. One huge advantage to storing shopping carts in cookies is that you don't need to write to a database to keep them. But one of the disadvantages is that you also need to keep reparsing and validating the cookie to ensure that it has the proper format and contains items that can actually be purchased. Yet another disadvantage is that cookies are passed with every request, which can slow down request sending and processing for large cookies.

Because we've had such good luck with session cookies and recently viewed items, we'll push our shopping cart information into Redis. Since we're already keeping user session cookies in Redis (along with recently viewed items), we can use the same cookie ID for referencing the shopping cart.

The shopping cart that we'll use is simple: it's a HASH that maps an item ID to the quantity of that item that the customer would like to purchase. We'll have the web application handle validation for item count, so we only need to update counts in the cart as they change. If the user wants more than 0 items, we add the item(s) to the HASH (replacing an earlier count if it existed). If not, we remove the entry from the hash. Our add_to_cart() function can be seen in this listing.

Listing 2.4 The add_to_cart() function

```
def add_to_cart(conn, session, item, count):
    if count <= 0:
        conn.hrem('cart:' + session, item)              Remove the item
                                                         from the cart.
    else:
        conn.hset('cart:' + session, item, count)       Add the item to the cart.
```

While we're at it, we'll update our session cleanup function to include deleting old shopping carts as clean_full_sessions() in the next listing.

Listing 2.5   The `clean_full_sessions()` function

```
def clean_full_sessions(conn):
    while not QUIT:
        size = conn.zcard('recent:')
        if size <= LIMIT:
            time.sleep(1)
            continue

        end_index = min(size - LIMIT, 100)
        sessions = conn.zrange('recent:', 0, end_index-1)

        session_keys = []
        for sess in sessions:
            session_keys.append('viewed:' + sess)
            session_keys.append('cart:' + sess)

        conn.delete(*session_keys)
        conn.hdel('login:', *sessions)
        conn.zrem('recent:', *sessions)
```

> The required added line to delete the shopping cart for old sessions

We now have both sessions and the shopping cart stored in Redis, which helps to reduce request size, as well as allows the performing of statistical calculations on visitors to our site based on what items they looked at, what items ended up in their shopping carts, and what items they finally purchased. All of this lets us build (if we want to) features similar to many other large web retailers: "People who looked at this item ended up buying this item X% of the time," and "People who bought this item also bought these other items." This can help people to find other related items, which is ultimately good for business.

With both session and shopping cart cookies in Redis, we now have two major pieces for performing useful data analysis. Continuing on, let's look at how we can further reduce our database and web front-end load with caching.

2.3   *Web page caching*

When producing web pages dynamically, it's common to use a templating language to simplify page generation. Gone are the days when each page would be written by hand. Modern web pages are generated from page templates with headers, footers, side menus, toolbars, content areas, and maybe even generated JavaScript.

Despite being capable of dynamically generating content, the majority of pages that are served on Fake Web Retailer's website don't change much on a regular basis. Sure, some new items are added to the catalog, old items are removed, sometimes there are specials, and sometimes there are even "hot items" pages. But really, only a handful of account settings, past orders, shopping cart/checkout, and similar pages have content that needs to be generated on every page load.

By looking at their view numbers, Fake Web Retailer has determined that 95% of the web pages that they serve change at most once per day, and don't actually require content to be dynamically generated. It's our job to stop generating 95% of pages for every load. By reducing the amount of time we spend generating static content, we can reduce the number of servers necessary to handle the same load, and we can serve our site faster. (Research has shown that reducing the time users spend waiting for pages to load increases their desire to use a site and improves how they rate the site.)

All of the standard Python application frameworks offer the ability to add layers that can pre- or post-process requests as they're handled. These layers are typically called *middleware* or *plugins*. Let's create one of these layers that calls out to our Redis caching function. If a web request can't be cached, we'll generate the page and return the content. If a request can be cached, we'll try to fetch and return the page from the cache; otherwise we'll generate the page, cache the result in Redis for up to 5 minutes, and return the content. Our simple caching method can be seen in the next listing.

Listing 2.6 The `cache_request()` function

```
def cache_request(conn, request, callback):
    if not can_cache(conn, request):
        return callback(request)

    page_key = 'cache:' + hash_request(request)
    content = conn.get(page_key)

    if not content:
        content = callback(request)
        conn.setex(page_key, content, 300)

    return content
```

If we can't cache the request, immediately call the callback.

Convert the request into a simple string key for later lookups.

Fetch the cached content if we can, and it's available.

Generate the content if we can't cache the page, or if it wasn't cached.

Cache the newly generated content if we can cache it.

Return the content.

For that 95% of content that could be cached and is loaded often, this bit of code removes the need to dynamically generate viewed pages for 5 minutes. Depending on the complexity of content, this one change could reduce the latency for a data-heavy page from maybe 20–50ms, down to one round trip to Redis (under 1ms for a local connection, under 5ms for computers close to each other in the same data center). For pages that used to hit the database for data, this can further reduce page load time and database load.

Now that we've cut loading time for pages that don't change often, can we keep using Redis to cut loading time for pages that do change often? Of course we can! Keep reading to find out how.

2.4 *Database row caching*

In this chapter so far, we've moved login and visitor sessions from our relational database and web browser to Redis, we've taken shopping carts out of the relational database and put them into Redis, and we've cached entire pages in Redis. This has helped us improve performance and reduce the load on our relational database, which has also lowered our costs.

Individual product pages that we're displaying to a user typically only load one or two rows from the database: the user information for the user who's logged in (with our generated pages, we can load that with an AJAX call to keep using our cache), and the information about the item itself. Even for pages where we may not want to cache the whole page (customer account pages, a given user's past orders, and so on), we could instead cache the individual rows from our relational database.

As an example of where caching rows like this would be useful, let's say that Fake Web Retailer has decided to start a new promotion to both clean out some older inventory and get people coming back to spend money. To make this happen, we'll start performing daily deal sales for certain items until they run out. In the case of a deal, we can't cache the full page, because then someone might see a version of the page with an incorrect count of items remaining. And though we could keep reading the item's row from the database, that could push our database to become over-utilized, which would then increase our costs because we'd need to scale our databases up again.

To cache database rows in preparation for a heavy load, we'll write a daemon function that will run continuously, whose purpose will be to cache specific database rows in Redis, updating them on a variable schedule. The rows themselves will be JSON-encoded dictionaries stored as a plain Redis value. We'll map column names and row values to the dictionary keys and values. An example row can be seen in figure 2.1.

In order to know when to update the cache, we'll use two ZSETs. Our first ZSET, the scheduleZSET, will use the row ID from the original database row as the member of the ZSET. We'll use a timestamp for our schedule scores, which will tell us when the row should be copied to Redis next. Our second ZSET, the delayZSET, will use the same row ID for the members, but the score will be how many seconds to wait between cache updates.

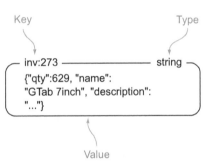

Figure 2.1   **A cached database row for an item to be sold online**

USING JSON INSTEAD OF OTHER FORMATS   Our use of JSON instead of XML, Google's protocol buffers, Thrift, BSON, MessagePack, or other serialization formats is a subjective one. We generally use JSON because it's human readable, somewhat concise, and it has fast encoding and decoding libraries available in every language with an existing Redis client (as far as we know). If your situation requires the use of another format, or if you'd prefer to use a different format, then feel free to do so.

NESTED STRUCTURES   One feature that users of other non-relational databases sometime expect is the ability to nest structures. Specifically, some new users of Redis expect that a HASH should be able to have a value that's a ZSET or LIST. Though conceptually this is fine, there's a question that comes up early

in such a discussion that boils down to a simple example, "How do I increment a value in a HASH that's nested five levels deep?" As a matter of keeping
the syntax of commands simple, Redis doesn't allow nested structures. If necessary, you can use key names for this (user:123 could be a HASH and
user:123:posts could be a ZSET of recent posts from that user). Or you can
explicitly store your nested structures using JSON or some other serialization
library of your choice (Lua scripting, covered in chapter 11, supports server-
side manipulation of JSON and MessagePack encoded data).

In order for rows to be cached on a regular basis by the caching function, we'll first
add the row ID to our delay ZSET with the given delay. This is because our actual caching function will require the delay, and if it's missing, will remove the scheduled item.
When the row ID is in the delay ZSET, we'll then add the row ID to our schedule ZSET
with the current timestamp. If we want to stop a row from being synced to Redis and
remove it from the cache, we can set the delay to be less than or equal to 0, and our
caching function will handle it. Our function to schedule or stop caching can be seen
in the following listing.

Listing 2.7 The `schedule_row_cache()` function

```
def schedule_row_cache(conn, row_id, delay):
    conn.zadd('delay:', row_id, delay)
    conn.zadd('schedule:', row_id, time.time())
```

Set the delay for the item first.

Schedule the item to be cached now.

Now that we have the scheduling part done, how do we cache the rows? We'll pull the
first item from the schedule ZSET with its score. If there are no items, or if the timestamp returned is in the future, we'll wait 50 milliseconds and try again. When we
have an item that should be updated now, we'll check the row's delay. If the delay for
the next caching time is less than or equal to 0, we'll remove the row ID from the delay
and schedule ZSETs, as well as delete the cached row and try again. Finally, for any row
that should be cached, we'll update the row's schedule, pull the row from the database, and save a JSON-encoded version of the row to Redis. Our function for doing
this can be seen in this listing.

Listing 2.8 The `cache_rows()` daemon function

```
def cache_rows(conn):
    while not QUIT:
        next = conn.zrange('schedule:', 0, 0, withscores=True)
        now = time.time()
        if not next or next[0][1] > now:
            time.sleep(.05)
            continue

        row_id = next[0][0]
```

Find the next row that should be cached (if any), including the timestamp, as a list of tuples with zero or one items.

No rows can be cached now, so wait 50 milliseconds and try again.

```
                    delay = conn.zscore('delay:', row_id)              Get the delay before
                    if delay <= 0:                                     the next schedule.
                        conn.zrem('delay:', row_id)
                        conn.zrem('schedule:', row_id)             The item shouldn't be cached
                        conn.delete('inv:' + row_id)               anymore; remove it from the cache.
                        continue
    Update the      row = Inventory.get(row_id)                        Get the database row.
schedule and set    conn.zadd('schedule:', row_id, now + delay)
the cache value.    conn.set('inv:' + row_id, json.dumps(row.to_dict()))
```

With the combination of a scheduling function and a continuously running caching function, we've added a repeating scheduled autocaching mechanism. With these two functions, inventory rows can be updated as frequently as we think is reasonable. For a daily deal with inventory counts being reduced and affecting whether someone can buy the item, it probably makes sense to update the cached row every few seconds if there are many buyers. But if the data doesn't change often, or when back-ordered items are acceptable, it may make sense to only update the cache every minute. Both are possible with this simple method.

Now that we're caching individual rows in Redis, could it be possible to further reduce our memory load by caching only some of our pages?

2.5   *Web page analytics*

As people come to the websites that we build, interact with them, maybe even purchase something from them, we can learn valuable information. For example, if we only pay attention to pages that get the most views, we can try to change the way the pages are formatted, what colors are being used, maybe even change what other links are shown on the pages. Each one of these changes can lead to a better or worse experience on a page or subsequent pages, or even affect buying behavior.

In sections 2.1 and 2.2, we talked about gathering information about items that a user has looked at or added to their cart. In section 2.3, we talked about caching generated web pages in order to reduce page load times and improve responsiveness. Unfortunately, we went overboard with our caching for Fake Web Retailer; we cached every one of the 100,000 available product pages, and now we're running out of memory. After some work, we've determined that we can only reasonably hold about 10,000 pages in the cache.

If you remember from section 2.1, we kept a reference to every item that was visited. Though we can use that information directly to help us decide what pages to cache, actually calculating that could take a long time to get good numbers. Instead, let's add one line to the update_token() function from listing 2.2, which we see next.

Listing 2.9   The updated update_token() function

```
def update_token(conn, token, user, item=None):
    timestamp = time.time()
    conn.hset('login:', token, user)
    conn.zadd('recent:', token, timestamp)
```

```
if item:
    conn.zadd('viewed:' + token, item, timestamp)
    conn.zremrangebyrank('viewed:' + token, 0, -26)
    conn.zincrby('viewed:', item, -1)
```

The line we need to add to update_token()

With this one line added, we now have a record of all of the items that are viewed. Even more useful, that list of items is ordered by the number of times that people have seen the items, with the most-viewed item having the lowest score, and thus having an index of 0. Over time, some items will be seen many times and others rarely. Obviously we only want to cache commonly seen items, but we also want to be able to discover new items that are becoming popular, so we know when to cache them.

To keep our top list of pages fresh, we need to trim our list of viewed items, while at the same time adjusting the score to allow new items to become popular. You already know how to remove items from the ZSET from section 2.1, but rescaling is new. ZSETs have a function called ZINTERSTORE, which lets us combine one or more ZSETs and multiply every score in the input ZSETs by a given number. (Each input ZSET can be multiplied by a different number.) Every 5 minutes, let's go ahead and delete any item that isn't in the top 20,000 items, and rescale the view counts to be half has much as they were before. The following listing will both delete items and rescale remaining scores.

Listing 2.10 The `rescale_viewed()` daemon function

Remove any item not in the top 20,000 viewed items.

```
def rescale_viewed(conn):
    while not QUIT:
        conn.zremrangebyrank('viewed:', 20000, -1)
        conn.zinterstore('viewed:', {'viewed:': .5})
        time.sleep(300)
```

Rescale all counts to be 1/2 of what they were before.

Do it again in 5 minutes.

With the rescaling and the counting, we now have a constantly updated list of the most-frequently viewed items at Fake Web Retailer. Now all we need to do is to update our `can_cache()` function to take into consideration our new method of deciding whether a page can be cached, and we're done. You can see our new `can_cache()` function here.

Listing 2.11 The `can_cache()` function

Get the item ID for the page, if any.

Check whether the page can be statically cached and whether this is an item page.

```
def can_cache(conn, request):
    item_id = extract_item_id(request)
    if not item_id or is_dynamic(request):
        return False
    rank = conn.zrank('viewed:', item_id)
    return rank is not None and rank < 10000
```

Get the rank of the item.

Return whether the item has a high enough view count to be cached.

And with that final piece, we're now able to take our actual viewing statistics and only cache those pages that are in the top 10,000 product pages. If we wanted to store even more pages with minimal effort, we could compress the pages before storing them in Redis, use a technology called *edge side includes* to remove parts of our pages, or we could pre-optimize our templates to get rid of unnecessary whitespace. Each of these techniques and more can reduce memory use and increase how many pages we could store in Redis, all for additional performance improvements as our site grows.

2.6   Summary

In this chapter, we've covered a few methods for reducing database and web server load for Fake Web Retailer. The ideas and methods used in these examples are currently in use in real web applications today.

If there's one thing that you should take away from this chapter, it's that as you're building new pieces that fit within your application, you shouldn't be afraid to revisit and update old components that you've already written. Sometimes you may find that your earlier solutions got you a few steps toward what you need now (as was the case with both shopping cart cookies and web analytics combined with our initial login session cookies code). As we continue through this book, we'll keep introducing new topics, and we'll occasionally revisit them later to improve performance or functionality, or to reuse ideas we already understand.

Now that you've gotten a taste for what Redis can do as part of a real application, the next chapter will go over a wider variety of commands available in Redis. After you learn more about each structure and what can be done with them, you'll be ready to build even more useful components for other layers of your application or stack of services. So what are you waiting for? Keep reading!

Part 2

Core concepts

Through these next several chapters, we'll dig into standard Redis commands, how they manipulate data, and how to configure Redis. In the latter chapters, we'll build ever-growing pieces of support tools and applications, until we finally build a simple social network completely within Redis.

Commands in Redis

This chapter covers

- String, list, and set commands
- Hash and sorted set commands
- Publish/subscribe commands
- Other commands

In this chapter, we'll primarily cover commands that we haven't already covered in chapters 1 and 2. By learning about Redis through its commands, you'll be able to build on the examples provided and have a better understanding of how to solve your own problems. If you're looking for short examples that are more than the simple interactions I show here, you'll find some in chapter 2.

The commands that are highlighted in this chapter are broken down by structure or concept, and were chosen because they include 95% or more of the typical Redis calls in a variety of applications. The examples are interactions in the console, similar to the way I introduced each of the structures in chapter 1. Where appropriate, I'll reference earlier or later sections that use those commands.

In the section for each of the different data types, I'll show commands that are unique to the different structures, primarily focusing on what makes those structures and commands distinct. Let's start by seeing how Redis STRINGs offer more than just GET and SET operations.

ADDITIONAL DOCUMENTATION FOR COMMANDS NOT COVERED   In this chapter, I only cover the most commonly used commands or those commands that we'll use in later chapters. If you're looking for a full command and documentation reference, you can visit http://redis.io/commands.

REDIS 2.4 AND 2.6   As mentioned in appendix A, as of the time of this writing, precompiled versions of Redis for Windows are from the 2.4 series. In this and other chapters, we use features that are only available in Redis 2.6 and later. The primary differences between Redis 2.4 and 2.6 include (but aren't limited to) Lua scripting (which we'll discuss in chapter 11), millisecond-level precision for expiration (PTTL, PEXPIRE, and PEXPIREAT, described in this chapter), some bit operations (BITOP and BITCOUNT), and some commands now taking multiple arguments where they previously only took one argument (RPUSH, LPUSH, SADD, SREM, HDEL, ZADD, and ZREM).

3.1   *Strings*

You'll remember from chapters 1 and 2 that STRINGs hold sequences of bytes, not significantly different from strings in many programming languages, or even C/C++–style char arrays. In Redis, STRINGs are used to store three types of values:

- Byte string values
- Integer values
- Floating-point values

Integers and floats can be incremented or decremented by an arbitrary numeric value (integers turning into floats as necessary). Integers have ranges that are equivalent to the platform's long integer range (signed 32-bit integers on 32-bit platforms, and signed 64-bit integers on 64-bit platforms), and floats have ranges and values limited to IEEE 754 floating-point doubles. This three-way ability to look at the simplest of Redis values can be an advantage; it offers more flexibility in data representation than if only byte string values were allowed.

In this section, we'll talk about the simplest structure available to Redis, the STRING. We'll cover the basic numeric increment and decrement operations, followed later by the bit and substring manipulation calls, and you'll come to understand that even the simplest of structures has a few surprises that can make it useful in a variety of powerful ways.

In table 3.1, you can see the available integer and float increment/decrement operations available on Redis STRINGs.

Table 3.1   Increment and decrement commands in Redis

Command	Example use and description
INCR	INCR key-name—Increments the value stored at the key by 1
DECR	DECR key-name—Decrements the value stored at the key by 1

Table 3.1 Increment and decrement commands in Redis *(continued)*

Command	Example use and description
INCRBY	INCRBY key-name amount—Increments the value stored at the key by the provided integer value
DECRBY	DECRBY key-name amount—Decrements the value stored at the key by the provided integer value
INCRBYFLOAT	INCRBYFLOAT key-name amount—Increments the value stored at the key by the provided float value (available in Redis 2.6 and later)

When setting a STRING value in Redis, if that value could be interpreted as a base-10 integer or a floating-point value, Redis will detect this and allow you to manipulate the value using the various INCR* and DECR* operations. If you try to increment or decrement a key that doesn't exist or is an empty string, Redis will operate as though that key's value were zero. If you try to increment or decrement a key that has a value that can't be interpreted as an integer or float, you'll receive an error. In the next listing, you can see some interactions with these commands.

Listing 3.1 A sample interaction showing INCR and DECR operations in Redis

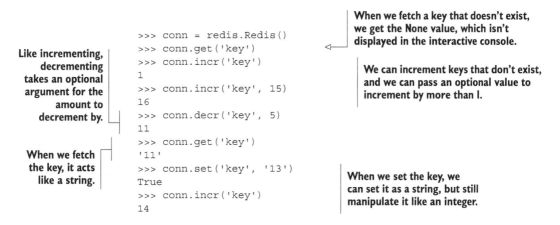

After reading other chapters, you may notice that we really only call incr(). Internally, the Python Redis libraries call INCRBY with either the optional second value passed, or 1 if the value is omitted. As of this writing, the Python Redis client library supports the full command set of Redis 2.6, and offers INCRBYFLOAT support via an incrbyfloat() method that works the same as incr().

Redis additionally offers methods for reading and writing parts of byte string values (integer and float values can also be accessed as though they're byte strings, though that use is somewhat uncommon). This can be useful if we were to use Redis STRING values to pack structured data in an efficient fashion, which we'll talk about in chapter 9. Table 3.2 shows some methods that can be used to manipulate substrings and individual bits of STRINGs in Redis.

Table 3.2 Substring manipulation commands available to Redis

Command	Example use and description
APPEND	APPEND key-name value—Concatenates the provided value to the string already stored at the given key
GETRANGE	GETRANGE key-name start end—Fetches the substring, including all characters from the start offset to the end offset, inclusive
SETRANGE	SETRANGE key-name offset value—Sets the substring starting at the provided offset to the given value
GETBIT	GETBIT key-name offset—Treats the byte string as a bit string, and returns the value of the bit in the string at the provided bit offset
SETBIT	SETBIT key-name offset value—Treats the byte string as a bit string, and sets the value of the bit in the string at the provided bit offset
BITCOUNT	BITCOUNT key-name [start end]—Counts the number of 1 bits in the string, optionally starting and finishing at the provided byte offsets
BITOP	BITOP operation dest-key key-name [key-name ...]—Performs one of the bitwise operations, AND, OR, XOR, or NOT, on the strings provided, storing the result in the destination key

GETRANGE AND SUBSTR In the past, GETRANGE was named SUBSTR, and the Python client continues to use the substr() method name to fetch ranges from the string. When using a version of Redis later than 2.6, you should use the get-range() method, and use substr() for Redis versions before 2.6.

When writing to strings using SETRANGE and SETBIT, if the STRING wasn't previously long enough, Redis will automatically extend the STRING with nulls before updating and writing the new data. When reading STRINGs with GETRANGE, any request for data beyond the end of the STRING won't be returned, but when reading bits with GETBIT, any bit beyond the end of the STRING is considered zero. In the following listing, you can see some uses of these STRING manipulation commands.

Listing 3.2 A sample interaction showing substring and bit operations in Redis

When appending a value, Redis returns the length of the string so far.

Let's append the string 'hello ' to the previously nonexistent key 'new-string-key'.

```
>>> conn.append('new-string-key', 'hello ')
6L
>>> conn.append('new-string-key', 'world!')
12L
>>> conn.substr('new-string-key', 3, 7)
'lo wo'
>>> conn.setrange('new-string-key', 0, 'H')
```

Redis uses 0-indexing, and when accessing ranges, is inclusive of the endpoints by default.

Let's set a couple string ranges.

The string 'lo wo' is from the middle of 'hello world!'

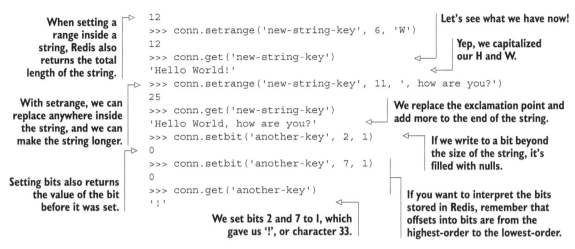

When setting a range inside a string, Redis also returns the total length of the string.

```
12
>>> conn.setrange('new-string-key', 6, 'W')
12
>>> conn.get('new-string-key')
'Hello World!'
```

Let's see what we have now!

Yep, we capitalized our H and W.

With setrange, we can replace anywhere inside the string, and we can make the string longer.

```
>>> conn.setrange('new-string-key', 11, ', how are you?')
25
>>> conn.get('new-string-key')
'Hello World, how are you?'
>>> conn.setbit('another-key', 2, 1)
```

We replace the exclamation point and add more to the end of the string.

Setting bits also returns the value of the bit before it was set.

```
0
>>> conn.setbit('another-key', 7, 1)
0
>>> conn.get('another-key')
'!'
```

If we write to a bit beyond the size of the string, it's filled with nulls.

If you want to interpret the bits stored in Redis, remember that offsets into bits are from the highest-order to the lowest-order.

We set bits 2 and 7 to 1, which gave us '!', or character 33.

In many other key-value databases, data is stored as a plain string with no opportunities for manipulation. Some other key-value databases do allow you to prepend or append bytes, but Redis is unique in its ability to read and write substrings. In many ways, even if Redis only offered STRINGs and these methods to manipulate strings, Redis would be more powerful than many other systems; enterprising users could use the substring and bit manipulation calls along with WATCH/MULTI/EXEC (which we'll briefly introduce in section 3.7.2, and talk about extensively in chapter 4) to build arbitrary data structures. In chapter 9, we'll talk about using STRINGs to store a type of simple mappings that can greatly reduce memory use in some situations.

With a little work, we can store some types of sequences, but we're limited in the kinds of manipulations we can perform. But if we use LISTs, we have a wider range of commands and ways to manipulate LIST items.

3.2 Lists

As you may remember from chapter 1, LISTs allow you to push and pop items from both ends of a sequence, fetch individual items, and perform a variety of other operations that are expected of lists. LISTs by themselves can be great for keeping a queue of work items, recently viewed articles, or favorite contacts.

In this section, we'll talk about LISTs, which store an ordered sequence of STRING values. We'll cover some of the most commonly used LIST manipulation commands for pushing and popping items from LISTs. After reading this section, you'll know how to manipulate LISTs using the most common commands. We'll start by looking at table 3.3, where you can see some of the most frequently used LIST commands.

Table 3.3 Some commonly used LIST commands

Command	Example use and description
RPUSH	RPUSH key-name value [value ...]—Pushes the value(s) onto the right end of the list
LPUSH	LPUSH key-name value [value ...]—Pushes the value(s) onto the left end of the list

Table 3.3 Some commonly used `LIST` commands *(continued)*

Command	Example use and description
RPOP	RPOP key-name—Removes and returns the rightmost item from the list
LPOP	LPOP key-name—Removes and returns the leftmost item from the list
LINDEX	LINDEX key-name offset—Returns the item at the given offset
LRANGE	LRANGE key-name start end—Returns the items in the list at the offsets from start to end, inclusive
LTRIM	LTRIM key-name start end—Trims the list to only include items at indices between start and end, inclusive

The semantics of the `LIST` push commands shouldn't be surprising, and neither should the pop commands. We covered a couple of these, along with both `LINDEX` and `LRANGE`, back in chapter 1. The next listing shows some uses of these push and pop commands.

Listing 3.3   A sample interaction showing `LIST` push and pop commands in Redis

When we push items onto the list, it returns the length of the list after the push has completed.

```
>>> conn.rpush('list-key', 'last')
1L
>>> conn.lpush('list-key', 'first')
2L
>>> conn.rpush('list-key', 'new last')
3L
>>> conn.lrange('list-key', 0, -1)
['first', 'last', 'new last']
>>> conn.lpop('list-key')
'first'
>>> conn.lpop('list-key')
'last'
>>> conn.lrange('list-key', 0, -1)
['new last']
>>> conn.rpush('list-key', 'a', 'b', 'c')
4L
>>> conn.lrange('list-key', 0, -1)
['new last', 'a', 'b', 'c']
>>> conn.ltrim('list-key', 2, -1)
True
>>> conn.lrange('list-key', 0, -1)
['b', 'c']
```

We can easily push on both ends of the list.

Semantically, the left end of the list is the beginning, and the right end of the list is the end.

Popping off the left items repeatedly will return items from left to right.

We can push multiple items at the same time.

We can trim any number of items from the start, end, or both.

The `LTRIM` command is new in this example, and we can combine it with `LRANGE` to give us something that functions much like an `LPOP` or `RPOP` call that returns and pops multiple items at once. We'll talk more about how to make these kinds of composite commands atomic[1] later in this chapter, as well as dive deeper into more advanced Redis-style transactions in chapter 4.

---

[1] In Redis, when we talk about a group of commands as being *atomic*, we mean that no other client can read or change data while we're reading or changing that same data.

Among the LIST commands we didn't introduce in chapter 1 are a few commands that allow you to move items from one list to another, and even block while waiting for other clients to add items to LISTs. Table 3.4 shows our blocking pop and item moving commands.

Table 3.4   Some LIST commands for blocking LIST pops and moving items between LISTs

Command	Example use and description
BLPOP	BLPOP key-name [key-name ...] timeout—Pops the leftmost item from the first non-empty LIST, or waits the timeout in seconds for an item
BRPOP	BRPOP key-name [key-name ...] timeout—Pops the rightmost item from the first non-empty LIST, or waits the timeout in seconds for an item
RPOPLPUSH	RPOPLPUSH source-key dest-key—Pops the rightmost item from the source and LPUSHes the item to the destination, also returning the item to the user
BRPOPLPUSH	BRPOPLPUSH source-key dest-key timeout—Pops the rightmost item from the source and LPUSHes the item to the destination, also returning the item to the user, and waiting up to the timeout if the source is empty

This set of commands is particularly useful when we talk about queues in chapter 6. The following listing shows some examples of moving items around with BRPOPLPUSH and popping items from multiple lists with BLPOP.

Listing 3.4   Blocking LIST pop and movement commands in Redis

```
>>> conn.rpush('list', 'item1')
1
>>> conn.rpush('list', 'item2')
2
>>> conn.rpush('list2', 'item3')
1
>>> conn.brpoplpush('list2', 'list', 1)
'item3'
>>> conn.brpoplpush('list2', 'list', 1)
>>> conn.lrange('list', 0, -1)
['item3', 'item1', 'item2']
>>> conn.brpoplpush('list', 'list2', 1)
'item2'
>>> conn.blpop(['list', 'list2'], 1)
('list', 'item3')
>>> conn.blpop(['list', 'list2'], 1)
('list', 'item1')
>>> conn.blpop(['list', 'list2'], 1)
('list2', 'item2')
>>> conn.blpop(['list', 'list2'], 1)
>>>
```

Let's move an item from one list to the other, also returning the item.

When a list is empty, the blocking pop will stall for the timeout, and return None (which isn't displayed in the interactive console).

Let's add some items to a couple of lists to start.

We popped the rightmost item from "list2" and pushed it to the left of "list".

Blocking left-popping items from these will check lists for items in the order that they are passed until they are empty.

The most common use case for using blocking pop commands as well as the pop/push combination commands is in the development of messaging and task queues, which we'll cover in chapter 6.

Exercise: Reducing memory use with LISTS

Back in sections 2.1 and 2.5, we used ZSETs to keep a listing of recently viewed items. Those recently viewed items included timestamps as scores to allow us to perform analytics during cleanup or after purchase. But including these timestamps takes space, and if timestamps aren't necessary for our analytics, then using a ZSET just wastes space. Try to replace the use of ZSETs in update_token() with LISTs, while keeping the same semantics. Hint: If you find yourself stuck, you can skip ahead to section 6.1.1 for a push in the right direction.

One of the primary benefits of LISTs is that they can contain multiple string values, which can allow you to group data together. SETs offer a similar feature, but with the caveat that all items in a given SET are unique. Let's look at how that changes what we can do with SETs.

3.3   Sets

You'll remember from chapter 1 that SETs hold unique items in an unordered fashion. You can quickly add, remove, and determine whether an item is in the SET. Among the many uses of SETs are storing who voted for an article and which articles belong to a specific group, as seen in chapter 1.

In this section, we'll discuss some of the most frequently used commands that operate on SETs. You'll learn about the standard operations for inserting, removing, and moving members between SETs, as well as commands to perform intersection, union, and differences on SETs. When finished with this section, you'll be better prepared to fully understand how our search examples in chapter 7 work.

Let's take a look at table 3.5 to see some of the more commonly used set commands.

Table 3.5   Some commonly used SET commands

Command	Example use and description
SADD	SADD key-name item [item ...]—Adds the items to the set and returns the number of items added that weren't already present
SREM	SREM key-name item [item ...]—Removes the items and returns the number of items that were removed
SISMEMBER	SISMEMBER key-name item—Returns whether the item is in the SET
SCARD	SCARD key-name—Returns the number of items in the SET
SMEMBERS	SMEMBERS key-name—Returns all of the items in the SET as a Python set
SRANDMEMBER	SRANDMEMBER key-name [count]—Returns one or more random items from the SET. When count is positive, Redis will return count distinct randomly chosen items, and when count is negative, Redis will return count randomly chosen items that may not be distinct.

Table 3.5   Some commonly used `SET` **commands** *(continued)*

Command	Example use and description
SPOP	`SPOP key-name`—Removes and returns a random item from the `SET`
SMOVE	`SMOVE source-key dest-key item`—If the item is in the source, removes the item from the source and adds it to the destination, returning if the item was moved

Some of those commands should be familiar from chapter 1, so let's jump to the next listing to see some of these commands in action.

Listing 3.5   A sample interaction showing some common `SET` **commands in Redis**

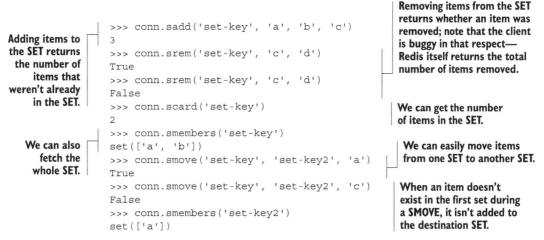

Adding items to the SET returns the number of items that weren't already in the SET.

We can also fetch the whole SET.

Removing items from the SET returns whether an item was removed; note that the client is buggy in that respect— Redis itself returns the total number of items removed.

We can get the number of items in the SET.

We can easily move items from one SET to another SET.

When an item doesn't exist in the first set during a SMOVE, it isn't added to the destination SET.

```
>>> conn.sadd('set-key', 'a', 'b', 'c')
3
>>> conn.srem('set-key', 'c', 'd')
True
>>> conn.srem('set-key', 'c', 'd')
False
>>> conn.scard('set-key')
2
>>> conn.smembers('set-key')
set(['a', 'b'])
>>> conn.smove('set-key', 'set-key2', 'a')
True
>>> conn.smove('set-key', 'set-key2', 'c')
False
>>> conn.smembers('set-key2')
set(['a'])
```

Using just these commands, we can keep track of unique events and items like we did in chapter 1 with voting and article groups. But the real power of `SET`s is in the commands that combine multiple `SET`s at the same time. Table 3.6 shows some of the ways that you can relate multiple `SET`s to each other.

Table 3.6   Operations for combining and manipulating `SET`s **in Redis**

Command	Example use and description
SDIFF	`SDIFF key-name [key-name ...]`—Returns the items in the first `SET` that weren't in any of the other `SET`s (mathematical set difference operation)
SDIFFSTORE	`SDIFFSTORE dest-key key-name [key-name ...]`—Stores at the `dest-key` the items in the first `SET` that weren't in any of the other `SET`s (mathematical set difference operation)
SINTER	`SINTER key-name [key-name ...]`—Returns the items that are in all of the `SET`s (mathematical set intersection operation)

Table 3.6   Operations for combining and manipulating SETs in Redis *(continued)*

Command	Example use and description
SINTERSTORE	SINTERSTORE dest-key key-name [key-name ...]—Stores at the dest-key the items that are in all of the SETs (mathematical set intersection operation)
SUNION	SUNION key-name [key-name ...]—Returns the items that are in at least one of the SETs (mathematical set union operation)
SUNIONSTORE	SUNIONSTORE dest-key key-name [key-name ...]—Stores at the dest-key the items that are in at least one of the SETs (mathematical set union operation)

This group of commands are three fundamental SET operations, with both "return the result" and "store the result" versions. Let's see a sample of what these commands are able to do.

Listing 3.6   A sample interaction showing SET difference, intersection, and union in Redis

We can calculate the result of removing all of the items in the second SET from the first SET.

```
>>> conn.sadd('skey1', 'a', 'b', 'c', 'd')
4
>>> conn.sadd('skey2', 'c', 'd', 'e', 'f')
4
>>> conn.sdiff('skey1', 'skey2')
set(['a', 'b'])
>>> conn.sinter('skey1', 'skey2')
set(['c', 'd'])
>>> conn.sunion('skey1', 'skey2')
set(['a', 'c', 'b', 'e', 'd', 'f'])
```

First we'll add a few items to a couple of SETs.

We can also find out which items exist in both SETs.

And we can find out all of the items that are in either of the SETs.

If you're comparing with Python sets, Redis SETs offer many of the same semantics and functionality, but are available remotely to potentially many clients. We'll dig more deeply into what SETs are capable of in chapter 7, where we build a type of search engine with them.

Coming up next, we'll talk about commands that manipulate HASHes, which allow us to group related keys and values together for easy fetching and updating.

3.4   *Hashes*

As introduced in chapter 1, HASHes in Redis allow you to store groups of key-value pairs in a single higher-level Redis key. Functionally, the values offer some of the same features as values in STRINGs and can be useful to group related data together. This data grouping can be thought of as being similar to a row in a relational database or a document in a document store.

In this section, we'll talk about the most commonly used commands that manipulate HASHes. You'll learn more about the operations for adding and removing key-value pairs to HASHes, as well as commands to fetch all of the HASH contents along with the ability to increment or decrement values. When finished with this section, you'll better understand the usefulness of storing your data in HASHes and how to do so. Look at table 3.7 to see some commonly used HASH commands.

Table 3.7 Operations for adding and removing items from HASHes

Command	Example use and description
HMGET	HMGET key-name key [key ...]—Fetches the values at the fields in the HASH
HMSET	HMSET key-name key value [key value ...]—Sets the values of the fields in the HASH
HDEL	HDEL key-name key [key ...]—Deletes the key-value pairs in the HASH, returning the number of pairs that were found and deleted
HLEN	HLEN key-name—Returns the number of key-value pairs in the HASH

Some of those commands should be familiar from chapter 1, but we have a couple of new ones for getting and setting multiple keys at the same time. These bulk commands are mostly a matter of convenience and to improve Redis's performance by reducing the number of calls and round trips between a client and Redis. Look at the next listing to see some of them in action.

Listing 3.7 A sample interaction showing some common HASH commands in Redis

```
>>> conn.hmset('hash-key', {'k1':'v1', 'k2':'v2', 'k3':'v3'})
True
>>> conn.hmget('hash-key', ['k2', 'k3'])
['v2', 'v3']
>>> conn.hlen('hash-key')
3
>>> conn.hdel('hash-key', 'k1', 'k3')
True
```

We can add multiple items to the hash in one call.

We can fetch a subset of the values in a single call.

The HLEN command is typically used for debugging very large HASHes.

The HDEL command handles multiple arguments without needing an HMDEL counterpart and returns True if any fields were removed.

The HMGET/HMSET commands are similar to their single-argument versions that we introduced in chapter 1, only differing in that they take a list or dictionary for arguments instead of the single entries.

Table 3.8 shows some other bulk commands and more STRING-like operations on HASHes.

With the availability of HGETALL, it may not seem as though HKEYS and HVALUES would be that useful, but when you expect your values to be large, you can fetch the keys, and then get the values one by one to keep from blocking other requests.

Table 3.8   More bulk operations and `STRING`-like calls over `HASH`es

Command	Example use and description
HEXISTS	`HEXISTS key-name key`—Returns whether the given key exists in the HASH
HKEYS	`HKEYS key-name`—Fetches the keys in the HASH
HVALS	`HVALS key-name`—Fetches the values in the HASH
HGETALL	`HGETALL key-name`—Fetches all key-value pairs from the HASH
HINCRBY	`HINCRBY key-name key increment`—Increments the value stored at the given key by the integer increment
HINCRBYFLOAT	`HINCRBYFLOAT key-name key increment`—Increments the value stored at the given key by the float increment

HINCRBY and HINCRBYFLOAT should remind you of the INCRBY and INCRBYFLOAT operations available on STRING keys, and they have the same semantics, applied to HASH values. Let's look at some of these commands being used in the next listing.

Listing 3.8   A sample interaction showing some more advanced features of Redis HASHes

```
>>> conn.hmset('hash-key2', {'short':'hello', 'long':1000*'1'})
True
>>> conn.hkeys('hash-key2')
['long', 'short']
>>> conn.hexists('hash-key2', 'num')
False
>>> conn.hincrby('hash-key2', 'num')
1L
>>> conn.hexists('hash-key2', 'num')
True
```

Fetching keys can be useful to keep from needing to transfer large values when we're looking into HASHes.

We can also check the existence of specific keys.

Incrementing a previously nonexistent key in a hash behaves just like on strings; Redis operates as though the value had been 0.

As we described earlier, when confronted with a large value in a HASH, we can fetch the keys and only fetch values that we're interested in to reduce the amount of data that's transferred. We can also perform key checks, as we could perform member checks on SETs with SISMEMBER. And back in chapter 1, we used HINCRBY to keep track of the number of votes an article had received, which we just revisited.

Let's look at a structure that we'll be using fairly often in the remaining chapters: sorted sets.

3.5   *Sorted sets*

ZSETs offer the ability to store a mapping of members to scores (similar to the keys and values of HASHes). These mappings allow us to manipulate the numeric scores,[2] and fetch and scan over both members and scores based on the sorted order of the scores. In chapter 1, we showed a brief example that used ZSETs as a way of sorting submitted

---

[2] Scores are actually stored inside Redis as IEEE 754 floating-point doubles.

articles based on time and how many up-votes they had received, and in chapter 2, we had an example that used ZSETs as a way of handling the expiration of old cookies.

In this section, we'll talk about commands that operate on ZSETs. You'll learn how to add and update items in ZSETs, as well as how to use the ZSET intersection and union commands. When finished with this section, you'll have a much clearer understanding about how ZSETs work, which will help you to better understand what we did with them in chapter 1, and how we'll use them in chapters 5, 6, and 7.

Let's look at some commonly used ZSET commands in table 3.9.

Table 3.9   Some common ZSET commands

Command	Example use and description
ZADD	ZADD key-name score member [score member ...]—Adds members with the given scores to the ZSET
ZREM	ZREM key-name member [member ...]—Removes the members from the ZSET, returning the number of members that were removed
ZCARD	ZCARD key-name—Returns the number of members in the ZSET
ZINCRBY	ZINCRBY key-name increment member—Increments the member in the ZSET
ZCOUNT	ZCOUNT key-name min max—Returns the number of members with scores between the provided minimum and maximum
ZRANK	ZRANK key-name member—Returns the position of the given member in the ZSET
ZSCORE	ZSCORE key-name member—Returns the score of the member in the ZSET
ZRANGE	ZRANGE key-name start stop [WITHSCORES]—Returns the members and optionally the scores for the members with ranks between start and stop

We've used some of these commands in chapters 1 and 2, so they should already be familiar to you. Let's quickly revisit the use of some of our commands.

Listing 3.9   A sample interaction showing some common ZSET commands in Redis

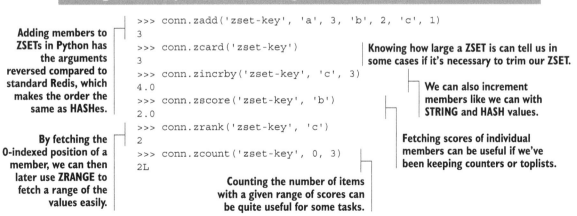

Adding members to ZSETs in Python has the arguments reversed compared to standard Redis, which makes the order the same as HASHes.

```
>>> conn.zadd('zset-key', 'a', 3, 'b', 2, 'c', 1)
3
>>> conn.zcard('zset-key')
3
>>> conn.zincrby('zset-key', 'c', 3)
4.0
>>> conn.zscore('zset-key', 'b')
2.0
>>> conn.zrank('zset-key', 'c')
2
>>> conn.zcount('zset-key', 0, 3)
2L
```

Knowing how large a ZSET is can tell us in some cases if it's necessary to trim our ZSET.

We can also increment members like we can with STRING and HASH values.

Fetching scores of individual members can be useful if we've been keeping counters or toplists.

By fetching the 0-indexed position of a member, we can then later use ZRANGE to fetch a range of the values easily.

Counting the number of items with a given range of scores can be quite useful for some tasks.

Removing members is as easy as adding them.

```
>>> conn.zrem('zset-key', 'b')
True
>>> conn.zrange('zset-key', 0, -1, withscores=True)
[('a', 3.0), ('c', 4.0)]
```

For debugging, we usually fetch the entire ZSET with this ZRANGE call, but real use cases will usually fetch items a relatively small group at a time.

You'll likely remember our use of ZADD, ZREM, ZINCRBY, ZSCORE, and ZRANGE from chapters 1 and 2, so their semantics should come as no surprise. The ZCOUNT command is a little different than the others, primarily meant to let you discover the number of values whose scores are between the provided minimum and maximum scores.

Table 3.10 shows several more ZSET commands in Redis that you'll find useful.

Table 3.10 Commands for fetching and deleting ranges of data from ZSETs and offering SET-like intersections

Command	Example use and description
ZREVRANK	ZREVRANK key-name member—Returns the position of the member in the ZSET, with members ordered in reverse
ZREVRANGE	ZREVRANGE key-name start stop [WITHSCORES]—Fetches the given members from the ZSET by rank, with members in reverse order
ZRANGEBYSCORE	ZRANGEBYSCORE key min max [WITHSCORES] [LIMIT offset count]—Fetches the members between min and max
ZREVRANGEBYSCORE	ZREVRANGEBYSCORE key max min [WITHSCORES] [LIMIT offset count]—Fetches the members in reverse order between min and max
ZREMRANGEBYRANK	ZREMRANGEBYRANK key-name start stop—Removes the items from the ZSET with ranks between start and stop
ZREMRANGEBYSCORE	ZREMRANGEBYSCORE key-name min max—Removes the items from the ZSET with scores between min and max
ZINTERSTORE	ZINTERSTORE dest-key key-count key [key ...] [WEIGHTS weight [weight ...]] [AGGREGATE SUM|MIN|MAX]—Performs a SET-like intersection of the provided ZSETs
ZUNIONSTORE	ZUNIONSTORE dest-key key-count key [key ...] [WEIGHTS weight [weight ...]] [AGGREGATE SUM|MIN|MAX]—Performs a SET-like union of the provided ZSETs

This is the first time that you've seen a few of these commands. If some of the ZREV* commands are confusing, remember that they work the same as their nonreversed counterparts, except that the ZSET behaves as if it were in reverse order (sorted by score from high to low). You can see a few examples of their use in the next listing.

Listing 3.10   A sample interaction showing ZINTERSTORE and ZUNIONSTORE

We'll start out by creating
a couple of ZSETs.

```
>>> conn.zadd('zset-1', 'a', 1, 'b', 2, 'c', 3)
3
>>> conn.zadd('zset-2', 'b', 4, 'c', 1, 'd', 0)
3
>>> conn.zinterstore('zset-i', ['zset-1', 'zset-2'])
2L
>>> conn.zrange('zset-i', 0, -1, withscores=True)
[('c', 4.0), ('b', 6.0)]
>>> conn.zunionstore('zset-u', ['zset-1', 'zset-2'], aggregate='min')
4L
>>> conn.zrange('zset-u', 0, -1, withscores=True)
[('d', 0.0), ('a', 1.0), ('c', 1.0), ('b', 2.0)]
>>> conn.sadd('set-1', 'a', 'd')
2
>>> conn.zunionstore('zset-u2', ['zset-1', 'zset-2', 'set-1'])
4L
>>> conn.zrange('zset-u2', 0, -1, withscores=True)
[('d', 1.0), ('a', 2.0), ('c', 4.0), ('b', 6.0)]
```

When performing
ZINTERSTORE or
ZUNIONSTORE, our
default aggregate is
sum, so scores of items
that are in multiple
ZSETs are added.

It's easy
to provide
different
aggregates,
though
we're
limited to
sum, min,
and max.

We can also pass SETs as inputs to ZINTERSTORE
and ZUNIONSTORE; they behave as though they
were ZSETs with all scores equal to 1.

ZSET union and intersection can be difficult to understand at first glance, so let's look at some figures that show what happens during the processes of both intersection and union. Figure 3.1 shows the intersection of the two ZSETs and the final ZSET result. In this case, our aggregate is the default of sum, so scores are added.

Unlike intersection, when we perform a union operation, items that exist in at least one of the input ZSETs are included in the output. Figure 3.2 shows the result of performing a union operation with a different aggregate function, min, which takes the minimum score if a member is in multiple input ZSETs.

In chapter 1, we used the fact that we can include SETs as part of ZSET union and intersection operations. This feature allowed us to easily add and remove articles from groups without needing to propagate scoring and insertion times into additional ZSETs. Figure 3.3 shows a ZUNIONSTORE call that combines two ZSETs with one SET to produce a final ZSET.

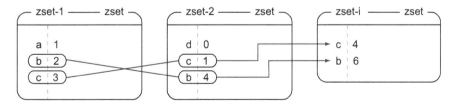

Figure 3.1   What happens when calling conn.zinterstore('zset-i', ['zset-1', 'zset-2']); **elements that exist in both zset-1 and zset-2 are added together to get zset-i**

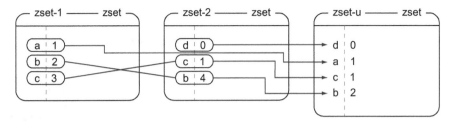

Figure 3.2   What happens when calling `conn.zunionstore('zset-u', ['zset-1',` `'zset-2'], aggregate='min');` **elements that exist in either zset-1 or zset-2 are combined with the** `minimum` **function to get zset-u**

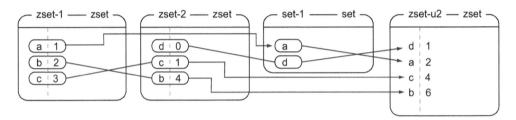

Figure 3.3   What happens when calling `conn.zunionstore('zset-u2', ['zset-1', 'zset-2',` `'set-1']);` **elements that exist in any of zset-1, zset-2, or set-1 are combined via addition to get zset-u2**

In chapter 7, we'll use ZINTERSTORE and ZUNIONSTORE as parts of a few different types of search. We'll also talk about a few different ways to combine ZSET scores with the optional WEIGHTS parameter to further extend the types of problems that can be solved with SETs and ZSETs.

As you're developing applications, you may have come upon a pattern known as publish/subscribe, also referred to as *pub/sub*. Redis includes this functionality, which we'll cover next.

3.6   *Publish/subscribe*

If you're confused because you can't remember reading about publish or subscribe yet, don't be—this is the first time we've talked about it. Generally, the concept of publish/subscribe, also known as pub/sub, is characterized by listeners *subscribing* to channels, with publishers sending binary string messages to channels. Anyone listening to a given channel will receive all messages sent to that channel while they're connected and listening. You can think of it like a radio station, where subscribers can listen to multiple radio stations at the same time, and publishers can send messages on any radio station.

In this section, we'll discuss and use operations involving publish and subscribe. When finished with this section, you'll know how to use these commands, and why we use other similar solutions in later chapters.

In Redis, the pub/sub concept has been included through the use of a collection of the five commands shown in table 3.11.

Table 3.11 Commands for handling pub/sub in Redis

Command	Example use and description
SUBSCRIBE	SUBSCRIBE channel [channel ...]—Subscribes to the given channels
UNSUBSCRIBE	UNSUBSCRIBE [channel [channel ...]]—Unsubscribes from the provided channels, or unsubscribes all channels if no channel is given
PUBLISH	PUBLISH channel message—Publishes a message to the given channel
PSUBSCRIBE	PSUBSCRIBE pattern [pattern ...]—Subscribes to messages broadcast to channels that match the given pattern
PUNSUBSCRIBE	PUNSUBSCRIBE [pattern [pattern ...]]—Unsubscribes from the provided patterns, or unsubscribes from all subscribed patterns if none are given

With the way the PUBLISH and SUBSCRIBE commands are implemented on the Python side of things, it's easier to demonstrate the feature if we use a helper thread to handle the PUBLISHing. You can see an example of PUBLISH/SUBSCRIBE in the next listing.[3]

Listing 3.11 Using PUBLISH and SUBSCRIBE in Redis

We sleep initially in the function to let the SUBSCRIBEr connect and start listening for messages.

Let's start the publisher thread to send three messages.

After publishing, we'll pause for a moment so that we can see this happen over time.

We'll set up the pubsub object and subscribe to a channel.

```
>>> def publisher(n):
...     time.sleep(1)
...     for i in xrange(n):
...         conn.publish('channel', i)
...         time.sleep(1)
...
>>> def run_pubsub():
...     threading.Thread(target=publisher, args=(3,)).start()
...     pubsub = conn.pubsub()
...     pubsub.subscribe(['channel'])
...     count = 0
...     for item in pubsub.listen():
...         print item
...         count += 1
...         if count == 4:
...             pubsub.unsubscribe()
...         if count == 5:
...             break
...
```

We can listen to subscription messages by iterating over the result of pubsub.listen().

We'll print every message that we receive.

We'll stop listening for new messages after the subscribe message and three real messages by unsubscribing.

When we receive the unsubscribe message, we need to stop receiving messages.

```
>>> run_pubsub()
{'pattern': None, 'type': 'subscribe', 'channel': 'channel', 'data': 1L}
```

Actually run the functions to see them work.

When subscribing, we receive a message on the listen channel.

---

[3] If you'd like to run this code yourself, you can: I included the publisher() and run_pubsub() functions in the source code for this chapter.

```
{'pattern': None, 'type': 'message', 'channel': 'channel', 'data': '0'}
{'pattern': None, 'type': 'message', 'channel': 'channel', 'data': '1'}
{'pattern': None, 'type': 'message', 'channel': 'channel', 'data': '2'}
{'pattern': None, 'type': 'unsubscribe', 'channel': 'channel', 'data':
0L}
```

When we unsubscribe, we receive a message telling us which channels we have unsubscribed from and the number of channels we are still subscribed to.

These are the structures that are produced as items when we iterate over pubsub.listen().

The publish/subscribe pattern and its Redis implementation can be useful. If you skip ahead and scan around other chapters, you'll notice that we only use publish/subscribe in one other section, section 8.5. If PUBLISH and SUBSCRIBE are so useful, why don't we use them very much? There are two reasons.

One reason is because of Redis system reliability. In older versions of Redis, a client that had subscribed to channels but didn't read sent messages fast enough could cause Redis itself to keep a large outgoing buffer. If this outgoing buffer grew too large, it could cause Redis to slow down drastically or crash, could cause the operating system to kill Redis, and could even cause the operating system itself to become unusable. Modern versions of Redis don't have this issue, and will disconnect subscribed clients that are unable to keep up with the client-output-buffer-limit pubsub configuration option (which we'll talk about in chapter 8).

The second reason is for data transmission reliability. Within any sort of networked system, you must operate under the assumption that your connection could fail at some point. Typically, this is handled by one side or the other reconnecting as a result of a connection error. Our Python Redis client will normally handle connection issues well by automatically reconnecting on failure, automatically handling connection pooling (we'll talk about this more in chapter 4), and more. But in the case of clients that have subscribed, if the client is disconnected and a message is sent before it can reconnect, the client will never see the message. When you're relying on receiving messages over a channel, the semantics of PUBLISH/SUBSCRIBE in Redis may let you down.

It's for these two reasons that we write two different methods to handle reliable message delivery in chapter 6, which works in the face of network disconnections, and which won't cause Redis memory to grow (even in older versions of Redis) unless you want it to.

If you like the simplicity of using PUBLISH/SUBSCRIBE, and you're okay with the chance that you may lose a little data, then feel free to use pub/sub instead of our methods, as we also do in section 8.5; just remember to configure client-output-buffer-limit pubsub reasonably before starting.

At this point, we've covered the majority of commands that you'll use on a regular basis that are related to individual data types. There are a few more commands that you'll also likely use, which don't fit into our nice five structures-plus-pub/sub theme.

3.7 Other commands

So far we've gone through the five structures that Redis provides, as well as shown a bit of pub/sub. The commands in this section are commands that operate on multiple types of data. We'll first cover SORT, which can involve STRINGs, SETs or LISTs, and HASHes all at the same time. We'll then cover basic transactions with MULTI and EXEC, which can allow you to execute multiple commands together as though they were just one command. Finally, we'll cover the variety of automatic expiration commands for automatically deleting unnecessary data.

After reading this section, you should have a better idea of how to combine and manipulate multiple data types at the same time.

3.7.1 Sorting

Sorting in Redis is similar to sorting in other languages: we want to take a sequence of items and order them according to some comparison between elements. SORT allows us to sort LISTs, SETs, and ZSETs according to data in the LIST/SET/ZSET data stored in STRING keys, or even data stored in HASHes. If you're coming from a relational database background, you can think of SORT as like the order by clause in a SQL statement that can reference other rows and tables. Table 3.12 shows the SORT command definition.

Table 3.12   The SORT command definition

Command	Example use and description
SORT	SORT source-key [BY pattern] [LIMIT offset count] [GET pattern [GET pattern ...]] [ASC|DESC] [ALPHA] [STORE dest-key]—Sorts the input LIST, SET, or ZSET according to the options provided, and returns or stores the result

Some of the more basic options with SORT include the ability to order the results in descending order rather than the default ascending order, consider items as though they were numbers, compare as though items were binary strings (the sorted order of the strings '110' and '12' are different than the sorted order of the numbers 110 and 12), sorting by values not included in the original sequence, and even fetching values outside of the input LIST, SET, or ZSET.

You can see some examples that use SORT in listing 3.12. The first few lines of the listing show the addition of some initial data, and basic sorting (by numeric value and by string order). The remaining parts show how we can store data to be sorted by and/or fetched inside HASHes using a special syntax.

Listing 3.12   A sample interaction showing some uses of SORT

```
>>> conn.rpush('sort-input', 23, 15, 110, 7)          Start by adding some
4                                                     items to a LIST.
>>> conn.sort('sort-input')            We can sort the
['7', '15', '23', '110']               items numerically.
```

```
>>> conn.sort('sort-input', alpha=True)
['110', '15', '23', '7']
>>> conn.hset('d-7', 'field', 5)
1L
>>> conn.hset('d-15', 'field', 1)
1L
>>> conn.hset('d-23', 'field', 9)
1L
>>> conn.hset('d-110', 'field', 3)
1L
>>> conn.sort('sort-input', by='d-*->field')
['15', '110', '7', '23']
>>> conn.sort('sort-input', by='d-*->field', get='d-*->field')
['1', '3', '5', '9']
```

And we can sort the items alphabetically.

We are just adding some additional data for SORTing and fetching.

We can sort our data by fields of HASHes.

And we can even fetch that data and return it instead of or in addition to our input data.

Sorting can be used to sort LISTs, but it can also sort SETs, turning the result into a LIST. In this example, we sorted numbers character by character (via the alpha keyword argument), we sorted some items based on external data, and we were even able to fetch external data to return. When combined with SET intersection, union, and difference, along with storing data externally inside HASHes, SORT is a powerful command. We'll spend some time talking about how to combine SET operations with SORT in chapter 7.

Though SORT is the only command that can manipulate three types of data at the same time, basic Redis transactions can let you manipulate multiple data types with a series of commands without interruption.

3.7.2   *Basic Redis transactions*

Sometimes we need to make multiple calls to Redis in order to manipulate multiple structures at the same time. Though there are a few commands to copy or move items between keys, there isn't a single command to move items between types (though you can copy from a SET to a ZSET with ZUNIONSTORE). For operations involving multiple keys (of the same or different types), Redis has five commands that help us operate on multiple keys without interruption: WATCH, MULTI, EXEC, UNWATCH, and DISCARD.

For now, we'll only talk about the simplest version of a Redis transaction, which uses MULTI and EXEC. If you want to see an example that uses WATCH, MULTI, EXEC, and UNWATCH, you can skip ahead to section 4.4, where I explain why you'd need to use WATCH and UNWATCH with MULTI and EXEC.

WHAT IS A BASIC TRANSACTION IN REDIS?

In Redis, a basic transaction involving MULTI and EXEC is meant to provide the opportunity for one client to execute multiple commands A, B, C, ... without other clients being able to interrupt them. This isn't the same as a relational database transaction, which can be executed partially, and then rolled back or committed. In Redis, every command passed as part of a basic MULTI/EXEC transaction is executed one after another until they've completed. After they've completed, other clients may execute their commands.

To perform a transaction in Redis, we first call MULTI, followed by any sequence of commands we intend to execute, followed by EXEC. When seeing MULTI, Redis will queue up commands from that same connection until it sees an EXEC, at which point Redis will execute the queued commands sequentially without interruption. Semantically, our Python library handles this by the use of what's called a *pipeline*. Calling the pipeline() method on a connection object will create a transaction, which when used correctly will automatically wrap a sequence of commands with MULTI and EXEC. Incidentally, the Python Redis client will also store the commands to send until we actually want to send them. This reduces the number of round trips between Redis and the client, which can improve the performance of a sequence of commands.

As was the case with PUBLISH and SUBSCRIBE, the simplest way to demonstrate the result of using a transaction is through the use of threads. In the next listing, you can see the result of parallel increment operations without a transaction.

Listing 3.13 What can happen without transactions during parallel execution

```
>>> def notrans():                              Increment the 'notrans:'
...     print conn.incr('notrans:')             counter and print the result.
...     time.sleep(.1)
...     conn.incr('notrans:', -1)
...                                              Decrement the
>>> if 1:                                        'notrans:' counter.
...     for i in xrange(3):
...         threading.Thread(target=notrans).start()
...     time.sleep(.5)
...
1
2
3
```

Wait for 100 milliseconds. → (points to time.sleep(.1))

Start three threads to execute the non-transactional increment/sleep/decrement. → (points to for loop)

Wait half a second for everything to be done. → (points to time.sleep(.5))

Because there's no transaction, each of the threaded commands can interleave freely, causing the counter to steadily grow in this case.

Without transactions, each of the three threads are able to increment the notrans: counter before the decrement comes through. We exaggerate potential issues here by including a 100ms sleep, but if we needed to be able to perform these two calls without other commands getting in the way, we'd have issues. The following listing shows these same operations with a transaction.

Listing 3.14 What can happen with transactions during parallel execution

```
>>> def trans():
...     pipeline = conn.pipeline()
...     pipeline.incr('trans:')
...     time.sleep(.1)
```

Create a transactional pipeline. → (points to pipeline = conn.pipeline())

Queue up the 'trans:' counter increment.

Wait for 100 milliseconds.

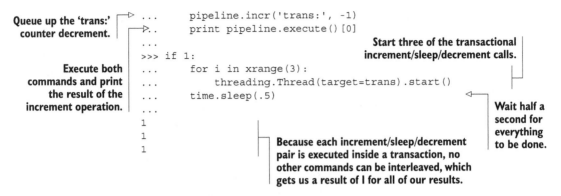

Queue up the 'trans:' counter decrement.

Execute both commands and print the result of the increment operation.

Start three of the transactional increment/sleep/decrement calls.

Wait half a second for everything to be done.

Because each increment/sleep/decrement pair is executed inside a transaction, no other commands can be interleaved, which gets us a result of 1 for all of our results.

```
     ... pipeline.incr('trans:', -1)
     ... print pipeline.execute()[0]
     ...
>>> if 1:
     ...     for i in xrange(3):
     ...         threading.Thread(target=trans).start()
     ...     time.sleep(.5)
     ...
1
1
1
```

As you can see, by using a transaction, each thread is able to execute its entire sequence of commands without other threads interrupting it, despite the delay between the two calls. Again, this is because Redis waits to execute all of the provided commands between MULTI and EXEC until all of the commands have been received and followed by an EXEC.

There are both benefits and drawbacks to using transactions, which we'll discuss further in section 4.4.

Exercise: Removing of race conditions

One of the primary purposes of MULTI/EXEC transactions is removing what are known as *race conditions*, which you saw exposed in listing 3.13. It turns out that the article_vote() function from chapter 1 has a race condition and a second related bug. The race condition can cause a memory leak, and the bug can cause a vote to not be counted correctly. The chances of either of them happening is very small, but can you spot and fix them? Hint: If you're having difficulty finding the memory leak, check out section 6.2.5 while consulting the post_article() function.

Exercise: Improving performance

A secondary purpose of using pipelines in Redis is to improve performance (we'll talk more about this in sections 4.4–4.6). In particular, by reducing the number of round trips between Redis and our client that occur over a sequence of commands, we can significantly reduce the amount of time our client is waiting for a response. In the get_articles() function we defined in chapter 1, there will actually be 26 round trips between Redis and the client to fetch a full page of articles. This is a waste. Can you change get_articles() so that it only makes two round trips?

When writing data to Redis, sometimes the data is only going to be useful for a short period of time. We can manually delete this data after that time has elapsed, or we can have Redis automatically delete the data itself by using key expiration.

3.7.3 *Expiring keys*

When writing data into Redis, there may be a point at which data is no longer needed. We can remove the data explicitly with DEL, or if we want to remove an entire key after a specified timeout, we can use what's known as *expiration*. When we say that a key has a *time to live*, or that it'll *expire* at a given time, we mean that Redis will automatically delete the key when its expiration time has arrived.

Having keys that will expire after a certain amount of time can be useful to handle the cleanup of cached data. If you look through other chapters, you won't see the use of key expiration in Redis often (except in sections 6.2, 7.1, and 7.2). This is mostly due to the types of structures that are used; few of the commands we use offer the ability to set the expiration time of a key automatically. And with containers (LISTs, SETs, HASHes, and ZSETs), we can only expire entire keys, not individual items (this is also why we use ZSETs with timestamps in a few places).

In this section, we'll cover commands that are used to expire and delete keys from Redis automatically after a specified timeout, or at a specified time. After reading this section, you'll be able to use expiration as a way of keeping Redis memory use low, and for cleaning up data you no longer need.

Table 3.13 shows the list of commands that we use to set and check the expiration times of keys in Redis.

Table 3.13 Commands for handling expiration in Redis

Command	Example use and description
PERSIST	PERSIST key-name—Removes the expiration from a key
TTL	TTL key-name—Returns the amount of time remaining before a key will expire
EXPIRE	EXPIRE key-name seconds—Sets the key to expire in the given number of seconds
EXPIREAT	EXPIREAT key-name timestamp—Sets the expiration time as the given Unix timestamp
PTTL	PTTL key-name—Returns the number of milliseconds before the key will expire (available in Redis 2.6 and later)
PEXPIRE	PEXPIRE key-name milliseconds—Sets the key to expire in the given number of milliseconds (available in Redis 2.6 and later)
PEXPIREAT	PEXPIREAT key-name timestamp-milliseconds—Sets the expiration time to be the given Unix timestamp specified in milliseconds (available in Redis 2.6 and later)

You can see a few examples of using expiration times on keys in the next listing.

Listing 3.15 A sample interaction showing the use of expiration-related commands in Redis

```
>>> conn.set('key', 'value')
True
>>> conn.get('key')
'value'
```

We're starting with a very simple STRING value.

```
>>> conn.expire('key', 2)
True
>>> time.sleep(2)
>>> conn.get('key')
>>> conn.set('key', 'value2')
True
>>> conn.expire('key', 100); conn.ttl('key')
True
100
```

If we set a key to expire in the future and we wait long enough for the key to expire, when we try to fetch the key, it's already been deleted.

We can also easily find out how long it will be before a key will expire.

Exercise: Replacing timestamp ZSETs with EXPIRE

In sections 2.1, 2.2, and 2.5, we used a ZSET with timestamps to keep a listing of session IDs to clean up. By using this ZSET, we could optionally perform analytics over our items when we cleaned sessions out. But if we aren't interested in analytics, we can instead get similar semantics with expiration, without needing a cleanup function. Can you update the update_token() and add_to_cart() functions to expire keys instead of using a "recent" ZSET and cleanup function?

3.8   Summary

In this chapter, we've looked at commands that typically should cover at least 95% of your command usage in Redis. We started with each of the different datatypes, and then discussed PUBLISH and SUBSCRIBE, followed by SORT, MULTI/EXEC transactions, and key expiration.

If there's one thing that you should learn from this chapter, it's that a wide variety of commands can be used to manipulate Redis structures in numerous ways. Although this chapter presents more than 70 of the most important commands, still more are listed and described at http://redis.io/commands.

If there's a second thing you should take away from this chapter, it's that I sometimes don't offer the perfect answer to every problem. In revisiting a few of our examples from chapters 1 and 2 in the exercises (whose answers you can see in the downloadable source code), I'm giving you an opportunity to try your hand at taking our already pretty-good answers, and making them better overall, or making them suit your problems better.

One large group of commands that we didn't cover in this chapter was configuration-related commands. In the next chapter, we get into configuring Redis to ensure your data stays healthy, and we give pointers on how to ensure that Redis performs well.

Keeping data safe and ensuring performance

This chapter covers

- Persisting data to disk
- Replicating data to other machines
- Dealing with system failures
- Redis transactions
- Non-transactional pipelines
- Diagnosing performance issues

In the last few chapters, you've learned about the variety of commands available in Redis and how they manipulate structures, and you've even solved a few problems using Redis. This chapter will prepare you for building real software with Redis by showing you how to keep your data safe, even in the face of system failure, and I'll point out methods that you can use to improve Redis performance while preserving data integrity.

We'll start by exploring the various Redis persistence options available to you for getting your data on disk. We'll then talk about the use of replication to keep up-to-date copies of your data on additional machines for both performance and data reliability. Combining replication and persistence, we'll talk about trade-offs you may need to make, and we'll walk through a few examples of choosing persistence and replication options to suit your needs. We'll then talk about Redis transactions and pipelines, and we'll finish out the chapter by discussing how to diagnose some performance issues.

As we go through this chapter, our focus is understanding more about how Redis works so that we can first ensure that our data is correct, and then work toward making our operations on the data fast.

To start, let's examine how Redis stores our information on disk so that, after restart, it's still there.

4.1   *Persistence options*

Within Redis, there are two different ways of persisting data to disk. One is a method called *snapshotting* that takes the data as it exists at one moment in time and writes it to disk. The other method is called *AOF*, or *append-only file*, and it works by copying incoming write commands to disk as they happen. These methods can be used together, separately, or not at all in some circumstances. Which to choose will depend on your data and your application.

One of the primary reasons why you'd want to store in-memory data on disk is so that you have it later, or so that you can back it up to a remote location in the case of failure. Additionally, the data that's stored in Redis may have taken a long time to compute, or may be in the process of computation, and you may want to have access to it later without having to compute it again. For some Redis uses, "computation" may simply involve an act of copying data from another database into Redis (as was the case in section 2.4), but for others, Redis could be storing aggregate analytics data from billions of log lines.

Two different groups of configuration options control how Redis will write data to disk. All of these configuration options with example configuration values can be seen in the following listing. We'll talk about them all more specifically in sections 4.1.1 and 4.1.2, but for now, we'll just look at the options so you can get familiar with them.

> **Listing 4.1   Options for persistence configuration available in Redis**

```
save 60 1000
stop-writes-on-bgsave-error no          Snapshotting
rdbcompression yes                      persistence options
dbfilename dump.rdb

appendonly no
appendfsync everysec
no-appendfsync-on-rewrite no            Append-only file          Shared option,
auto-aof-rewrite-percentage 100         persistence options       where to store
auto-aof-rewrite-min-size 64mb                                    the snapshot or
                                                                  append-only file
dir ./
```

As you saw in listing 4.1, the first few options deal with basic snapshotting, like what to name the snapshot on disk, how often to perform an automatic snapshot, whether to compress the snapshot, and whether to keep accepting writes on failure. The second group of options configure the AOF subsystem, telling Redis whether to use it, how often to sync writes to disk, whether to sync during AOF compaction, and how often to compact the AOF. In the next section, we'll talk about using snapshots to keep our data safe.

4.1.1 Persisting to disk with snapshots

In Redis, we can create a point-in-time copy of in-memory data by creating a snapshot. After creation, these snapshots can be backed up, copied to other servers to create a clone of the server, or left for a future restart.

On the configuration side of things, snapshots are written to the file referenced as `dbfilename` in the configuration, and stored in the path referenced as `dir`. Until the next snapshot is performed, data written to Redis since the last snapshot started (and completed) would be lost if there were a crash caused by Redis, the system, or the hardware.

As an example, say that we have Redis running with 10 gigabytes of data currently in memory. A previous snapshot had been started at 2:35 p.m. and had finished. Now a snapshot is started at 3:06 p.m., and 35 keys are updated before the snapshot completes at 3:08 p.m. If some part of the system were to crash and prevent Redis from completing its snapshot operation between 3:06 p.m. and 3:08 p.m., any data written between 2:35 p.m. and now would be lost. But if the system were to crash just *after* the snapshot had completed, then only the updates to those 35 keys would be lost.

There are five methods to initiate a snapshot, which are listed as follows:

- Any Redis client can initiate a snapshot by calling the `BGSAVE` command. On platforms that support `BGSAVE` (basically all platforms except for Windows), Redis will *fork*,[1] and the child process will write the snapshot to disk while the parent process continues to respond to commands.
- A Redis client can also initiate a snapshot by calling the `SAVE` command, which causes Redis to stop responding to any/all commands until the snapshot completes. This command isn't commonly used, except in situations where we need our data on disk, and either we're okay waiting for it to complete, or we don't have enough memory for a `BGSAVE`.
- If Redis is configured with `save` lines, such as `save 60 10000`, Redis will automatically trigger a `BGSAVE` operation if 10,000 writes have occurred within 60 seconds since the last successful save has started (using the configuration option described). When multiple `save` lines are present, any time one of the rules match, a `BGSAVE` is triggered.

---

[1] When a process forks, the underlying operating system makes a copy of the process. On Unix and Unix-like systems, the copying process is optimized such that, initially, all memory is shared between the child and parent processes. When either the parent or child process writes to memory, that memory will stop being shared.

- When Redis receives a request to shut down by the SHUTDOWN command, or it receives a standard TERM signal, Redis will perform a SAVE, blocking clients from performing any further commands, and then shut down.
- If a Redis server connects to another Redis server and issues the SYNC command to begin replication, the master Redis server will start a BGSAVE operation if one isn't already executing or recently completed. See section 4.2 for more information about replication.

When using only snapshots for saving data, you must remember that if a crash were to happen, you'd lose any data changed since the last snapshot. For some applications, this kind of loss isn't acceptable, and you should look into using append-only file persistence, as described in section 4.1.2. But if your application can live with data loss, snapshots can be the right answer. Let's look at a few scenarios and how you may want to configure Redis to get the snapshot persistence behavior you're looking for.

DEVELOPMENT

For my personal development server, I'm mostly concerned with minimizing the overhead of snapshots. To this end, and because I generally trust my hardware, I have a single rule: save 900 1. The save option tells Redis that it should perform a BGSAVE operation based on the subsequent two values. In this case, if at least one write has occurred in at least 900 seconds (15 minutes) since the last BGSAVE, Redis will automatically start a new BGSAVE.

If you're planning on using snapshots on a production server, and you're going to be storing a lot of data, you'll want to try to run a development server with the same or similar hardware, the same save options, a similar set of data, and a similar expected load. By setting up an environment equivalent to what you'll be running in production, you can make sure that you're not snapshotting too often (wasting resources) or too infrequently (leaving yourself open for data loss).

AGGREGATING LOGS

In the case of aggregating log files and analysis of page views, we really only need to ask ourselves how much time we're willing to lose if something crashes between dumps. If we're okay with losing up to an hour of work, then we can use save 3600 1 (there are 3600 seconds in an hour). But how might we recover if we were processing logs?

To recover from data loss, we need to know what we lost in the first place. To know what we lost, we need to keep a record of our progress while processing logs. Let's imagine that we have a function that's called when new logs are ready to be processed. This function is provided with a Redis connect, a path to where log files are stored, and a callback that will process individual lines in the log file. With our function, we can record which file we're working on and the file position information as we're processing. A log-processing function that records this information can be seen in the next listing.

Listing 4.2   The process_logs() function that keeps progress information in Redis

Get the current progress.

```
def process_logs(conn, path, callback):
    current_file, offset = conn.mget(
        'progress:file', 'progress:position')

    pipe = conn.pipeline()

    def update_progress():
        pipe.mset({
            'progress:file': fname,
            'progress:position': offset
        })
        pipe.execute()

    for fname in sorted(os.listdir(path)):
        if fname < current_file:
            continue

        inp = open(os.path.join(path, fname), 'rb')
        if fname == current_file:
            inp.seek(int(offset, 10))
        else:
            offset = 0

        current_file = None

        for lno, line in enumerate(inp):
            callback(pipe, line)
            offset = int(offset) + len(line)

            if not (lno+1) % 1000:
                update_progress()
        update_progress()

        inp.close()
```

Our function will be provided with a callback that will take a connection and a log line, calling methods on the pipeline as necessary.

This closure is meant primarily to reduce the number of duplicated lines later.

We want to update our file and line number offsets into the log file.

This will execute any outstanding log updates, as well as actually write our file and line number updates to Redis.

Iterate over the log files in sorted order.

Skip over files that are before the current file.

If we're continuing a file, skip over the parts that we've already processed.

Handle the log line.

The enumerate function iterates over a sequence (in this case lines from a file), and produces pairs consisting of a numeric sequence starting from 0, and the original data.

Update our information about the offset into the file.

Write our progress back to Redis every 1000 lines, or when we're done with a file.

By keeping a record of our progress in Redis, we can pick up with processing logs if at any point some part of the system crashes. And because we used MULTI/EXEC pipelines as introduced in chapter 3, we ensure that the dump will only include processed log information when it also includes progress information.

BIG DATA

When the amount of data that we store in Redis tends to be under a few gigabytes, snapshotting can be the right answer. Redis will fork, save to disk, and finish the snapshot faster than you can read this sentence. But as our Redis memory use grows over time, so does the time to perform a fork operation for the BGSAVE. In situations where Redis is using tens of gigabytes of memory, there isn't a lot of free memory, or if we're running on a virtual machine, letting a BGSAVE occur may cause the system to pause for extended periods of time, or may cause heavy use of system virtual memory, which could degrade Redis's performance to the point where it's unusable.

This extended pausing (and how significant it is) will depend on what kind of system we're running on. Real hardware, VMWare virtualization, or KVM virtualization will generally allow us to create a fork of a Redis process at roughly 10–20ms per gigabyte of memory that Redis is using. If our system is running within Xen virtualization, those numbers can be closer to 200–300ms per gigabyte of memory used by Redis, depending on the Xen configuration. So if we're using 20 gigabytes of memory with Redis, running BGSAVE on standard hardware will pause Redis for 200–400 milliseconds for the fork. If we're using Redis inside a Xen-virtualized machine (as is the case with Amazon EC2 and some other cloud providers), that same fork will cause Redis to pause for 4–6 seconds. You need to decide for your application whether this pause is okay.

To prevent forking from causing such issues, we may want to disable automatic saving entirely. When automatic saving is disabled, we then need to manually call BGSAVE (which has all of the same potential issues as before, only now we know when they will happen), or we can call SAVE. With SAVE, Redis does block until the save is completed, but because there's no fork, there's no fork delay. And because Redis doesn't have to fight with itself for resources, the snapshot will finish faster.

As a point of personal experience, I've run Redis servers that used 50 gigabytes of memory on machines with 68 gigabytes of memory inside a cloud provider running Xen virtualization. When trying to use BGSAVE with clients writing to Redis, forking would take 15 seconds or more, followed by 15–20 minutes for the snapshot to complete. But with SAVE, the snapshot would finish in 3–5 minutes. For our use, a daily snapshot at 3 a.m. was sufficient, so we wrote scripts that would stop clients from trying to access Redis, call SAVE, wait for the SAVE to finish, back up the resulting snapshot, and then signal to the clients that they could continue.

Snapshots are great when we can deal with potentially substantial data loss in Redis, but for many applications, 15 minutes or an hour or more of data loss or processing time is too much. To allow Redis to keep more up-to-date information about data in memory stored on disk, we can use append-only file persistence.

4.1.2 *Append-only file persistence*

In basic terms, append-only log files keep a record of data changes that occur by writing each change to the end of the file. In doing this, anyone could recover the entire dataset by replaying the append-only log from the beginning to the end. Redis has functionality that does this as well, and it's enabled by setting the configuration option appendonly yes, as shown in listing 4.1. Table 4.1 shows the appendfsync options and how they affect file-write syncing to disk.

> **FILE SYNCING** When writing files to disk, at least three things occur. The first is writing to a buffer, and this occurs when calling file.write() or its equivalent in other languages. When the data is in the buffer, the operating system can take that data and write it to disk at some point in the future. We can optionally take a second step and ask the operating system to write the data provided to disk when it next has a chance, with file.flush(), but this is only a request. Because data isn't actually on disk until the operating system writes it to disk, we can tell the operating system to "sync" the files to disk, which will block until it's completed. When that sync is completed, we can be fairly certain that our data is on disk and we can read it later if the system otherwise fails.

Table 4.1 Sync options to use with `appendfsync`

Option	How often syncing will occur
`always`	Every write command to Redis results in a write to disk. This slows Redis down substantially if used.
`everysec`	Once per second, explicitly syncs write commands to disk.
`no`	Lets the operating system control syncing to disk.

If we were to set `appendfsync always`, every write to Redis would result in a write to disk, and we can ensure minimal data loss if Redis were to crash. Unfortunately, because we're writing to disk with every write to Redis, we're limited by disk performance, which is roughly 200 writes/second for a spinning disk, and maybe a few tens of thousands for an SSD (a solid-state drive).

> **WARNING: SSDS AND** `appendfsync always` You'll want to be careful if you're using SSDs with `appendfsync always`. Writing every change to disk as they happen, instead of letting the operating system group writes together as is the case with the other `appendfsync` options, has the potential to cause an extreme form of what is known as *write amplification*. By writing small amounts of data to the end of a file, you can reduce the lifetime of SSDs from years to just a few months in some cases.

As a reasonable compromise between keeping data safe and keeping our write performance high, we can also set `appendfsync everysec`. This configuration will sync the append-only log once every second. For most common uses, we'll likely not find significant performance penalties for syncing to disk every second compared to not using any sort of persistence. By syncing to disk every second, if the system were to crash, we could lose at most one second of data that had been written or updated in Redis. Also, in the case where the disk is unable to keep up with the write volume that's happening, Redis would gracefully slow down to accommodate the maximum write rate of the drive.

As you may guess, when setting `appendfsync  no`, Redis doesn't perform any explicit file syncing, leaving everything up to the operating system. There should be no performance penalties in this case, though if the system were to crash in one way or another, we'd lose an unknown and unpredictable amount of data. And if we're using a hard drive that isn't fast enough for our write load, Redis would perform fine until the buffers to write data to disk were filled, at which point Redis would get very slow as it got blocked from writing. For these reasons, I generally discourage the use of this configuration option, and include its description and semantics here for completeness.

Append-only files are flexible, offering a variety of options to ensure that almost every level of paranoia can be addressed. But there's a dark side to AOF persistence, and that is file size.

4.1.3   Rewriting/compacting append-only files

After reading about AOF persistence, you're probably wondering why snapshots exist at all. If by using append-only files we can minimize our data losses to one second (or essentially none at all), and minimize the time it takes to have data persisted to disk on a regular basis, it would seem that our choice should be clear. But the choice is actually not so simple: because every write to Redis causes a log of the command to be written to disk, the append-only log file will continuously grow. Over time, a growing AOF could cause your disk to run out of space, but more commonly, upon restart, Redis will be executing every command in the AOF in order. When handling large AOFs, Redis can take a very long time to start up.

To solve the growing AOF problem, we can use BGREWRITEAOF, which will rewrite the AOF to be as short as possible by removing redundant commands. BGREWRITEAOF works similarly to the snapshotting BGSAVE: performing a fork and subsequently rewriting the append-only log in the child. As such, all of the same limitations with snapshotting performance regarding fork time, memory use, and so on still stand when using append-only files. But even worse, because AOFs can grow to be many times the size of a dump (if left uncontrolled), when the AOF is rewritten, the OS needs to delete the AOF, which can cause the system to hang for multiple seconds while it's deleting an AOF of tens of gigabytes.

With snapshots, we could use the save configuration option to enable the automatic writing of snapshots using BGSAVE. Using AOFs, there are two configuration options that enable automatic BGREWRITEAOF execution: auto-aof-rewrite-percentage and auto-aof-rewrite-min-size. Using the example values of auto-aof-rewrite-percentage 100 and auto-aof-rewrite-min-size 64mb, when AOF is enabled, Redis will initiate a BGREWRITEAOF when the AOF is at least 100% larger than it was when Redis last finished rewriting the AOF, and when the AOF is at least 64 megabytes in size. As a point of configuration, if our AOF is rewriting too often, we can increase the 100 that represents 100% to something larger, though it will cause Redis to take longer to start up if it has been a while since a rewrite happened.

Regardless of whether we choose append-only files or snapshots, having the data on disk is a great first step. But unless our data has been backed up somewhere else (preferably to multiple locations), we're still leaving ourselves open to data loss. Whenever possible, I recommend backing up snapshots and newly rewritten append-only files to other servers.

By using either append-only files or snapshots, we can keep our data between system reboots or crashes. As load increases, or requirements for data integrity become more stringent, we may need to look to replication to help us.

4.2   Replication

Over their years of scaling platforms for higher loads, engineers and administrators have added *replication* to their bag of tricks to help systems scale. Replication is a method by which other servers receive a continuously updated copy of the data as it's being written, so that the replicas can service read queries. In the relational database world, it's not uncommon for a single *master* database to send writes out to multiple *slaves*, with the slaves performing all of the read queries. Redis has adopted this method of replication as a way of helping to scale, and this section will discuss configuring replication in Redis, and how Redis operates during replication.

Though Redis may be fast, there are situations where one Redis server running isn't fast enough. In particular, operations over SETs and ZSETs can involve dozens of SETs/ZSETs over tens of thousands or even millions of items. When we start getting millions of items involved, set operations can take seconds to finish, instead of milliseconds or microseconds. But even if single commands can complete in 10 milliseconds, that still limits us to 100 commands/second from a single Redis instance.

> **EXAMPLE PERFORMANCE FOR SUNIONSTORE** As a point to consider for the performance to expect from Redis, on a 2.4 GHz Intel Core 2 Duo, Redis will take 7–8 milliseconds to perform a SUNIONSTORE of two 10,000-item SETs that produces a single 20,000 item SET.

For situations where we need to scale out read queries, or where we may need to write temporary data (we'll talk about some of those in chapter 7), we can set up additional slave Redis servers to keep copies of our dataset. After receiving an initial copy of the data from the master, slaves are kept up to date in real time as clients write data to the master. With a master/slave setup, instead of connecting to the master for reading data, clients will connect to one of the slaves to read their data (typically choosing them in a random fashion to try to balance the load).

Let's talk about configuring Redis for master/slave operation, and how Redis behaves during the entire process.

4.2.1 Configuring Redis for replication

As I mentioned in section 4.1.1, when a slave connects to the master, the master will start a BGSAVE operation. To configure replication on the master side of things, we only need to ensure that the path and filename listed under the dir and dbfilename configuration options shown in listing 4.1 are to a path and file that are writable by the Redis process.

Though a variety of options control behavior of the slave itself, only one option is really necessary to enable slaving: slaveof. If we were to set slaveof host port in our configuration file, the Redis that's started with that configuration will use the provided host and port as the master Redis server it should connect to. If we have an already running system, we can tell a Redis server to stop slaving, or even to slave to a new or different master. To connect to a new master, we can use the SLAVEOF host port command, or if we want to stop updating data from the master, we can use SLAVEOF no one.

There's not a lot to configuring Redis for master/slave operation, but what's interesting and useful to know is what happens to Redis when it becomes a master or slave.

4.2.2 *Redis replication startup process*

I briefly described what happens when a slave connects—that the master starts a snapshot and sends that to the slave—but that's the simple version. Table 4.2 lists all of the operations that occur on both the master and slave when a slave connects to a master.

Table 4.2   What happens when a slave connects to a master

Step	Master operations	Slave operations
1	(waiting for a command)	(Re-)connects to the master; issues the SYNC command
2	Starts BGSAVE operation; keeps a backlog of all write commands sent after BGSAVE	Serves old data (if any), or returns errors to commands (depending on configuration)
3	Finishes BGSAVE; starts sending the snapshot to the slave; continues holding a backlog of write commands	Discards all old data (if any); starts loading the dump as it's received
4	Finishes sending the snapshot to the slave; starts sending the write command backlog to the slave	Finishes parsing the dump; starts responding to commands normally again
5	Finishes sending the backlog; starts live streaming of write commands as they happen	Finishes executing backlog of write commands from the master; continues executing commands as they happen

With the method outlined in table 4.2, Redis manages to keep up with most loads during replication, except in cases where network bandwidth between the master and slave instances isn't fast enough, or when the master doesn't have enough memory to fork and keep a backlog of write commands. Though it isn't necessary, it's generally considered to be a good practice to have Redis masters only use about 50–65% of the memory in our system, leaving approximately 30–45% for spare memory during BGSAVE and command backlogs.

On the slave side of things, configuration is also simple. To configure the slave for master/slave replication, we can either set the configuration option SLAVEOF host port, or we can configure Redis during runtime with the SLAVEOF command. If we use the configuration option, Redis will initially load whatever snapshot/AOF is currently available (if any), and then connect to the master to start the replication process outlined in table 4.2. If we run the SLAVEOF command, Redis will immediately try to connect to the master, and upon success, will start the replication process outlined in table 4.2.

> **DURING SYNC, THE SLAVE FLUSHES ALL OF ITS DATA** Just to make sure that we're all on the same page (some users forget this the first time they try using slaves): when a slave initially connects to a master, any data that had been in memory will be lost, to be replaced by the data coming from the master.

WARNING: REDIS DOESN'T SUPPORT MASTER-MASTER REPLICATION When shown master/slave replication, some people get the mistaken idea that because we can set slaving options after startup using the SLAVEOF command, that means we can get what's known as *multi-master replication* by setting two Redis instances as being SLAVEOF each other (some have even considered more than two in a loop). Unfortunately, *this does not work.* At best, our two Redis instances will use as much processor as they can, will be continually communicating back and forth, and depending on which server we connect and try to read/write data from/to, we may get inconsistent data or no data.

When multiple slaves attempt to connect to Redis, one of two different scenarios can occur. Table 4.3 describes them.

Table 4.3 When a slave connects to an existing master, sometimes it can reuse an existing dump file.

When additional slaves connect	Master operation
Before step 3 in table 4.2	All slaves will receive the same dump and same backlogged write commands.
On or after step 3 in table 4.2	While the master is finishing up the five steps for earlier slaves, a new sequence of steps 1-5 will start for the new slave(s).

For the most part, Redis does its best to ensure that it doesn't have to do more work than is necessary. In some cases, slaves may try to connect at inopportune times and cause the master to do more work. On the other hand, if multiple slaves connect at the same time, the outgoing bandwidth used to synchronize all of the slaves initially may cause other commands to have difficulty getting through, and could cause general network slowdowns for other devices on the same network.

4.2.3 *Master/slave chains*

Some developers have found that when they need to replicate to more than a handful of slaves, some networks are unable to keep up—especially when replication is being performed over the internet or between data centers. Because there's nothing particularly special about being a master or a slave in Redis, slaves can have their own slaves, resulting in master/slave chaining.

Operationally, the only difference in the replication process that occurs is that if a slave X has its own slave Y, when slave X hits step 4 from table 4.2, slave X will disconnect slave Y, causing Y to reconnect and resync.

When read load significantly outweighs write load, and when the number of reads pushes well beyond what a single Redis server can handle, it's common to keep adding slaves to help deal with the load. As load continues to increase, we can run into situations where the single master can't write to all of its slaves fast enough, or is overloaded with slaves reconnecting and resyncing. To alleviate such issues, we may want to set up a layer of intermediate Redis master/slave nodes that can help with replication duties similar to figure 4.1.

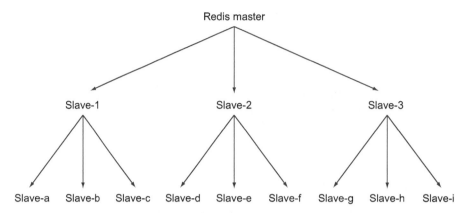

Figure 4.1   An example Redis master/slave replica tree with nine lowest-level slaves and three intermediate replication helper servers

Though the example shown in figure 4.1 may not necessarily need to be in a tree structure, remembering and understanding that this is both possible and reasonable for Redis replication can help you later.

Back in section 4.1.2, we talked about using append-only files with syncing to limit the opportunities for us to lose data. We could prevent data loss almost entirely (except for system or hard drive crashes) by syncing every write to disk, but then we end up limiting performance severely. If we tell Redis to sync every second, we're able to get the performance we need, but we could lose up to a second of writes if bad things happen. But by combining replication and append-only files, we can ensure that data gets to disk on multiple machines.

In order to ensure that data gets to disk on multiple machines, we must obviously set up a master with slaves. By configuring our slaves (and optionally our master) with `appendonly yes` and `appendfsync everysec`, we now have a group of machines that will sync to disk every second. But that's only the first part: we must wait for the write to reach the slave(s) and check to make sure that the data reached disk before we can continue.

4.2.4   *Verifying disk writes*

Verifying that the data we wrote to the master made it to the slave is easy: we merely need to write a unique dummy value after our important data, and then check for it on the slave. But verifying that the data made it to disk is more difficult. If we wait at least one second, we know that our data made it to disk. But if we're careful, we may be able to wait less time by checking the output of `INFO` for the value of `aof_pending_bio_fsync`, which will be 0 if all data that the server knows about has been written to disk. To automate this check, we can use the function provided in the next listing, which we'd call after writing our data to the master by passing both the master and slave connections.

Listing 4.3 The `wait_for_sync()` function

```
def wait_for_sync(mconn, sconn):
    identifier = str(uuid.uuid4())
    mconn.zadd('sync:wait', identifier, time.time())

    while not sconn.info()['master_link_status'] != 'up':
        time.sleep(.001)

    while not sconn.zscore('sync:wait', identifier):
        time.sleep(.001)

    deadline = time.time() + 1.01
    while time.time() < deadline:
        if sconn.info()['aof_pending_bio_fsync'] == 0:
            break
        time.sleep(.001)

    mconn.zrem('sync:wait', identifier)
    mconn.zremrangebyscore('sync:wait', 0, time.time()-900)
```

> Add the token to the master.

> Wait for the slave to sync (if necessary).

> Wait for the slave to receive the data change.

> Wait up to one second.

> Check to see if the data is known to be on disk.

> Clean up our status and clean out older entries that may have been left there.

OTHER INFORMATION FROM THE `INFO` COMMAND The `INFO` command can offer a wide range of information about the current status of a Redis server—memory used, the number of connected clients, the number of keys in each database, the number of commands executed since the last snapshot, and more. Generally speaking, `INFO` is a good source of information about the general state of our Redis servers, and many resources online can explain more.

To ensure correct operation, this function will first verify that the slave is connected to the master. It'll then poll the slave, looking for the value that it had added to the sync wait `ZSET`. After it has found that the value has made it to the slave, it'll then check on the status of the Redis write buffer, waiting for it to either say that there are no pending syncs to disk (signaling that the change had made it to disk), or wait for up to one second. We wait for one second under the assumption that after one second, the data had been synced to disk, but there's so much writing to Redis that we didn't catch when the data had been synced. After verifying the write to disk, we then clean up after ourselves.

By combining replication and append-only files, we can configure Redis to be resilient against system failures.

4.3 Handling system failures

In order to be able to handle system failures in Redis, we need to prepare ourselves for the failure. The reason we've spent so much time talking about these topics is because if we're going to rely on Redis as the sole data store for our application, then we must ensure that we never lose any data. Unlike a traditional relational database that offers ACID[2] guarantees, when choosing to architect on top of a Redis back end,

---

[2] ACID—or atomicity, consistency, isolation, and durability—is a functional description of what a database must guarantee to offer reliable transactions over data.

we need to do a little extra work to ensure data consistency. Redis is software, and it runs on hardware, and even if both were designed perfectly and couldn't fail, power can fail, generators can run out of fuel, and batteries can run out of power. In looking at what Redis offers, we spent a lot of time preparing for potential system failures. This section will talk about what we can do when failure does happen.

4.3.1   Verifying snapshots and append-only files

When confronted with system failures, we have tools to help us recover when either snapshotting or append-only file logging had been enabled. Redis includes two command-line applications for testing the status of a snapshot and an append-only file. These commands are `redis-check-aof` and `redis-check-dump`. If we run either command without arguments, we'll see the basic help that's provided:

```
$ redis-check-aof
Usage: redis-check-aof [--fix] <file.aof>
$ redis-check-dump
Usage: redis-check-dump <dump.rdb>
$
```

If we provide `--fix` as an argument to `redis-check-aof`, the command will fix the file. Its method to fix an append-only file is simple: it scans through the provided AOF, looking for an incomplete or incorrect command. Upon finding the first bad command, it trims the file to just before that command would've been executed. For most situations, this will discard the last partial write command.

Unfortunately, there's no currently supported method of repairing a corrupted snapshot. Though there's the potential to discover where the first error had occurred, because the snapshot itself is compressed, an error partway through the dump has the potential to make the remaining parts of the snapshot unreadable. It's for these reasons that I'd generally recommend keeping multiple backups of important snapshots, and calculating the SHA1 or SHA256 hashes to verify content during restoration. (Modern Linux and Unix platforms will have available `sha1sum` and `sha256sum` command-line applications for generating and verifying these hashes.)

CHECKSUMS AND HASHES   Redis versions including 2.6 and later include a CRC64 checksum of the snapshot as part of the snapshot. The use of a CRC-family checksum is useful to discover errors that are typical in some types of network transfers or disk corruption. The SHA family of cryptographic hashes is much better suited for discovering arbitrary errors. To the point, if we calculated the CRC64 of a file, then flipped any number of bits inside the file, we could later flip a subset of the last 64 bits of the file to produce the original checksum. There's no currently known method for doing the same thing with SHA1 or SHA256.

After we've verified that our backups are what we had saved before, and we've corrected the last write to AOF as necessary, we may need to replace a Redis server.

4.3.2 *Replacing a failed master*

When we're running a group of Redis servers with replication and persistence, there may come a time when some part of our infrastructure stops working for one reason or another. Maybe we get a bad hard drive, maybe bad memory, or maybe the power just went out. Regardless of what causes the system to fail, we'll eventually need to replace a Redis server. Let's look at an example scenario involving a master, a slave, and needing to replace the master.

Machine A is running a copy of Redis that's acting as the master, and machine B is running a copy of Redis that's acting as the slave. Unfortunately, machine A has just lost network connectivity for some reason that we haven't yet been able to diagnose. But we have machine C with Redis installed that we'd like to use as the new master.

Our plan is simple: We'll tell machine B to produce a fresh snapshot with SAVE. We'll then copy that snapshot over to machine C. After the snapshot has been copied into the proper path, we'll start Redis on machine C. Finally, we'll tell machine B to become a slave of machine C.[3] Some example commands to make this possible on this hypothetical set of systems are shown in the following listing.

> **Listing 4.4 An example sequence of commands for replacing a failed master node**

```
user@vpn-master ~:$ ssh root@machine-b.vpn
Last login: Wed Mar 28 15:21:06 2012 from ...
root@machine-b ~:$ redis-cli
redis 127.0.0.1:6379> SAVE
OK
redis 127.0.0.1:6379> QUIT
root@machine-b ~:$ scp \
> /var/local/redis/dump.rdb machine-c.vpn:/var/local/redis/
dump.rdb                   100%    525MB   8.1MB/s   01:05
root@machine-b ~:$ ssh machine-c.vpn
Last login: Tue Mar 27 12:42:31 2012 from ...
root@machine-c ~:$ sudo /etc/init.d/redis-server start
Starting Redis server...
root@machine-c ~:$ exit
root@machine-b ~:$ redis-cli
redis 127.0.0.1:6379> SLAVEOF machine-c.vpn 6379
OK
redis 127.0.0.1:6379> QUIT
root@machine-b ~:$ exit
user@vpn-master ~:$
```

Annotations:
- Connect to machine B on our VPN network.
- Start up the command-line redis client to do a few simple operations.
- Start a SAVE, and when it's done, QUIT so that we can continue.
- Copy the snapshot over to the new master, machine C.
- Connect to the new master and start Redis.
- Tell machine B's Redis that it should use C as the new master.

Most of these commands should be familiar to those who have experience using and maintaining Unix or Linux systems. The only interesting things in the commands being run here are that we can initiate a SAVE on machine B by running a command, and we later set up machine B to be a slave of machine C by running a command.

As an alternative to creating a new master, we may want to turn the slave into a master and create a new slave. Either way, Redis will be able to pick up where it left off,

---

[3] Because B was originally a slave, our clients shouldn't have been writing to B, so we won't have any race conditions with clients writing to B after the snapshot operation was started.

and our only job from then on is to update our client configuration to read and write to the proper servers, and optionally update the on-disk server configuration if we need to restart Redis.

> **REDIS SENTINEL** A relatively recent addition to the collection of tools available with Redis is *Redis Sentinel.* By the final publishing of this manuscript, Redis Sentinel should be complete. Generally, Redis Sentinel pays attention to Redis masters and the slaves of the masters and automatically handles failover if the master goes down. We'll discuss Redis Sentinel in chapter 10.

In the next section, we'll talk about keeping our data from being corrupted by multiple writers working on the same data, which is a necessary step toward keeping our data safe.

4.4   *Redis transactions*

Part of keeping our data correct is understanding that when other clients are working on the same data, if we aren't careful, we may end up with data corruption. In this section, we'll talk about using Redis transactions to prevent data corruption and, in some cases, to improve performance.

Transactions in Redis are different from transactions that exist in more traditional relational databases. In a relational database, we can tell the database server BEGIN, at which point we can perform a variety of read and write operations that will be consistent with respect to each other, after which we can run either COMMIT to make our changes permanent or ROLLBACK to discard our changes.

Within Redis, there's a simple method for handling a sequence of reads and writes that will be consistent with each other. We begin our transaction by calling the special command MULTI, passing our series of commands, followed by EXEC (as introduced in section 3.7.2). The problem is that this simple transaction doesn't actually do anything until EXEC is called, which means that we can't use data we read to make decisions until after we may have needed it. This may not seem important, but there's a class of problems that become difficult to solve because of not being able to read the data in a consistent fashion, or allow for transactions to fail where they should succeed (as is the case when we have multiple simultaneous transactions against a single object when using two-phase commit, a common solution to the problem). One of these problems is the process of purchasing an item from a marketplace. Let's see an example of this in action.

> **DELAYED EXECUTION WITH MULTI/EXEC CAN IMPROVE PERFORMANCE** Because of Redis's delaying execution of commands until EXEC is called when using MULTI/EXEC, many clients (including the Python client that we're using) will hold off on even sending commands until all of them are known. When all of the commands are known, the client will send MULTI, followed by the series of commands to be executed, and EXEC, all at the same time. The client will then wait until all of the replies from all of the commands are received. This method of sending multiple commands at once and waiting for all of the replies is generally referred to as *pipelining*, and has the ability to improve Redis's performance when executing multiple commands by reducing the number of network round trips that a client needs to wait for.

In the last few months, Fake Game Company has seen major growth in their web-based RPG that's played on YouTwitFace, a fictional social network. Because it pays attention to the needs and desires of its community, it has determined that the players need the ability to buy and sell items in a marketplace. It's our job to design and build a marketplace that can scale to the needs of the community.

4.4.1 Defining users and their inventory

We'll start by showing some structures that define our users and their inventory. User information is stored as a HASH, with keys and values that store user attributes like name, funds, and anything else. A user's inventory will be a SET that holds unique identifiers for each item, which can be seen in figure 4.2.

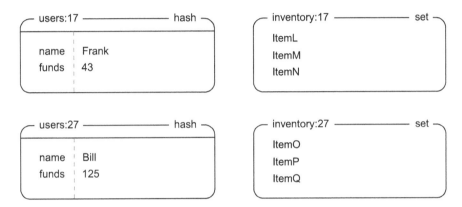

Figure 4.2   Example user inventory and user information. Frank has 43 e-dollars and an item that he's considering selling from his inventory.

Our requirements for the market are simple: a user can list an item for a given price, and when another user purchases the item, the seller receives the money. We'll also say that the part of the market we'll be worrying about only needs to be ordered by selling price. In chapter 7, we'll cover some topics for handling other orders.

To include enough information to sell a given item in the market, we'll concatenate the item ID for the item with the user ID of the seller and use that as a member of a market ZSET, with the score being the item's selling price. By including all of this information together, we greatly simplify our data structures and what we need to look up, and get the benefit of being able to easily paginate through a presorted market. A small version of the marketplace is shown in figure 4.3.

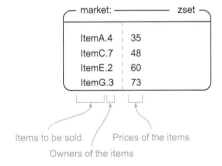

Figure 4.3   Our basic marketplace that includes an ItemA being sold by user 4 for 35 e-dollars

Now that we know what structures our marketplace uses, let's list items in the market.

4.4.2 *Listing items in the marketplace*

In the process of listing, we'll use a Redis operation called WATCH, which we combine with MULTI and EXEC, and sometimes UNWATCH or DISCARD. When we've watched keys with WATCH, if at any time some other client replaces, updates, or deletes any keys that we've WATCHed before we have performed the EXEC operation, our operations against Redis will fail with an error message when we try to EXEC (at which point we can retry or abort the operation). By using WATCH, MULTI/EXEC, and UNWATCH/DISCARD, we can ensure that the data that we're working with doesn't change while we're doing something important, which protects us from data corruption.

> **WHAT IS DISCARD?**   In the same way that UNWATCH will let us reset our connection if sent after WATCH but before MULTI, DISCARD will also reset the connection if sent after MULTI but before EXEC. That is to say, if we'd WATCHed a key or keys, fetched some data, and then started a transaction with MULTI followed by a group of commands, we could cancel the WATCH and clear out any queued commands with DISCARD. We don't use DISCARD here, primarily because we know whether we want to perform a MULTI/EXEC or UNWATCH, so a DISCARD is unnecessary for our purposes.

Let's go about listing an item in the marketplace. To do so, we add the item to the market ZSET, while WATCHing the seller's inventory to make sure that the item is still available to be sold. The function to list an item is shown here.

Listing 4.5   The `list_item()` function

```
def list_item(conn, itemid, sellerid, price):
    inventory = "inventory:%s"%sellerid
    item = "%s.%s"%(itemid, sellerid)
    end = time.time() + 5
    pipe = conn.pipeline()

    while time.time() < end:
        try:
            pipe.watch(inventory)                           # Watch for changes to
                                                            # the user's inventory.
            if not pipe.sismember(inventory, itemid):       # Verify that the
                pipe.unwatch()                              # user still has the
                return None                                 # item to be listed.

            pipe.multi()
            pipe.zadd("market:", item, price)               # Actually list the item.
            pipe.srem(inventory, itemid)
            pipe.execute()                                  # If execute returns without
            return True                                     # a WatchError being raised,
        except redis.exceptions.WatchError:                 # then the transaction is
            pass                                            # complete and the inventory
    return False                                            # key is no longer watched.
```

If the item isn't in the user's inventory, stop watching the inventory key and return.

Actually list the item.

The user's inventory was changed; retry.

After some initial setup, we'll do what we described earlier. We'll tell Redis that we want to watch the seller's inventory, verify that the seller can still sell the item, and if so, add the item to the market and remove the item from their inventory. If there's an update or change to the inventory while we're looking at it, we'll receive an error and retry, as is shown by the `while` loop outside of our actual operation.

Let's look at the sequence of operations that are performed when Frank (user 17) wants to sell ItemM for 97 e-dollars in figure 4.4.

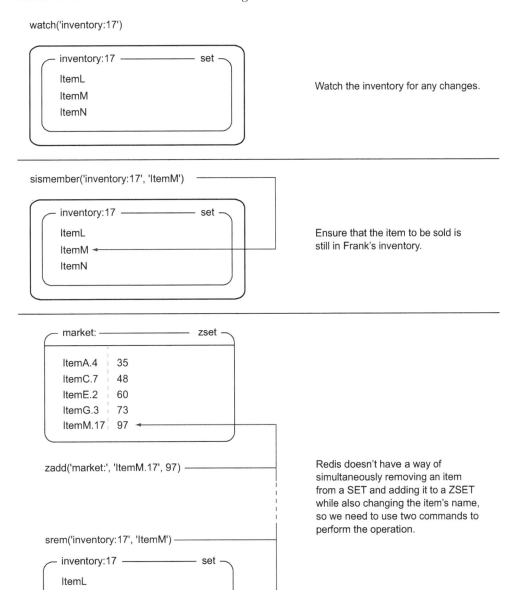

Figure 4.4 `list_item(conn, "ItemM", 17, 97)`

Generally, listing an item should occur without any significant issue, since only the user should be selling their own items (which is enforced farther up the application stack). But as I mentioned before, if a user's inventory were to change between the WATCH and EXEC, our attempt to list the item would fail, and we'd retry.

Now that you know how to list an item, it's time to purchase an item.

4.4.3   Purchasing items

To process the purchase of an item, we first WATCH the market and the user who's buying the item. We then fetch the buyer's total funds and the price of the item, and verify that the buyer has enough money. If they don't have enough money, we cancel the transaction. If they do have enough money, we perform the transfer of money between the accounts, move the item into the buyer's inventory, and remove the item from the market. On WATCH error, we retry for up to 10 seconds in total. We can see the function which handles the purchase of an item in the following listing.

> **Listing 4.6   The `purchase_item()` function**

```
def purchase_item(conn, buyerid, itemid, sellerid, lprice):
    buyer = "users:%s"%buyerid
    seller = "users:%s"%sellerid
    item = "%s.%s"%(itemid, sellerid)
    inventory = "inventory:%s"%buyerid
    end = time.time() + 10
    pipe = conn.pipeline()

    while time.time() < end:
        try:
            pipe.watch("market:", buyer)                    #  Watch for changes to the
                                                            #  market and to the buyer's
                                                            #  account information.
            price = pipe.zscore("market:", item)
            funds = int(pipe.hget(buyer, "funds"))          #  Check for a sold/repriced
            if price != lprice or price > funds:            #  item or insufficient funds.
                pipe.unwatch()
                return None

            pipe.multi()
            pipe.hincrby(seller, "funds", int(price))       #  Transfer funds from the buyer
            pipe.hincrby(buyer, "funds", int(-price))       #  to the seller, and transfer the
            pipe.sadd(inventory, itemid)                    #  item to the buyer.
            pipe.zrem("market:", item)
            pipe.execute()
            return True
        except redis.exceptions.WatchError:                 #  Retry if the buyer's account
            pass                                            #  or the market changed.

    return False
```

To purchase an item, we need to spend more time preparing the data, and we need to watch both the market and the buyer's information. We watch the market to ensure that the item can still be bought (or that we can notice that it has already been bought), and we watch the buyer's information to verify that they have enough money.

When we've verified that the item is still there, and that the buyer has enough money, we go about actually moving the item into their inventory, as well as moving money from the buyer to the seller.

After seeing the available items in the market, Bill (user 27) decides that he wants to buy ItemM from Frank through the marketplace. Let's follow along to see how our data changes through figures 4.5 and 4.6.

If either the market ZSET or Bill's account information changes between our WATCH and our EXEC, the purchase_item() function will either retry or abort, based on how long it has been trying to purchase the item, as shown in listing 4.6.

> **WHY DOESN'T REDIS IMPLEMENT TYPICAL LOCKING?** When accessing data for writing (SELECT FOR UPDATE in SQL), relational databases will place a lock on rows that are accessed until a transaction is completed with COMMIT or ROLL-BACK. If any other client attempts to access data for writing on any of the same rows, that client will be blocked until the first transaction is completed. This form of locking works well in practice (essentially all relational databases implement it), though it can result in long wait times for clients waiting to acquire locks on a number of rows if the lock holder is slow.

Because there's potential for long wait times, and because the design of Redis minimizes wait time for clients (except in the case of blocking LIST pops), Redis doesn't lock data during WATCH. Instead, Redis will notify clients if some-one else modified the data first, which is called *optimistic locking* (the actual locking that relational databases perform could be viewed as *pessimistic*). Optimistic locking also works well in practice because clients are never waiting on the first holder of the lock; instead they retry if some other client was faster.

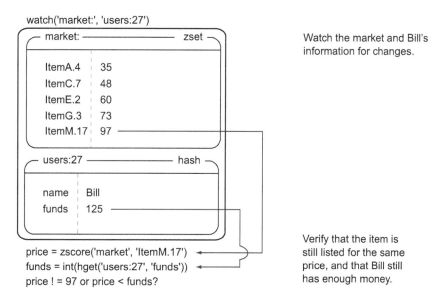

Figure 4.5 Before the item can be purchased, we must watch the market and the buyer's information to verify that the item is still available, and that the buyer has enough money.

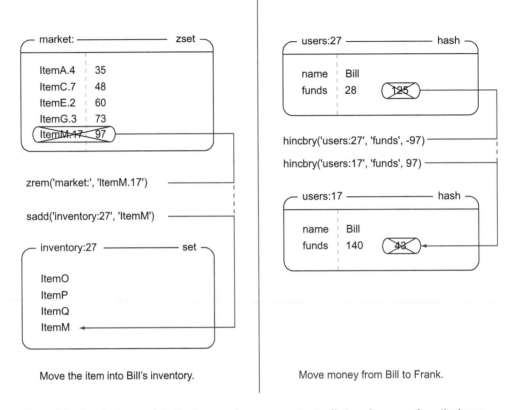

Figure 4.6 **In order to complete the item purchase, we must actually transfer money from the buyer to the seller, and we must remove the item from the market while adding it to the buyer's inventory.**

In this section, we've discussed combining WATCH, MULTI, and EXEC to handle the manipulation of multiple types of data so that we can implement a marketplace. Given this functionality as a basis, it wouldn't be out of the question to make our marketplace into an auction, add alternate sorting options, time out old items in the market, or even add higher-level searching and filtering based on techniques discussed in chapter 7.

As long as we consistently use transactions in Redis, we can keep our data from being corrupted while being operated on by multiple clients. Let's look at how we can make our operations even faster when we don't need to worry about other clients altering our data.

4.5   *Non-transactional pipelines*

When we first introduced MULTI/EXEC in chapter 3, we talked about them as having a "transaction" property—everything between the MULTI and EXEC commands will execute without other clients being able to do anything. One benefit to using transactions is the underlying library's use of a pipeline, which improves performance. This section will show how to use a pipeline without a transaction to further improve performance.

You'll remember from chapter 2 that some commands take multiple arguments for adding/updating—commands like MGET, MSET, HMGET, HMSET, RPUSH/LPUSH, SADD, ZADD, and others. Those commands exist to streamline calls to perform the same operation repeatedly. As you saw in chapter 2, this can result in significant performance improvements. Though not as drastic as these commands, the use of non-transactional pipelines offers many of the same performance advantages, and allows us to run a variety of commands at the same time.

In the case where we don't need transactions, but where we still want to do a lot of work, we could still use MULTI/EXEC for their ability to send all of the commands at the same time to minimize round trips and latency. Unfortunately, MULTI and EXEC aren't free, and can delay other important commands from executing. But we can gain all the benefits of pipelining without using MULTI/EXEC. When we used MULTI/EXEC in Python in chapter 3 and in section 4.4, you may have noticed that we did the following:

```
pipe = conn.pipeline()
```

By passing True to the pipeline() method (or omitting it), we're telling our client to wrap the sequence of commands that we'll call with a MULTI/EXEC pair. If instead of passing True we were to pass False, we'd get an object that prepared and collected commands to execute similar to the transactional pipeline, only it wouldn't be wrapped with MULTI/EXEC. For situations where we want to send more than one command to Redis, the result of one command doesn't affect the input to another, and we don't need them all to execute transactionally, passing False to the pipeline() method can further improve overall Redis performance. Let's look at an example.

Way back in sections 2.1 and 2.5, we wrote and updated a function called update_token(), which kept a record of recent items viewed and recent pages viewed, and kept the user's login cookie updated. The updated code from section 2.5 is shown in listing 4.7. Note how the function will make three or five calls to Redis for every call of the function. As written, that will result in three or five round trips between Redis and our client.

Listing 4.7   The update_token() function from section 2.5

```
                      def update_token(conn, token, user, item=None):       ⟵┐ Get the
Keep a mapping from the    timestamp = time.time()                             │ timestamp.
token to the logged-in user. └⟶ conn.hset('login:', token, user)
                          conn.zadd('recent:', token, timestamp)            ⟵┐ Record
Record that the user      if item:                                            │ when the
viewed the item. └⟶           conn.zadd('viewed:' + token, item, timestamp)   │ token was
                              conn.zremrangebyrank('viewed:' + token, 0, -26) │ last seen.
Remove old items, ┌⟶          conn.zincrby('viewed:', item, -1)    ⟵┐
keeping the most  │                                                 └ Update the number
recent 25. │                                                         of times the given
                                                                     item was viewed.
```

If our Redis and web servers are connected over LAN with only one or two steps, we could expect that the round trip between the web server and Redis would be around 1–2 milliseconds. With three to five round trips between Redis and the web server, we could expect that it would take 3–10 milliseconds for update_token() to execute. At that speed, we could only expect a single web server thread to be able to handle 100–333 requests per second. This is great, but we could do better. Let's quickly create a non-transactional pipeline and make all of our requests over that pipeline. You can see the updated function in the next listing.

Listing 4.8 The update_token_pipeline() function

```
def update_token_pipeline(conn, token, user, item=None):
    timestamp = time.time()
    pipe = conn.pipeline(False)                                    ◁─── Set up the pipeline.
    pipe.hset('login:', token, user)
    pipe.zadd('recent:', token, timestamp)
    if item:
        pipe.zadd('viewed:' + token, item, timestamp)
        pipe.zremrangebyrank('viewed:' + token, 0, -26)           ⎤ Execute the commands
        pipe.zincrby('viewed:', item, -1)                         ⎦ in the pipeline.
    pipe.execute()                                            ◁───
```

By replacing our standard Redis connection with a pipelined connection, we can reduce our number of round trips by a factor of 3–5, and reduce the expected time to execute update_token_pipeline() to 1–2 milliseconds. At that speed, a single web server thread could handle 500–1000 requests per second if it only had to deal with updating item view information. Theoretically, this is great, but what about in reality?

Let's test both of these functions by performing a simple benchmark. We'll test the number of requests that can be processed per second against a copy of Redis that's on the same machine, across a fast and low-latency network connection, and across a slow and higher latency connection. We'll first start with the benchmark code that we'll use to test the performance of these connections. In our benchmark, we'll call either update_token() or update_token_pipeline() repeatedly until we reach a prespecified timeout, and then calculate the number of requests we can service at a given time. The following listing shows the code that we'll use to run our two update_token commands.

Listing 4.9 The benchmark_update_token() function

```
def benchmark_update_token(conn, duration):
    for function in (update_token, update_token_pipeline):       ◁⎤ Execute both the
        count = 0                                                  │ update_token() and the
        start = time.time()                                        │ update_token_pipeline()
        end = start + duration                                     │ functions.
        while time.time() < end:
            count += 1
            function(conn, 'token', 'user', 'item')              ◁⎤ Calculate the duration.
        delta = time.time() - start                              ◁⎦
        print function.__name__, count, delta, count / delta     ◁⎤ Print information
                                                                    ⎦ about the results.
```

Set up our counters and our ending conditions.

Call one of the two functions.

When we run the benchmark function across a variety of connections with the given available bandwidth (gigabits or megabits) and latencies, we get data as shown in table 4.4.

Table 4.4 Performance of pipelined and nonpipelined connections over different types of connections. For high-speed connections, we'll tend to run at the limit of what a single processor can perform for encoding/decoding commands in Redis. For slower connections, we'll run at the limit of bandwidth and/or latency.

Description	Bandwidth	Latency	update_table() calls per second	update_table_ pipeline() calls per second
Local machine, Unix domain socket	>1 gigabit	0.015ms	3,761	6,394
Local machine, local-host	>1 gigabit	0.015ms	3,257	5,991
Remote machine, shared switch	1 gigabit	0.271ms	739	2,841
Remote machine, connected through VPN	1.8 megabit	48ms	3.67	18.2

Looking at the table, note that for high-latency connections, we can multiply performance by a factor of five using pipelines over not using pipelines. Even with very low-latency remote connections, we're able to improve performance by almost four times. For local connections, we actually run into the single-core performance limit of Python sending and receiving short command sequences using the Redis protocol (we'll talk about this more in section 4.6).

You now know how to push Redis to perform better without transactions. Beyond using pipelines, are there any other standard ways of improving the performance of Redis?

4.6 *Performance considerations*

When coming from a relational database background, most users will be so happy with improving performance by a factor of 100 times or more by adding Redis, they won't realize that they can make Redis perform even better. In the previous section, we introduced non-transactional pipelines as a way to minimize the number of round trips between our application and Redis. But what if we've already built an application, and we know that it could perform better? How do we find ways to improve performance?

Improving performance in Redis requires having an understanding of what to expect in terms of performance for the types of commands that we're sending to Redis. To get a better idea of what to expect from Redis, we'll quickly run a benchmark that's included with Redis, redis-benchmark, as can be seen in listing 4.10. Feel free to explore redis-benchmark on your own to discover the performance characteristics of your server and of Redis.

Listing 4.10   Running `redis-benchmark` on an Intel Core-2 Duo 2.4 GHz desktop

```
$ redis-benchmark  -c 1 -q
PING (inline): 34246.57 requests per second
PING: 34843.21 requests per second
MSET (10 keys): 24213.08 requests per second
SET: 32467.53 requests per second
GET: 33112.59 requests per second
INCR: 32679.74 requests per second
LPUSH: 33333.33 requests per second
LPOP: 33670.04 requests per second
SADD: 33222.59 requests per second
SPOP: 34482.76 requests per second
LPUSH (again, in order to bench LRANGE): 33222.59 requests per second
LRANGE (first 100 elements): 22988.51 requests per second
LRANGE (first 300 elements): 13888.89 requests per second
LRANGE (first 450 elements): 11061.95 requests per second
LRANGE (first 600 elements): 9041.59 requests per second
```

> ◁ **We run with the '-q' option to get simple output and '-c l' to use a single client.**

The output of `redis-benchmark` shows a group of commands that are typically used in Redis, as well as the number of commands of that type that can be run in a single second. A standard run of this benchmark without any options will try to push Redis to its limit using 50 clients, but it's a lot easier to compare performance of a single benchmark client against one copy of our own client, rather than many.

When looking at the output of `redis-benchmark`, we must be careful not to try to directly compare its output with how quickly our application performs. This is because `redis-benchmark` doesn't actually process the result of the commands that it performs, which means that the results of some responses that require substantial parsing overhead aren't taken into account. Generally, compared to `redis-benchmark` running with a single client, we can expect the Python Redis client to perform at roughly 50–60% of what `redis-benchmark` will tell us for a single client and for non-pipelined commands, depending on the complexity of the command to call.

If you find that your commands are running at about half of what you'd expect given `redis-benchmark` (about 25–30% of what `redis-benchmark` reports), or if you get errors reporting "Cannot assign requested address," you may be accidentally creating a new connection for every command.

I've listed some performance numbers relative to a single `redis-benchmark` client using the Python client, and have described some of the most likely causes of slowdowns and/or errors in table 4.5.

This list of possible performance issues and solutions is short, but these issues amount to easily 95% of the performance-related problems that users report on a regular basis (aside from using Redis data structures incorrectly). If we're experiencing slowdowns that we're having difficulty in diagnosing, and we know it isn't one of the problems listed in table 4.5, we should request help by one of the ways described in section 1.4.

Table 4.5 A table of general performance comparisons against a single `redis-benchmark` client and what may be causing potential slowdowns

Performance or error	Likely cause	Remedy
50–60% of `redis-benchmark` for a single client	Expected performance without pipelining	N/A
25–30% of `redis-benchmark` for a single client	Connecting for every command/group of commands	Reuse your Redis connections
Client error: "Cannot assign requested address"	Connecting for every command/group of commands	Reuse your Redis connections

Most client libraries that access Redis offer some level of connection pooling built in. For Python, we only need to create a single `redis.Redis()` for every unique Redis server we need to connect to (we need to create a new connection for each numbered database we're using). The `redis.Redis()` object itself will handle creating connections as necessary, reusing existing connections, and discarding timed-out connections. As written, the Python client connection pooling is both thread safe and `fork()` safe.

4.7   Summary

Through this chapter, we've covered topics that can help keep Redis performing well while keeping your data secure against system failures. The first half of the chapter primarily discussed the use of persistence and replication to prepare for failures and deal with failures. The latter half dealt with keeping your data from being corrupted, using pipelines to improve performance, and diagnosing potential performance problems.

If there are two things you should take from this chapter, they are that the use of replication and append-only files can go a long way toward keeping your data safe, and that using `WATCH`/`MULTI`/`EXEC` can keep your data from being corrupted by multiple clients working on the same data.

Hopefully our discussion of `WATCH`/`MULTI`/`EXEC` introduced in chapter 3 has helped you to better understand how to fully utilize transactions in Redis. In chapter 6, we'll revisit transactions, but now let's move on to chapter 5, where you'll learn more about using Redis to help with system administration tasks.

Using Redis for
application support

This chapter covers

- Logging to Redis
- Counters and statistics
- Discovering city and country from IP address
- Service discovery and configuration

In the last chapter, we spent most of our time talking about how to keep Redis up and running as part of a larger group of systems. In this chapter, we'll talk about using Redis to support other parts of your environment: from gathering information about the current state of the system with logs and counters, to discovering information about the clients using your system, all the way to configuring your system by using Redis as a directory.

Overall, this chapter offers control of and insight into how your system operates during runtime. As you read along, keep in mind that we're looking to support the continued running of higher-level applications—that the components we build in this chapter aren't the applications themselves, but will help to support those applications. This support comes by way of recording information about the applications and application visitors, and a method of configuring applications. Let's look at the first level of monitoring that we can add through logging.

5.1 Logging to Redis

As we build applications and services, being able to discover information about the running system becomes increasingly important. Being able to dig into that information to diagnose problems, discover problems before they become severe, or even just to discover information about users—these all necessitate logging.

In the world of Linux and Unix, there are two common logging methods. The first is logging to a file, where over time we write individual log lines to a file, and every once in a while, we write to a new file. Many thousands of pieces of software have been written do this (including Redis itself). But this method can run into issues because we have many different services writing to a variety of log files, each with a different way of rolling them over, and no common way of easily taking all of the log files and doing something useful with them.

Running on TCP and UDP port 514 of almost every Unix and Linux server available is a service called *syslog*, the second common logging method. Syslog accepts log messages from any program that sends it a message and routes those messages to various on-disk log files, handling rotation and deletion of old logs. With configuration, it can even forward messages to other servers for further processing. As a service, it's far more convenient than logging to files directly, because all of the special log file rotation and deletion is already handled for us.

> **REPLACING SYSLOG** Whether you end up using the logging methods described here, you owe it to yourself to consider replacing your current syslog daemon (which is likely `Rsyslogd`) with `syslog-ng`. Having used and configured both systems, I find that the configuration language that `syslog-ng` provides for directing log messages is easier to use. And though I don't have the space or time to build it in this book, building a service that consumes syslog messages and puts them into Redis is a great way to offer a layer of indirection between what needs to happen now for processing a request, and what can happen later (like logging or updating counters).

Having logs available in files on a single server (thanks to syslog forwarding) is a great long-term plan with logging (remember to back them up). In this section, we'll talk about using Redis as a way of keeping more time-sensitive logs, to function as a replacement for syslog messages being stored in the short term. Our first view into changing logs is a continuously updated stream of recent log messages.

5.1.1 Recent logs

When building a system, knowing what's important to record can be difficult. Do you record every time someone logs in? What about when they log out? Do you log every time someone changes their account information? Or do you only log errors and exceptions? I can't answer those questions for you directly, but I can offer a method of keeping a recent list of log messages in Redis, which will let you get a snapshot view of your logs at any time.

To keep a recent list of logs, we'll LPUSH log messages to a LIST and then trim that LIST to a fixed size. Later, if we want to read the log messages, we can perform a simple LRANGE to fetch the messages. We'll take a few extra steps to support different named log message queues and to support the typical log severity levels, but you can remove either of those in your own code if you need to. The code for writing recent logs to Redis is shown in the next listing.

Listing 5.1   The `log_recent()` function

```
SEVERITY = {
    logging.DEBUG: 'debug',
    logging.INFO: 'info',                    Set up a mapping that
    logging.WARNING: 'warning',              should help turn most
    logging.ERROR: 'error',                  logging severity levels into      Actually try to
    logging.CRITICAL: 'critical',            something consistent.             turn a logging
}                                                                              level into a
SEVERITY.update((name, name) for name in SEVERITY.values())                    simple string.

def log_recent(conn, name, message, severity=logging.INFO, pipe=None):
    severity = str(SEVERITY.get(severity, severity)).lower()
    destination = 'recent:%s:%s'%(name, severity)                  Create
    message = time.asctime() + ' ' + message    Set up a pipeline so we        the key that
    pipe = pipe or conn.pipeline()              only need one round trip.      messages will
    pipe.lpush(destination, message)                                           be written to.
    pipe.ltrim(destination, 0, 99)
    pipe.execute()

         Execute the two commands.      Trim the log list to     Add the message to the
                                        only include the most    beginning of the log list.
                                        recent 100 messages.
```

Add the current time so that we know when the message was sent.

Aside from the part that handles turning the different log levels into useful strings like info and debug, the `log_recent()` function is simple—a quick LPUSH followed by an LTRIM. Now that you have a better idea of what's going on right now, can we discover the most common (and maybe the most important) messages?

5.1.2   Common logs

If you've been running `log_recent()`, you'll probably discover that although it's useful for getting an idea of what's happening right now, it's not very good at telling you whether any important messages were lost in the noise. By recording information about how often a particular message appears, you could then look through the messages ordered by how often they happened to help you determine what's important.

A simple and useful way of knowing how often a message appears is by storing the message as a member of a ZSET, with the score being how often the message appears. To make sure that we only see recent common messages, we'll rotate our record of common messages every hour. So that we don't lose *everything*, we'll keep the previous hour's worth of common messages. Our code for keeping track of and rotating common log messages is shown next.

Listing 5.2　The `log_common()` function

Handle the logging level. →
We'll watch the start of the hour key for changes that only happen at the beginning of the hour. →
...move the old common log information to the archive.
Call the log_recent() function to record these, and rely on its call to execute(). →

```
def log_common(conn, name, message, severity=logging.INFO, timeout=5):
    severity = str(SEVERITY.get(severity, severity)).lower()
    destination = 'common:%s:%s'%(name, severity)
    start_key = destination + ':start'
    pipe = conn.pipeline()
    end = time.time() + timeout
    while time.time() < end:
        try:
            pipe.watch(start_key)
            now = datetime.utcnow().timetuple()
            hour_start = datetime(*now[:4]).isoformat()

            existing = pipe.get(start_key)
            pipe.multi()
            if existing and existing < hour_start:
                pipe.rename(destination, destination + ':last')
                pipe.rename(start_key, destination + ':pstart')
                pipe.set(start_key, hour_start)

            pipe.zincrby(destination, message)
            log_recent(pipe, name, message, severity, pipe)
            return
        except redis.exceptions.WatchError:
            continue
```

Set up the destination key for keeping recent logs.
Keep a record of the start of the hour for this set of messages.
Get the current time.
Find the current start hour.
Set up the transaction.
If the current list of common logs is for a previous hour...
Update the start of the current hour for the common logs.
Actually increment our common counter.
If we got a watch error from someone else archiving, try again.

This logging function was more involved than the recent logging function, primarily due to being careful when taking care of old logs. That's why we used the WATCH/MULTI/EXEC transaction to rename the ZSET and rewrite the key that tells us what hour the current data is for. We also passed the pipeline through to the log_recent() function to minimize round trips to Redis while keeping track of common and recent logs.

Now that we've started to gather information about running software in Redis by storing recent and common logs, what other kinds of information would be useful to keep in Redis?

5.2　*Counters and statistics*

As you saw way back in chapter 2 when I introduced the concept of counting individual page visits, having basic hit count information can (for example) change the way we choose our caches. But our example from chapter 2 was very simple, and reality is rarely that simple, especially when it involves a real website.

The fact that our site received 10,000 hits in the last 5 minutes, or that the database handled 200 writes and 600 reads in the last 5 seconds, is useful information to know. If we add the ability to see that information over time, we can notice sudden or gradual increases in traffic, predict when server upgrades are necessary, and ultimately save ourselves from downtime due to an overloaded system.

This section will work through two different methods for recording both counters and statistics in Redis, and will finish by discussing how to simplify the collection of our example statistics. Both of these examples are driven by real use cases and requirements. Our next stop on the road of application introspection is collecting time series counters in Redis.

5.2.1   Storing counters in Redis

As we monitor our application, being able to gather information over time becomes ever more important. Code changes (that can affect how quickly our site responds, and subsequently how many pages we serve), new advertising campaigns, or new users to our system can all radically change the number of pages that are loaded on a site. Subsequently, any number of other performance metrics may change. But if we aren't recording any metrics, then it's impossible to know how they're changing, or whether we're doing better or worse.

In an attempt to start gathering metrics to watch and analyze, we'll build a tool to keep named counters over time (counters with names like *site hits*, *sales*, or *database queries* can be crucial). Each of these counters will store the most recent 120 samples at a variety of time precisions (like 1 second, 5 seconds, 1 minute, and so on). Both the number of samples and the selection of precisions to record can be customized as necessary.

The first step for keeping counters is actually storing the counters themselves.

UPDATING A COUNTER

In order to update counters, we'll need to store the actual counter information. For each counter and precision, like *site hits* and *5 seconds*, we'll keep a HASH that stores information about the number of site hits that have occurred in each 5-second time slice. The keys in the hash will be the start of the time slice, and the value will be the number of hits. Figure 5.1 shows a selection of data from a hit counter with 5-second time slices.

As we start to use counters, we need to record what counters have been written to so that we can clear out old data. For this, we need an ordered sequence that lets us iterate one by one over its entries, and that also doesn't allow duplicates. We could use a LIST combined with a SET, but that would take extra code and round trips to Redis. Instead, we'll use a ZSET, where the members are the combinations of precisions and names that have been written to, and the scores are all 0. By setting all scores to 0 in a ZSET, Redis will try to sort by score, and finding them all equal, will then sort by member name. This gives us a fixed order for a given set of members, which will make it easy to sequentially scan them. An example ZSET of known counters can be seen in figure 5.2.

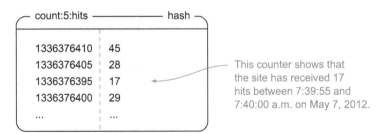

Figure 5.1   A HASH that shows the number of web page hits over 5-second time slices around 7:40 a.m. on May 7, 2012

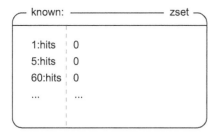

When scores are equal as they are in this ZSET, Redis sorts by member name.

Figure 5.2 A ZSET that shows some known counters

Now that we know what our structures for counters look like, what goes on to make that happen? For each time slice precision, we'll add a reference to the precision and the name of the counter to the known ZSET, and we'll increment the appropriate time window by the count in the proper HASH. Our code for updating a counter looks like this.

Listing 5.3 The update_counter() function

The precision of the counters in seconds: I second, 5 seconds, I minute, 5 minutes, I hour, 5 hours, I day—adjust as necessary.

Get the current time to know which time slice to increment.

Add entries for all precisions that we record.

Record a reference to the counters into a ZSET with the score 0 so we can clean up after ourselves.

Create a transactional pipeline so that later cleanup can work correctly.

Get the start of the current time slice.

Create the named hash where this data will be stored.

Update the counter for the given name and time precision.

```python
PRECISION = [1, 5, 60, 300, 3600, 18000, 86400]

def update_counter(conn, name, count=1, now=None):
    now = now or time.time()
    pipe = conn.pipeline()
    for prec in PRECISION:
        pnow = int(now / prec) * prec
        hash = '%s:%s'%(prec, name)
        pipe.zadd('known:', hash, 0)
        pipe.hincrby('count:' + hash, pnow, count)
    pipe.execute()
```

Updating the counter information isn't so bad; just a ZADD and HINCRBY for each time slice precision. And fetching the information for a named counter and a specific precision is also easy. We fetch the whole HASH with HGETALL, convert our time slices and counters back into numbers (they're all returned as strings), sort them by time, and finally return the values. The next listing shows our code for fetching counter data.

Listing 5.4 The get_counter() function

Get the name of the key where we'll be storing counter data.

Fetch the counter data from Redis.

Convert the counter data into something more expected.

Sort our data so that older samples are first.

```python
def get_counter(conn, name, precision):
    hash = '%s:%s'%(precision, name)
    data = conn.hgetall('count:' + hash)
    to_return = []
    for key, value in data.iteritems():
        to_return.append((int(key), int(value)))
    to_return.sort()
    return to_return
```

We did exactly what we said we were going to do. We fetched the data, ordered it sequentially based on time, and converted it back into integers. Let's look at how we prevent these counters from keeping too much data.

CLEANING OUT OLD COUNTERS

Now we have all of our counters written to Redis and we can fetch our counters with ease. But as we update our counters, at some point we're going to run out of memory if we don't perform any cleanup. Because we were thinking ahead, we wrote to our known ZSET the listing of known counters. To clean out the counters, we need to iterate over that listing and clean up old entries.

> **WHY NOT USE** EXPIRE?   One limitation of the EXPIRE command is that it only applies to whole keys; we can't expire parts of keys. And because we chose to structure our data so that counter X of precision Y is in a single key for all time, we have to clean out the counters periodically. If you feel ambitious, you may want to try restructuring the counters to change the data layout to use standard Redis expiration instead.

As we process and clean up old counters, a few things are important to pay attention to. The following list shows a few of the more important items that we need to be aware of as we clean out old counters:

- New counters can be added at any time.
- Multiple cleanups may be occurring at the same time.
- Trying to clean up daily counters every minute is a waste of effort.
- If a counter has no more data, we shouldn't try to clean it up any more.

With all of those things in mind, we'll build a daemon function similar in operation to the daemon functions that we wrote back in chapter 2. As before, we'll repeatedly loop until the system is told to quit. To help minimize load during cleanup, we'll attempt to clean out old counters roughly once per minute, and will also clean up old counters at roughly the schedule that they're creating new entries, except for counters that get new entries more often than once per minute. If a counter has a time slice of 5 minutes, we'll try to clean out old entries from that counter every 5 minutes. Counters that have new entries more often (1 second and 5 seconds in our example), we'll clean out every minute.

To iterate over the counters, we'll fetch known counters one by one with ZRANGE. To clean a counter, we'll fetch all of the start times for a given counter, calculate which items are before a calculated cutoff (120 samples ago), and remove them. If there's no more data for a given counter, we'll remove the counter reference from the known ZSET. Explaining what goes on is simple, but the details of the code show some corner cases. Check out this listing to see the cleanup code in full detail.

Listing 5.5   The clean_counters() **function**

Keep cleaning out counters until we're told to stop.

Keep a record of the number of passes so that we can balance cleaning out per-second vs. per-day counters.

```
def clean_counters(conn):
    pipe = conn.pipeline(True)
    passes = 0
    while not QUIT:
```

Incrementally iterate over all known counters.

We'll take a pass every 60 seconds or so, so we'll try to clean out counters at roughly the rate that they're written to.

Try the next counter if we aren't supposed to check this one on this pass (for example, we've taken three passes, but the counter has a precision of 5 minutes).

Find the cutoff time for the earliest sample that we should keep, given the precision and number of samples that we want to keep.

Remove the samples as necessary.

Watch the counter hash for changes.

Verify that the counter hash is empty, and if so, remove it from the known counters.

The hash isn't empty; keep it in the list of known counters.

Someone else changed the counter hash by adding counters, which means that it has data, so we'll leave the counter in the list of known counters.

Get the start time of the pass to calculate the total duration.

Get the next counter to check.

Get the precision of the counter.

Fetch the times of the samples, and convert the strings to integers.

Determine the number of samples that should be deleted.

The data HASH may be empty.

If we deleted a counter, then we can use the same index next pass.

Sleep the remainder of the 60 seconds, or at least I second, just to offer a bit of a rest.

Update our passes and duration variables for the next pass to clean out counters as often as they're seeing updates.

```python
start = time.time()
index = 0
while index < conn.zcard('known:'):
    hash = conn.zrange('known:', index, index)
    index += 1
    if not hash:
        break
    hash = hash[0]
    prec = int(hash.partition(':')[0])
    bprec = int(prec // 60) or 1
    if passes % bprec:
        continue
    hkey = 'count:' + hash
    cutoff = time.time() - SAMPLE_COUNT * prec
    samples = map(int, conn.hkeys(hkey))
    samples.sort()
    remove = bisect.bisect_right(samples, cutoff)
    if remove:
        conn.hdel(hkey, *samples[:remove])
        if remove == len(samples):
            try:
                pipe.watch(hkey)
                if not pipe.hlen(hkey):
                    pipe.multi()
                    pipe.zrem('known:', hash)
                    pipe.execute()
                    index -= 1
                else:
                    pipe.unwatch()
            except redis.exceptions.WatchError:
                pass

passes += 1
duration = min(int(time.time() - start) + 1, 60)
time.sleep(max(60 - duration, 1))
```

As described earlier, we iterate one by one over the ZSET of counters, looking for items to clean out. We only clean out counters that should be cleaned in this pass, so we perform that check early. We then fetch the counter data and determine what (if anything) should be cleaned up. After cleaning out old data as necessary, if we don't believe that there should be any remaining data, we verify that there's no more data for the counter and remove it from our ZSET of counters. Finally, after passing over all of the counters, we calculate how long it took to perform a pass, and sleep roughly the remainder of the minute we left for ourselves to perform the full cleanup, until the next pass.

Now that we have counter data, are cleaning it up, and can fetch it, it's just a matter of building an interface for consuming the data. Sadly, that part is out of the scope of this book, but there are a few usable JavaScript plotting libraries that can help you out on the web side of things (I've had good experiences with jqplot [http://www.jqplot.com/], Highcharts [http://www.highcharts.com/], dygraphs [http://dygraphs.com/], and D3 [http://d3js.org/] for personal and professional uses).

When dealing with the depth of complexity in a real website, knowing that a page gets hit thousands of times a day can help us to decide that the page should be cached. But if that page takes 2 milliseconds to render, whereas another page gets one tenth the traffic but takes 2 seconds to render, we can instead direct our attention to optimizing the slower page. In the next section, we change our approach from keeping precise counters that give us data over time, to keeping aggregate statistics to help us make more nuanced decisions about what to optimize.

5.2.2 *Storing statistics in Redis*

Truth be told, I've personally implemented five different methods of storing statistics in Redis. The method described here takes many of the good ideas from those methods and combines them in a way that allows for the greatest flexibility and opportunity to scale. What are we going to build?

We'll build a method to store statistics that have a similar scope to our `log_common()` function from section 5.1.2 (the current hour and the last hour). We'll collect enough information to keep track of the minimum, maximum, average value, standard deviation, sample count, and the sum of values that we're recording. We record so much information because we can just about guarantee that if we aren't recording it, we'll probably need it.

For a given named context and type, we'll store a group of values in a ZSET. We won't use the ZSET for its ability to sort scores, but instead for its ability to be unioned against another ZSET, keeping only the MIN or MAX of items that intersect. The precise information that we'll store for that context and type is the minimum value, the maximum value, the count of values, the sum of the values, and the sum of the squares of the values. With that information, we can calculate the average and standard deviation. Figure 5.3 shows an example of a ZSET holding this information for the ProfilePage context with statistics on AccessTime.

Now that we know the type of data that we'll be storing, how do we get the data in there? We'll start like we did with our common logs by checking to make sure that our current data is for the correct hour, moving the old data to an archive if it's not for the current hour. We'll then construct two temporary ZSETs—one with the minimum

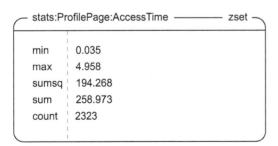

stats:ProfilePage:AccessTime ──────── zset

min	0.035
max	4.958
sumsq	194.268
sum	258.973
count	2323

Figure 5.3 Example access time stats for the profile page. Remember that ZSETs are sorted by score, which is why our order seems strange compared to our description.

value, the other with the maximum value—and ZUNIONSTORE them with the current stats with an aggregate of MIN and MAX, respectively. That'll allow us to quickly update the data without needing to WATCH a potentially heavily updated stats key. After cleaning up those temporary ZSETs, we'll then ZINCRBY the count, sum, and sumsq members of the statsZSET. Our code for performing this operation is shown next.

Listing 5.6 The `update_stats()` function

```
def update_stats(conn, context, type, value, timeout=5):          Set up the destination
    destination = 'stats:%s:%s'%(context, type)          ◄─┘      statistics key.
    start_key = destination + ':start'                        ◄─
    pipe = conn.pipeline(True)
    end = time.time() + timeout                                       Handle the current
    while time.time() < end:                                          hour/last hour like
        try:                                                          in common_log().
            pipe.watch(start_key)
            now = datetime.utcnow().timetuple()
            hour_start = datetime(*now[:4]).isoformat()

            existing = pipe.get(start_key)
            pipe.multi()
            if existing and existing < hour_start:
                pipe.rename(destination, destination + ':last')
                pipe.rename(start_key, destination + ':pstart')
                pipe.set(start_key, hour_start)

            tkey1 = str(uuid.uuid4())
            tkey2 = str(uuid.uuid4())
            pipe.zadd(tkey1, 'min', value)          Add the value to the
            pipe.zadd(tkey2, 'max', value)          temporary keys.
            pipe.zunionstore(destination,
                [destination, tkey1], aggregate='min')     Union the temporary keys with the
            pipe.zunionstore(destination,                  destination stats key, using the
                [destination, tkey2], aggregate='max')     appropriate min/max aggregate.

            pipe.delete(tkey1, tkey2)                ◄─┐    Clean up the
            pipe.zincrby(destination, 'count')          │  temporary keys.
            pipe.zincrby(destination, 'sum', value)
            pipe.zincrby(destination, 'sumsq', value*value)

            return pipe.execute()[-3:]                ◄─    Return the base counter
        except redis.exceptions.WatchError:                 info so that the caller
            continue                                  ◄─┐    can do something
                                                           interesting if necessary.
```

Update the count, sum, and sum of squares members of the ZSET.

If the hour just turned over and the stats have already been shuffled over, try again.

We can ignore almost all of the first half of the code listing, since it's a verbatim copy of the rollover code from our log_common() function from section 5.1.2. The latter half does exactly what we described: creating temporary ZSETs, ZUNIONSTOREing them with our destination ZSET with the proper aggregates, cleaning the temporary ZSETs, and then adding our standard statistics information. But what about pulling the statistics information back out?

To pull the information back out, we need to pull all of the values from the ZSET and then calculate the average and standard deviation. The average is simply the sum member divided by the count member. But the standard deviation is more difficult. With a bit of work, we can derive the standard deviation from the information we have, though for the sake of brevity I won't explain the math behind it. Our code for fetching stats is shown here.

Listing 5.7   The get_stats() function

```
def get_stats(conn, context, type):
    key = 'stats:%s:%s'%(context, type)
    data = dict(conn.zrange(key, 0, -1, withscores=True))
    data['average'] = data['sum'] / data['count']
    numerator = data['sumsq'] - data['sum'] ** 2 / data['count']
    data['stddev'] = (numerator / (data['count'] - 1 or 1)) ** .5
    return data
```

Set up the key that we're fetching our statistics from.

Calculate the average.

Fetch our basic statistics and package them as a dictionary.

Prepare the first part of the calculation of standard deviation.

Finish our calculation of standard deviation.

Aside from the calculation of the standard deviation, the get_stats() function isn't surprising. And for those who've spent some time on the Wikipedia page for standard deviation, even calculating the standard deviation shouldn't be all that surprising. But with all of this statistical information being stored, how do we know what information to look at? We'll be answering that question and more in the next section.

5.2.3   *Simplifying our statistics recording and discovery*

Now we have our statistics stored in Redis—what next? More specifically, now that we have information about (for example) access time on every page, how do we discover which pages take a long time on average to generate? Or how do we know when it takes significantly longer to generate a page than it did on previous occasions? The simple answer is that we need to store more information in a way that lets us discover when both situations happen, which we'll explore in this section.

If we want to record access times, then we need to calculate access times. We can spend our time adding access time calculations in various places and then adding code to record the access times, or we can implement something to help us to calculate and record the access times. That same helper could then also make that information available in (for example) a ZSET of the slowest pages to access on average, and could even report on pages that take a long time to access compared to other times that page was accessed.

To help us calculate and record access times, we'll write a Python context manager[1] that will wrap our code that we want to calculate and record access times for.

---

[1] In Python, a *context manager* is a specially defined function or class that will have parts of it executed before and after a given block of code is executed. This allows, for example, the easy opening and automatic closing of files.

This context manager will get the current time, let the wrapped code execute, and then calculate the total time of execution, record it in Redis, and also update a ZSET of the highest access time contexts. The next listing shows our context manager for performing this set of operations.

Listing 5.8   The `access_time()` context manager

Record the start time.

Let the block of code that we're wrapping run.

Update the stats for this context.

Add the average to a ZSET that holds the slowest access times.

```
@contextlib.contextmanager
def access_time(conn, context):
    start = time.time()
    yield

    delta = time.time() - start
    stats = update_stats(conn, context, 'AccessTime', delta)
    average = stats[1] / stats[0]

    pipe = conn.pipeline(True)
    pipe.zadd('slowest:AccessTime', context, average)
    pipe.zremrangebyrank('slowest:AccessTime', 0, -101)
    pipe.execute()
```

Make this Python generator into a context manager.

Calculate the time that the block took to execute.

Calculate the average.

Keep the slowest 100 items in the AccessTime ZSET.

There's some magic going on in the `access_time()` context manager, and it'll probably help to see it in use to understand what's going on. The following code shows the `access_time()` context manager being used to record access times of web pages that are served through a similar kind of callback method as part of a middleware layer or plugin that was used in our examples from chapter 2:

This is how we'd use the access time context manager to wrap a block of code.

```
def process_view(conn, callback):
    with access_time(conn, request.path):
        return callback()
```

This web view takes the Redis connection as well as a callback to generate content.

This is executed when the yield statement is hit from within the context manager.

After seeing the example, even if you don't yet understand how to create a context manager, you should at least know how to use one. In this example, we used the access time context manager to calculate the total time to generate a web page. This context manager could also be used to record the time it takes to make a database query or the amount of time it takes to render a template. As an exercise, can you think of other types of context managers that could record statistics that would be useful? Or can you add reporting of access times that are more than two standard deviations above average to the `recent_log()`?

GATHERING STATISTICS AND COUNTERS IN THE REAL WORLD   I know that we just spent several pages talking about how to gather fairly important statistics about how our production systems operate, but let me remind you that there are pre-existing software packages designed for collecting and plotting counters and statistics. My personal favorite is Graphite (http://graphite.wikidot.com/), which you should probably download and install before spending too much time building your own data-plotting library.

Now that we've been recording diverse and important information about the state of our application into Redis, knowing more about our visitors can help us to answer other questions.

5.3   IP-to-city and -country lookup

While we've been collecting statistics and logs in Redis, we've been gathering information about visitor behavior in our system. But we've been ignoring one of the most important parts of visitor behavior—where the visitor is coming from. In this section, we'll build a set of functions that we can use to parse an IP-to-location database, and we'll write a function to look up IP addresses to determine the visitor's city, region (state), and country. Let's look at an example.

As visitors to Fake Game Company's game have multiplied, players have been coming from all over the world to visit and play. Though tools like Google Analytics have helped Fake Game Company to understand which major countries their users are from, they want to know cities and states to better understand their users. It's our job to use one of the IP address-to-city databases and combine it with Redis to discover the locations of players.

We use Redis instead of a typical relational database because Redis will generally be faster for this (and other) use cases. And we use Redis over local lookup tables because the amount of information necessary to locate users is large enough to make loading tables on application startup a relatively expensive operation. To start using our lookup tables, we first need to load the tables into Redis.

5.3.1   Loading the location tables

For development data, I've downloaded a free IP-to-city database available from http://dev.maxmind.com/geoip/geolite. This database contains two important files: GeoLiteCity-Blocks.csv, which contains information about ranges of IP addresses and city IDs for those ranges, and GeoLiteCity-Location.csv, which contains a mapping of city IDs to the city name, the name of the region/state/province, the name of the country, and some other information that we won't use.

We'll first construct the lookup table that allows us to take an IP address and convert it to a city ID. We'll then construct a second lookup table that allows us to take the city ID and convert it to actual city information (city information will also include region and country information).

The table that allows us to find an IP address and turn it into a city ID will be constructed from a single ZSET, which has a special city ID as the member, and an integer value of the IP address as the score. To allow us to map from IP address to city ID, we convert dotted-quad format IP addresses to an integer score by taking each octet as a byte in an unsigned 32-bit integer, with the first octet being the highest bits. Code to perform this operation can be seen here.

Listing 5.9 The `ip_to_score()` function

```
def ip_to_score(ip_address):
    score = 0
    for v in ip_address.split('.'):
        score = score * 256 + int(v, 10)
    return score
```

After we have the score, we'll add the IP address mapping to city IDs first. To construct a unique city ID from each normal city ID (because multiple IP address ranges can map to the same city ID), we'll append a _ character followed by the number of entries we've added to the ZSET already, as can be seen in the next listing.

Listing 5.10 The `import_ips_to_redis()` function

```
def import_ips_to_redis(conn, filename):
    csv_file = csv.reader(open(filename, 'rb'))        ◁──┐ Should be run with the location
    for count, row in enumerate(csv_file):                │ of the GeoLiteCity-Blocks.csv file.
        start_ip = row[0] if row else ''
        if 'i' in start_ip.lower():
            continue
        if '.' in start_ip:                                  Convert the IP address
            start_ip = ip_to_score(start_ip)                 to a score as necessary.
        elif start_ip.isdigit():
            start_ip = int(start_ip, 10)
        else:                                              ┌ Header row or
            continue                                    ◁─┘ malformed entry.

        city_id = row[2] + '_' + str(count)            ◁──┐ Construct the
        conn.zadd('ip2cityid:', city_id, start_ip)     ◁─┐│ unique city ID.
                                                         ││
                          Add the IP address ───────────┘│
                          score and city ID.             │
```

When our IP addresses have all been loaded by calling `import_ips_to_redis()`, we'll create a HASH that maps city IDs to city information, as shown in the next listing. We'll store the city information as a list encoded with JSON, because all of our entries are of a fixed format that won't be changing over time.

Listing 5.11 The `import_cities_to_redis()` function

```
def import_cities_to_redis(conn, filename):          ◁──┐ Should be run with the location
    for row in csv.reader(open(filename, 'rb')):        │ of the GeoLiteCity-Location.csv
        if len(row) < 4 or not row[0].isdigit():        │ file.
            continue
        row = [i.decode('latin-1') for i in row]
        city_id = row[0]
        country = row[1]                                  Prepare the information
        region = row[2]                                   for adding to the hash.
        city = row[3]
        conn.hset('cityid2city:', city_id,                Actually add the city
            json.dumps([city, region, country]))          information to Redis.
```

Now that we have all of our information in Redis, we can start looking up IP addresses.

5.3.2   *Looking up cities*

To support looking up IP addresses, we added integer scores to a ZSET to represent the beginning of IP address ranges for a given city ID. In order to find a city given an IP address, we map the IP address to a similarly calculated score and then find the city ID that has the largest starting IP address less than or equal to the IP address we pass. We can use ZREVRANGEBYSCORE with the optional START and NUM arguments set to 0 and 1, respectively, to fetch this information. After we've discovered the city ID, we can fetch the city information from our HASH. Our function for finding which city an IP address is in can be seen next.

Listing 5.12   The find_city_by_ip() function

```
def find_city_by_ip(conn, ip_address):
    if isinstance(ip_address, str):            Convert the IP address to a
        ip_address = ip_to_score(ip_address)   score for zrevrangebyscore.

    city_id = conn.zrevrangebyscore(           Find the
        'ip2cityid:', ip_address, 0, start=0, num=1)   unique city ID.

    if not city_id:                            Convert the unique city
        return None                            ID to the common city ID.

    city_id = city_id[0].partition('_')[0]     ◄─┘
    return json.loads(conn.hget('cityid2city:', city_id))   ◄─┐ Fetch the city
                                                               information
                                                               from the hash.
```

We can now look up city information based on IP address and begin to analyze where our users are coming from. This method of converting data into integers for use with a ZSET is useful, and can greatly simplify the discovery of individual items or ranges. We'll talk more about these kinds of data transformations in chapter 7. But for now, let's look at how we can use Redis to help us find and connect to other servers and services.

5.4   *Service discovery and configuration*

As your use of Redis and other services grows over time, you'll eventually come to a situation where keeping configuration information can get out of hand. It's not a big deal when you have one Redis server, one database server, and one web server. But when you have a Redis master with a few slaves, or different Redis servers for different applications, or even master and slave database servers, keeping all of that configuration can be a pain.

Typically, configuration information for connecting to different services and servers is contained in configuration files that are stored on disk. And in situations where a machine breaks down, a network connection goes down, or something else causes us to need to connect to a different server, we'll usually need to update a number of configuration files in one of a number of locations. In this section, we'll talk about how we can move much of our configuration out of files and into Redis, which will let applications almost configure themselves.

Let's start with a simple live configuration to see how Redis can help us.

5.4.1 *Using Redis to store configuration information*

To see how generally difficult configuration management can be, we only need to look at the simplest of configurations: a flag to tell our web servers whether we're under maintenance. If so, we shouldn't make requests against the database, and should instead return a simple "Sorry, we're under maintenance; try again later" message to visitors. If the site isn't under maintenance, all of the normal web-serving behavior should happen.

In a typical situation, updating that single flag can force us to push updated configuration files to all of our web servers, and may force us to reload configurations on all of our servers, if not force us to restart our application servers themselves.

Instead of trying to write and maintain configuration files as our number of services grows, let's instead write our configuration to Redis. By putting our configuration in Redis and by writing our application to fetch configuration information from Redis, we no longer need to write tools to push out configuration information and cause our servers and services to reload that configuration.

To implement this simple behavior, we'll assume that we've built a middleware layer or plugin like we used for caching in chapter 2 that will return our maintenance page if a simple is_under_maintenance() function returns True, or will handle the request like normal if it returns False. Our actual function will check for a key called is-under-maintenance. If the key has any value stored there, we'll return True; otherwise, we'll return False. To help minimize the load to Redis under heavy web server load (because people love to hit Refresh when they get maintenance pages), we'll only update our information once per second. Our function can be seen in this listing.

Listing 5.13 The is_under_maintenance() function

```
                              LAST_CHECKED = None
                              IS_UNDER_MAINTENANCE = False        Set the two variables as globals so
                                                                  we can write to them later.
        Check to see if       def is_under_maintenance(conn):
        it's been at least        global LAST_CHECKED, IS_UNDER_MAINTENANCE
        1 second since
        we last checked.          if LAST_CHECKED < time.time() - 1:
                                      LAST_CHECKED = time.time()
                                      IS_UNDER_MAINTENANCE = bool(        Update the last
        Find out                          conn.get('is-under-maintenance'))  checked time.
        whether the
        system is under           return IS_UNDER_MAINTENANCE        Return whether the system
        maintenance.                                                 is under maintenance.
```

With that one function plugged into the right place in our application, we could affect the behavior of thousands of web servers within 1 second. We chose 1 second to help reduce load against Redis for very heavily trafficked web sites, but we can reduce or remove that part of the function if our needs require faster updates. This seems like a toy example, but it demonstrates the power of keeping configuration information in a commonly accessible location. But what about more intricate configuration options?

5.4.2 *One Redis server per application component*

As countless developers have discovered during our increasing use of Redis, at some point we outgrow our first Redis server. Maybe we need to log more information, maybe we need more space for caching, or maybe we've already skipped ahead and are using one of the more advanced services described in later chapters. For whatever reason, we'll need more servers.

To help with the ease of transitioning to more servers, I recommend running one Redis server for every separate part of your application—one for logging, one for statistics, one for caching, one for cookies, and so forth. Note that you can run multiple Redis servers on a single machine; they just need to run on different ports. Alternatively, if you want to reduce your system administration load, you can also use different "databases" in Redis. Either way, by having different data split up into different key spaces, your transition to more or larger servers is somewhat simplified. Unfortunately, as your number of servers and/or Redis databases increases, managing and distributing configuration information for all of those servers becomes more of a chore.

In the previous section, we used Redis as our source for configuration information about whether we should serve a maintenance page. We can again use Redis to tell us information about other Redis servers. More specifically, let's use a single known Redis server as a directory of configuration information to discover how to connect to all of the other Redis servers that provide data for different application or service components. While we're at it, we'll build it in such a way that when configurations change, we'll connect to the correct servers. Our implementation will be more generic than this example calls for, but I'm sure that after you start using this method for getting configuration information, you'll start using it for non-Redis servers and services.

We'll build a function that will fetch a JSON-encoded configuration value from a key that's named after the type of service and the application component that service is for. For example, if we wanted to fetch connection information for the Redis server that holds statistics, we'd fetch the key `config:redis:statistics`. The following listing shows the code for setting configurations.

Listing 5.14 The `set_config()` function

```
def set_config(conn, type, component, config):
    conn.set(
        'config:%s:%s'%(type, component),
        json.dumps(config))
```

With this `set_config()` function, we can set any JSON-encodable configuration that we may want. With a slight change in semantics and a `get_config()` function structured similarly to our earlier `is_under_maintenance()` function, we could replace `is_under_maintenance()`. Consult the following listing for a function that matches `set_config()` and will allow us to locally cache configuration information for 1 second, 10 seconds, or 0 seconds, depending on our needs.

Listing 5.15   The `get_config()` function

```
                    CONFIGS = {}
                    CHECKED = {}                                    Check to see if we
                                                                    should update the
                    def get_config(conn, type, component, wait=1):  configuration
                        key = 'config:%s:%s'%(type, component)      information about
 We can, so                                                         this component.
 update the last        if CHECKED.get(key) < time.time() - wait:  ◄──
 time we checked             CHECKED[key] = time.time()
 this connection. └─►        config = json.loads(conn.get(key) or '{}')    ◄──┐
                            config = dict((str(k), config[k]) for k in config)
 Convert potentially Unicode ┌─►  old_config = CONFIGS.get(key)
 keyword arguments into  ┌─►                                       Fetch the configuration
 string keyword arguments. │      if config != old_config:      ◄──  for this component.
                           │           CONFIGS[key] = config    ◄──┐
 Get the old configuration │  return CONFIGS.get(key)             If the configurations
 for this component.       │                                     are different...
                                                      ...update the
                                                      configuration.
```

Now that we have a pair of functions for getting and setting configurations, we can go farther. We started down this path of storing and fetching configurations in order to set up and create connections to a variety of different Redis servers. But the first argument to almost every function that we've written so far is a connection argument. Rather than needing to manually fetch connections for the variety of services that we're using, let's build a method to help us automatically connect to these services.

5.4.3 Automatic Redis connection management

Manually creating and passing connections to Redis can be tough. Not only do we need to repeatedly refer to configuration information, but if we're using our configuration management functions from the last section, we still need to fetch the configuration, connect to Redis, and somehow deal with the connection when we're done. To simplify the management of all of these connections, we'll write a decorator that will take care of connecting to all of our Redis servers (except for the configuration server).

> **DECORATORS**   Within Python there's a syntax for passing a function X into another function Y. This function Y is called a *decorator*. Decorators are given an opportunity to alter the behavior of function X. Some decorators validate arguments, other decorators register callbacks, and even others manage connections like we intend to.

Our decorator will take a named configuration as an argument, which will generate a wrapper that, when called on the actual function, will wrap the function such that later calls will automatically connect to the appropriate Redis server, and that connection will be passed to the wrapped function with all of the other arguments that were later provided. The next listing has the source for our `redis_connection()` function.

Listing 5.16   The `redis_connection()` function/decorator

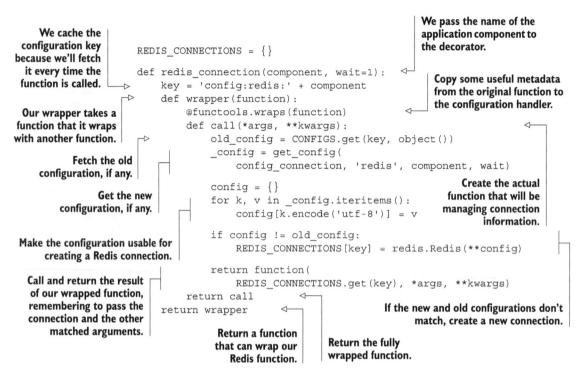

We cache the configuration key because we'll fetch it every time the function is called.

We pass the name of the application component to the decorator.

Copy some useful metadata from the original function to the configuration handler.

Our wrapper takes a function that it wraps with another function.

Fetch the old configuration, if any.

Get the new configuration, if any.

Make the configuration usable for creating a Redis connection.

Create the actual function that will be managing connection information.

Call and return the result of our wrapped function, remembering to pass the connection and the other matched arguments.

Return a function that can wrap our Redis function.

Return the fully wrapped function.

If the new and old configurations don't match, create a new connection.

```
REDIS_CONNECTIONS = {}

def redis_connection(component, wait=1):
    key = 'config:redis:' + component
    def wrapper(function):
        @functools.wraps(function)
        def call(*args, **kwargs):
            old_config = CONFIGS.get(key, object())
            _config = get_config(
                config_connection, 'redis', component, wait)

            config = {}
            for k, v in _config.iteritems():
                config[k.encode('utf-8')] = v

            if config != old_config:
                REDIS_CONNECTIONS[key] = redis.Redis(**config)

            return function(
                REDIS_CONNECTIONS.get(key), *args, **kwargs)
        return call
    return wrapper
```

COMBINING `*args` AND `**kwargs`   Way back in chapter 1, we first looked at default arguments in Python. But here, we're combining two different forms of argument passing. If you're having difficulty understanding what's going on (which is essentially capturing all positional and named arguments in the args and kwargs variables in the function definition, and passing all positional and named parameters to the called function), then you should spend some time with the Python language tutorial via this shortened URL: http://mng.bz/KM5x.

I know that this group of nested functions can be confusing at first, but it really isn't that bad. We have a function, `redis_connection()`, that takes the named application component and returns a wrapper function. That wrapper function is then called with the function we want to pass a connection to (the wrapped function), which then returns the function caller. This caller handles all of the work of getting configuration information, connecting to Redis, and calling our wrapped function. Though it's a mouthful to describe, actually using it is convenient, as you can see by applying it in the next listing to our `log_recent()` function from section 5.1.1.

Listing 5.17 The decorated `log_recent()` function

**The function
definition
doesn't change.**

```
@redis_connection('logs')
def log_recent(conn, app, message):
    'the old log_recent() code'

log_recent('main', 'User 235 logged in')
```

**The redis_connection()
decorator is very easy to use.**

**We no longer need to worry
about passing the log server
connection when calling
log_recent().**

DECORATORS In addition to the strange argument passing with `*args` and
`**kwargs` from listing 5.16, we're also using syntax to "decorate" the log function. That is to say, we pass a function to a decorator, which performs some
manipulation on the function before returning the original function, or
something else. You can read up on the details of what's going on and why at
http://www.python.org/dev/peps/pep-0318/.

Now that you've seen how to use the `redis_connection()` decorator on `log_recent()`,
it doesn't seem so bad, does it? With this better method of handling connections and
configuration, we've just removed a handful of lines from almost every function that
we'll be calling. As an exercise, try to add this decorator to the `access_time()` context
manager from section 5.2.3 so that we don't need to pass a connection. Feel free to reuse
this decorator with all of the other examples in the book.

5.5 *Summary*

All of the topics that we've covered in this chapter have directly or indirectly been
written to support applications. These functions and decorators are meant to help you
start using Redis as a way of supporting different parts of your application over time.
Logging, counters, and statistics are there to offer direct insight into how your application is performing. IP-to-location lookup can tell you where your consumers are
located. And storing service discovery and configuration can save a lot of effort
because of not needing to manually handle connections.

Now that we have a solid foundation for supporting applications in Redis, chapter 6 will continue down this path to functions that can be used as building blocks of
your application.

Application
components in Redis

6

This chapter covers

- Building two prefix-matching autocomplete methods
- Creating a distributed lock to improve performance
- Developing counting semaphores to control concurrency
- Two task queues for different use cases
- Pull messaging for delayed message delivery
- Handling file distribution

In the last few chapters, we've gone through some basic use cases and tools to help build applications in Redis. In this chapter, we'll get into more useful tools and techniques, working toward building bigger pieces of applications in Redis.

We'll begin by building autocomplete functions to quickly find users in short and long lists of items. We'll then take some time to carefully build two different types of locks to reduce data contention, improve performance, prevent data corruption, and reduce wasted work. We'll construct a delayed task queue, only to augment it later to allow for executing a task at a specific time with the use of the lock we just created. Building on the task queues, we'll build two different messaging systems to offer point-to-point and broadcast messaging services. We'll then reuse our earlier IP-address-to-city/-country lookup from chapter 5, and apply it to billions of log entries that are stored and distributed via Redis.

Each component offers usable code and solutions for solving these specific problems in the context of two example companies. But our solutions contain techniques that can be used for other problems, and our specific solutions can be applied to a variety of personal, public, or commercial projects.

To start, let's look at a fictional web-based game company called Fake Game Company, which currently has more than a million daily players of its games on YouTwit-Face, a fictional social network. Later we'll look at a web/mobile startup called Fake Garage Startup that does mobile and web instant messaging.

6.1   *Autocomplete*

In the web world, *autocomplete* is a method that allows us to quickly look up things that we want to find without searching. Generally, it works by taking the letters that we're typing and finding all words that start with those letters. Some autocomplete tools will even let us type the beginning of a phrase and finish the phrase for us. As an example, autocomplete in Google's search shows us that Betty White's SNL appearance is still popular, even years later (which is no surprise—she's a firecracker). It shows us the URLs we've recently visited and want to revisit when we type in the address bar, and it helps us remember login names. All of these functions and more are built to help us access information faster. Some of them, like Google's search box, are backed by many terabytes of remote information. Others, like our browser history and login boxes, are backed by much smaller local databases. But they all get us what we want with less work.

We'll build two different types of autocomplete in this section. The first uses lists to remember the most recent 100 contacts that a user has communicated with, trying to minimize memory use. Our second autocomplete offers better performance and scalability for larger lists, but uses more memory per list. They differ in their structure, the methods used, and the time it takes for the operations to complete. Let's first start with an autocomplete for recent contacts.

6.1.1   *Autocomplete for recent contacts*

The purpose of this autocomplete is to keep a list of the most recent users that each player has been in contact with. To increase the social aspect of the game and to allow people to quickly find and remember good players, Fake Game Company is looking to create a contact list for their client to remember the most recent 100 people that each user has chatted with. On the client side, when someone is trying to start a chat, they can start typing the name of the person they want to chat with, and autocomplete will show the list of users whose screen names start with the characters they've typed. Figure 6.1 shows an example of this kind of autocompletion.

Because each of the millions of users on the server will have their own list of their most recent 100 contacts, we need to try to minimize memory use, while still offering the ability to quickly add and remove users from the list. Because Redis LISTs keep the order of items consistent, and because LISTs use minimal memory compared to some other structures, we'll use them to store our autocomplete lists.

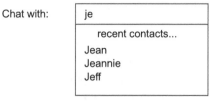

Chat with: je

recent contacts...
Jean
Jeannie
Jeff

Figure 6.1   A recent contacts autocomplete showing users with names starting with *je*

Unfortunately, LISTs don't offer enough functionality to actually perform the autocompletion inside Redis, so we'll perform the actual autocomplete outside of Redis, but inside of Python. This lets us use Redis to store and update these lists using a minimal amount of memory, leaving the relatively easy filtering to Python.

Generally, three operations need to be performed against Redis in order to deal with the recent contacts autocomplete lists. The first operation is to add or update a contact to make them the most recent user contacted. To perform this operation, we need to perform these steps:

1 Remove the contact from the list if it exists.
2 Add the contact to the beginning of the list.
3 Trim the list if it now has more than 100 items.

We can perform these operations with LREM, LPUSH, and LTRIM, in that order. To make sure that we don't have any race conditions, we'll use a MULTI/EXEC transaction around our commands like I described in chapter 3. The complete function is shown in this next listing.

Listing 6.1   The add_update_contact() function

```
                       def add_update_contact(conn, user, contact):
Remove the                 ac_list = 'recent:' + user               Set up the atomic
contact from the           pipeline = conn.pipeline(True)           operation.
list if it exists.         pipeline.lrem(ac_list, contact)
                           pipeline.lpush(ac_list, contact)         Push the item onto
Remove anything            pipeline.ltrim(ac_list, 0, 99)           the front of the list.
beyond the 100th item.     pipeline.execute()

                                                                    Actually execute everything.
```

As I mentioned, we removed the user from the LIST (if they were present), pushed the user onto the left side of the LIST; then we trimmed the LIST to ensure that it didn't grow beyond our limit.

The second operation that we'll perform is to remove a contact if the user doesn't want to be able to find them anymore. This is a quick LREM call, which can be seen as follows:

```
def remove_contact(conn, user, contact):
    conn.lrem('recent:' + user, contact)
```

The final operation that we need to perform is to fetch the autocomplete list itself to find the matching users. Again, because we'll perform the actual autocomplete processing in Python, we'll fetch the whole LIST, and then process it in Python, as shown next.

Listing 6.2   The `fetch_autocomplete_list()` function

```
                   def fetch_autocomplete_list(conn, user, prefix):
                       candidates = conn.lrange('recent:' + user, 0, -1)    ◁──  Fetch the
Check each             matches = []                                               autocomplete
candidate. ┌┐          for candidate in candidates:                              list.
           └┘              if candidate.lower().startswith(prefix):
            ┌─▷               matches.append(candidate)
We found a match. │    return matches    ◁──  Return all of the matches.
```

Again, we fetch the entire autocomplete LIST, filter it by whether the name starts with the necessary prefix, and return the results. This particular operation is simple enough that we could even push it off to the client if we find that our server is spending too much time computing it, only requiring a refetch on update.

This autocomplete will work fine for our specific example. It won't work as well if the lists grow significantly larger, because to remove an item takes time proportional to the length of the list. But because we were concerned about space, and have explicitly limited our lists to 100 users, it'll be fast enough. If you find yourself in need of much larger most- or least-recently-used lists, you can use ZSETs with timestamps instead.

6.1.2   *Address book autocomplete*

In the previous example, Redis was used primarily to keep track of the contact list, not to actually perform the autocomplete. This is okay for short lists, but for longer lists, fetching thousands or millions of items to find just a handful would be a waste. Instead, for autocomplete lists with many items, we must find matches inside Redis.

Going back to Fake Game Company, the recent contacts chat autocomplete is one of the most-used social features of our game. Our number-two feature, in-game mailing, has been gaining momentum. To keep the momentum going, we'll add an autocomplete for mailing. But in our game, we only allow users to send mail to other users that are in the same in-game social group as they are, which we call a *guild*. This helps to prevent abusive and unsolicited messages between users.

Guilds can grow to thousands of members, so we can't use our old LIST-based autocomplete method. But because we only need one autocomplete list per guild, we can use more space per member. To minimize the amount of data to be transferred to clients who are autocompleting, we'll perform the autocomplete prefix calculation inside Redis using ZSETs.

To store each autocomplete list will be different than other ZSET uses that you've seen before. Mostly, we'll use ZSETs for their ability to quickly tell us whether an item is in the ZSET, what position (or index) a member occupies, and to quickly pull ranges of items from anywhere inside the ZSET. What makes this use different is that all of our scores will be zero. By setting our scores to zero, we use a secondary feature of ZSETs:

ZSETs sort by member names when scores are equal. When all scores are zero, all members are sorted based on the binary ordering of the strings. In order to actually perform the autocomplete, we'll insert lowercased contact names. Conveniently enough, we've only ever allowed users to have letters in their names, so we don't need to worry about numbers or symbols.

What do we do? Let's start by thinking of names as a sorted sequence of strings like abc, abca, abcb, ... abd. If we're looking for words with a prefix of *abc*, we're really looking for strings that are after abbz... and before abd. If we knew the rank of the first item that is before abbz... and the last item after abd, we could perform a ZRANGE call to fetch items between them. But, because we don't know whether either of those items are there, we're stuck. To become unstuck, all we really need to do is to insert items that we know are after abbz... and before abd, find their ranks, make our ZRANGE call, and then remove our start and end members.

The good news is that finding an item that's before abd but still after all valid names with a prefix of abc is easy: we concatenate a { (left curly brace) character onto the end of our prefix, giving us abc{. Why {? Because it's the next character in ASCII after *z*. To find the start of our range for abc, we could also concatenate { to abb, getting abb{, but what if our prefix was aba instead of abc? How do we find a character before a? We take a hint from our use of the curly brace, and note that the character that precedes *a* in ASCII is ` (back quote). So if our prefix is aba, our start member will be ab`, and our end member will be aba{.

Putting it all together, we'll find the predecessor of our prefix by replacing the last character of our prefix with the character that came right before it. We'll find the successor of our prefix by concatenating a curly brace. To prevent any issues with two prefix searches happening at the same time, we'll concatenate a curly brace onto our prefix (for post-filtering out endpoint items if necessary). A function that will generate these types of ranges can be seen next.

Listing 6.3   The `find_prefix_range()` function

```
valid_characters = '`abcdefghijklmnopqrstuvwxyz{'    ← Set up our list of characters
                                                       that we know about.
def find_prefix_range(prefix):
    posn = bisect.bisect_left(valid_characters, prefix[-1:])    ← Find the position
    suffix = valid_characters[(posn or 1) - 1]                     of prefix character
    return prefix[:-1] + suffix + '{', prefix + '{'    ←           in our list of
                                    Return the range.              characters.
```

Find the predecessor character. (annotation for `suffix = valid_characters[(posn or 1) - 1]`)

I know, it can be surprising to have spent so many paragraphs describing what we're going to do, only to end up with just a few lines that actually implement it. But if we look at what we're doing, we're just finding the last character in the prefix in our presorted sequence of characters (using the bisect module), and then looking up the character that came just before it.

CHARACTER SETS AND INTERNATIONALIZATION This method of finding the preceding and following characters in ASCII works really well for languages with characters that only use characters *a-z*. But when confronted with characters that aren't in this range, you'll find a few new challenges.

First, you'll have to find a method that turns all of your characters into bytes; three common encodings include UTF-8, UTF-16, and UTF-32 (big-endian and little-endian variants of UTF-16 and UTF-32 are used, but only big-endian versions work in this situation). Second, you'll need to find the range of characters that you intend to support, ensuring that your chosen encoding leaves at least one character before your supported range and one character after your selected range in the encoded version. Third, you need to use these characters to replace the back quote character ` and the left curly brace character { in our example.

Thankfully, our algorithm doesn't care about the native sort order of the characters, only the encodings. So you can pick UTF-8 or big-endian UTF-16 or UTF-32, use a null to replace the back quote, and use the maximum value that your encoding and language supports to replace the left curly brace. (Some language bindings are somewhat limited, allowing only up to Unicode code point U+ffff for UTF-16 and Unicode code point U+2ffff for UTF-32.)

After we have the range of values that we're looking for, we need to insert our ending points into the ZSET, find the rank of those newly added items, pull some number of items between them (we'll fetch at most 10 to avoid overwhelming the user), and then remove our added items. To ensure that we're not adding and removing the same items, as would be the case if two members of the same guild were trying to message the same user, we'll also concatenate a 128-bit randomly generated UUID to our start and end members. To make sure that the ZSET isn't being changed when we try to find and fetch our ranges, we'll use WATCH with MULTI and EXEC after we've inserted our endpoints. The full autocomplete function is shown here.

Listing 6.4 The `autocomplete_on_prefix()` function

```
def autocomplete_on_prefix(conn, guild, prefix):
    start, end = find_prefix_range(prefix)          ← Find the start/
    identifier = str(uuid.uuid4())                     end range for
    start += identifier                                the prefix.
    end += identifier
    zset_name = 'members:' + guild

    conn.zadd(zset_name, start, 0, end, 0)   ← Add the start/end range items to the ZSET.
    pipeline = conn.pipeline(True)
    while 1:
        try:
            pipeline.watch(zset_name)
            sindex = pipeline.zrank(zset_name, start)   ← Find the ranks of
            eindex = pipeline.zrank(zset_name, end)        our end points.
            erange = min(sindex + 9, eindex - 2)
            pipeline.multi()
```

Get the values inside our range, and clean up.

```
pipeline.zrem(zset_name, start, end)
pipeline.zrange(zset_name, sindex, erange)
items = pipeline.execute()[-1]
break
except redis.exceptions.WatchError:
    continue
```

Retry if someone modified our autocomplete ZSET.

Remove start/end entries if an autocomplete was in progress.

```
return [item for item in items if '{' not in item]
```

Most of this function is bookkeeping and setup. The first part is just getting our start and ending points, followed by adding them to the guild's autocomplete ZSET. When we have everything in the ZSET, we WATCH the ZSET to ensure that we discover if someone has changed it, fetch the ranks of the start and end points in the ZSET, fetch items between the endpoints, and clean up after ourselves.

To add and remove members from a guild is straightforward: we only need to ZADD and ZREM the user from the guild's ZSET. Both of these functions are shown here.

Listing 6.5   The `join_guild()` and `leave_guild()` functions

```
def join_guild(conn, guild, user):
    conn.zadd('members:' + guild, user, 0)

def leave_guild(conn, guild, user):
    conn.zrem('members:' + guild, user)
```

Joining or leaving a guild, at least when it comes to autocomplete, is straightforward. We only need to add or remove names from the ZSET.

This method of adding items to a ZSET to create a range—fetching items in the range and then removing those added items—can be useful. Here we use it for autocomplete, but this technique can also be used for arbitrary sorted indexes. In chapter 7, we'll talk about a technique for improving these kinds of operations for a few different types of range queries, which removes the need to add and remove items at the endpoints. We'll wait to talk about the other method, because it only works on some types of data, whereas this method works on range queries over any type of data.

When we added our endpoints to the ZSET, we needed to be careful about other users trying to autocomplete at the same time, which is why we use the WATCH command. As our load increases, we may need to retry our operations often, which can be wasteful. The next section talks about a way to avoid retries, improve performance, and sometimes simplify our code by reducing and/or replacing WATCH with locks.

6.2   *Distributed locking*

Generally, when you "lock" data, you first *acquire* the lock, giving you exclusive access to the data. You then perform your operations. Finally, you *release* the lock to others. This sequence of acquire, operate, release is pretty well known in the context of shared-memory data structures being accessed by threads. In the context of Redis, we've been using WATCH as a replacement for a lock, and we call it *optimistic locking*, because rather than actually preventing others from modifying the data, we're notified if someone else changes the data before we do it ourselves.

With distributed locking, we have the same sort of acquire, operate, release operations, but instead of having a lock that's only known by threads within the same process, or processes on the same machine, we use a lock that different Redis clients on different machines can acquire and release. When and whether to use locks or WATCH will depend on a given application; some applications don't need locks to operate correctly, some only require locks for parts, and some require locks at every step.

One reason why we spend so much time building locks with Redis instead of using operating system–level locks, language-level locks, and so forth, is a matter of scope. Clients want to have exclusive access to data stored on Redis, so clients need to have access to a lock defined in a scope that all clients can see—Redis. Redis *does* have a basic sort of lock already available as part of the command set (SETNX), which we use, but it's not full-featured and doesn't offer advanced functionality that users would expect of a distributed lock.

Throughout this section, we'll talk about how an overloaded WATCHed key can cause performance issues, and build a lock piece by piece until we can replace WATCH for some situations.

6.2.1 *Why locks are important*

In the first version of our autocomplete, we added and removed items from a LIST. We did so by wrapping our multiple calls with a MULTI/EXEC pair. Looking all the way back to section 4.6, we first introduced WATCH/MULTI/EXEC transactions in the context of an in-game item marketplace. If you remember, the market is structured as a single ZSET, with members being an object and owner ID concatenated, along with the item price as the score. Each user has their own HASH, with columns for user name, currently available funds, and other associated information. Figure 6.2 shows an example of the marketplace, user inventories, and user information.

You remember that to add an item to the marketplace, we WATCH the seller's inventory to make sure the item is still available, add the item to the market ZSET, and

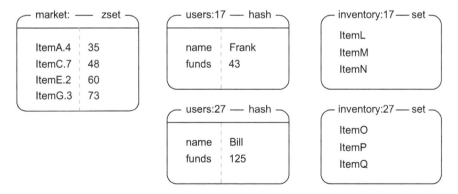

Figure 6.2   The structure of our marketplace from section 4.6. There are four items in the market on the left—ItemA, ItemC, ItemE, and ItemG—with prices 35, 48, 60, and 73, and seller IDs of 4, 7, 2, and 3, respectively. In the middle we have two users, Frank and Bill, and their current funds, with their inventories on the right.

remove it from the user's inventory. The core of our earlier `list_item()` function from section 4.4.2 is shown next.

Listing 6.6   The `list_item()` function from section 4.4.2

```
def list_item(conn, itemid, sellerid, price):
    #...
            pipe.watch(inv)
            if not pipe.sismember(inv, itemid):
                pipe.unwatch()
                return None

            pipe.multi()
            pipe.zadd("market:", item, price)
            pipe.srem(inv, itemid)
            pipe.execute()
            return True
    #...
```

Watch for changes to
the user's inventory.

Verify that the user still
has the item to be listed.

Actually list
the item.

The short comments in this code just hide a lot of the setup and WATCH/MULTI/EXEC handling that hide the core of what we're doing, which is why I omitted it here. If you feel like you need to see that code again, feel free to jump back to section 4.4.2 to refresh your memory.

Now, to review our purchasing of an item, we WATCH the market and the buyer's HASH. After fetching the buyer's total funds and the price of the item, we verify that the buyer has enough money. If the buyer has enough money, we transfer money between the accounts, add the item to the buyer's inventory, and remove the item from the market. If the buyer doesn't have enough money, we cancel the transaction. If a WATCH error is caused by someone else writing to the market ZSET or the buyer HASH changing, we retry. The following listing shows the core of our earlier `purchase_item()` function from section 4.4.3.

Listing 6.7   The `purchase_item()` function from section 4.4.3

```
def purchase_item(conn, buyerid, itemid, sellerid, lprice):
    #...
            pipe.watch("market:", buyer)

            price = pipe.zscore("market:", item)
            funds = int(pipe.hget(buyer, 'funds'))
            if price != lprice or price > funds:
                pipe.unwatch()
                return None

            pipe.multi()
            pipe.hincrby(seller, 'funds', int(price))
            pipe.hincrby(buyerid, 'funds', int(-price))
            pipe.sadd(inventory, itemid)
            pipe.zrem("market:", item)
            pipe.execute()
            return True
    #...
```

Watch for changes to the
market and the buyer's
account information.

Check for a sold/repriced
item or insufficient funds.

Transfer funds from the
buyer to the seller, and
transfer the item to
the buyer.

As before, we omit the setup and WATCH/MULTI/EXEC handling to focus on the core of what we're doing.

To see the necessity of locks at scale, let's take a moment to simulate the marketplace in a few different loaded scenarios. We'll have three different runs: one listing and one buying process, then five listing processes and one buying process, and finally five listing and five buying processes. Table 6.1 shows the result of running this simulation.

Table 6.1 Performance of a heavily loaded marketplace over 60 seconds

	Listed items	Bought items	Purchase retries	Average wait per purchase
1 lister, 1 buyer	145,000	27,000	80,000	14ms
5 listers, 1 buyer	331,000	<200	50,000	150ms
5 listers, 5 buyers	206,000	<600	161,000	498ms

As our overloaded system pushes its limits, we go from roughly a 3-to-1 ratio of retries per completed sale with one listing and buying process, all the way up to 250 retries for every completed sale. As a result, the latency to complete a sale increases from under 10 milliseconds in the moderately loaded system, all the way up to nearly 500 milliseconds in the overloaded system. This is a perfect example of why WATCH/MULTI/ EXEC transactions sometimes don't scale at load, and it's caused by the fact that while trying to complete a transaction, we fail and have to retry over and over. Keeping our data correct is important, but so is actually getting work done. To get past this limitation and actually start performing sales at scale, we must make sure that we only list or sell one item in the marketplace at any one time. We do this by using a lock.

6.2.2 *Simple locks*

In our first simple version of a lock, we'll take note of a few different potential failure scenarios. When we actually start building the lock, we won't handle all of the failures right away. We'll instead try to get the basic acquire, operate, and release process working right. After we have that working and have demonstrated how using locks can actually improve performance, we'll address any failure scenarios that we haven't already addressed.

While using a lock, sometimes clients can fail to release a lock for one reason or another. To protect against failure where our clients may crash and leave a lock in the acquired state, we'll eventually add a *timeout*, which causes the lock to be released automatically if the process that has the lock doesn't finish within the given time.

Many users of Redis already know about locks, locking, and lock timeouts. But sadly, many implementations of locks in Redis are only *mostly* correct. The problem with mostly correct locks is that they'll fail in ways that we don't expect, precisely when we don't expect them to fail. Here are some situations that can lead to incorrect behavior, and in what ways the behavior is incorrect:

- A process acquired a lock, operated on data, but took too long, and the lock was automatically released. The process doesn't know that it lost the lock, or may even release the lock that some other process has since acquired.
- A process acquired a lock for an operation that takes a long time and crashed. Other processes that want the lock don't know what process had the lock, so can't detect that the process failed, and waste time waiting for the lock to be released.
- One process had a lock, but it timed out. Other processes try to acquire the lock simultaneously, and multiple processes are able to get the lock.
- Because of a combination of the first and third scenarios, many processes now hold the lock and all believe that they are the only holders.

Even if each of these problems had a one-in-a-million chance of occurring, because Redis can perform 100,000 operations per second on recent hardware (and up to 225,000 operations per second on high-end hardware), those problems can come up when under heavy load,[1] so it's important to get locking right.

6.2.3 *Building a lock in Redis*

Building a *mostly* correct lock in Redis is easy. Building a *completely* correct lock in Redis isn't much more difficult, but requires being extra careful about the operations we use to build it. In this first version, we're not going to handle the case where a lock times out, or the case where the holder of the lock crashes and doesn't release the lock. Don't worry; we'll get to those cases in the next section, but for now, let's just get basic locking correct.

The first part of making sure that no other code can run is to acquire the lock. The natural building block to use for acquiring a lock is the SETNX command, which will only set a value if the key doesn't already exist. We'll set the value to be a unique identifier to ensure that no other process can get the lock, and the unique identifier we'll use is a 128-bit randomly generated UUID.

If we fail to acquire the lock initially, we'll retry until we acquire the lock, or until a specified timeout has passed, whichever comes first, as shown here.

> **Listing 6.8 The `acquire_lock()` function**

```
def acquire_lock(conn, lockname, acquire_timeout=10):
    identifier = str(uuid.uuid4())                              ◁── A 128-bit random identifier.

    end = time.time() + acquire_timeout
    while time.time() < end:
        if conn.setnx('lock:' + lockname, identifier):         ◁── Get the lock.
            return identifier

        time.sleep(.001)

    return False
```

---

[1] Having tested a few available Redis lock implementations that include support for timeouts, I was able to induce lock duplication on at least half of the lock implementations with just five clients acquiring and releasing the same lock over 10 seconds.

As described, we'll attempt to acquire the lock by using SETNX to set the value of the lock's key only if it doesn't already exist. On failure, we'll continue to attempt this until we've run out of time (which defaults to 10 seconds).

Now that we have the lock, we can perform our buying or selling without WATCH errors getting in our way. We'll acquire the lock and, just like before, check the price of the item, make sure that the buyer has enough money, and if so, transfer the money and item. When completed, we release the lock. The code for this can be seen next.

> ### Listing 6.9 The `purchase_item_with_lock()` function

```
def purchase_item_with_lock(conn, buyerid, itemid, sellerid):
    buyer = "users:%s"%buyerid
    seller = "users:%s"%sellerid
    item = "%s.%s"%(itemid, sellerid)
    inventory = "inventory:%s"%buyerid
    end = time.time() + 30

    locked = acquire_lock(conn, market)              Get the
        return False                                 lock.

    pipe = conn.pipeline(True)
    try:
        while time.time() < end:
            try:
                pipe.watch(buyer)
                pipe.zscore("market:", item)
                pipe.hget(buyer, 'funds')            Check for a sold item
                price, funds = pipe.execute()        or insufficient funds.
                if price is None or price > funds:
                    pipe.unwatch()
                    return None

                pipe.hincrby(seller, int(price))     Transfer funds from
                pipe.hincrby(buyerid, int(-price))   the buyer to the seller,
                pipe.sadd(inventory, itemid)         and transfer the item
                pipe.zrem("market:", item)           to the buyer.
                pipe.execute()
                return True
            except redis.exceptions.WatchError:
                pass
    finally:                                         Release
        release_lock(conn, market, locked)           the lock.
```

Looking through the code listing, it almost seems like we're locking the operation. But don't be fooled—we're locking the market data, and the lock must exist while we're operating on the data, which is why it surrounds the code performing the operation.

To release the lock, we have to be at least as careful as when acquiring the lock. Between the time when we acquired the lock and when we're trying to release it, someone may have done bad things to the lock. To release the lock, we need to WATCH the lock key, and then check to make sure that the value is still the same as what we set it to before we delete it. This also prevents us from releasing a lock multiple times. The release_lock() function is shown next.

Listing 6.10 The `release_lock()` function

```
def release_lock(conn, lockname, identifier):
    pipe = conn.pipeline(True)
    lockname = 'lock:' + lockname

    while True:
        try:
            pipe.watch(lockname)                         Check and verify
            if pipe.get(lockname) == identifier:         that we still have
                pipe.multi()                             the lock.
                pipe.delete(lockname)
                pipe.execute()                           Release the lock.
                return True

            pipe.unwatch()
            break

        except redis.exceptions.WatchError:             Someone else did something
            pass                                        with the lock; retry.

    return False                    ←—— We lost the lock.
```

We take many of the same steps to ensure that our lock hasn't changed as we did with our money transfer in the first place. But if you think about our release lock function for long enough, you'll (reasonably) come to the conclusion that, except in very rare situations, we don't need to repeatedly loop. But the next version of the acquire lock function that supports timeouts, if accidentally mixed with earlier versions (also unlikely, but anything is possible with code), could cause the release lock transaction to fail and could leave the lock in the acquired state for longer than necessary. So, just to be extra careful, and to guarantee correctness in as many situations as possible, we'll err on the side of caution.

After we've wrapped our calls with locks, we can perform the same simulation of buying and selling as we did before. In table 6.2, we have new rows that use the lock-based buying and selling code, which are shown below our earlier rows.

Though we generally have lower total number of items that finished being listed, we never retry, and our number of listed items compared to our number of purchased

Table 6.2 Performance of locking over 60 seconds

	Listed items	Bought items	Purchase retries	Average wait per purchase
1 lister, 1 buyer, no lock	145,000	27,000	80,000	14ms
1 lister, 1 buyer, with lock	51,000	50,000	0	1ms
5 listers, 1 buyer, no lock	331,000	<200	50,000	150ms
5 listers, 1 buyer, with lock	68,000	13,000	<10	5ms
5 listers, 5 buyers, no lock	206,000	<600	161,000	498ms
5 listers, 5 buyers, with lock	21,000	20,500	0	14ms

items is close to the ratio of number of listers to buyers. At this point, we're running at the limit of contention between the different listing and buying processes.

6.2.4 *Fine-grained locking*

When we introduced locks and locking, we only worried about providing the same type of locking granularity as the available WATCH command—on the level of the market key that we were updating. But because we're constructing locks manually, and we're less concerned about the market in its entirety than we are with whether an item is still in the market, we can actually lock on a finer level of detail. If we replace the market-level lock with one specific to the item to be bought or sold, we can reduce lock contention and increase performance.

Let's look at the results in table 6.3, which is the same simulation as produced table 6.2, only with locks over just the items being listed or sold individually, and not over the entire market.

Table 6.3   Performance of fine-grained locking over 60 seconds

	Listed items	Bought items	Purchase retries	Average wait per purchase
1 lister, 1 buyer, no lock	145,000	27,000	80,000	14ms
1 lister, 1 buyer, with lock	51,000	50,000	0	1ms
1 lister, 1 buyer, with fine-grained lock	113,000	110,000	0	<1ms
5 listers, 1 buyer, no lock	331,000	<200	50,000	150ms
5 listers, 1 buyer, with lock	68,000	13,000	<10	5ms
5 listers, 1 buyer, with fine-grained lock	192,000	36,000	0	<2ms
5 listers, 5 buyers, no lock	206,000	<600	161,000	498ms
5 listers, 5 buyers, with lock	21,000	20,500	0	14ms
5 listers, 5 buyers, with fine-grained lock	116,000	111,000	0	<3ms

With fine-grained locking, we're performing 220,000–230,000 listing and buying operations regardless of the number of listing and buying processes. We have no retries, and even under a full load, we're seeing less than 3 milliseconds of latency. Our listed-to-sold ratio is again almost exactly the same as our ratio of listing-to-buying processes. Even better, we never get into a situation like we did without locks where there's so much contention that latencies shoot through the roof and items are rarely sold.

Let's take a moment to look at our data as a few graphs so that we can see the relative scales. In figure 6.3, we can see that both locking methods result in much higher numbers of items being purchased over all relative loads than the WATCH-based method.

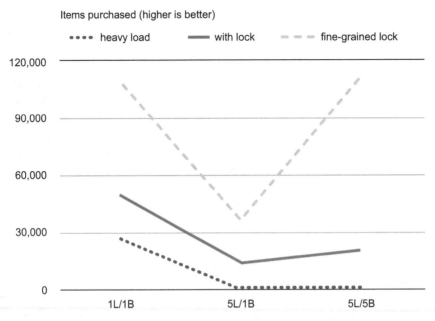

Figure 6.3   Items purchased completed in 60 seconds. This graph has an overall V shape because the system is overloaded, so when we have five listing processes to only one buying process (shown as 5L/ 1B in the middle samples), the ratio of listed items to bought items is roughly the same ratio, 5 to 1.

Looking at figure 6.4, we can see that the WATCH-based method has to perform many thousands of expensive retries in order to complete what few sales are completed.

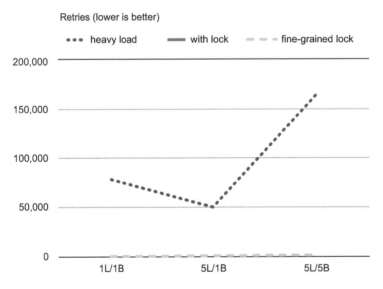

Figure 6.4   The number of retries when trying to purchase an item in 60 seconds. There are no retries for either types of locks, so we can't see the line for "with lock" because it's hidden behind the line for fine-grained locks.

And in figure 6.5, we can see that because of the WATCH contention, which caused the huge number of retries and the low number of purchase completions, latency without using a lock went up significantly.

What these simulations and these charts show overall is that when under heavy load, using a lock can reduce retries, reduce latency, improve performance, and be tuned at the granularity that we need.

Our simulation is limited. One major case that it doesn't simulate is where many more buyers are unable to buy items because they're waiting for others. It also doesn't simulate an effect known as *dogpiling*, when, as transactions take longer to complete, more transactions are overlapping and trying to complete. That will increase the time it takes to complete an individual transaction, and subsequently increase the chances for a time-limited transaction to fail. This will substantially increase the failure and retry rates for all transactions, but it's especially harmful in the WATCH-based version of our market buying and selling.

The choice to use a lock over an entire structure, or over just a small portion of a structure, can be easy. In our case, the critical data that we were watching was a small piece of the whole (one item in a marketplace), so locking that small piece made sense. There are situations where it's not just one small piece, or when it may make sense to lock multiple parts of structures. That's where the decision to choose locks over small pieces of data or an entire structure gets difficult; the use of multiple small locks can lead to deadlocks, which can prevent any work from being performed at all.

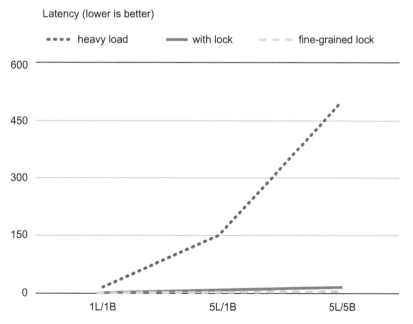

Figure 6.5 **Average latency for a purchase; times are in milliseconds. The maximum latency for either kind of lock is under 14ms, which is why both locking methods are difficult to see and hugging the bottom—our overloaded system without a lock has an average latency of nearly 500ms.**

6.2.5   *Locks with timeouts*

As mentioned before, our lock doesn't handle cases where a lock holder crashes without releasing the lock, or when a lock holder fails and holds the lock forever. To handle the crash/failure cases, we add a timeout to the lock.

In order to give our lock a timeout, we'll use EXPIRE to have Redis time it out automatically. The natural place to put the EXPIRE is immediately after the lock is acquired, and we'll do that. But if our client happens to crash (and the worst place for it to crash for us is between SETNX and EXPIRE), we still want the lock to eventually time out. To handle that situation, any time a client fails to get the lock, the client will check the expiration on the lock, and if it's not set, set it. Because clients are going to be checking and setting timeouts if they fail to get a lock, the lock will always have a timeout, and will eventually expire, letting other clients get a timed-out lock.

What if multiple clients set expiration times simultaneously? They'll run at essentially the same time, so expiration will be set for the same time.

Adding expiration to our earlier acquire_lock() function gets us the updated acquire_lock_with_timeout() function shown here.

Listing 6.11   The acquire_lock_with_timeout() function

```
def acquire_lock_with_timeout(
    conn, lockname, acquire_timeout=10, lock_timeout=10):          A 128-bit random
    identifier = str(uuid.uuid4())                                identifier.
    lock_timeout = int(math.ceil(lock_timeout))                   Only pass integers
                                                                  to our EXPIRE calls.
    end = time.time() + acquire_timeout
    while time.time() < end:
        if conn.setnx(lockname, identifier):                      Get the lock and
            conn.expire(lockname, lock_timeout)                   set the expiration.
            return identifier
        elif not conn.ttl(lockname):                              Check and update the
            conn.expire(lockname, lock_timeout)                   expiration time as necessary.

        time.sleep(.001)

    return False
```

This new acquire_lock_with_timeout() handling timeouts. It ensures that locks expire as necessary, and that they won't be stolen from clients that rightfully have them. Even better, we were smart with our release lock function earlier, which still works.

> **NOTE**   As of Redis 2.6.12, the SET command added options to support a combination of SETNX and SETEX functionality, which makes our lock acquire function trivial. We still need the complicated release lock to be correct.

In section 6.1.2 when we built the address book autocomplete using a ZSET, we went through a bit of trouble to create start and end entries to add to the ZSET in order to fetch a range. We also postprocessed our data to remove entries with curly braces ({}), because other autocomplete operations could be going on at the same time. And because other operations could be going on at the same time, we used WATCH so that we could retry. Each of those pieces added complexity to our functions, which could've been simplified if we'd used a lock instead.

In other databases, locking is a basic operation that's supported and performed automatically. As I mentioned earlier, using `WATCH`, `MULTI`, and `EXEC` is a way of having an optimistic lock—we aren't actually locking data, but we're notified and our changes are canceled if someone else modifies it before we do. By adding explicit locking on the client, we get a few benefits (better performance, a more familiar programming concept, easier-to-use API, and so on), but we need to remember that Redis itself doesn't respect our locks. It's up to us to consistently use our locks in addition to or instead of `WATCH`, `MULTI`, and `EXEC` to keep our data consistent and correct.

Now that we've built a lock with timeouts, let's look at another kind of lock called a *counting semaphore*. It isn't used in as many places as a regular lock, but when we need to give multiple clients access to the same information at the same time, it's the perfect tool for the job.

6.3 Counting semaphores

A *counting semaphore* is a type of lock that allows you to limit the number of processes that can concurrently access a resource to some fixed number. You can think of the lock that we just created as being a counting semaphore with a limit of 1. Generally, counting semaphores are used to limit the amount of resources that can be used at one time.

Like other types of locks, counting semaphores need to be acquired and released. First, we acquire the semaphore, then we perform our operation, and then we release it. But where we'd typically wait for a lock if it wasn't available, it's common to fail immediately if a semaphore isn't immediately available. For example, let's say that we wanted to allow for five processes to acquire the semaphore. If a sixth process tried to acquire it, we'd want that call to fail early and report that the resource is busy.

We'll move through this section similarly to how we went through distributed locking in section 6.2. We'll build a counting semaphore piece by piece until we have one that's complete and correct.

Let's look at an example with Fake Game Company. With the success of its marketplace continuously growing, Fake Game Company has had requests from users wanting to access information about the marketplace from outside the game so that they can buy and sell items without being logged into the game. The API to perform these operations has already been written, but it's our job to construct a mechanism that limits each account from accessing the marketplace from more than five processes at a time.

After we've built our counting semaphore, we make sure to wrap incoming API calls with a proper `acquire_semaphore()` and `release_semaphore()` pair.

6.3.1 Building a basic counting semaphore

When building a counting semaphore, we run into many of the same concerns we had with other types of locking. We must decide who got the lock, how to handle processes that crashed with the lock, and how to handle timeouts. If we don't care about timeouts,

semaphore:remote	zset
c5a58232-0d6c-467f-976f-d577163b24f2	1326437034.113
4cec3d88-a80e-4713-832c-42ec957fb845	1326437037.511
c73f379d-6a5b-48a6-9796-b6f9bbb55402	1326437037.621
40f93169-f8c7-40d3-a342-f0ec68b17dde	1326437038.765

Figure 6.6 Basic semaphore `ZSET`

or handling the case where semaphore holders can crash without releasing semaphores, we could build semaphores fairly conveniently in a few different ways. Unfortunately, those methods don't lead us to anything useful in the long term, so I'll describe one method that we'll incrementally improve to offer a full range of functionality.

In almost every case where we want to deal with timeouts in Redis, we'll generally look to one of two different methods. Either we'll use `EXPIRE` like we did with our standard locks, or we'll use `ZSET`s. In this case, we want to use `ZSET`s, because that allows us to keep information about multiple semaphore holders in a single structure.

More specifically, for each process that attempts to acquire the semaphore, we'll generate a unique identifier. This identifier will be the member of a `ZSET`. For the score, we'll use the timestamp for when the process attempted to acquire the semaphore. Our semaphore `ZSET` will look something like figure 6.6.

When a process wants to attempt to acquire a semaphore, it first generates an identifier, and then the process adds the identifier to the `ZSET` using the current timestamp as the score. After adding the identifier, the process then checks for its identifier's *rank*. If the rank returned is lower than the total allowed count (Redis uses 0-indexing on rank), then the caller has acquired the semaphore. Otherwise, the caller doesn't have the semaphore and must delete its identifier from the `ZSET`. To handle timeouts, before adding our identifier to the `ZSET`, we first clear out any entries that have timestamps that are older than our timeout number value. The code to acquire the semaphore can be seen next.

Listing 6.12 The `acquire_semaphore()` function

```
def acquire_semaphore(conn, semname, limit, timeout=10):
    identifier = str(uuid.uuid4())
    now = time.time()

    pipeline = conn.pipeline(True)
    pipeline.zremrangebyscore(semname, '-inf', now - timeout)
    pipeline.zadd(semname, identifier, now)
    pipeline.zrank(semname, identifier)
    if pipeline.execute()[-1] < limit:
        return identifier

    conn.zrem(semname, identifier)
    return None
```

- A 128-bit random identifier.
- Time out old semaphore holders.
- Try to acquire the semaphore.
- Check to see if we have it.
- We failed to get the semaphore; discard our identifier.

Our code proceeds as I've already described: generating the identifier, cleaning out any timed-out semaphores, adding its identifier to the ZSET, and checking its rank. Not too surprising.

Releasing the semaphore is easy: we remove the identifier from the ZSET, as can be seen in the next listing.

Listing 6.13 The `release_semaphore()` function

```
def release_semaphore(conn, semname, identifier):
    return conn.zrem(semname, identifier)
```

> **Returns True if the semaphore was properly released, False if it had timed out**

This basic semaphore works well—it's simple, and it's very fast. But relying on every process having access to the same system time in order to get the semaphore can cause problems if we have multiple hosts. This isn't a huge problem for our specific use case, but if we had two systems A and B, where A ran even 10 milliseconds faster than B, then if A got the last semaphore, and B tried to get a semaphore within 10 milliseconds, B would actually "steal" A's semaphore without A knowing it.

Any time we have a lock or a semaphore where such a slight difference in the system clock can drastically affect who can get the lock, the lock or semaphore is considered *unfair*. Unfair locks and semaphores can cause clients that should've gotten the lock or semaphore to never get it, and this is something that we'll fix in the next section.

6.3.2 *Fair semaphores*

Because we can't assume that all system clocks are exactly the same on all systems, our earlier basic counting semaphore will have issues where clients on systems with slower system clocks can steal the semaphore from clients on systems with faster clocks. Any time there's this kind of sensitivity, locking itself becomes unfair. We want to reduce the effect of incorrect system times on acquiring the semaphore to the point where as long as systems are within 1 second, system time doesn't cause semaphore theft or early semaphore expiration.

In order to minimize problems with inconsistent system times, we'll add a counter and a second ZSET. The counter creates a steadily increasing timer-like mechanism that ensures that whoever incremented the counter first should be the one to get the semaphore. We then enforce our requirement that clients that want the semaphore who get the counter first also get the semaphore by using an "owner" ZSET with the counter-produced value as the score, checking our identifier's rank in the new ZSET to determine which client got the semaphore. The new owner ZSET appears in figure 6.7.

We continue to handle timeouts the same way as our basic semaphore, by removing entries from the system time ZSET. We propagate those timeouts to the new owner ZSET by the use of ZINTERSTORE and the WEIGHTS argument.

Bringing it all together in listing 6.14, we first time out an entry by removing old entries from the timeout ZSET and then intersect the timeout ZSET with the owner

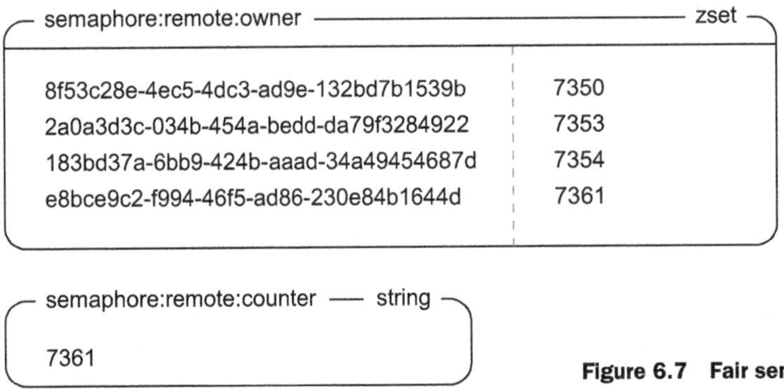

Figure 6.7   Fair semaphore owner ZSET

ZSET, saving to and overwriting the owner ZSET. We then increment the counter and add our counter value to the owner ZSET, while at the same time adding our current system time to the timeout ZSET. Finally, we check whether our rank in the owner ZSET is low enough, and if so, we have a semaphore. If not, we remove our entries from the owner and timeout ZSETs.

Listing 6.14   The `acquire_fair_semaphore()` function

```
def acquire_fair_semaphore(conn, semname, limit, timeout=10):
    identifier = str(uuid.uuid4())                              A 128-bit
    czset = semname + ':owner'                                  random
    ctr = semname + ':counter'                                  identifier.

    now = time.time()
    pipeline = conn.pipeline(True)
    pipeline.zremrangebyscore(semname, '-inf', now - timeout)   Time out old
    pipeline.zinterstore(czset, {czset: 1, semname: 0})         entries.

    pipeline.incr(ctr)                              Get the counter.
    counter = pipeline.execute()[-1]

    pipeline.zadd(semname, identifier, now)         Try to acquire the semaphore.
    pipeline.zadd(czset, identifier, counter)

    pipeline.zrank(czset, identifier)              Check the rank to determine
    if pipeline.execute()[-1] < limit:             if we got the semaphore.
        return identifier                          We got the semaphore.

    pipeline.zrem(semname, identifier)
    pipeline.zrem(czset, identifier)
    pipeline.execute()                             We didn't get the semaphore;
    return None                                    clean out the bad data.
```

This function has a few different pieces. We first clean up timed-out semaphores, updating the owner ZSET and fetching the next counter ID for this item. After we've added our time to the timeout ZSET and our counter value to the owner ZSET, we're ready to check to see whether our rank is low enough.

FAIR SEMAPHORES ON 32-BIT PLATFORMS On 32-bit Redis platforms, integer counters are limited to 2^{31} - 1, the standard signed integer limit. An overflow situation could occur on heavily used semaphores roughly once every 2 hours in the worst case. Though there are a variety of workarounds, the simplest is to switch to a 64-bit platform for any machine using any counter-based ID.

Let's look at figure 6.8, which shows the sequence of operations that are performed when process ID 8372 wants to acquire the semaphore at time 1326437039.100 when there's a limit of 5.

Releasing the semaphore is almost as easy as before, only now we remove our identifier from both the owner and timeout ZSETs, as can be seen in this next listing.

Listing 6.15 The `release_fair_semaphore()` function

```
def release_fair_semaphore(conn, semname, identifier):
    pipeline = conn.pipeline(True)
    pipeline.zrem(semname, identifier)
    pipeline.zrem(semname + ':owner', identifier)
    return pipeline.execute()[0]
```

Returns True if the semaphore was properly released, False if it had timed out

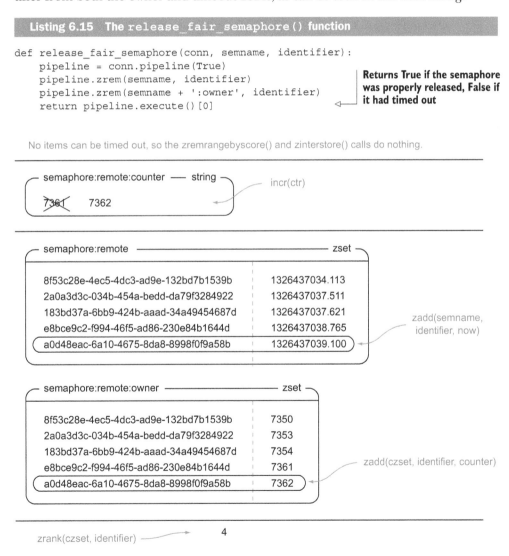

No items can be timed out, so the zremrangebyscore() and zinterstore() calls do nothing.

Figure 6.8 Call sequence for `acquire_fair_semaphore()`

If we wanted to be lazy, in most situations we could just remove our semaphore identifier from the timeout ZSET; one of our steps in the acquire sequence is to refresh the owner ZSET to remove identifiers that are no longer in the timeout ZSET. But by only removing our identifier from the timeout ZSET, there's a chance (rare, but possible) that we removed the entry, but the acquire_fair_semaphore() was between the part where it updated the owner ZSET and when it added its own identifiers to the timeout and owner ZSETs. If so, this could prevent it from acquiring the semaphore when it should've been able to. To ensure correct behavior in as many situations as possible, we'll stick to removing the identifier from both ZSETs.

Now we have a semaphore that doesn't require that all hosts have the same system time, though system times do need to be within 1 or 2 seconds in order to ensure that semaphores don't time out too early, too late, or not at all.

6.3.3   *Refreshing semaphores*

As the API for the marketplace was being completed, it was decided that there should be a method for users to stream all item listings as they happen, along with a stream for all purchases that actually occur. The semaphore method that we created only supports a timeout of 10 seconds, primarily to deal with timeouts and possible bugs on our side of things. But users of the streaming portion of the API will want to keep connected for much longer than 10 seconds, so we need a method for refreshing the semaphore so that it doesn't time out.

Because we already separated the timeout ZSET from the owner ZSET, we can actually refresh timeouts quickly by updating our time in the timeout ZSET, shown in the following listing.

> **Listing 6.16   The** refresh_fair_semaphore() **function**

```
def refresh_fair_semaphore(conn, semname, identifier):
    if conn.zadd(semname, identifier, time.time()):
        release_fair_semaphore(conn, semname, identifier)
        return False
    return True
```

Update our semaphore. → (points to `if conn.zadd(...)` and `release_fair_semaphore(...)`)

We lost our semaphore; report back. (points to `return False`)

We still have our semaphore. ←— (points to `return True`)

As long as we haven't already timed out, we'll be able to refresh the semaphore. If we were timed out in the past, we'll go ahead and let the semaphore be lost and report to the caller that it was lost. When using a semaphore that may be refreshed, we need to be careful to refresh often enough to not lose the semaphore.

Now that we have the ability to acquire, release, and refresh a fair semaphore, it's time to deal with our final race condition.

6.3.4   *Preventing race conditions*

As you saw when building locks in section 6.2, dealing with race conditions that cause retries or data corruption can be difficult. In this case, the semaphores that we created have race conditions that we alluded to earlier, which can cause incorrect operation.

We can see the problem in the following example. If we have two processes A and B that are trying to get one remaining semaphore, and A increments the counter first but B adds its identifier to the ZSETs and checks its identifier's rank first, then B will get the semaphore. When A then adds its identifier and checks its rank, it'll "steal" the semaphore from B, but B won't know until it tries to release or renew the semaphore.

When we were using the system clock as a way of getting a lock, the likelihood of this kind of a race condition coming up and resulting in more than the desired number of semaphore owners was related to the difference in system times—the greater the difference, the greater the likelihood. After introducing the counter with the owner ZSET, this problem became less likely (just by virtue of removing the system clock as a variable), but because we have multiple round trips, it's still possible.

To fully handle all possible race conditions for semaphores in Redis, we need to reuse the earlier distributed lock with timeouts that we built in section 6.2.5. We need to use our earlier lock to help build a correct counting semaphore. Overall, to acquire the semaphore, we'll first try to acquire the lock for the semaphore with a short timeout. If we got the lock, we then perform our normal semaphore acquire operations with the counter, owner ZSET, and the system time ZSET. If we failed to acquire the lock, then we say that we also failed to acquire the semaphore. The code for performing this operation is shown next.

> **Listing 6.17 The `acquire_semaphore_with_lock()` function**

```
def acquire_semaphore_with_lock(conn, semname, limit, timeout=10):
    identifier = acquire_lock(conn, semname, acquire_timeout=.01)
    if identifier:
        try:
            return acquire_fair_semaphore(conn, semname, limit, timeout)
        finally:
            release_lock(conn, semname, identifier)
```

I know, it can be disappointing to come so far only to end up needing to use a lock at the end. But that's the thing with Redis: there are usually a few ways to solve the same or a similar problem, each with different trade-offs. Here are some of the trade-offs for the different counting semaphores that we've built:

- If you're happy with using the system clock, never need to refresh the semaphore, and are okay with occasionally going over the limit, then you can use the first semaphore we created.
- If you can only really trust system clocks to be within 1 or 2 seconds, but are still okay with occasionally going over your semaphore limit, then you can use the second one.
- If you need your semaphores to be correct every single time, then you can use a lock to guarantee correctness.

Now that we've used our lock from section 6.2 to help us fix the race condition, we have varying options for how strict we want to be with our semaphore limits. Generally it's a good idea to stick with the last, strictest version. Not only is the last semaphore actually correct, but whatever time we may save using a simpler semaphore, we could lose by using too many resources.

In this section, we used semaphores to limit the number of API calls that can be running at any one time. Another common use case is to limit concurrent requests to databases to reduce individual query times and to prevent dogpiling like we talked about at the end of section 6.2.4. One other common situation is when we're trying to download many web pages from a server, but their robots.txt says that we can only make (for example) three requests at a time. If we have many clients downloading web pages, we can use a semaphore to ensure that we aren't pushing a given server too hard.

As we finish with building locks and semaphores to help improve performance for concurrent execution, it's now time to talk about using them in more situations. In the next section, we'll build two different types of task queues for delayed and concurrent task execution.

6.4   *Task queues*

When handling requests from web clients, sometimes operations take more time to execute than we want to spend immediately. We can defer those operations by putting information about our task to be performed inside a queue, which we process later. This method of deferring work to some task processor is called a *task queue*. Right now there are many different pieces of software designed specifically for task queues (ActiveMQ, RabbitMQ, Gearman, Amazon SQS, and others), but there are also ad hoc methods of creating task queues in situations where queues aren't expected. If you've ever had a cron job that scans a database table for accounts that have been modified/checked before or after a specific date/time, and you perform some operation based on the results of that query, you've already created a task queue.

In this section we'll talk about two different types of task queues. Our first queue will be built to execute tasks as quickly as possible in the order that they were inserted. Our second type of queue will have the ability to schedule tasks to execute at some specific time in the future.

6.4.1   *First-in, first-out queues*

In the world of queues beyond task queues, normally a few different kinds of queues are discussed—first-in, first-out (FIFO), last-in first-out (LIFO), and priority queues. We'll look first at a first-in, first-out queue, because it offers the most reasonable semantics for our first pass at a queue, can be implemented easily, and is fast. Later, we'll talk about adding a method for coarse-grained priorities, and even later, time-based queues.

Let's again look back to an example from Fake Game Company. To encourage users to play the game when they don't normally do so, Fake Game Company has decided to add the option for users to opt-in to emails about marketplace sales that have completed or that have timed out. Because outgoing email is one of those internet services that can have very high latencies and can fail, we need to keep the act of sending emails for completed or timed-out sales out of the typical code flow for those operations. To do this, we'll use a task queue to keep a record of people who need to be emailed and why, and will implement a worker process that can be run in parallel to send multiple emails at a time if outgoing mail servers become slow.

The queue that we'll write only needs to send emails out in a first-come, first-served manner, and will log both successes and failures. As we talked about in chapters 3 and 5, Redis LISTs let us push and pop items from both ends with RPUSH/LPUSH and RPOP/LPOP. For our email queue, we'll push emails to send onto the right end of the queue with RPUSH, and pop them off the left end of the queue with LPOP. (We do this because it makes sense visually for readers of left-to-right languages.) Because our worker processes are only going to be performing this emailing operation, we'll use the blocking version of our list pop, BLPOP, with a timeout of 30 seconds. We'll only handle item-sold messages in this version for the sake of simplicity, but adding support for sending timeout emails is also easy.

Our queue will simply be a list of JSON-encoded blobs of data, which will look like figure 6.9.

To add an item to the queue, we'll get all of the necessary information together, serialize it with JSON, and RPUSH the result onto our email queue.

queue:email ───────────── list

{'seller_id':17, 'item_id':'ItemM', 'price':97, 'buyer_id': 27, 'time' : 1322700540.934}
...

Figure 6.9 A first-in, first-out queue using a LIST

As in previous chapters, we use JSON because it's human readable and because there are fast libraries for translation to/from JSON in most languages. The function that pushes an email onto the item-sold email task queue appears in the next listing.

Listing 6.18 The send_sold_email_via_queue() function

```
def send_sold_email_via_queue(conn, seller, item, price, buyer):
    data = {
        'seller_id': seller,
        'item_id': item,                          Prepare
        'price': price,                           the item.
        'buyer_id': buyer,
        'time': time.time()
    }                                             Push the item
    conn.rpush('queue:email', json.dumps(data))   onto the queue.
```

Adding a message to a LIST queue shouldn't be surprising.

Sending emails from the queue is easy. We use BLPOP to pull items from the email queue, prepare the email, and finally send it. The next listing shows our function for doing so.

Listing 6.19 The process_sold_email_queue() function

```
def process_sold_email_queue(conn):
    while not QUIT:                                    Try to get a
        packed = conn.blpop(['queue:email'], 30)       message to send.
```

```
if not packed:
    continue
to_send = json.loads(packed[1])
try:
    fetch_data_and_send_sold_email(to_send)
except EmailSendError as err:
    log_error("Failed to send sold email", err, to_send)
else:
    log_success("Sent sold email", to_send)
```

| No message to send; try again. |

| Load the packed email information. |

| Send the email using our prewritten emailing function. |

Similarly, actually sending the email after pulling the message from the queue is also not surprising. But what about executing more than one type of task?

MULTIPLE EXECUTABLE TASKS

Because Redis only gives a single caller a popped item, we can be sure that none of the emails are duplicated and sent twice. Because we only put email messages to send in the queue, our worker process was simple. Having a single queue for each type of message is not uncommon for some situations, but for others, having a single queue able to handle many different types of tasks can be much more convenient. Take the worker process in listing 6.20: it watches the provided queue and dispatches the JSON-encoded function call to one of a set of known registered callbacks. The item to be executed will be of the form `['FUNCTION_NAME', [ARG1, ARG2, ...]]`.

Listing 6.20   The `worker_watch_queue()` function

```
def worker_watch_queue(conn, queue, callbacks):
    while not QUIT:
        packed = conn.blpop([queue], 30)
        if not packed:
            continue

        name, args = json.loads(packed[1])
        if name not in callbacks:
            log_error("Unknown callback %s"%name)
            continue
        callbacks[name](*args)
```

| Try to get an item from the queue. |

| There's nothing to work on; try again. |

⟵—— Unpack the work item.

| The function is unknown; log the error and try again. |

⟵—— Execute the task.

With this generic worker process, our email sender could be written as a callback and passed with other callbacks.

TASK PRIORITIES

Sometimes when working with queues, it's necessary to prioritize certain operations before others. In our case, maybe we want to send emails about sales that completed before we send emails about sales that expired. Or maybe we want to send password reset emails before we send out emails for an upcoming special event. Remember the BLPOP/BRPOP commands—we can provide multiple LISTs in which to pop an item from; the first LIST to have any items in it will have its first item popped (or last if we're using BRPOP).

Let's say that we want to have three priority levels: high, medium, and low. High-priority items should be executed if they're available. If there are no high-priority items, then items in the medium-priority level should be executed. If there are neither high- nor medium-priority items, then items in the low-priority level should be executed. Looking at our earlier code, we can change two lines to make that possible in the updated listing.

Listing 6.21 The `worker_watch_queues()` function

```
def worker_watch_queues(conn, queues, callbacks):
    while not QUIT:
        packed = conn.blpop(queues, 30)
        if not packed:
            continue
        name, args = json.loads(packed[1])
        if name not in callbacks:
            log_error("Unknown callback %s"%name)
            continue
        callbacks[name](*args)
```

This is the first changed line to add priority support.

This is the second changed line to add priority support.

By using multiple queues, priorities can be implemented easily. There are situations where multiple queues are used as a way of separating different queue items (announcement emails, notification emails, and so forth) without any desire to be "fair." In such situations, it can make sense to reorder the queue list occasionally to be more fair to all of the queues, especially in the case where one queue can grow quickly relative to the other queues.

If you're using Ruby, you can use an open source package called Resque that was put out by the programmers at GitHub. It uses Redis for Ruby-based queues using lists, which is similar to what we've talked about here. Resque offers many additional features over the 11-line function that we provided here, so if you're using Ruby, you should check it out. Regardless, there are many more options for queues in Redis, and you should keep reading.

6.4.2 Delayed tasks

With list-based queues, we can handle single-call per queue, multiple callbacks per queue, and we can handle simple priorities. But sometimes, we need a bit more. Fake Game Company has decided that they're going to add a new feature in their game: delayed selling. Rather than putting an item up for sale now, players can tell the game to put an item up for sale in the future. It's our job to change or replace our task queue with something that can offer this feature.

There are a few different ways that we could potentially add delays to our queue items. Here are the three most straightforward ones:

- We could include an execution time as part of queue items, and if a worker process sees an item with an execution time later than now, it can wait for a brief period and then re-enqueue the item.
- The worker process could have a local waiting list for any items it has seen that need to be executed in the future, and every time it makes a pass through

its while loop, it could check that list for any outstanding items that need to be executed.

- Normally when we talk about times, we usually start talking about ZSETs. What if, for any item we wanted to execute in the future, we added it to a ZSET instead of a LIST, with its score being the time when we want it to execute? We then have a process that checks for items that should be executed now, and if there are any, the process removes it from the ZSET, adding it to the proper LIST queue.

We can't wait/re-enqueue items as described in the first, because that'll waste the worker process's time. We also can't create a local waiting list as described in the second option, because if the worker process crashes for an unrelated reason, we lose any pending work items it knew about. We'll instead use a secondary ZSET as described in the third option, because it's simple, straightforward, and we can use a lock from section 6.2 to ensure that the move is safe.

Each delayed item in the ZSET queue will be a JSON-encoded list of four items: a unique identifier, the queue where the item should be inserted, the name of the callback to call, and the arguments to pass to the callback. We include the unique identifier in order to differentiate all calls easily, and to allow us to add possible reporting features later if we so choose. The score of the item will be the time when the item should be executed. If the item can be executed immediately, we'll insert the item into the list queue instead. For our unique identifier, we'll again use a 128-bit randomly generated UUID. The code to create an (optionally) delayed task can be seen next.

Listing 6.22   The execute_later() function

Generate a unique identifier.

Prepare the item for the queue.

Delay the item.

Return the identifier.

```
def execute_later(conn, queue, name, args, delay=0):
    identifier = str(uuid.uuid4())
    item = json.dumps([identifier, queue, name, args])
    if delay > 0:
        conn.zadd('delayed:', item, time.time() + delay)
    else:
        conn.rpush('queue:' + queue, item)
    return identifier
```

Execute the item immediately.

When the queue item is to be executed without delay, we continue to use the old list-based queue. But if we need to delay the item, we add the item to the delayed ZSET. An example of the delayed queue emails to be sent can be seen in figure 6.10.

Unfortunately, there isn't a convenient method in Redis to block on ZSETs until a score is lower than the current Unix timestamp, so we need to manually poll. Because delayed items are only going into a single queue, we can just fetch the first item with the score. If there's no item, or

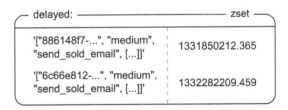

Figure 6.10   A delayed task queue using a ZSET

if the item still needs to wait, we'll wait a brief period and try again. If there is an item, we'll acquire a lock based on the identifier in the item (a fine-grained lock), remove the item from the ZSET, and add the item to the proper queue. By moving items into queues instead of executing them directly, we only need to have one or two of these running at any time (instead of as many as we have workers), so our polling overhead is kept low. The code for polling our delayed queue is in the following listing.

Listing 6.23 The `poll_queue()` function

```
def poll_queue(conn):
    while not QUIT:                                              Get the first item
        item = conn.zrange('delayed:', 0, 0, withscores=True)   in the queue.
        if not item or item[0][1] > time.time():     No item or the item is still
            time.sleep(.01)                          to be executed in the future.
            continue
        item = item[0][0]
        identifier, queue, function, args = json.loads(item)

        locked = acquire_lock(conn, identifier)           Get the lock for the item.
        if not locked:
            continue

        if conn.zrem('delayed:', item):          Move the item to the
            conn.rpush('queue:' + queue, item)   proper list queue.

        release_lock(conn, identifier, locked)            Release the lock.
```

Unpack the item so that we know where it should go.

We couldn't get the lock, so skip it and try again.

As is clear from listing 6.23, because ZSETs don't have a blocking pop mechanism like LISTs do, we need to loop and retry fetching items from the queue. This can increase load on the network and on the processors performing the work, but because we're only using one or two of these pollers to move items from the ZSET to the LIST queues, we won't waste too many resources. If we further wanted to reduce overhead, we could add an adaptive method that increases the sleep time when it hasn't seen any items in a while, or we could use the time when the next item was scheduled to help determine how long to sleep, capping it at 100 milliseconds to ensure that tasks scheduled only slightly in the future are executed in a timely fashion.

RESPECTING PRIORITIES

In the basic sense, delayed tasks have the same sort of priorities that our first-in, first-out queue had. Because they'll go back on their original destination queues, they'll be executed with the same sort of priority. But what if we wanted delayed tasks to execute as soon as possible after their time to execute has come up?

The simplest way to do this is to add some extra queues to make scheduled tasks jump to the front of the queue. If we have our high-, medium-, and low-priority queues, we can also create high-delayed, medium-delayed, and low-delayed queues, which are passed to the `worker_watch_queues()` function as `["high-delayed"`, `"high"`, `"medium-delayed"`, `"medium"`, `"low-delayed"`, `"low"]`. Each of the delayed queues comes just before its nondelayed equivalent.

Some of you may be wondering, "If we're having them jump to the front of the queue, why not just use LPUSH instead of RPUSH?" Suppose that all of our workers are working on tasks for the medium queue, and will take a few seconds to finish. Suppose also that we have three delayed tasks that are found and LPUSHed onto the front of the medium queue. The first is pushed, then the second, and then the third. But on the medium queue, the third task to be pushed will be executed first, which violates our expectations that things that we want to execute earlier should be executed earlier.

If you use Python and you're interested in a queue like this, I've written a package called RPQueue that offers delayed task execution semantics similar to the preceding code snippets. It does include more functionality, so if you want a queue and are already using Redis, give RPQueue a look at http://github.com/josiahcarlson/rpqueue/.

When we use task queues, sometimes we need our tasks to report back to other parts of our application with some sort of messaging system. In the next section, we'll talk about creating message queues that can be used to send to a single recipient, or to communicate between many senders and receivers.

6.5   Pull messaging

When sending and receiving messages between two or more clients, there are two common ways of looking at how the messages are delivered. One method, called *push messaging*, causes the sender to spend some time making sure that all of the recipients of the message receive it. Redis has built-in commands for handling push messaging called PUBLISH and SUBSCRIBE, whose drawbacks and use we discussed in chapter 3.[2] The second method, called *pull messaging*, requires that the recipients of the message fetch the messages instead. Usually, messages will wait in a sort of mailbox for the recipient to fetch them.

Though push messaging can be useful, we run into problems when clients can't stay connected all the time for one reason or another. To address this limitation, we'll write two different pull messaging methods that can be used as a replacement for PUBLISH/SUBSCRIBE.

We'll first start with single-recipient messaging, since it shares much in common with our first-in, first-out queues. Later in this section, we'll move to a method where we can have multiple recipients of a message. With multiple recipients, we can replace Redis PUBLISH and SUBSCRIBE when we need our messages to get to all recipients, even if they were disconnected.

6.5.1   Single-recipient publish/subscribe replacement

One common pattern that we find with Redis is that we have clients of one kind or another (server processes, users in a chat, and so on) that listen or wait for messages on their own channel. They're the only ones that receive those messages. Many

---

[2] Briefly, these drawbacks are that the client must be connected at all times to receive messages, disconnections can cause the client to lose messages, and older versions of Redis could become unusable, crash, or be killed if there was a slow subscriber.

programmers will end up using Redis PUBLISH and SUBSCRIBE commands to send messages and wait for messages, respectively. But if we need to receive messages, even in the face of connection issues, PUBLISH and SUBSCRIBE don't help us much.

Breaking from our game company focus, Fake Garage Startup wants to release a mobile messaging application. This application will connect to their web servers to send and receive SMS/MMS-like messages (basically a text or picture messaging replacement). The web server will be handling authentication and communication with the Redis back end, and Redis will be handling the message routing/storage.

Each message will only be received by a single client, which greatly simplifies our problem. To handle messages in this way, we use a single LIST for each mobile client. Senders cause messages to be placed in the recipient's LIST, and any time the recipient's client makes a request, it fetches the most recent messages. With HTTP 1.1's ability to pipeline requests, or with more modern web socket support, our mobile client can either make a request for all waiting messages (if any), can make requests one at a time, or can fetch 10 and use LTRIM to remove the first 10 items.

Because you already know how to push and pop items from lists from earlier sections, most recently from our first-in, first-out queues from section 6.4.1, we'll skip including code to send messages, but an example incoming message queue for user jack451 is illustrated in figure 6.11.

With LISTs, senders can also be notified if the recipient hasn't been connecting

```
┌─ mailbox:jack451 ──────────────────────── list ─┐
│ {'sender':'jill84', 'msg':'Are you coming or not?', 'ts':133066...} │
│ {'sender':'mom65', 'msg':'Did you hear about aunt Elly?', ...} │
└─────────────────────────────────────────────────┘
```

Figure 6.11 jack451 has some messages from Jill and his mother waiting for him.

recently, hasn't received their previous messages, or maybe has too many pending messages; all by checking the messages in the recipient's LIST. If the system were limited by a recipient needing to be connected all the time, as is the case with PUBLISH/SUBSCRIBE, messages would get lost, clients wouldn't know if their message got through, and slow clients could result in outgoing buffers growing potentially without limit (in older versions of Redis) or getting disconnected (in newer versions of Redis).

With single-recipient messaging out of the way, it's time to talk about replacing PUBLISH and SUBSCRIBE when we want to have multiple listeners to a given channel.

6.5.2 *Multiple-recipient publish/subscribe replacement*

Single-recipient messaging is useful, but it doesn't get us far in replacing the PUBLISH and SUBSCRIBE commands when we have multiple recipients. To do that, we need to turn our problem around. In many ways, Redis PUBLISH/SUBSCRIBE is like group chat where whether someone's connected determines whether they're in the group chat. We want to remove that "need to be connected all the time" requirement, and we'll implement it in the context of chatting.

Let's look at Fake Garage Startup's next problem. After quickly implementing their user-to-user messaging system, Fake Garage Startup realized that replacing SMS

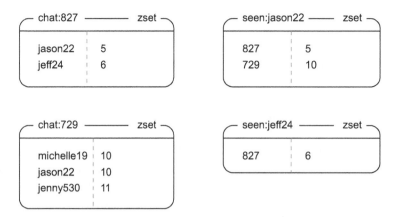

Figure 6.12   Some example chat and user data. The chat ZSETs show users and the maximum IDs of messages in that chat that they've seen. The seen ZSETs list chat IDs per user, again with the maximum message ID in the given chat that they've seen.

is good, but they've had many requests to add group chat functionality. Like before, their clients may connect or disconnect at any time, so we can't use the built-in PUBLISH/SUBSCRIBE method.

Each new group chat will have a set of original recipients of the group messages, and users can join or leave the group if they want. Information about what users are in the chat will be stored as a ZSET with members being the usernames of the recipients, and values being the highest message ID the user has received in the chat. Which chats an individual user is a part of will also be stored as a ZSET, with members being the groups that the user is a part of, and scores being the highest message ID that the user has received in that chat. Information about some users and chats can be seen in figure 6.12.

As you can see, user jason22 has seen five of six chat messages sent in chat:827, in which jason22 and jeff24 are participating.

CREATING A CHAT SESSION

The content of chat sessions themselves will be stored in ZSETs, with messages as members and message IDs as scores. To create and start a chat, we'll increment a global counter to get a new chat ID. We'll then create a ZSET with all of the users that we want to include with seen IDs being 0, and add the group to each user's group list ZSET. Finally, we'll send the initial message to the users by placing the message in the chat ZSET. The code to create a chat is shown here.

Listing 6.24   The `create_chat()` function

```
def create_chat(conn, sender, recipients, message, chat_id=None):
    chat_id = chat_id or str(conn.incr('ids:chat:'))        ←── Get a new chat ID.

    recipients.append(sender)                              Set up a dictionary of users-to-
    recipientsd = dict((r, 0) for r in recipients)         scores to add to the chat ZSET.
```

```
pipeline = conn.pipeline(True)
pipeline.zadd('chat:' + chat_id, **recipientsd)
for rec in recipients:
    pipeline.zadd('seen:' + rec, chat_id, 0)
pipeline.execute()

return send_message(conn, chat_id, sender, message)
```

Create the set with the list of people participating.

Initialize the seen ZSETs.

Send the message.

About the only thing that may be surprising is our use of what's called a *generator expression* from within a call to the dict() object constructor. This shortcut lets us quickly construct a dictionary that maps users to an initially 0-valued score, which ZADD can accept in a single call.

> **GENERATOR EXPRESSIONS AND DICTIONARY CONSTRUCTION** Python dictionaries can be easily constructed by passing a sequence of pairs of values. The first item in the pair becomes the key; the second item becomes the value. Listing 6.24 shows some code that looks odd, where we actually generate the sequence to be passed to the dictionary in-line. This type of sequence generation is known as a *generator expression*, which you can read more about at http://mng.bz/TTKb.

SENDING MESSAGES

To send a message, we must get a new message ID, and then add the message to the chat's messages ZSET. Unfortunately, there's a race condition in sending messages, but it's easily handled with the use of a lock from section 6.2. Our function for sending a message using a lock is shown next.

Listing 6.25   The send_message() function

```
def send_message(conn, chat_id, sender, message):
    identifier = acquire_lock(conn, 'chat:' + chat_id)
    if not identifier:
        raise Exception("Couldn't get the lock")
    try:
        mid = conn.incr('ids:' + chat_id)
        ts = time.time()
        packed = json.dumps({
            'id': mid,
            'ts': ts,
            'sender': sender,
            'message': message,
        })

        conn.zadd('msgs:' + chat_id, packed, mid)
    finally:
        release_lock(conn, 'chat:' + chat_id, identifier)
    return chat_id
```

Prepare the message.

Send the message to the chat.

Most of the work involved in sending a chat message is preparing the information to be sent itself; actually sending the message involves adding it to a ZSET. We use locking around the packed message construction and addition to the ZSET for the same reasons that we needed a lock for our counting semaphore earlier. Generally, when we use a value from Redis in the construction of another value we need to add to Redis, we'll either need to use a WATCH/MULTI/EXEC transaction or a lock to remove race conditions. We use a lock here for the same performance reasons that we developed it in the first place.

Now that we've created the chat and sent the initial message, users need to find out information about the chats they're a part of and how many messages are pending, and they need to actually receive the messages.

FETCHING MESSAGES

To fetch all pending messages for a user, we need to fetch group IDs and message IDs seen from the user's ZSET with ZRANGE. When we have the group IDs and the messages that the user has seen, we can perform ZRANGEBYSCORE operations on all of the message ZSETs. After we've fetched the messages for the chat, we update the seen ZSET with the proper ID and the user entry in the group ZSET, and we go ahead and clean out any messages from the group chat that have been received by everyone in the chat, as shown in the following listing.

Listing 6.26   The fetch_pending_messages() function

```
def fetch_pending_messages(conn, recipient):
    seen = conn.zrange('seen:' + recipient, 0, -1, withscores=True)     Get the last
                                                                        message IDs
    pipeline = conn.pipeline(True)                                      received.

    for chat_id, seen_id in seen:                        Fetch all new
        pipeline.zrangebyscore(                          messages.
            'msgs:' + chat_id, seen_id+1, 'inf')
    chat_info = zip(seen, pipeline.execute())            Prepare
                                                         information
    for i, ((chat_id, seen_id), messages) in enumerate(chat_info):   about the data
        if not messages:                                             to be returned.
            continue
        messages[:] = map(json.loads, messages)
        seen_id = messages[-1]['id']                     Update the "chat" ZSET with the
        conn.zadd('chat:' + chat_id, recipient, seen_id)  most recently received message.

        min_id = conn.zrange(                            Discover messages that have
            'chat:' + chat_id, 0, 0, withscores=True)    been seen by all users.

        pipeline.zadd('seen:' + recipient, chat_id, seen_id)   Update the
        if min_id:                                             "seen" ZSET.
            pipeline.zremrangebyscore(
                'msgs:' + chat_id, 0, min_id[0][1])      Clean out messages that
        chat_info[i] = (chat_id, messages)               have been seen by all users.
    pipeline.execute()

    return chat_info
```

Fetching pending messages is primarily a matter of iterating through all of the chats for the user, pulling the messages, and cleaning up messages that have been seen by all users in a chat.

JOINING AND LEAVING THE CHAT

We've sent and fetched messages from group chats; all that remains is joining and leaving the group chat. To join a group chat, we fetch the most recent message ID for the chat, and we add the chat information to the user's seen ZSET with the score being the most recent message ID. We also add the user to the group's member list, again with the score being the most recent message ID. See the next listing for the code for joining a group.

Listing 6.27   The `join_chat()` function

```
def join_chat(conn, chat_id, user):
    message_id = int(conn.get('ids:' + chat_id))

    pipeline = conn.pipeline(True)
    pipeline.zadd('chat:' + chat_id, user, message_id)
    pipeline.zadd('seen:' + user, chat_id, message_id)
    pipeline.execute()
```

Add the user to the chat member list.

Get the most recent message ID for the chat.

Add the chat to the user's seen list.

Joining a chat only requires adding the proper references to the user to the chat, and the chat to the user's seen ZSET.

To remove a user from the group chat, we remove the user ID from the chat ZSET, and we remove the chat from the user's seen ZSET. If there are no more users in the chat ZSET, we delete the messages ZSET and the message ID counter. If there are users remaining, we'll again take a pass and clean out any old messages that have been seen by all users. The function to leave a chat is shown in the following listing.

Listing 6.28   The `leave_chat()` function

```
def leave_chat(conn, chat_id, user):
    pipeline = conn.pipeline(True)
    pipeline.zrem('chat:' + chat_id, user)
    pipeline.zrem('seen:' + user, chat_id)
    pipeline.zcard('chat:' + chat_id)

    if not pipeline.execute()[-1]:
        pipeline.delete('msgs:' + chat_id)
        pipeline.delete('ids:' + chat_id)
        pipeline.execute()
    else:
        oldest = conn.zrange(
            'chat:' + chat_id, 0, 0, withscores=True)
        conn.zremrangebyscore('chat:' + chat_id, 0, oldest)
```

Find the number of remaining group members.

Remove the user from the chat.

Delete the chat.

Find the oldest message seen by all users.

Delete old messages from the chat.

Cleaning up after a user when they leave a chat isn't that difficult, but requires taking care of a lot of little details to ensure that we don't end up leaking a ZSET or ID somewhere.

We've now finished creating a complete multiple-recipient pull messaging system in Redis. Though we're looking at it in terms of chat, this same method can be used to replace the PUBLISH/SUBSCRIBE functions when you want your recipients to be able to receive messages that were sent while they were disconnected. With a bit of work, we could replace the ZSET with a LIST, and we could move our lock use from sending a message to old message cleanup. We used a ZSET instead, because it saves us from having to fetch the current message ID for every chat. Also, by making the sender do more work (locking around sending a message), the multiple recipients are saved from having to request more data and to lock during cleanup, which will improve performance overall.

We now have a multiple-recipient messaging system to replace PUBLISH and SUB-SCRIBE for group chat. In the next section, we'll use it as a way of sending information about key names available in Redis.

6.6   *Distributing files with Redis*

When building distributed software and systems, it's common to need to copy, distribute, or process data files on more than one machine. There are a few different common ways of doing this with existing tools. If we have a single server that will always have files to be distributed, it's not uncommon to use NFS or Samba to mount a path or drive. If we have files whose contents change little by little, it's also common to use a piece of software called Rsync to minimize the amount of data to be transferred between systems. Occasionally, when many copies need to be distributed among machines, a protocol called BitTorrent can be used to reduce the load on the server by partially distributing files to multiple machines, which then share their pieces among themselves.

Unfortunately, all of these methods have a significant setup cost and value that's somewhat relative. NFS and Samba can work well, but both can have significant issues when network connections aren't perfect (or even if they are perfect), due to the way both of these technologies are typically integrated with operating systems. Rsync is designed to handle intermittent connection issues, since each file or set of files can be partially transferred and resumed, but it suffers from needing to download complete files before processing can start, and requires interfacing our software with Rsync in order to fetch the files (which may or may not be a problem). And though BitTorrent is an amazing technology, it only really helps if we're running into limits sending from our server, or if our network is underutilized. It also relies on interfacing our software with a BitTorrent client that may not be available on all platforms, and which may not have a convenient method to fetch files.

Each of the three methods described also require setup and maintenance of users, permissions, and/or servers. Because we already have Redis installed, running, and available, we'll use Redis to distribute files instead. By using Redis, we bypass issues that some other software has: our client handles connection issues well, we can fetch the data directly with our clients, and we can start processing data immediately (no need to wait for an entire file).

6.6.1   *Aggregating users by location*

Let's take a moment and look back at an earlier problem that we solved for Fake Game Company. With the ability to discover where users are accessing the game from thanks to our IP-to-city lookup in chapter 5, Fake Game Company has found itself needing to reparse many gigabytes of log files. They're looking to aggregate user visitation patterns over time in a few different dimensions: per country, per region, per city, and more. Because we need this to be run in real time over new data, we've already implemented callbacks to perform the aggregate operations.

As you may remember from chapter 5, Fake Game Company has been around for about 2 years. They have roughly 1,000,000 users per day, but they have roughly 10 events per user per day. That gives us right around 7.3 billion log lines to process. If we were to use one of the earlier methods, we'd copy the log files to various machines that need to process the data, and then go about processing the log files. This works, but then we need to copy the data, potentially delaying processing, and using storage space on every machine that processes the data, which later needs to be cleaned up.

In this particular case, instead of copying files around, we could write a one-time map-reduce[3] process to handle all of this data. But because map-reduces are designed to not share memory between items to be processed (each item is usually one log line), we can end up taking more time with map-reduce than if we spent some time writing it by hand to share memory. More specifically, if we load our IP-to-city lookup table into memory in Python (which we'd only want to do if we had a lot of processing to do, and we do), we can perform about 200k IP-to-city ID lookups per second, which is faster than we could expect a single Redis instance to respond to the same queries. Also, to scale with map-reduce, we'd have to run at least a few instances of Redis to keep up with the map-reduces.

With the three standard methods of handling this already discounted (NFS/Samba, copying files, map-reduce), let's look at some other practical pieces that we'll need to solve to actually perform all of our lookups.

AGGREGATING DATA LOCALLY

In order to process that many log entries efficiently, we'll need to locally cache aggregates before updating Redis in order to minimize round trips. Why? If we have roughly 10 million log lines to process for each day, then that's roughly 10 million writes to Redis. If we perform the aggregates locally on a per-country basis for the entire day (being that there are around 300 countries), we can instead write 300 values to Redis. This will significantly reduce the number of round trips between Redis, reducing the number of commands processed, which in turn will reduce the total processing time.

If we don't do anything intelligent about local caching, and we have 10 aggregates that we want to calculate, we're looking at around 10 days to process all of the data. But anything on the country or region level can be aggregated completely (for the day) before being sent to Redis. And generally because the top 10% of cities (there are roughly 350,000 cities in our sample dataset) amount for more than 90% of our game's users, we can also locally cache any city-level aggregates. So by performing local caching of aggregates, we're not limited by Redis on aggregate throughput.

Assuming that we've already cached a copy of our ZSET and HASH table for IP lookups from section 5.3, we only need to worry about aggregating the data. Let's start

---

[3] MapReduce (or Map/Reduce) is a type of distributed computation popularized by Google, which can offer high performance and simplicity for some problems.

with the log lines that contain an IP address, date, time, and the operation that was performed, similar to the following snippet:

```
173.194.38.137 2011-10-10 13:55:36 achievement-762
```

Given log lines of that form, let's aggregate those lines on a daily basis per country. To do this, we'll receive the line as part of a call and increment the appropriate counter. If the log line is empty, then we'll say that the day's worth of data is done, and we should write to Redis. The source code for performing this aggregate is shown next.

Listing 6.29   A locally aggregating callback for a daily country-level aggregate

```
                aggregates = defaultdict(lambda: defaultdict(int))        ◁──┐  Prepare the
                                                                             │  local aggregate
                def daily_country_aggregate(conn, line):                     │  dictionary.
                    if line:
                        line = line.split()
                        ip = line[0]
                        day = line[1]
                        country = find_city_by_ip_local(ip)[2]        ◁──┐  Find the
                        aggregates[day][country] += 1                     │  country from
                        return                                           │  the IP address.

                    for day, aggregate in aggregates.items():
                        conn.zadd('daily:country:' + day, **aggregate)
                        del aggregates[day]

                                              The day file is done; write
                                              our aggregate to Redis.
```

- Extract the information from our log lines. (annotation for line/ip/day extraction)
- Increment our local aggregate. (annotation for `aggregates[day][country] += 1`)

Now that we've written and seen one of these aggregate functions, the rest are fairly similar and just as easy to write. Let's move on to more interesting topics, like how we're going to send files through Redis.

6.6.2   Sending files

In order to get the log data to our logs processors, we'll have two different components operating on the data. The first is a script that will be taking the log files and putting them in Redis under named keys, publishing the names of the keys to a chat channel using our group chat method from section 6.5.2, and waiting for notification when they're complete (to not use more memory than our Redis machine has). It'll be waiting for a notification that a key with a name similar to the file stored in Redis has a value equal to 10, which is our number of aggregation processes. The function that copies logs and cleans up after itself is shown in the following listing.

Listing 6.30   The `copy_logs_to_redis()` function

```
def copy_logs_to_redis(conn, path, channel, count=10,         Create the chat that
                       limit=2**30, quit_when_done=True):      will be used to send
    bytes_in_redis = 0                                         messages to clients.
    waiting = deque()
    create_chat(conn, 'source', map(str, range(count)), '', channel)        ◁──┘
    count = str(count)
```

```
    for logfile in sorted(os.listdir(path)):        <-- Iterate over all
        full_path = os.path.join(path, logfile)         of the log files.

        fsize = os.stat(full_path).st_size
        while bytes_in_redis + fsize > limit:
            cleaned = _clean(conn, channel, waiting, count)    Clean out
            if cleaned:                                        finished files
                bytes_in_redis -= cleaned                      if we need
            else:                                              more room.
                time.sleep(.25)

        with open(full_path, 'rb') as inp:
            block = ' '
            while block:                                       Upload the
                block = inp.read(2**17)                        file to Redis.
                conn.append(channel+logfile, block)

Notify the listeners that the file is ready.
    --> send_message(conn, channel, 'source', logfile)

        bytes_in_redis += fsize                  Update our local information
        waiting.append((logfile, fsize))         about Redis' memory use.

    if quit_when_done:                                      We are out of files, so
        send_message(conn, channel, 'source', ':done')      signal that it's done.

    while waiting:
        cleaned = _clean(conn, channel, waiting, count)
        if cleaned:                                         Clean up the
            bytes_in_redis -= cleaned                       files when
        else:                                               we're done.
            time.sleep(.25)

def _clean(conn, channel, waiting, count):
    if not waiting:
        return 0                                                 How we
    w0 = waiting[0][0]                                           actually
    if conn.get(channel + w0 + ':done') == count:                perform
        conn.delete(channel + w0, channel + w0 + ':done')        the cleanup
        return waiting.popleft()[1]                              from Redis.
    return 0
```

Copying logs to Redis requires a lot of detailed steps, mostly involving being careful to not put too much data into Redis at one time and properly cleaning up after ourselves when a file has been read by all clients. The actual aspect of notifying logs processors that there's a new file ready is easy, but the setup, sending, and cleanup are pretty detailed.

6.6.3 Receiving files

The second part of the process is a group of functions and generators that will fetch log filenames from the group chat. After receiving each name, it'll process the log files directly from Redis, and will update the keys that the copy process is waiting on. This will also call our callback on each incoming line, updating our aggregates. The next listing shows the code for the first of these functions.

Listing 6.31   The `process_logs_from_redis()` function

```
def process_logs_from_redis(conn, id, callback):
    while 1:
        fdata = fetch_pending_messages(conn, id)

        for ch, mdata in fdata:
            for message in mdata:
                logfile = message['message']

                if logfile == ':done':
                    return
                elif not logfile:
                    continue

                block_reader = readblocks
                if logfile.endswith('.gz'):
                    block_reader = readblocks_gz

                for line in readlines(conn, ch+logfile, block_reader):
                    callback(conn, line)
                callback(conn, None)

                conn.incr(ch + logfile + ':done')

        if not fdata:
            time.sleep(.1)
```

Fetch the list of files.

No more log files.

Choose a block reader.

Iterate over the lines.

Force a flush of our aggregate caches.

Pass each line to the callback.

Report that we're finished with the log.

Receiving information about log files is straightforward, though we do defer a lot of the hard work of actually reading the file from Redis to helper functions that generate sequences of log lines. We also need to be careful to notify the file sender by incrementing the counter for the log file; otherwise the file sending process won't know to clean up finished log files.

6.6.4   Processing files

We're deferring some of the work of decoding our files to functions that return generators over data. The `readlines()` function takes the connection, key, and a block-iterating callback. It'll iterate over blocks of data yielded by the block-iterating callback, discover line breaks, and yield lines. When provided with blocks as in listing 6.32, it finds the last line ending in the block, and then splits the lines up to that last line ending, yielding the lines one by one. When it's done, it keeps any partial lines to prepend onto the next block. If there's no more data, it yields the last line by itself. There are other ways of finding line breaks and extracting lines in Python, but the `rfind()`/`split()` combination is faster than other methods.

Listing 6.32   The `readlines()` function

```
def readlines(conn, key, rblocks):
    out = ''
    for block in rblocks(conn, key):
        out += block
        posn = out.rfind('\n')
        if posn >= 0:
```

Find the rightmost line break if any; rfind() returns -1 on failure.

We found a line break.

```
                               for line in out[:posn].split('\n'):
Split on all of the ┌─────▷        yield line + '\n'                              ◁─── Yield each line.
line breaks.        │          out = out[posn+1:]                          ◁──┐
                         ┌──▷ if not block:                                     │ Keep track of
We're out of data. │           yield out                                       │ the trailing data.
                   │           break
```

For our higher-level line-generating function, we're iterating over blocks produced by one of two readers, which allows us to focus on finding line breaks.

GENERATORS WITH YIELD Listing 6.32 offers our first real use of Python generators with the `yield` statement. Generally, this allows Python to suspend and resume execution of code primarily to allow for easy iteration over sequences or pseudo-sequences of data. For more details on how generators work, you can visit the Python language tutorial with this short URL: http://mng.bz/Z2b1.

Each of the two block-yielding callbacks, `readblocks()` and `readblocks_gz()`, will read blocks of data from Redis. The first yields the blocks directly, whereas the other automatically decompresses gzip files. We'll use this particular layer separation in order to offer the most useful and reusable data reading method possible. The following listing shows the `readblocks()` generator.

Listing 6.33 The `readblocks()` generator

```
def readblocks(conn, key, blocksize=2**17):
    lb = blocksize
    pos = 0
    while lb == blocksize:                                    ◁─┘ Keep fetching
        block = conn.substr(key, pos, pos + blocksize - 1)      more data as long
        yield block                                    ◁──┐     as we don't have a
        lb = len(block)                                   │     partial read.
        pos += lb                     Prepare for         │ Fetch the
    yield ''                          the next pass.        block.
```

The `readblocks()` generator is primarily meant to offer an abstraction over our block reading, which allows us to replace it later with other types of readers, like maybe a filesystem reader, a memcached reader, a `ZSET` reader, or in our case, a block reader that handles gzip files in Redis. The next listing shows the `readblocks_gz()` generator.

Listing 6.34 The `readblocks_gz()` generator

```
def readblocks_gz(conn, key):
    inp = ''
    decoder = None
    for block in readblocks(conn, key, 2**17):       ◁──┐ Read the raw
        if not decoder:                                   data from Redis.
            inp += block
            try:
                if inp[:3] != "\x1f\x8b\x08":            ┐ Parse the header infor-
                    raise IOError("invalid gzip data")   │ mation so that we can
                i = 10                                   │ get the compressed data.
                flag = ord(inp[3])                       ▽
```

```
        if flag & 4:
            i += 2 + ord(inp[i]) + 256*ord(inp[i+1])
        if flag & 8:
            i = inp.index('\0', i) + 1
        if flag & 16:
            i = inp.index('\0', i) + 1
        if flag & 2:
            i += 2

        if i > len(inp):
            raise IndexError("not enough data")
    except (IndexError, ValueError):
        continue

    else:
        block = inp[i:]
        inp = None
        decoder = zlib.decompressobj(-zlib.MAX_WBITS)
        if not block:
            continue

if not block:
    yield decoder.flush()
    break

yield decoder.decompress(block)
```

> Parse the header information so that we can get the compressed data.

> We haven't read the full header yet.

> We found the header; prepare the decompresser.

> We're out of data; yield the last chunk.

> Yield a decompressed block.

Much of the body of readblocks_gz() is gzip header parsing code, which is unfortunately necessary. For log files (like we're parsing), gzip can offer a reduction of 2–5 times in storage space requirements, while offering fairly high-speed decompression. Though more modern compression methods are able to compress better (bzip2, lzma/xz, and many others) or faster (lz4, lzop, snappy, QuickLZ, and many others), no other method is as widely available (bzip2 comes close) or has such a useful range of compression ratio and CPU utilization trade-off options.

6.7   Summary

In this chapter we've gone through six major topics, but in looking at those topics, we actually solved nine different problems. Whenever possible, we've taken steps to borrow ideas and functionality from previous sections to keep building more useful tools, while trying to highlight that many of the techniques that we use in one solution can also be used to solve other problems.

If there's one concept that you should take away from this entire chapter, it's that although WATCH is a useful command, is built in, convenient, and so forth, having access to a working distributed lock implementation from section 6.2 can make concurrent Redis programming so much easier. Being able to lock at a finer level of detail than an entire key can reduce contention, and being able to lock around related operations can reduce operation complexity. We saw both performance improvements and operation simplicity in our revisited marketplace example from section 4.6, and in our delayed task queue from section 6.4.2.

If there's a second concept that you should remember, take to heart, and apply in the future, it's that with a little work, you can build reusable components with Redis. We reused locks explicitly in counting semaphores, delayed task queues, and in our multiple-recipient pub/sub replacement. And we reused our multiple-recipient pub/sub replacement when we distributed files with Redis.

In the next chapter, we'll continue with building more advanced tools with Redis, writing code that can be used to back entire applications from document indexing and search with scored indexing and sorting, all the way to an ad targeting system, and a job search system. Going forward, we'll reuse some of these components in later chapters, so keep an eye out, and remember that it's not difficult to build reusable components for Redis.

Search-based applications

Over the last several chapters, I've introduced a variety of topics and problems that can be solved with Redis. Redis is particularly handy in solving a class of problems that I generally refer to as *search-based problems*. These types of problems primarily involve the use of SET and ZSET intersection, union, and difference operations to find items that match a specified criteria.

In this chapter, I'll introduce the concept of searching for content with Redis SETs. We'll then talk about scoring and sorting our search results based on a few different options. After getting all of the basics out of the way, we'll dig into creating an ad-targeting engine using Redis, based on what we know about search. Before finishing the chapter, we'll talk about a method for matching or exceeding a set of requirements as a part of job searching.

Overall, the set of problems in this chapter will show you how to search and filter data quickly and will expand your knowledge of techniques that you can use to organize and search your own information. First, let's talk about what we mean by searching in Redis.

7.1 Searching in Redis

In a text editor or word processor, when you want to search for a word or phrase, the software will scan the document for that word or phrase. If you've ever used grep in Linux, Unix, or OS X, or if you've used Windows' built-in file search capability to find files with words or phrases, you've noticed that as the number and size of documents to be searched increases, it takes longer to search your files.

Unlike searching our local computer, searching for web pages or other content on the web is very fast, despite the significantly larger size and number of documents. In this section, we'll examine how we can change the way we think about searching through data, and subsequently reduce search times over almost any kind of word or keyword-based content search with Redis.

As part of their effort to help their customers find help in solving their problems, Fake Garage Startup has created a knowledge base of troubleshooting articles for user support. As the number and variety of articles has increased over the last few months, the previous database-backed search has slowed substantially, and it's time to come up with a method to search over these documents quickly. We've decided to use Redis, because it has all of the functionality necessary to build a content search engine.

Our first step is to talk about how it's even possible for us to search so much faster than scanning documents word by word.

7.1.1 Basic search theory

Searching for words in documents faster than scanning over them requires preprocessing the documents in advance. This preprocessing step is generally known as *indexing*, and the structures that we create are called *inverted indexes*. In the search world, inverted indexes are well known and are the underlying structure for almost every search engine that we've used on the internet. In a lot of ways, we can think of this process as producing something similar to the index at the end of this book. We create inverted indexes in Redis primarily because Redis has native structures that are ideally suited for inverted indexes: the SET and ZSET.[1]

More specifically, an inverted index of a collection of documents will take the words from each of the documents and create tables that say which documents contain what words. So if we have two documents, docA and docB, containing just the titles *lord of the rings* and *lord of the dance*, respectively, we'll create a SET in Redis for *lord* that contains both docA and docB. This signifies that both docA and docB contain the word *lord*. The full inverted index for our two documents appears in figure 7.1.

---

[1] Though SETs and ZSETs could be emulated with a properly structured table and unique index in a relational database, emulating a SET or ZSET intersection, union, or difference using SQL for more than a few terms is cumbersome.

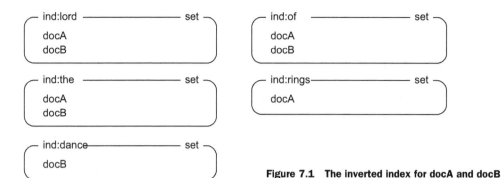

Figure 7.1   The inverted index for docA and docB

Knowing that the ultimate result of our index operation is a collection of Redis SETs is helpful, but it's also important to know how we get to those SETs.

BASIC INDEXING

In order to construct our SETs of documents, we must first examine our documents for words. The process of extracting words from documents is known as *parsing* and *tokenization*; we're producing a set of tokens (or words) that identify the document.

There are many different ways of producing tokens. The methods used for web pages could be different from methods used for rows in a relational database, or from documents from a document store. We'll keep it simple and consider words of alphabetic characters and apostrophes (') that are at least two characters long. This accounts for the majority of words in the English language, except for *I* and *a*, which we'll ignore.

One common addition to a tokenization process is the removal of words known as *stop words*. Stop words are words that occur so frequently in documents that they don't offer a substantial amount of information, and searching for those words returns too many documents to be useful. By removing stop words, not only can we improve the performance of our searches, but we can also reduce the size of our index. Figure 7.2 shows the process of tokenization and stop word removal.

Original content:

> In order to construct our SETs of documents, we must first examine our documents for words. The process of extracting words from documents is known as parsing and tokenization; we are producing a set of tokens (or words) that identify the document.

Tokenization

Tokenized content:

> and are as construct document documents examine extracting first for from identify in is known must of or order our parsing process producing set sets that the to tokenization tokens we words

Remove stop words

Stop words removed:

> construct document documents examine extracting first identify known order parsing process producing set sets tokenization tokens words

Figure 7.2   The process of tokenizing text into words, then removing stop words, as run on a paragraph from an early version of this section

One challenge in this process is coming up with a useful list of stop words. Every group of documents will have different statistics on what words are most common, which may or may not affect stop words. As part of listing 7.1, we include a list of stop words (fetched from http://www.textfixer.com/resources/), as well as functions to both tokenize and index a document, taking into consideration the stop words that we want to remove.

Listing 7.1   Functions to tokenize and index a document

```
STOP_WORDS = set('''able about across after all almost also am among
an and any are as at be because been but by can cannot could dear did
do does either else ever every for from get got had has have he her
hers him his how however if in into is it its just least let like
likely may me might most must my neither no nor not of off often on
only or other our own rather said say says she should since so some
than that the their them then there these they this tis to too twas us
wants was we were what when where which while who whom why will with
would yet you your'''.split())

WORDS_RE = re.compile("[a-z']{2,}")

def tokenize(content):
    words = set()
    for match in WORDS_RE.finditer(content.lower()):
        word = match.group().strip("'")
        if len(word) >= 2:
            words.add(word)
    return words - STOP_WORDS

def index_document(conn, docid, content):
    words = tokenize(content)

    pipeline = conn.pipeline(True)
    for word in words:
        pipeline.sadd('idx:' + word, docid)
    return len(pipeline.execute())
```

Our Python set of words that we have found in the document content.

Iterate over all of the words in the content.

Return the set of words that remain that are also not stop words.

We predeclare our known stop words; these were fetched from http://www.textfixer.com/resources/.

A regular expression that extracts words as we defined them.

Strip any leading or trailing single-quote characters.

Keep any words that are still at least two characters long.

Get the tokenized words for the content.

Add the documents to the appropriate inverted index entries.

Return the number of unique non-stop words that were added for the document.

If we were to run our earlier docA and docB examples through the updated tokenization and indexing step in listing 7.1, instead of having the five SETs corresponding to lord, of, the, rings, and dance, we'd only have lord, rings, and dance, because of and the are both stop words.

REMOVING A DOCUMENT FROM THE INDEX   If you're in a situation where your document may have its content changed over time, you'll want to add functionality to automatically remove the document from the index prior to reindexing the item, or a method to intelligently update only those inverted indexes that the document should be added or removed from. A simple way of doing this would be to use the SET command to update a key with a JSON-encoded list of words that the document had been indexed under, along with a bit of code to un-index as necessary at the start of index_document().

Now that we have a way of generating inverted indexes for our knowledge base documents, let's look at how we can search our documents.

BASIC SEARCHING

Searching the index for a single word is easy: we fetch the set of documents in that word's SET. But what if we wanted to find documents that contained two or more words? We could fetch the SETs of documents for all of those words, and then try to find those documents that are in all of the SETs, but as we discussed in chapter 3, there are two commands in Redis that do this directly: SINTER and SINTERSTORE. Both commands will discover the items that are in all of the provided SETs and, for our example, will discover the SET of documents that contain all of the words.

One of the amazing things about using inverted indexes with SET intersections is not so much what we can find (the documents we're looking for), and it's not even how quickly it can find the results—it's how much information the search completely ignores. When searching text the way a text editor does, a lot of useless data gets examined. But with inverted indexes, we already know what documents have each individual word, and it's only a matter of filtering through the documents that have *all* of the words we're looking for.

Sometimes we want to search for items with similar meanings and have them considered the same, which we call *synonyms* (at least in this context). To handle that situation, we could again fetch all of the document SETs for those words and find all of the unique documents, or we could use another built-in Redis operation: SUNION or SUNIONSTORE.

Occasionally, there are times when we want to search for documents with certain words or phrases, but we want to remove documents that have other words. There are also Redis SET operations for that: SDIFF and SDIFFSTORE.

With Redis SET operations and a bit of helper code, we can perform arbitrarily intricate word queries over our documents. Listing 7.2 provides a group of helper functions that will perform SET intersections, unions, and differences over the given words, storing them in temporary SETs with an expiration time that defaults to 30 seconds.

Listing 7.2 SET intersection, union, and difference operation helpers

Set up a transactional pipeline so that we have consistent results for each individual call.

Create a new temporary identifier.

Add the 'idx:' prefix to our terms.

Instruct Redis to expire the SET in the future.

```
def _set_common(conn, method, names, ttl=30, execute=True):
    id = str(uuid.uuid4())
    pipeline = conn.pipeline(True) if execute else conn
    names = ['idx:' + name for name in names]
    getattr(pipeline, method)('idx:' + id, *names)
    pipeline.expire('idx:' + id, ttl)
    if execute:
        pipeline.execute()
    return id
```

Set up the call for one of the operations.

Actually execute the operation.

Return the ID for the caller to process the results.

Helper function to perform SET intersections.

Helper function to perform SET unions.

```
def intersect(conn, items, ttl=30, _execute=True):
    return _set_common(conn, 'sinterstore', items, ttl, _execute)

def union(conn, items, ttl=30, _execute=True):
    return _set_common(conn, 'sunionstore', items, ttl, _execute)

def difference(conn, items, ttl=30, _execute=True):
    return _set_common(conn, 'sdiffstore', items, ttl, _execute)
```

Helper function to perform SET differences.

Each of the `intersect()`, `union()`, and `difference()` functions calls another helper function that actually does all of the heavy lifting. This is because they all essentially do the same thing: set up the keys, make the appropriate SET call, update the expiration, and return the new SET's ID. Another way of visualizing what happens when we perform the three different SET operations SINTER, SUNION, and SDIFF can be seen in figure 7.3, which shows the equivalent operations on Venn diagrams.

This is everything necessary for programming the search engine, but what about parsing a search query?

PARSING AND EXECUTING A SEARCH

We almost have all of the pieces necessary to perform indexing and search. We have tokenization, indexing, and the basic functions for intersection, union, and differences. The remaining piece is to take a text query and turn it into a search operation. Like our earlier tokenization of documents, there are many ways to tokenize search queries. We'll use a method that allows for searching for documents that contain all of the provided words, supporting both synonyms and unwanted words.

A basic search will be about finding documents that contain all of the provided words. If we have just a list of words, that's a simple `intersect()` call. In the case where we want to remove unwanted words, we'll say that any word with a leading minus character (-) will be removed with `difference()`. To handle synonyms, we

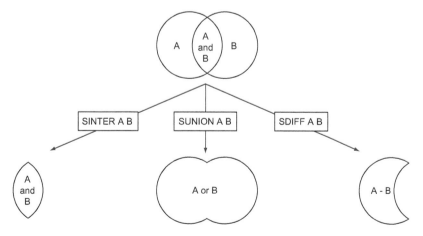

Figure 7.3 The SET intersection, union, and difference calls as if they were operating on Venn diagrams

need a way of saying "This word is a synonym," which we'll denote by the use of the plus (+) character prefix on a word. If we see a plus character leading a word, it's considered a synonym of the word that came just before it (skipping over any unwanted words), and we'll group synonyms together to perform a `union()` prior to the higher-level `intersect()` call.

Putting it all together where + denotes synonyms and - denotes unwanted words, the next listing shows the code for parsing a query into a Python list of lists that describes words that should be considered the same, and a list of words that are unwanted.

Listing 7.3   A function for parsing a search query

A unique set of unwanted words.

Our final result of words that we're looking to intersect.

Our regular expression for finding wanted, unwanted, and synonym words.

The current unique set of words to consider as synonyms.

Iterate over all words in the search query.

Discover +/- prefixes, if any.

Strip any leading or trailing single quotes, and skip anything that's a stop word.

If the word is unwanted, add it to the unwanted set.

Add the current word to the current set.

Set up a new synonym set if we have no synonym prefix and we already have words.

Add any remaining words to the final intersection.

```python
QUERY_RE = re.compile("[+-]?[a-z']{2,}")

def parse(query):
    unwanted = set()
    all = []
    current = set()
    for match in QUERY_RE.finditer(query.lower()):
        word = match.group()
        prefix = word[:1]
        if prefix in '+-':
            word = word[1:]
        else:
            prefix = None

        word = word.strip("'")
        if len(word) < 2 or word in STOP_WORDS:
            continue

        if prefix == '-':
            unwanted.add(word)
            continue

        if current and not prefix:
            all.append(list(current))
            current = set()
        current.add(word)

    if current:
        all.append(list(current))

    return all, list(unwanted)
```

To give this parsing function a bit of exercise, let's say that we wanted to search our knowledge base for chat connection issues. What we really want to search for is an article with connect, connection, disconnect, or disconnection, along with chat, but because we aren't using a proxy, we want to skip any documents that include proxy or proxies. Here's an example interaction that shows the query (formatted into groups for easier reading):

```python
>>> parse('''
connect +connection +disconnect +disconnection
chat
-proxy -proxies''')
```

```
([['disconnection', 'connection', 'disconnect', 'connect'], ['chat']],
['proxies', 'proxy'])
>>>
```

Our parse function properly extracted the synonyms for connect/disconnect, kept chat separate, and discovered our unwanted proxy and proxies. We aren't going to be passing that parsed result around (except for maybe debugging as necessary), but instead are going to be calling our parse() function as part of a parse_and_search() function that union()s the individual synonym lists as necessary, intersect()ing the final list, and removing the unwanted words with difference() as necessary. The full parse_and_search() function is shown in the next listing.

Listing 7.4   A function to parse a query and search documents

```
def parse_and_search(conn, query, ttl=30):
    all, unwanted = parse(query)              ◁── Parse the query.
    if not all:
        return None

    to_intersect = []
    for syn in all:                           ◁── Iterate over each list of synonyms.
        if len(syn) > 1:
            to_intersect.append(union(conn, syn, ttl=ttl))
        else:
            to_intersect.append(syn[0])
    if len(to_intersect) > 1:
        intersect_result = intersect(conn, to_intersect, ttl=ttl)
    else:
        intersect_result = to_intersect[0]
    if unwanted:
        unwanted.insert(0, intersect_result)
        return difference(conn, unwanted, ttl=ttl)

    return intersect_result                   ◁── Otherwise, return the intersection result.
```

If there are only stop words, we don't have a result.

If the synonym list is more than one word long, perform the union operation.

Otherwise, use the individual word directly.

If we have more than one word/result to intersect, intersect them.

Otherwise, use the individual word/result directly.

If we have any unwanted words, remove them from our earlier result and return it.

Like before, the final result will be the ID of a SET that includes the documents that match the parameters of our search. Assuming that Fake Garage Startup has properly indexed all of their documents using our earlier index_document() function, parse_and_search() will perform the requested search.

We now have a method that's able to search for documents with a given set of criteria. But ultimately, when there are a large number of documents, we want to see them in a specific order. To do that, we need to learn how to sort the results of our searches.

7.1.2   *Sorting search results*

We now have the ability to arbitrarily search for words in our indexed documents. But searching is only the first step in retrieving information that we're looking for. After we have a list of documents, we need to decide what's important enough about each of the documents to determine its position relative to other matching documents. This question is generally known as *relevance* in the search world, and one way of determining whether one article is more relevant than another is which article has been updated more recently. Let's see how we could include this as part of our search results.

If you remember from chapter 3, the Redis SORT call allows us to sort the contents of a LIST or SET, possibly referencing external data. For each article in Fake Garage Startup's knowledge base, we'll also include a HASH that stores information about the article. The information we'll store about the article includes the title, the creation timestamp, the timestamp for when the article was last updated, and the document's ID. An example document appears in figure 7.4.

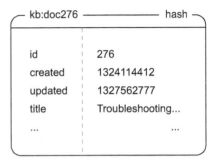

With documents stored in this format, we can then use the SORT command to sort by one of a few different attributes. We've been giving our result SETs expiration times as a way of cleaning them out shortly after we've finished

Figure 7.4   An example document stored in a HASH

using them. But for our final SORTed result, we could keep that result around longer, while at the same time allowing for the ability to re-sort, and even paginate over the results without having to perform the search again. Our function for integrating this kind of caching and re-sorting can be seen in the following listing.

Listing 7.5   A function to parse and search, sorting the results

We'll optionally take a previous result ID, a way to sort the results, and options for paginating over the results.

Determine which attribute to sort by and whether to sort ascending or descending.

We need to tell Redis whether we're sorting by a number or alphabetically.

```
def search_and_sort(conn, query, id=None, ttl=300, sort="-updated",
                    start=0, num=20):
    desc = sort.startswith('-')
    sort = sort.lstrip('-')
    by = "kb:doc:*->" + sort
    alpha = sort not in ('updated', 'id', 'created')
```

Perform the search if we didn't have a past search ID, or if our results expired.

```
    if id and not conn.expire(id, ttl):
        id = None

    if not id:
        id = parse_and_search(conn, query, ttl=ttl)
```

If there was a previous result, try to update its expiration time if it still exists.

Fetch the total number of results.

```
    pipeline = conn.pipeline(True)
    pipeline.scard('idx:' + id)
    pipeline.sort('idx:' + id, by=by, alpha=alpha,
        desc=desc, start=start, num=num)
    results = pipeline.execute()

    return results[0], results[1], id
```

Sort the result list by the proper column and fetch only those results we want.

Return the number of items in the results, the results we wanted, and the ID of the results so that we can fetch them again later.

When searching and sorting, we can paginate over results by updating the start and num arguments; alter the sorting attribute (and order) with the sort argument; cache the results for longer or shorter with the ttl argument; and reference previous search results (to save time) with the id argument.

Though these functions won't let us create a search engine to compete with Google, this problem and solution are what brought me to use Redis in the first place. Limitations on SORT lead to using ZSETs to support more intricate forms of document sorting, including combining scores for a composite sort order.

7.2 *Sorted indexes*

In the previous section, we talked primarily about searching, with the ability to sort results by referencing data stored in HASHes. This kind of sorting works well when we have a string or number that represents the actual sort order we're interested in. But what if our sort order is a composite of a few different scores? In this section, we'll talk about ways to combine multiple scores using SETs and ZSETs, which can offer greater flexibility than calling SORT.

Stepping back for a moment, when we used SORT and fetched data to sort by from HASHes, the HASHes behaved much like rows in a relational database. If we were to instead pull all of the updated times for our articles into a ZSET, we could similarly order our articles by updated times by intersecting our earlier result SET with our update time ZSET with ZINTERSTORE, using an aggregate of MAX. This works because SETs can participate as part of a ZSET intersection or union as though every element has a score of 1.

7.2.1 *Sorting search results with ZSETs*

As we saw in chapter 1 and talked about in chapter 3, SETs can actually be provided as arguments to the ZSET commands ZINTERSTORE and ZUNIONSTORE. When we pass SETs to these commands, Redis will consider the SET members to have scores of 1. For now, we aren't going to worry about the scores of SETs in our operations, but we will later.

In this section, we'll talk about using SETs and ZSETs together for a two-part search-and-sort operation. When you've finished reading this section, you'll understand why and how we'd want to combine scores together as part of a document search.

Let's consider a situation in which we've already performed a search and have our result SET. We can sort our results with the SORT command, but that means we can only sort based on a single value at a time. Being able to easily sort by a single value is one of the reasons why we started out sorting with our indexes in the first place.

But say that we want to add the ability to vote on our knowledge base articles to indicate if they were useful. We could put the vote count in the article hash and use SORT as we did before. That's reasonable. But what if we also wanted to sort based on a combination of recency *and* votes? We could do as we did in chapter 1 and predefine the score increase for each vote. But if we don't have enough information about how much scores should increase with each vote, then picking a score early on will force us to have to recalculate later when we find the right number.

Instead, we'll keep a ZSET of the times that articles were last updated, as well as a ZSET for the number of votes that an article has received. Both will use the article IDs of the knowledge base articles as members of the ZSETs, with update times or vote count as scores, respectively. We'll also pass similar arguments to an updated search_and_zsort() function defined in the next listing, in order to calculate the resulting sort order for only update times, only vote counts, or almost any relative balance between the two.

Listing 7.6   An updated function to search and sort based on votes and updated times

Like before, we'll optionally take a previous result ID for pagination if the result is still available.

```
def search_and_zsort(conn, query, id=None, ttl=300, update=1, vote=0,
                     start=0, num=20, desc=True):
    if id and not conn.expire(id, ttl):
        id = None

    if not id:
        id = parse_and_search(conn, query, ttl=ttl)

        scored_search = {
            id: 0,
            'sort:update': update,
            'sort:votes': vote
        }
        id = zintersect(conn, scored_search, ttl)

    pipeline = conn.pipeline(True)
    pipeline.zcard('idx:' + id)
    if desc:
        pipeline.zrevrange('idx:' + id, start, start + num - 1)
    else:
        pipeline.zrange('idx:' + id, start, start + num - 1)
    results = pipeline.execute()

    return results[0], results[1], id
```

We'll refresh the search result's TTL if possible.

If our search result expired, or if this is the first time we've searched, perform the standard SET search.

We use the "id" key for the intersection, but we don't want it to count toward weights.

Set up the scoring adjustments for balancing update time and votes. Remember: votes can be adjusted to 1, 10, 100, or higher, depending on the sorting result desired.

Intersect using our helper function that we define in listing 7.7.

Fetch the size of the result ZSET.

Handle fetching a "page" of results.

Return the results and the ID for pagination.

Our search_and_zsort() works much like the earlier search_and_sort(), differing primarily in how we sort/order our results. Rather than calling SORT, we perform a ZINTERSTORE operation, balancing the search result SET, the updated time ZSET, and the vote ZSET.

As part of search_and_zsort(), we used a helper function for handling the creation of a temporary ID, the ZINTERSTORE call, and setting the expiration time of the result ZSET. The zintersect() and zunion() helper functions are shown next.

Listing 7.7   Some helper functions for performing ZSET intersections and unions

```
def _zset_common(conn, method, scores, ttl=30, **kw):
    id = str(uuid.uuid4())
    execute = kw.pop('_execute', True)
    pipeline = conn.pipeline(True) if execute else conn
    for key in scores.keys():
        scores['idx:' + key] = scores.pop(key)
```

Allow the passing of an argument to determine whether we should defer pipeline execution.

Create a new temporary identifier.

Add the 'idx:' prefix to our inputs.

Set up a transactional pipeline so that we have consistent results for each individual call.

Set up the call for one of the operations.

Actually execute the operation, unless explicitly instructed not to by the caller.

Helper function to perform ZSET intersections.

Instruct Redis to expire the ZSET in the future.

Return the ID for the caller to process the results.

Helper function to perform ZSET unions.

```
        getattr(pipeline, method)('idx:' + id, scores, **kw)
        pipeline.expire('idx:' + id, ttl)
        if execute:
            pipeline.execute()
        return id
    def zintersect(conn, items, ttl=30, **kw):
        return _zset_common(conn, 'zinterstore', dict(items), ttl, **kw)

    def zunion(conn, items, ttl=30, **kw):
        return _zset_common(conn, 'zunionstore', dict(items), ttl, **kw)
```

These helper functions are similar to our SET-based helpers, the primary difference being that we're passing a dictionary through to specify scores, so we need to do more work to properly prefix all of our input keys.

> ### Exercise: Article voting
>
> In this section, we used ZSETs to handle combining a time and a vote count for an article. You remember that we did much the same thing back in chapter 1 without search, though we did handle groups of articles. Can you update article_vote(), post_articles(), get_articles(), and get_group_articles() to use this new method so that we can update our score per vote whenever we want?

In this section, we talked about how to combine SETs and ZSETs to calculate a simple composite score based on vote count and updated time. Though we used 2 ZSETs as sources for scores, there's no reason why we couldn't have used 1 or 100. It's all a question of what we want to calculate.

If we try to fully replace SORT and HASHes with the more flexible ZSET, we run into one problem almost immediately: scores in ZSETs must be floating-point numbers. But we can handle this issue in many cases by converting our non-numeric data to numbers.

7.2.2   *Non-numeric sorting with ZSETs*

Typical comparison operations between strings will examine two strings character by character until one character is different, one string runs out of characters, or until they're found to be equal. In order to offer the same sort of functionality with string data, we need to turn strings into numbers. In this section, we'll talk about methods of converting strings into numbers that can be used with Redis ZSETs in order to sort based on string prefixes. After reading this section, you should be able to sort your ZSET search results with strings.

Our first step in translating strings into numbers is understanding the limitations of what we can do. Because Redis uses IEEE 754 double-precision floating-point values to store scores, we're limited to at most 64 bits worth of storage. Due to some subtleties in the way doubles represent numbers, we can't use all 64 bits. Technically, we could use more than the equivalent of 63 bits, but that doesn't buy us significantly more than 63 bits, and for our case, we'll only use 48 bits for the sake of simplicity. Using 48 bits limits us to prefixes of 6 bytes on our data, which is often sufficient.

To convert our string into an integer, we'll trim our string down to six characters (as necessary), converting each character into its ASCII value. We'll then extend the values to six entries for strings shorter than six characters. Finally, we'll combine all of the values into an integer. Our code for converting a string into a score can be seen next.

Listing 7.8   A function to turn a string into a numeric score

Convert the first six characters of the string into their numeric values, null being 0, tab being 9, capital A being 65, and so on.

We can handle optional case-insensitive indexes easily, so we will.

For strings that aren't at least six characters long, we'll add placeholder values to represent that the strings are short.

For each value in the converted string values, we add it to the score, taking into consideration that a null is different from a placeholder.

Because we have an extra bit, we can also signify whether the string is exactly six characters or more, allowing us to differentiate "robber" and "robbers", though not "robbers" and "robbery".

```python
def string_to_score(string, ignore_case=False):
    if ignore_case:
        string = string.lower()
    pieces = map(ord, string[:6])
    while len(pieces) < 6:
        pieces.append(-1)
    score = 0
    for piece in pieces:
        score = score * 257 + piece + 1
    return score * 2 + (len(string) > 6)
```

Most of our `string_to_score()` function should be straightforward, except for maybe our use of -1 as a filler value for strings shorter than six characters, and our use of 257 as a multiplier before adding each character value to the score. For many applications, being able to differentiate between `hello\\0` and `hello` can be important, so we take steps to differentiate the two, primarily by adding 1 to all ASCII values (making null 1), and using 0 (-1 + 1) as a filler value for short strings. As a bonus, we use an extra bit to tell us whether a string is more than six characters long, which helps us with similar six-character prefixes.[2]

By mapping strings to scores, we're able to get a prefix comparison of a little more than the first six characters of our string. For non-numeric data, this is more or less what we can reasonably do without performing extensive numeric gymnastics, and without running into issues with how a non-Python library transfers large integers (that may or may not have been converted to a double).

When using scores derived from strings, the scores aren't always useful for combining with other scores and are typically only useful for defining a single sort order. Note

---

[2] If we didn't care about differentiating between `hello\\0` and `hello`, then we wouldn't need the filler. If we didn't need the filler, we could replace our multiplier of 257 with 256 and get rid of the +1 adjustment. But with the filler, we actually use .0337 additional bits to let us differentiate short strings from strings that have nulls. And when combined with the extra bit we used to distinguish whether we have strings longer than six characters, we actually use 49.0337 total bits.

> ### Exercise: Autocompleting with strings as scores
>
> Back in section 6.1.2, we used ZSETs with scores set to 0 to allow us to perform prefix matching on user names. We had to add items to the ZSET and either use WATCH/MULTI/EXEC or the lock that we covered in section 6.2 to make sure that we fetched the correct range. But if instead we added names with scores being the result of string_to_score() on the name itself, we could bypass the use of WATCH/MULTI/EXEC and locks when someone is looking for a prefix of at most six characters by using ZRANGEBYSCORE, with the endpoints we had calculated before being converted into scores as just demonstrated. Try rewriting our find_prefix_range() and autocomplete_on_prefix() functions to use ZRANGEBYSCORE instead.

> ### Exercise: Autocompleting with longer strings
>
> In this section and for the previous exercise, we converted arbitrary binary strings to scores, which limited us to six-character prefixes. By reducing the number of valid characters in our input strings, we don't need to use a full 8+ bits per input character. Try to come up with a method that would allow us to use more than a six-character prefix if we only needed to autocomplete on lowercase alphabetic characters.

that this is because the score that we produced from the string doesn't really mean anything, aside from defining a sort order.

Now that we can sort on arbitrary data, and you've seen how to use weights to adjust and combine numeric data, you're ready to read about how we can use Redis SETs and ZSETs to target ads.

7.3 Ad targeting

On countless websites around the internet, we see advertisements in the form of text snippets, images, and videos. Those ads exist as a method of paying website owners for their service—whether it's search results, information about travel destinations, or even finding the definition of a word.

In this section, we'll talk about using SETs and ZSETs to implement an ad-targeting engine. When you finish reading this section, you'll have at least a basic understanding of how to build an ad-serving platform using Redis. Though there are a variety of ways to build an ad-targeting engine without Redis (custom solutions written with C++, Java, or C# are common), building an ad-targeting engine with Redis is one of the quickest methods to get an ad network running.

If you've been reading these chapters sequentially, you've seen a variety of problems and solutions, almost all of which were simplified versions of much larger projects and problems. But in this section, we won't be simplifying anything. We'll build an almost-complete ad-serving platform based on software that I built and ran in a production setting for a number of months. The only major missing parts are the web server, ads, and traffic.

Before we get into building the ad server itself, let's first talk about what an ad server is and does.

7.3.1 What's an ad server?

When we talk about an ad server, what we really mean is a sometimes-small, but sophisticated piece of technology. Whenever we visit a web page with an ad, either the web server itself or our web browser makes a request to a remote server for that ad. This ad server will be provided a variety of information about how to find an ad that can earn the most money through clicks, views, or actions (I'll explain these shortly).

In order to choose a specific ad, our server must be provided with targeting parameters. Servers will typically receive at least basic information about the viewer's location (based on our IP address at minimum, and occasionally based on GPS information from our phone or computer), what operating system and web browser we're using, maybe the content of the page we're on, and maybe the last few pages we've visited on the current website.

We'll focus on building an ad-targeting platform that has a small amount of basic information about viewer location and the content of the page visited. After we've seen how to pick an ad from this information, we can add other targeting parameters later.

ADS WITH BUDGETS In a typical ad-targeting platform, each ad is provided with a budget to be spent over time. We don't address budgeting or accounting here, so both need to be built. Generally, budgets should at least attempt to be spread out over time, and as a practical approach, I've found that adding a portion of the ad's total budget on an hourly basis (with different ads getting budgeted at different times through the hour) works well.

Our first step in returning ads to the user is getting the ads into our platform in the first place.

7.3.2 Indexing ads

The process of indexing an ad is not so different from the process of indexing any other content. The primary difference is that we aren't looking to return a list of ads (or search results); we want to return a single ad. There are also some secondary differences in that ads will typically have required targeting parameters such as location, age, or gender.

As mentioned before, we'll only be targeting based on location and content, so this section will discuss how to index ads based on location and content. When you've seen how to index and target based on location and content, targeting based on, for example, age, gender, or recent behavior should be similar (at least on the indexing and targeting side of things).

Before we can talk about indexing an ad, we must first determine how to measure the value of an ad in a consistent manner.

CALCULATING THE VALUE OF AN AD

Three major types of ads are shown on web pages: *cost per view, cost per click*, and *cost per action* (or acquisition). Cost per view ads are also known as *CPM* or *cost per mille*, and are paid a fixed rate per 1,000 views of the ad itself. Cost per click, or *CPC*, ads are paid a fixed rate per click on the ad itself. Cost per action, or *CPA*, ads are paid a sometimes varying rate based on actions performed on the ad-destination site.

Making values consistent

To greatly simplify our calculations as to the value of showing a given ad, we'll convert all of our types of ads to have values relative to 1,000 views, generating what's known as an *estimated CPM*, or *eCPM*. CPM ads are the easiest because their value per thousand views is already provided, so eCPM = CPM. But for both CPC and CPA ads, we must calculate the eCPMs.

Calculating the estimated CPM of a CPC ad

If we have a CPC ad, we start with its cost per click, say $.25. We then multiply that cost by the click-through rate (CTR) on the ad. Click-through rate is the number of clicks that an ad received divided by the number of views the ad received. We then multiply that result by 1,000 to get our estimated CPM for that ad. If our ad gets .2% CTR, or .002, then our calculation looks something like this: .25 x .002 x 1000 = $.50 eCPM.

Calculating the estimated CPM of a CPA ad

When we have a CPA ad, the calculation is somewhat similar to the CPC value calculation. We start with the CTR of the ad, say .2%. We multiply that against the probability that the user will perform an action on the advertiser's destination page, maybe 10% or .1. We then multiply that times the value of the action performed, and again multiply that by 1,000 to get our estimated CPM. If our CPA is $3, our calculation would look like this: .002 x .1 x 3 x 1000 = $.60 eCPM.

Two helper functions for calculating the eCPM of CPC and CPA ads are shown next.

Listing 7.9 Helper functions for turning information about CPC and CPA ads into eCPM

```
def cpc_to_ecpm(views, clicks, cpc):
    return 1000. * cpc * clicks / views

def cpa_to_ecpm(views, actions, cpa):
    return 1000. * cpa * actions / views
```

Because click-through rate is clicks/ views, and action rate is actions/ clicks, when we multiply them together we get actions/views.

Notice that in our helper functions we used clicks, views, and actions directly instead of the calculated CTR. This lets us keep these values directly in our accounting system, only calculating the eCPM as necessary. Also notice that for our uses, CPC and CPA are similar, the major difference being that for most ads, the number of actions is significantly lower than the number of clicks, but the value per action is typically much larger than the value per click.

Now that we've calculated the basic value of an ad, let's index an ad in preparation for targeting.

INSERTING AN AD INTO THE INDEX

When targeting an ad, we'll have a group of optional and required targeting parameters. In order to properly target an ad, our indexing of the ad must reflect the targeting requirements. Since we have two targeting options—location and content—we'll say that location is required (either on the city, state, or country level), but any matching terms between the ad and the content of the page will be optional and a bonus.[3]

We'll use the same search functions we defined in sections 7.1 and 7.2, with slightly different indexing options. We'll also assume that you've taken my advice from chapter 4 by splitting up your different types of services to different machines (or databases) as necessary, so that your ad-targeting index doesn't overlap with your other content indexes.

As in section 7.1, we'll create inverted indexes that use SETs and ZSETs to hold ad IDs. Our SETs will hold the required location targeting, which provides no additional bonus. When we talk about learning from user behavior, we'll get into how we calculate our per-matched-word bonus, but initially we won't include any of our terms for targeting bonuses, because we don't know how much they may contribute to the overall value of the ad. Our ad-indexing function is shown here.

Listing 7.10   A method for indexing an ad that's targeted on location and ad content

```
TO_ECPM = {                                          Set up the pipeline so
    'cpc': cpc_to_ecpm,                              that we only need a single
    'cpa': cpa_to_ecpm,                              round trip to perform the
    'cpm': lambda *args:args[-1],                    full index operation.
}

def index_ad(conn, id, locations, content, type, value):
    pipeline = conn.pipeline(True)

    for location in locations:
        pipeline.sadd('idx:req:'+location, id)                    Index the words
                                                                  for the ad.
    words = tokenize(content)
    for word in tokenize(content):
        pipeline.zadd('idx:' + word, id, 0)                      Record what
                                                                  type of ad
    rvalue = TO_ECPM[type](                                      this is.
        1000, AVERAGE_PER_1K.get(type, 1), value)
    pipeline.hset('type:', id, type)
    pipeline.zadd('idx:ad:value:', id, rvalue)                   Add the ad's
    pipeline.zadd('ad:base_value:', id, value)                   eCPM to a ZSET
    pipeline.sadd('terms:' + id, *list(words))                   of all ads.
    pipeline.execute()
```

Add the ad ID to all of the relevant location SETs for targeting.

We'll keep a dictionary that stores the average number of clicks or actions per 1000 views on our network, for estimating the performance of new ads.

Keep a record of the words that could be targeted for the ad.

Add the ad's base value to a ZSET of all ads.

As shown in the listing and described in the annotations, we made three important additions to the listing. The first is that an ad can actually have multiple targeted locations. This is necessary to allow a single ad to be targeted for any one of multiple locations at the same time (like multiple cities, states, or countries).

---

[3]   If ad copy matches page content, then the ad looks like the page and will be more likely to be clicked on than an ad that doesn't look like the page content.

The second is that we'll keep a dictionary that holds information about the average number of clicks and actions across the entire system. This lets us come up with a reasonable estimate on the eCPM for CPC and CPA ads before they've even been seen in the system.[4]

Finally, we'll also keep a SET of all of the terms that we can optionally target in the ad. I include this information as a precursor to learning about user behavior a little later.

It's now time to search for and discover ads that match an ad request.

7.3.3 Targeting ads

As described earlier, when we receive a request to target an ad, we're generally looking to find the highest eCPM ad that matches the viewer's location. In addition to matching an ad based on a location, we'll gather and use statistics about how the content of a page matches the content of an ad, and what that can do to affect the ad's CTR. Using these statistics, content in an ad that matches a web page can result in bonuses that contribute to the calculated eCPM of CPC and CPA ads, which can result in those types of ads being shown more.

Before showing any ads, we won't have any bonus scoring for any of our web page content. But as we show ads, we'll learn about what terms in the ads help or hurt the ad's expected performance, which will allow us to change the relative value of each of the optional targeting terms.

To execute the targeting, we'll union all of the relevant location SETs to produce an initial group of ads that should be shown to the viewer. Then we'll parse the content of the page on which the ad will be shown, add any relevant bonuses, and finally calculate a total eCPM for all ads that a viewer could be shown. After we've calculated those eCPMs, we'll fetch the ad ID for the highest eCPM ad, record some statistics about our targeting, and return the ad itself. Our code for targeting an ad looks like this.

Listing 7.11   Ad targeting by location and page content bonuses

Find all ads that fit the location targeting parameter, and their eCPMs.

Finish any bonus scoring based on matching the content.

Get an ID that can be used for reporting and recording of this particular ad target.

```
def target_ads(conn, locations, content):
    pipeline = conn.pipeline(True)
    matched_ads, base_ecpm = match_location(pipeline, locations)
    words, targeted_ads = finish_scoring(
        pipeline, matched_ads, base_ecpm, content)

    pipeline.incr('ads:served:')
    pipeline.zrevrange('idx:' + targeted_ads, 0, 0)
    target_id, targeted_ad = pipeline.execute()[-2:]
```

Fetch the top-eCPM ad ID.

---

[4] It may seem strange to be estimating an expectation (which is arguably an estimate), but everything about targeting ads is fundamentally predicated on statistics of one kind or another. This is one of those cases where the basics can get us pretty far.

Record the results of our targeting efforts as part of our learning process.

```
if not targeted_ad:
    return None, None

ad_id = targeted_ad[0]
record_targeting_result(conn, target_id, ad_id, words)

return target_id, ad_id
```

If there were no ads that matched the location targeting, return nothing.

Return the target ID and the ad ID to the caller.

In this first version, we hide away the details of exactly how we're matching based on location and adding bonuses based on terms so that we can understand the general flow. The only part I didn't mention earlier is that we'll also generate a *target ID*, which is an ID that represents this particular execution of the ad targeting. This ID will allow us to track clicks later, helping us learn about which parts of the ad targeting may have contributed to the overall total clicks.

As mentioned earlier, in order to match based on location, we'll perform a SET union over the locations (city, state, country) that the viewer is coming from. While we're here, we'll also calculate the base eCPM of these ads without any bonuses applied. The code for performing this operation is shown next.

Listing 7.12 A helper function for targeting ads based on location

Calculate the SET key names for all of the provided locations.

Calculate the SET of matched ads that are valid for this location.

```
def match_location(pipe, locations):
    required = ['req:' + loc for loc in locations]
    matched_ads = union(pipe, required, ttl=300, _execute=False)
    return matched_ads, zintersect(pipe,
        {matched_ads: 0, 'ad:value:': 1}, _execute=False)
```

Return the matched ads SET ID, as well as the ID of the ZSET that includes the base eCPM of all of the matched ads.

This code listing does exactly what I said it would do: it finds ads that match the location of the viewer, and it calculates the eCPM of all of those ads without any bonuses based on page content applied. The only thing that may be surprising about this listing is our passing of the funny _execute keyword argument to the zintersect() function, which delays the actual execution of calculating the eCPM of the ad until later. The purpose of waiting until later is to help minimize the number of round trips between our client and Redis.

CALCULATING TARGETING BONUSES

The interesting part of targeting isn't the location matching; it's calculating the bonuses. We're trying to discover the amount to add to an ad's eCPM, based on words in the page content that matched words in the ad. We'll assume that we've precalculated a bonus for each word in each ad (as part of the learning phase), stored in ZSETs for each word, with members being ad IDs and scores being what should be added to the eCPM.

These word-based, per-ad eCPM bonuses have values such that the average eCPM of the ad, when shown on a page with that word, is the eCPM bonus from the word plus the known average CPM for the ad. Unfortunately, when more than one word in an ad matches the content of the page, adding all of the eCPM bonuses gives us a total eCPM bonus that probably isn't close to reality.

We have eCPM bonuses based on word matching for each word that are based on single word matching page content alone, or with any one or a number of other words in the ad. What we really want to find is the weighted average of the eCPMs, where the weight of each word is the number of times the word matched the page content. Unfortunately, we can't perform the weighted average calculation with Redis ZSETs, because we can't divide one ZSET by another.

Numerically speaking, the weighted average lies between the geometric average and the arithmetic average, both of which would be reasonable estimates of the combined eCPM. But we can't calculate either of those averages when the count of matching words varies. The best estimate of the ad's true eCPM is to find the maximum and minimum bonuses, calculate the average of those two, and use that as the bonus for multiple matching words.

> **BEING MATHEMATICALLY RIGOROUS** Mathematically speaking, our method of averaging the maximum and minimum word bonuses to determine an overall bonus isn't rigorous. The true mathematical expectation of the eCPM with a collection of matched words is different than what we calculated. We chose to use this mathematically nonrigorous method because it gets us to a reasonable answer (the weighted average of the words *is* between the minimum and maximum), with relatively little work. If you choose to use this bonus method along with our later learning methods, remember that there are better ways to target ads and to learn from user behavior. I chose this method because it's easy to write, easy to learn, and easy to improve.

We can calculate the maximum and minimum bonuses by using ZUNIONSTORE with the MAX and MIN aggregates. And we can calculate their average by using them as part of a ZUNIONSTORE operation with an aggregate of SUM, and their weights each being .5. Our function for combining bonus word eCPMs with the base eCPM of the ad can be seen in the next listing.

Listing 7.13   Calculating the eCPM of ads including content match bonuses

```
def finish_scoring(pipe, matched, base, content):
    bonus_ecpm = {}
    words = tokenize(content)                          ◁─┘  Tokenize the content for
    for word in words:                                       matching against ads.
        word_bonus = zintersect(
            pipe, {matched: 0, word: 1}, _execute=False)    Find the ads that are location
        bonus_ecpm[word_bonus] = 1                           targeted that also have one
                                                             of the words in the content.
    if bonus_ecpm:
        minimum = zunion(
            pipe, bonus_ecpm, aggregate='MIN', _execute=False)   Find the minimum
        maximum = zunion(                                         and maximum eCPM
            pipe, bonus_ecpm, aggregate='MAX', _execute=False)    bonuses for each ad.
```

```
        return words, zunion(
                pipe, {base:1, minimum:.5, maximum:.5}, _execute=False)
        return words, base
```

If there were no words in the content to match against, return just the known eCPM.

Compute the total of the base, plus half of the minimum eCPM bonus, plus half of the maximum eCPM bonus.

As before, we continue to pass the _execute parameter to delay execution of our various ZINTERSTORE and ZUNIONSTORE operations until after the function returns to the calling target_ads(). One thing that may be confusing is our use of ZINTERSTORE between the location-targeted ads and the bonuses, followed by a final ZUNIONSTORE call. Though we could perform fewer calls by performing a ZUNIONSTORE over all of our bonus ZSETs, followed by a single ZINTERSTORE call at the end (to match location), the majority of ad-targeting calls will perform better by performing many smaller intersections followed by a union.

The difference between the two methods is illustrated in figure 7.5, which shows that essentially all of the data in all of the relevant word bonus ZSETs is examined when we union and then intersect. Compare that with figure 7.6, which shows that when we intersect and then union, Redis will examine far less data to produce the same result.

After we have an ad targeted, we're given a target_id and an ad_id. These IDs would then be used to construct an ad response that includes both pieces of information, in addition to fetching the ad copy, formatting the result, and returning the result to the web page or client that requested it.

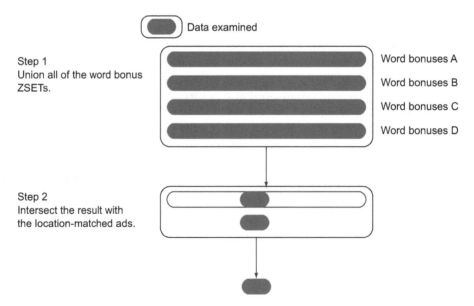

Figure 7.5   The data that's examined during a union-then-intersect calculation of ad-targeting bonuses includes all ads in the relevant word bonus ZSETs, even ads that don't meet the location matching requirements.

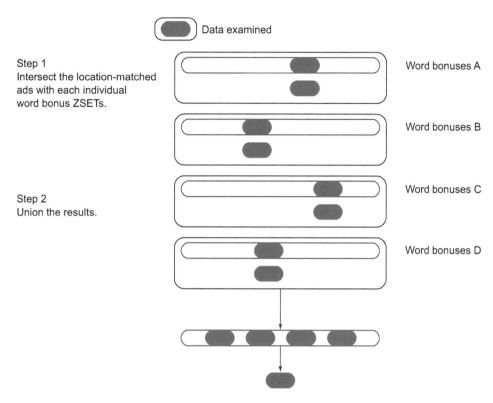

Figure 7.6   The data that's examined during an intersect-then-union calculation of ad-targeting bonuses only includes those ads that previously matched, which significantly cuts down on the amount of data that Redis will process.

> ### Exercise: No matching content
>
> If you pay careful attention to the flow of `target_ads()` through `finish_scoring()` in listings 7.11 and 7.13, you'll notice that we don't make any effort to deal with the case where an ad has zero matched words in the content. In that situation, the eCPM produced will actually be the average eCPM over all calls that returned that ad itself. It's not difficult to see that this may result in an ad being shown that shouldn't. Can you alter `finish_scoring()` to take into consideration ads that don't match any content?

The only part of our `target_ads()` function from listing 7.11 that we haven't defined is `record_targeting_result()`, which we'll now examine as part of the learning phase of ad targeting.

7.3.4   *Learning from user behavior*

As ads are shown to users, we have the opportunity to gain insight into what can cause someone to click on an ad. In the last section, we talked about using words as bonuses to ads that have already matched the required location. In this section, we'll talk about how we can record information about those words and the ads that were targeted to discover basic patterns about user behavior in order to develop per-word, per-ad-targeting bonuses.

A crucial question you should be asking yourself is "Why are we using words in the web page content to try to find better ads?" The simple reason is that ad placement is all about context. If a web page has content related to the safety of children's toys, showing an ad for a sports car probably won't do well. By matching words in the ad with words in the web page content, we get a form of context matching quickly and easily.

One thing to remember during this discussion is that we aren't trying to be perfect. We aren't trying to solve the ad-targeting and learning problem completely; we're trying to build something that will work "pretty well" with simple and straightforward methods. As such, our note about the fact that this isn't mathematically rigorous still applies.

RECORDING VIEWS

The first step in our learning process is recording the results of our ad targeting with the `record_targeting_result()` function that we called earlier from listing 7.11. Overall, we'll record some information about the ad-targeting results, which we'll later use to help us calculate click-through rates, action rates, and ultimately eCPM bonuses for each word. We'll record the following:

- Which words were targeted with the given ad
- The total number of times that a given ad has been targeted
- The total number of times that a word in the ad was part of the bonus calculation

To record this information, we'll store a SET of the words that were targeted and keep counts of the number of times that the ad and words were seen as part of a single ZSET per ad. Our code for recording this information is shown next.

Listing 7.14   A method for recording the result after we've targeted an ad

```
def record_targeting_result(conn, target_id, ad_id, words):        Find the words in
    pipeline = conn.pipeline(True)                                  the content that
                                                                    matched with the
    terms = conn.smembers('terms:' + ad_id)                        words in the ad.
    matched = list(words & terms)
    if matched:                                    If any words in the ad matched the
        matched_key = 'terms:matched:%s' % target_id    content, record that information
        pipeline.sadd(matched_key, *matched)            and keep it for 15 minutes.
        pipeline.expire(matched_key, 900)

                  type = conn.hget('type:', ad_id)          Keep a per-type count of the number
     Every        pipeline.incr('type:%s:views:' % type)    of views that each ad received.
    100th time    for word in matched:
  that the ad         pipeline.zincrby('views:%s' % ad_id, word)    Record view information
  was shown,    pipeline.zincrby('views:%s' % ad_id, '')           for each word in the ad,
   update the                                                       as well as the ad itself.
   ad's eCPM.   if not pipeline.execute()[-1] % 100:
                     update_cpms(conn, ad_id)
```

That function does everything we said it would do, and you'll notice a call to update_cpms(). This update_cpms() function is called every 100th time the ad is returned from a call. This function really is the core of the learning phase—it writes back to our per-word, per-ad-targeting bonus ZSETs.

We'll get to updating the eCPM of an ad in a moment, but first, let's see what happens when an ad is clicked.

RECORDING CLICKS AND ACTIONS

As we record views, we're recording half of the data for calculating CTRs. The other half of the data that we need to record is information about the clicks themselves, or in the case of a cost per action ad, the action. Numerically, this is because our eCPM calculations are based on this formula: (value of a click or action) x (clicks or actions) / views. Without recording clicks and actions, the numerator of our value calculation is 0, so we can't discover anything useful.

When someone actually clicks on an ad, prior to redirecting them to their final destination, we'll record the click in the total aggregates for the type of ad, as well as whether the ad got a click and which words matched the clicked ad. We'll record the same information for actions. Our function for recording clicks is shown next.

Listing 7.15 A method for recording clicks on an ad

```
def record_click(conn, target_id, ad_id, action=False):
    pipeline = conn.pipeline(True)
    click_key = 'clicks:%s'%ad_id

    match_key = 'terms:matched:%s'%target_id

    type = conn.hget('type:', ad_id)
    if type == 'cpa':
        pipeline.expire(match_key, 900)
        if action:
            click_key = 'actions:%s' % ad_id

    if action and type == 'cpa':
        pipeline.incr('type:cpa:actions:' % type)
        pipeline.incr('type:%s:clicks:' % type)

    matched = list(conn.smembers(match_key))
    matched.append('')
    for word in matched:
        pipeline.zincrby(click_key, word)
    pipeline.execute()

    update_cpms(conn, ad_id)
```

If the ad was a CPA ad, refresh the expiration time of the matched terms if it's still available.

Record actions instead of clicks.

Keep a global count of clicks/ actions for ads based on the ad type.

Record clicks (or actions) for the ad and for all words that had been targeted in the ad.

Update the eCPM for all words that were seen in the ad.

You'll notice there are a few parts of the recording function that we didn't mention earlier. In particular, when we receive a click or an action for a CPA ad, we'll refresh the expiration of the words that were a part of the ad-targeting call. This will let an action following a click count up to 15 minutes after the initial click-through to the destination site happened.

Another change is that we'll optionally be recording actions in this call for CPA ads; we'll assume that this function is called with the `action` parameter set to `True` in that case.

And finally, we'll call the `update_cpms()` function for every click/action because they should happen roughly once every 100–2000 views (or more), so each individual click/action is important relative to a view.

> ### Exercise: Changing the way we count clicks and actions
>
> In listing 7.15, we define a `record_click()` function to add 1 to every word that was targeted as part of an ad that was clicked on. Can you think of a different number to add to a word that may make more sense? Hint: You may want to consider this number to be related to the count of matched words. Can you update `finish_scoring()` and `record_click()` to take into consideration this new click/action value?

To complete our learning process, we only need to define our final `update_cpms()` function.

UPDATING ECPMS

We've been talking about and using the `update_cpms()` function for a couple of sections now, and hopefully you already have an idea of what happens inside of it. Regardless, we'll walk through the different parts of how we'll update our per-word, per-ad bonus eCPMs, as well as how we'll update our per-ad eCPMs.

The first part to updating our eCPMs is to know the click-through rate of an ad by itself. Because we've recorded both the clicks and views for each ad overall, we have the click-through rate by pulling both of those scores from the relevant ZSETs. By combining that click-through rate with the ad's actual value, which we fetch from the ad's base value ZSET, we can calculate the eCPM of the ad over all clicks and views.

The second part to updating our eCPMs is to know the CTR of words that were matched in the ad itself. Again, because we recorded all views and clicks involving the ad, we have that information. And because we have the ad's base value, we can calculate the eCPM. When we have the word's eCPM, we can subtract the ad's eCPM from it to determine the bonus that the word matching contributes. This difference is what's added to the per-word, per-ad bonus ZSETs.

The same calculation is performed for actions as was performed for clicks, the only difference being that we use the action count ZSETs instead of the click count ZSETs. Our method for updating eCPMs for clicks and actions can be seen in the next listing.

> **Listing 7.16   A method for updating eCPMs and per-word eCPM bonuses for ads**

```
def update_cpms(conn, ad_id):
    pipeline = conn.pipeline(True)
```

```
pipeline.hget('type:', ad_id)
pipeline.zscore('ad:base_value:', ad_id)
pipeline.smembers('terms:' + ad_id)
type, base_value, words = pipeline.execute()
```
Fetch the type and value of the ad, as well as all of the words in the ad.

```
which = 'clicks'
if type == 'cpa':
    which = 'actions'
```
Determine whether the eCPM of the ad should be based on clicks or actions.

Write back to our global dictionary the click-through rate or action rate for the ad.
```
pipeline.get('type:%s:views:' % type)
pipeline.get('type:%s:%s' % (type, which))
type_views, type_clicks = pipeline.execute()
AVERAGE_PER_1K[type] = (
    1000. * int(type_clicks or '1') / int(type_views or '1'))
```
Fetch the current number of views and clicks/actions for the given ad type.

```
if type == 'cpm':
    return
```
If we're processing a CPM ad, then we don't update any of the eCPMs; they're already updated.

```
view_key = 'views:%s' % ad_id
click_key = '%s:%s' % (which, ad_id)

to_ecpm = TO_ECPM[type]
```

Use the existing eCPM if the ad hasn't received any clicks yet.

Calculate the ad's eCPM and update the ad's value.
```
pipeline.zscore(view_key, '')
pipeline.zscore(click_key, '')
ad_views, ad_clicks = pipeline.execute()
if (ad_clicks or 0) < 1:
    ad_ecpm = conn.zscore('idx:ad:value:', ad_id)
else:
    ad_ecpm = to_ecpm(ad_views or 1, ad_clicks or 0, base_value)
    pipeline.zadd('idx:ad:value:', ad_id, ad_ecpm)
```
Fetch the per-ad view and click/action scores.

```
for word in words:
    pipeline.zscore(view_key, word)
    pipeline.zscore(click_key, word)
    views, clicks = pipeline.execute()[-2:]
```
Fetch the view and click/action scores for the word.

```
    if (clicks or 0) < 1:
        continue
```
Don't update eCPMs when the ad hasn't received any clicks.

Calculate the word's eCPM.
```
    word_ecpm = to_ecpm(views or 1, clicks or 0, base_value)
    bonus = word_ecpm - ad_ecpm
    pipeline.zadd('idx:' + word, ad_id, bonus)
pipeline.execute()
```
⟵ **Calculate the word's bonus.**

Write the word's bonus back to the per-word, per-ad ZSET.

Exercise: Optimizing eCPM calculations

In listing 7.16, we perform a number of round trips to Redis that's relative to the number of words that were targeted. More specifically, we perform the number of words plus three round trips. In most cases, this should be relatively small (considering that most ads won't have a lot of content or related keywords). But even so, some of these round trips can be avoided. Can you update the update_cpms() function to perform a total of only three round trips?

In our update_cpms() function, we updated the global per-type click-through and action rates, the per-ad eCPMs, and the per-word, per-ad bonus eCPMs.

With the learning portion of our ad-targeting process now complete, we've now built a complete ad-targeting engine from scratch. This engine will learn over time, adapt the ads it returns over time, and more. We can make many possible additions or changes to this engine to make it perform even better, some of which are mentioned in the exercises, and several of which are listed next. These are just starting points for building with Redis:

- Over time, the total number of clicks and views for each ad will stabilize around a particular ratio, and subsequent clicks and views won't alter that ratio significantly. The real CTR of an ad will vary based on time of day, day of week, and more. Consider degrading an ad's click/action and view count on a regular basis, as we did in section 2.5 with our rescale_viewed() call. This same concept applies to our global expected CTRs.

- To extend the learning ability beyond just a single count, consider keeping counts over the last day, week, and other time slices. Also consider ways of weighing those time slices differently, depending on their age. Can you think of a method to learn proper weights of different ages of counts?

- All of the big ad networks use second-price auctions in order to charge for a given ad placement. More specifically, rather than charging a fixed rate per click, per thousand views, or per action, you charge a rate that's relative to the second-highest value ad that was targeted.

- In most ad networks, there'll be a set of ads that rotate through the highest-value slot for a given set of keywords as each of them runs out of money. These ads are there because their high value and CTR earn the top slot. This means that new ads that don't have sufficiently high values will never be seen, so the network will never discover them. Rather than picking the highest-eCPM ads 100% of the time, fetch the top 100 ads and choose ads based on the relative values of their eCPMs anywhere from 10%-50% of the time (depending on how you want to balance learning true eCPMs and earning the most money).

- When ads are initially placed into the system, we know little about what to expect in terms of eCPM. We addressed this briefly by using the average CTR of all ads of the same type, but this is moot the moment a single click comes in. Another method mixes the average CTR for a given ad type, along with the seen CTR for the ad based on the number of views that the ad has seen. A simple inverse linear or inverse sigmoid relationship between the two can be used until the ad has had sufficient views (2,000–5,000 views is typically enough to determine a reliable CTR).

- In addition to mixing the average CTR for a given ad type with the CTR of the ad during the learning process, ads that are in the process of reaching an initial 2,000–5,000 views can have their CTR/eCPM artificially boosted. This can ensure sufficient traffic for the system to learn the ads' actual eCPMs.

- Our method of learning per-word bonuses is similar to Bayesian statistics. We could use real Bayesian statistics, neural networks, association rule learning, clustering, or other techniques to calculate the bonuses. These other methods may offer more mathematically rigorous results, which may result in better CTRs, and ultimately more money earned.

- In our code listings, we recorded views, clicks, and actions as part of the calls that return the ads or handle any sort of redirection. These operations may take a long time to execute, so should be handled after the calls have returned by being executed as an external task, as we discussed in section 6.4.

As you can see from our list, many additions and improvements can and should be made to this platform. But as an initial pass, what we've provided can get you started in learning about and building the internet's next-generation ad-targeting platform.

Now that you've learned about how to build an ad-targeting platform, let's keep going to see how to use search tools to find jobs that candidates are qualified for as part of a job-search tool.

7.4 Job search

If you're anything like me, at some point in your past you've spent time looking through classifieds and online job-search pages, or have used a recruiting agency to try to find work. One of the first things that's checked (after location) is required experience and/or skills.

In this section, we'll talk about using Redis SETs and ZSETs to find jobs for which a candidate has all of the required skills. When you're finished reading this section, you'll understand another way of thinking about your problem that fits the Redis data model.

As a way of approaching this problem, we'll say that Fake Garage Startup is branching out in their offerings, trying to pull their individual and group chat customers into using their system to find work. Initially, they're only offering the ability for users to search for positions in which they're qualified.

7.4.1 Approaching the problem one job at a time

At first glance, we might consider a straightforward solution to this problem. Start with every job having its own SET, with members being the skills that the job requires. To check whether a candidate has all of the requirements for a given job, we'd add the candidate's skills to a SET and then perform the SDIFF of the job and the candidate's skills. If there are no skills in the resulting SDIFF, then the user has all of the qualifications necessary to complete the job. The code for adding a job and checking whether a given set of skills is sufficient for that job looks like this next listing.

Listing 7.17 A potential solution for finding jobs when a candidate meets all requirements

```
def add_job(conn, job_id, required_skills):
    conn.sadd('job:' + job_id, *required_skills)

def is_qualified(conn, job_id, candidate_skills):
```

Add all required job skills to the job's SET.

```
temp = str(uuid.uuid4())
pipeline = conn.pipeline(True)
pipeline.sadd(temp, *candidate_skills)
pipeline.expire(temp, 5)
pipeline.sdiff('job:' + job_id, temp)
return not pipeline.execute()[-1]
```

> Add the candidate's skills to a temporary SET with an expiration time.

> Calculate the SET of skills that the job requires that the candidate doesn't have.

> Return True if there are no skills that the candidate doesn't have.

Explaining that again, we're checking whether a job requires any skills that the candidate doesn't have. This solution is okay, but it suffers from the fact that to find all of the jobs for a given candidate, we must check each job individually. This won't scale, but there are solutions that will.

7.4.2 *Approaching the problem like search*

In section 7.3.3, we used SETs and ZSETs as holders for additive bonuses for optional targeting parameters. If we're careful, we can do the same thing for groups of required targeting parameters.

Rather than talk about jobs with skills, we need to flip the problem around like we did with the other search problems described in this chapter. We start with one SET per skill, which stores all of the jobs that require that skill. In a required skills ZSET, we store the total number of skills that a job requires. The code that sets up our index looks like the next listing.

> **Listing 7.18   A function for indexing jobs based on the required skills**

```
def index_job(conn, job_id, skills):
    pipeline = conn.pipeline(True)
    for skill in skills:
        pipeline.sadd('idx:skill:' + skill, job_id)
    pipeline.zadd('idx:jobs:req', job_id, len(set(skills)))
    pipeline.execute()
```

> Add the job ID to all appropriate skill SETs.

> Add the total required skill count to the required skills ZSET.

This indexing function should remind you of the text indexing function we used in section 7.1. The only major difference is that we're providing index_job() with pretokenized skills, and we're adding a member to a ZSET that keeps a record of the number of skills that each job requires.

To perform a search for jobs that a candidate has all of the skills for, we need to approach the search like we did with the bonuses to ad targeting in section 7.3.3. More specifically, we'll perform a ZUNIONSTORE operation over skill SETs to calculate a total score for each job. This score represents how many skills the candidate has for each of the jobs.

Because we have a ZSET with the total number of skills required, we can then perform a ZINTERSTORE operation between the candidate's ZSET and the required skills ZSET with weights -1 and 1, respectively. Any job ID with a score equal to 0 in that final result ZSET is a job that the candidate has all of the required skills for. The code for implementing the search operation is shown in the following listing.

Listing 7.19 Find all jobs that a candidate is qualified for

Calculate
the scores
for each
of the
jobs.

```
def find_jobs(conn, candidate_skills):
    skills = {}
    for skill in set(candidate_skills):
        skills['skill:' + skill] = 1

    job_scores = zunion(conn, skills)
    final_result = zintersect(
        conn, {job_scores:-1, 'jobs:req':1})

    return conn.zrangebyscore('idx:' + final_result, 0, 0)
```

Set up the dictionary
for scoring the jobs.

Calculate how many more skills the
job requires than the candidate has.

Return the jobs
that the candidate
has the skills for.

Again, we first find the scores for each job. After we have the scores for each job, we subtract each job score from the total score necessary to match. In that final result, any job with a ZSET score of 0 is a job that the candidate has all of the skills for.

Depending on the number of jobs and searches that are being performed, our job-search system may or may not perform as fast as we need it to, especially with large numbers of jobs or searches. But if we apply sharding techniques that we'll discuss in chapter 9, we can break the large calculations into smaller pieces and calculate partial results bit by bit. Alternatively, if we first find the SET of jobs in a location to search for jobs, we could perform the same kind of optimization that we performed with ad targeting in section 7.3.3, which could greatly improve job-search performance.

Exercise: Levels of experience

A natural extension to the simple required skills listing is an understanding that skill levels vary from beginner to intermediate, to expert, and beyond. Can you come up with a method using additional SETs to offer the ability, for example, for someone who has as intermediate level in a skill to find jobs that require either beginner or intermediate-level candidates?

Exercise: Years of experience

Levels of expertise can be useful, but another way to look at the amount of experience someone has is the number of years they've used it. Can you build an alternate version that supports handling arbitrary numbers of years of experience?

7.5 *Summary*

In this chapter, you've learned how to perform basic searching using SET operations, and then ordered the results based on either values in HASHes, or potentially composite values with ZSETs. You continued through the steps necessary to build and update information in an ad-targeting network, and you finished with job searching that turned the idea of scoring search results on its head.

Though the problems introduced in this chapter may have been new, one thing that you should've gotten used to by now is Redis's ability to help you solve an unexpectedly wide variety of problems. With the data modeling options available in other databases, you really only have one tool to work with. But with Redis, the five data structures and pub/sub are an entire toolbox for you to work with.

In the next chapter, we'll continue to use Redis HASHes and ZSETs as building blocks in our construction of a fully functional Twitter clone.

Building a
simple social network

This chapter covers

- Users and statuses
- Home timeline
- Followers/following lists
- Posting or deleting a status update
- Streaming API

In this chapter, we'll cover the data structures and concepts necessary to build a system that offers almost all of the back-end-level functionality of Twitter. This chapter isn't intended to allow you to build a site that scales to the extent of Twitter, but the methods that we cover should give you a much better understanding of how social networking sites can be built from simple structures and data.

We'll begin this chapter by talking about user and status objects, which are the basis of almost all of the information in our application. From there, we'll discuss the home timeline and followers/following lists, which are sequences of status messages or users. Continuing on, we'll work through posting status messages, following/unfollowing someone, and deleting posts, which involves manipulating those lists. Finally, we'll build out a fully functioning streaming API with web server to encourage users of the social network to use and play with the data.

In the last chapter, we spent much of our time building an ad-targeting engine that combined user-entered data (the ads and their prices) with click behavior data in order to optimize ad earnings. The ad-targeting engine was query-intensive, in that every request could cause a lot of computation. In this Twitter-like platform, we'll do our best to perform as little work as possible when someone is interested in viewing a page.

To get started, let's build the basic structures that will hold much of the data that our users are interested in.

8.1 Users and statuses

As users interact with Twitter, two types of objects hold the most important information: users and status messages. User objects hold basic identity information, as well as aggregate data about the number of followers, number of status messages posted, and more. The user objects are important because they're the starting point for every other kind of data that's available or interesting. Status messages are also important because they're how individuals express themselves and interact with each other, and are the true content of social networks.

In this section, we'll talk about what data will be stored in the user and status message objects and how we'll store them. We'll also look at a function to create a new user.

Our first step is to define and create the structure for a user.

8.1.1 User information

In a variety of online services and social networks, user objects can be the basic building blocks from which everything else is derived. Our Twitter work-alike is no different.

We'll store user information inside of Redis as a HASH, similar to how we stored articles in chapter 1. Data that we'll store includes the username of the user, how many followers they have, how many people they're following, how many status messages they've posted, their sign-up date, and any other meta-information we decide to store down the line. A sample HASH that includes this information for a user with the username of dr_josiah (my Twitter username) is shown in figure 8.1.

From this figure, you can see that I have a modest number of followers, along with other information. When a new user signs up, we only need to create an object with the following, followers, and post count set to zero, a new timestamp for the sign-up time, and the relevant username. The function to perform this initial creation is shown next.

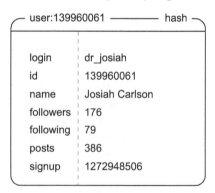

user:139960061 ———— hash	
login	dr_josiah
id	139960061
name	Josiah Carlson
followers	176
following	79
posts	386
signup	1272948506

Figure 8.1   Example user information stored in a HASH

Listing 8.1　How to create a new user profile HASH

We also store a
HASH of lowercased
login names to user
IDs, so if there's
already a login
name that maps to
an ID, we know and
won't give it to a
second person.

Try to acquire the lock for the
lowercased version of the
login name. This function is
defined in chapter 6.

If we couldn't get the lock,
then someone else already
has the same login name.

Add the
lowercased login
name to the
HASH that maps
from login names
to user IDs.

Each user is given a
unique ID, generated
by incrementing a
counter.

Add the user information
to the user's HASH.

Return
the ID of
the user.

Release the
lock over the
login name.

```
def create_user(conn, login, name):
    llogin = login.lower()
    lock = acquire_lock_with_timeout(conn, 'user:' + llogin, 1)
    if not lock:
        return None

    if conn.hget('users:', llogin):
        return None

    id = conn.incr('user:id:')
    pipeline = conn.pipeline(True)
    pipeline.hset('users:', llogin, id)
    pipeline.hmset('user:%s'%id, {
        'login': login,
        'id': id,
        'name': name,
        'followers': 0,
        'following': 0,
        'posts': 0,
        'signup': time.time(),
    })
    pipeline.execute()
    release_lock(conn, 'user:' + llogin, lock)
    return id
```

In our function, we perform the expected setting of the initial user information in the user's HASH, but we also acquire a lock around the user's login name. This lock is necessary: it guarantees that we won't have two requests trying to create a user with the same login at the same time. After locking, we verify that the login name hasn't been taken by another user. If the name hasn't been taken, we generate a new unique ID for the user, add the login name to the mapping of login names to user IDs, and then create the user's HASH.

> **SENSITIVE USER INFORMATION** Because the user HASH will be fetched countless times for rendering a template, or for returning directly as a response to an API request, we don't store sensitive user information in this HASH. For now, we'll assume that hashed passwords, email addresses, and more are stored at other keys, or in a different database entirely.

We've finished creating the user and setting all of the necessary meta-information about them. From here, the next step in building our Twitter work-alike is the status message itself.

8.1.2　Status messages

As we mentioned earlier, whereas user profiles store information about an individual, the ideas that people are trying to express are stored in status messages. As was the case with user information, we'll store status message information inside a HASH.

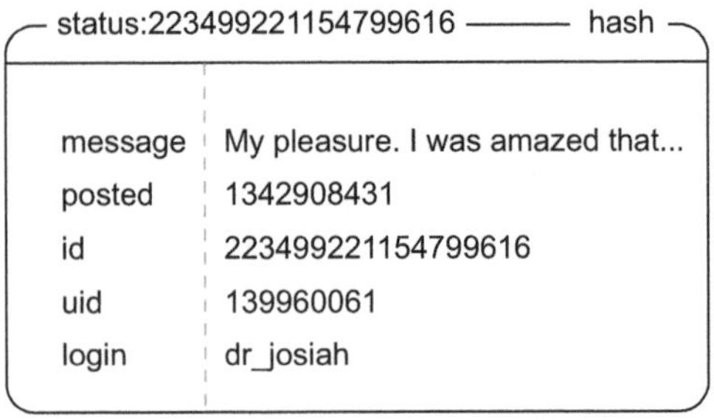

In addition to the message itself, we'll store when the status message was posted, the user ID and login of the user who posted it (so that if we have a status object, we don't need to fetch the user object of the poster to discover their login name), and any additional information that should be stored about the status message. Figure 8.2 shows an example status message.

And that's everything necessary for a basic status message. The code to create such a status message can be seen in the next listing.

Figure 8.2   Example status message stored in a HASH

Listing 8.2   How to create a status message HASH

```
def create_status(conn, uid, message, **data):
    pipeline = conn.pipeline(True)
    pipeline.hget('user:%s'%uid, 'login')
    pipeline.incr('status:id:')
    login, id = pipeline.execute()

    if not login:
        return None

    data.update({
        'message': message,
        'posted': time.time(),
        'id': id,
        'uid': uid,
        'login': login,
    })
    pipeline.hmset('status:%s'%id, data)
    pipeline.hincrby('user:%s'%uid, 'posts')
    pipeline.execute()
    return id
```

Create a new ID for the status message.

Get the user's login name from their user ID.

Verify that we have a proper user account before posting.

Record the fact that a status message has been posted.

Prepare and set the data for the status message.

Return the ID of the newly created status message.

There isn't anything surprising going on in the status creation function. The function fetches the login name of the user, gets a new ID for the status message, and then combines everything together and stores it as a HASH.

We'll talk about making the status message visible to followers in section 8.4, so sit tight for now, as we now examine the most commonly used view into lists of status messages: a user's *home timeline*.

8.2   Home timeline

When people visit Twitter after logging in, the first view that they see is what's referred to as their *home timeline*. This is a list of status messages that have been posted by the user and all of the people they're following. As the primary entry point to what users see, this data should be as easy to retrieve as possible.

In this section, we'll talk about the data to be stored in the home timeline and how to fetch information to display the home timeline quickly. We'll also talk about other important status message timelines.

As mentioned earlier in this chapter, we want to be able to fetch all of the data required for a given view as quickly as possible. For the home timeline, which will store the list of status messages that have been posted by the people that the current user is following, we'll use a ZSET to store status IDs as ZSET members, with the timestamp of when the message was posted being used as the score. Figure 8.3 shows an example home timeline.

home:139960061	zset
...	...
227138379358277633	1342988984
227140001668935680	1342989371
227143088878014464	1342990107

Figure 8.3 When someone visits their home timeline on a site like Twitter, they see the most recently posted messages that people they follow have written. This information is stored as a ZSET of status ID/timestamp pairs. Timestamp information provides the sort order, and the status ID shows us what information to pull in a second step.

Because the home timeline is just referencing status messages—it doesn't contain the status messages themselves—our function to fetch the most recently posted status messages must also fetch the status message data. The next listing shows the code to fetch a page of messages from the home timeline.

Listing 8.3   A function to fetch a page of recent status messages from a timeline

```
def get_status_messages(conn, uid, timeline='home:', page=1, count=30):
    statuses = conn.zrevrange(
        '%s%s'%(timeline, uid), (page-1)*count, page*count-1)

    pipeline = conn.pipeline(True)
    for id in statuses:
        pipeline.hgetall('status:%s'%id)

    return filter(None, pipeline.execute())
```

Fetch the most recent status IDs in the timeline.

We'll take an optional "timeline" argument, as well as page size and status message counts.

Actually fetch the status messages themselves.

Filter will remove any "missing" status messages that had been previously deleted.

That function will fetch status messages in reverse chronological order from the provided timeline, which defaults to the home timeline.

A second important timeline is the timeline of posts that a user has posted. Where the home timeline includes posts from other people, the user's timeline will include only those posts from the user. These timelines can be seen when visiting a user's profile, and are the primary entry point for finding someone interesting. To fetch a page of statuses from a given user, we can call the same get_messages() function, but we'll pass profile: as the timeline argument in our call.

Now that a user can fetch the home timeline, we should discuss how to manage the list of users that someone is following, and the list of users that are following them.

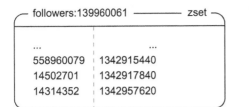

Figure 8.4   To know who's following a user, we store user ID/timestamp pairs in a ZSET. The user IDs are the people who're following that user, and the timestamp is when they started following the user. Similarly, the users that a user is following are stored as a ZSET of user ID/timestamp pairs of the user ID of the person being followed, and the timestamp of when the user followed them.

8.3   *Followers/following lists*

One of the primary services of a platform like Twitter is for users to share their thoughts, ideas, and dreams with others. Following someone means that you're interested in reading about what they're saying, with the hope that others will want to follow you.

In this section, we'll discuss how to manage the lists of users that each user follows, and the users that follow them. We'll also discuss what happens to a user's home timeline when they start or stop following someone.

When we looked at the home and profile timelines in the last section, we stored status IDs and timestamps in a ZSET. To keep a list of followers and a list of those people that a user is following, we'll also store user IDs and timestamps in ZSETs as well, with members being user IDs, and scores being the timestamp of when the user was followed. Figure 8.4 shows an example of the followers and those that a user is following.

As we start or stop following a user, there are following and followers ZSETs that need to be updated, as well as counts in the two user profile HASHes. After those ZSETs and HASHes have been updated, we then need to copy the newly followed user's status message IDs from their profile timeline into our home timeline. This is to ensure that after we've followed someone, we get to see their status messages immediately. The next listing shows the code for following someone.

Listing 8.4   Update the following user's home timeline

```
HOME_TIMELINE_SIZE = 1000
def follow_user(conn, uid, other_uid):
    fkey1 = 'following:%s'%uid
    fkey2 = 'followers:%s'%other_uid

    if conn.zscore(fkey1, other_uid):
        return None

    now = time.time()

    pipeline = conn.pipeline(True)
    pipeline.zadd(fkey1, other_uid, now)
    pipeline.zadd(fkey2, uid, now)
```

Cache the following and followers key names.

If the other_uid is already being followed, return.

Add the uids to the proper following and followers ZSETs.

```
pipeline.zcard(fkey1)
pipeline.zcard(fkey2)
pipeline.zrevrange('profile:%s'%other_uid,
    0, HOME_TIMELINE_SIZE-1, withscores=True)
following, followers, status_and_score = pipeline.execute()[-3:]

pipeline.hset('user:%s'%uid, 'following', following)
pipeline.hset('user:%s'%other_uid, 'followers', followers)
if status_and_score:
    pipeline.zadd('home:%s'%uid, **dict(status_and_score))
pipeline.zremrangebyrank('home:%s'%uid, 0, -HOME_TIMELINE_SIZE-1)

pipeline.execute()
return True
```

Find the size of the following and followers ZSETs.

Update the known size of the following and followers ZSETs in each user's HASH.

Fetch the most recent HOME_TIMELINE_SIZE status messages from the newly followed user's profile timeline.

Update the home timeline of the following user, keeping only the most recent 1000 status messages.

Return that the user was correctly followed.

CONVERTING A LIST OF TUPLES INTO A DICTIONARY   As part of our follow_user() function, we fetched a list of status message IDs along with their timestamp scores. Because this is a sequence of pairs, we can pass them directly to the dict() type, which will create a dictionary of keys and values, as passed.

This function proceeds in the way we described earlier: we add the appropriate user IDs to the following and followers ZSETs, get the size of the following and followers ZSETs, and fetch the recent status message IDs from the followed user's profile time-line. After we've fetched all of the data, we then update counts inside the user profile HASHes, and update the following user's home timeline.

After following someone and reading their status messages for a while, we may get to a point where we decide we don't want to follow them anymore. To stop following someone, we perform essentially the reverse operations of what we've discussed: removing UIDs from followers and following lists, removing status messages, and again updating the followers/following counts. The code to stop following someone is shown in the following listing.

Listing 8.5   A function to stop following a user

```
def unfollow_user(conn, uid, other_uid):
    fkey1 = 'following:%s'%uid
    fkey2 = 'followers:%s'%other_uid

    if not conn.zscore(fkey1, other_uid):
        return None

    pipeline = conn.pipeline(True)
    pipeline.zrem(fkey1, other_uid)
    pipeline.zrem(fkey2, uid)
    pipeline.zcard(fkey1)
    pipeline.zcard(fkey2)
    pipeline.zrevrange('profile:%s'%other_uid,
        0, HOME_TIMELINE_SIZE-1)
    following, followers, statuses = pipeline.execute()[-3:]
```

Cache the following and followers key names.

If the other_uid isn't being followed, return.

Remove the uids from the proper following and followers ZSETs.

Find the size of the following and followers ZSETs.

Fetch the most recent HOME_TIMELINE_SIZE status messages from the user that we stopped following.

Update the known size of the following and followers ZSETs in each user's HASH.

```
pipeline.hset('user:%s'%uid, 'following', following)
pipeline.hset('user:%s'%other_uid, 'followers', followers)
if statuses:
    pipeline.zrem('home:%s'%uid, *statuses)

pipeline.execute()
return True
```

Update the home timeline, removing any status messages from the previously followed user.

Return that the unfollow executed successfully.

In that function, we updated the following and followers lists, updated the followers and following counts, and updated the home timeline to remove status messages that should no longer be there. As of now, that completes all of the steps necessary to start and stop following a user.

> **Exercise: Refilling timelines**
>
> When someone stops following another user, some number of status messages will be removed from the former follower's home timeline. When this happens, we can either say that it's okay that fewer than the desired number of status messages are in the timeline, or we can make an effort to add status messages from the other people that the user is still following. Can you write a function that will add status messages to the user's timeline to keep it full? Hint: You may want to use tasks like we defined in section 6.4 to reduce the time it takes to return from an unfollow call.

> **Exercise: Lists of users**
>
> In addition to the list of users that someone follows, Twitter also supports the ability to create additional named lists of users that include the timeline of posts for just those users. Can you update follow_user() and unfollow_user() to take an optional "list ID" for storing this new information, create functions to create a custom list, and fetch the custom list? Hint: Think of it like a different type of follower. Bonus points: can you also update your function from the "Refilling timelines" exercise?

Now that we can start or stop following a user while keeping the home timeline updated, it's time to see what happens when someone posts a new status update.

8.4   *Posting or deleting a status update*

One of the most fundamental operations on a service like Twitter is posting status messages. People post to share their ideas, and people read because they're interested in what's going on with others. Section 8.1.2 showed how to create a status message as a prerequisite for knowing the types of data that we'll be storing, but didn't show how to get that status message into a profile timeline or the home timeline of the user's followers.

In this section, we'll discuss what happens to a status message when it's posted so it can find its way into the home timelines of that user's followers. We'll also talk about how to delete a status message.

You already know how to create the status message itself, but we now need to get the status message ID into the home timeline of all of our followers. How we should perform this operation will depend on the number of followers that the posting user happens to have. If the user has a relatively small number of followers (say, up to 1,000 or so), we can update their home timelines immediately. But for users with larger number of followers (like 1 million, or even the 25 million that some users have on Twitter), attempting to perform those insertions directly will take longer than is reasonable for a user to wait.

To allow for our call to return quickly, we'll do two things. First, we'll add the status ID to the home timelines of the first 1,000 followers as part of the call that posts the status message. Based on statistics from a site like Twitter, that should handle at least 99.9% of all users who post (Twitter-wide analytics suggest that there are roughly 100,000–250,000 users with more than 1,000 followers, which amounts to roughly .1% of the active user base). This means that only the top .1% of users will need another step.

Second, for those users with more than 1,000 followers, we'll start a deferred task using a system similar to what we built back in section 6.4. The next listing shows the code for pushing status updates to followers.

Listing 8.6   Update a user's profile timeline

```
                    def post_status(conn, uid, message, **data):
If the creation         id = create_status(conn, uid, message, **data)    ◁─┐  Create a status
failed, return.         if not id:                                           │  message using
                            return None                                      │  the earlier
                                                                             │  function.
Get the time that       posted = conn.hget('status:%s'%id, 'posted')
the message was         if not posted:
posted.                     return None                          ─┐  If the post wasn't
                                                                  │  found, return.
                        post = {str(id): float(posted)}
Add the status          conn.zadd('profile:%s'%uid, **post)        Actually push the status message
message to the user's                                              out to the followers of the user.
profile timeline.       syndicate_status(conn, uid, post)    ◁─┘
                        return id
```

Notice that we broke our status updating into two parts. The first part calls the create_status() function from listing 8.2 to actually create the status message, and then adds it to the poster's profile timeline. The second part actually adds the status message to the timelines of the user's followers, which can be seen next.

Listing 8.7   Update a user's followers' home timelines

```
POSTS_PER_PASS = 1000                                    ◁─┐  Only send to
def syndicate_status(conn, uid, post, start=0):            │  1000 users
                                                           │  per pass.
```

Fetch the next group of 1000 followers, starting at the last person to be updated last time.

Add the status to the home timelines of all of the fetched followers, and trim the home timelines so they don't get too big.

```
followers = conn.zrangebyscore('followers:%s'%uid, start, 'inf',
    start=0, num=POSTS_PER_PASS, withscores=True)

pipeline = conn.pipeline(False)
for follower, start in followers:
    pipeline.zadd('home:%s'%follower, **post)
    pipeline.zremrangebyrank(
        'home:%s'%follower, 0, -HOME_TIMELINE_SIZE-1)
pipeline.execute()

if len(followers) >= POSTS_PER_PASS:
    execute_later(conn, 'default', 'syndicate_status',
        [conn, uid, post, start])
```

Iterating through the followers results will update the "start" variable, which we can later pass on to subsequent syndicate_status() calls.

If at least 1000 followers had received an update, execute the remaining updates in a task.

This second function is what actually handles pushing status messages to the first 1,000 followers' home timelines, and starts a delayed task using the API we defined in section 6.4 for followers past the first 1,000. With those new functions, we've now completed the tools necessary to actually post a status update and send it to all of a user's followers.

> ### Exercise: Updating lists
>
> In the last section, I suggested an exercise to build named lists of users. Can you extend the `syndicate_message()` function to also support updating the list timelines from before?

Let's imagine that we posted a status message that we weren't proud of; what would we need to do to delete it?

It turns out that deleting a status message is pretty easy. Before returning the fetched status messages from a user's home or profile timeline in get_messages(), we're already filtering "empty" status messages with the Python filter() function. So to delete a status message, we only need to delete the status message HASH and update the number of status messages posted for the user. The function that deletes a status message is shown in the following listing.

Listing 8.8   A function to delete a previously posted status message

Delete the status message.

```
def delete_status(conn, uid, status_id):
    key = 'status:%s'%status_id
    lock = acquire_lock_with_timeout(conn, key, 1)
    if not lock:
        return None

    if conn.hget(key, 'uid') != str(uid):
        return None

    pipeline = conn.pipeline(True)
    pipeline.delete(key)
    pipeline.zrem('profile:%s'%uid, status_id)
```

Acquire a lock around the status object to ensure that no one else is trying to delete it when we are.

If we didn't get the lock, return.

If the user doesn't match the user stored in the status message, return.

Remove the status message id from the user's profile timeline.

```
pipeline.zrem('home:%s'%uid, status_id)
pipeline.hincrby('user:%s'%uid, 'posts', -1)
pipeline.execute()

release_lock(conn, key, lock)
return True
```

Remove the status message ID from the user's home timeline.

Reduce the number of posted messages in the user information HASH.

While deleting the status message and updating the status count, we also went ahead and removed the message from the user's home timeline and profile timeline. Though this isn't technically necessary, it does allow us to keep both of those timelines a little cleaner without much effort.

> ### Exercise: Cleaning out deleted IDs
>
> As status messages are deleted, "zombie" status message IDs will still be in the home timelines of all followers. Can you clean out these status IDs? Hint: Think about how we sent the messages out in the first place. Bonus points: also handle lists.

Being able to post or delete status messages more or less completes the primary functionality of a Twitter-like social network from a typical user's perspective. But to complete the experience, you may want to consider adding a few other features:

- Private users, along with the ability to request to follow someone
- Favorites (keeping in mind the privacy of a tweet)
- Direct messaging between users
- Replying to messages resulting in conversation flow
- Reposting/retweeting of messages
- The ability to @mention users or #tag ideas
- Keeping a record of who @mentions someone
- Spam and abuse reporting and controls

These additional features would help to round out the functionality of a site like Twitter, but may not be necessary in every situation. Expanding beyond those features that Twitter provides, some social networks have chosen to offer additional functionality that you may want to consider:

- Liking/+1 voting status messages
- Moving status messages around the timeline depending on "importance"
- Direct messaging between a prespecified group of people (like in section 6.5.2)
- Groups where users can post to and/or follow a group timeline (public groups, private groups, or even announcement-style groups)

Now that we've built the last piece of the standard functional API for actually servicing a site like Twitter, let's see what it'd take to build a system for processing streaming API requests.

8.5 *Streaming API*

As development of our social network continues, at some point we'll want to learn more about what's going on—maybe to discover how many posts are made every hour, the most-talked-about topics, or even who's being mentioned all the time. One way of doing this is to make calls to gather this information. Another way is to record this information inside the functions that perform all of the operations. The third way, which we'll explore in this section, is to build our functions to broadcast simple events, which are received and processed by event listeners to analyze the data.

In this section, I'll describe how to build the back end for a streaming API that functions similar to the streaming API offered by Twitter.

Unlike the other parts of the system that we've already built, the streaming API is a different group of functionalities altogether. The functions that we built to support the typical operations of a site like Twitter in the last several sections were meant to execute and complete quickly. On the other hand, a streaming API request is meant to return data over a longer period of time.

Most modern social networks offer the ability to gather information from their system via some sort of API. One advantage that Twitter has shown over the last several years is that by offering real-time events to third parties, those third parties can develop unique and interesting analyses of the data that Twitter itself may not have had the time or interest to develop.

The first step in building a streaming API is understanding what kind of data we'll be processing and producing.

8.5.1 *Data to be streamed*

As people perform a variety of actions within our social network, those actions are seen at the various functions that defined our API. In particular, we spent most of our time building out the ability to follow/unfollow users, and post/delete messages. If we'd built other pieces of our social network, we'd also find a variety of other *events* that occur as the result of user behavior. A streaming API is meant to produce a sequence of these events over time as a way of keeping clients or other services updated about a subset of what's going on across the entire network.

In the process of building a streaming API, a variety of decisions must be made, which can be generally reduced to three major questions:

- Which events should be exposed?
- What access restrictions (if any) should exist?
- What kinds of filtering options should be provided?

For now, I won't answer the second question about access restrictions. That's a question that we need to answer when we're building our social network based on expectations of privacy and system resources. But I'll answer the other two questions.

Because we focused on posting/deleting messages and following/unfollowing users, we should offer at least some of those events. To keep things simple for now, we'll only produce message posting and deletion events. But based on the structures that we create and pass around, adding functionality to support follow/unfollow events or events for other actions that we've added should be easy.

The types of filtering options that we'll provide will overlap significantly with the API features and functionality that Twitter provides on the public side of things. In particular, we'll offer the ability to filter over messages with an equivalent of follow (users), track (keywords), and location filters, in addition to a randomly selected subset of messages, similar to Twitter's *firehose* and *sample* streams.

Now that we know what data we'll have access to, let's start looking at how we'll serve the data.

8.5.2 Serving the data

In preceding sections and chapters, when we showed functions that made calls to Redis, we built on the assumption that we had an existing web server that would be calling these functions at just the right time. In the case of a streaming API, the details of streaming data to a client can be more complicated than just plugging these functions into an existing web service stack. In particular, most web servers operate under the assumption that we'll be returning the entire response to a request at once, but this is definitely not the case with a streaming API.

Responses from a streaming API are received status message by status message as they're produced and matched. Though modern technologies like WebSockets and SPDY can offer incremental data production, or even server-side push messages, the protocols involved are still in the process of being finalized, and client-side support in many programming languages is incomplete. But there is a method of producing incremental content with an HTTP server—sending data using the *chunked* transfer encoding.

In this section, we'll build a simple web server that supports streaming to clients that can handle chunked HTTP responses. This is to support our later sections which will actually implement filtering options for streamed message data.

To build this streaming HTTP web server, we have to delve deeper into the Python programming language. In the past, we've attempted to keep everything to standard functions, and in chapter 6, we even started using generators (that was the code that included `yield`). But here, we'll have to use Python classes. This is primarily because we don't want to have to build an entire web server from scratch, and Python already includes servers that we can mix together to handle all of the difficult parts of web serving. If you've used classes in other languages, you'll be comfortable with Python, because classes in Python are similar. They're meant to encapsulate data, with methods to manipulate the data. In our case, most of the functionality that we want to use is already available in existing libraries; we just need to plug them together.

A STREAMING HTTP SERVER

Within Python we have a series of socket server libraries that can be mixed together to offer varying types of functionality. To start, we'll create a server that uses threads in order to process each incoming request separately. When the server receives a request, the server will create a thread to execute a request handler. This request handler is where we'll perform some initial basic routing for GET and POST HTTP requests. Both the threaded server and the request handler are shown in the next listing.

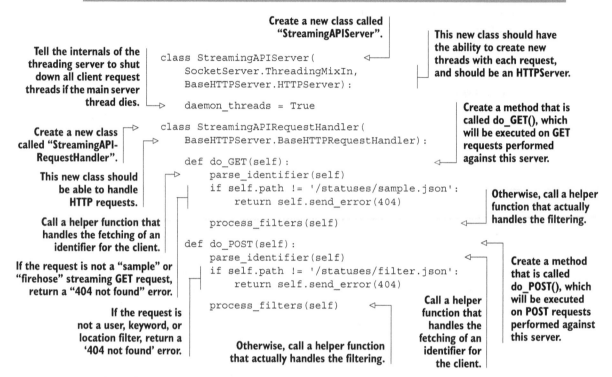

Listing 8.9　Server and request handler for our streaming HTTP server

What we didn't write is the code that actually starts up the server, but we'll get to that in a moment. For now, you can see that we defined a server that created threads on each request. Those threads execute methods on a request handler object, which eventually lead to either do_GET() or do_POST(), which handle the two major types of streaming API requests: filtered and sampled.

To actually run this server, we'll use a bit of Python magic. This magic allows us to later import a module to use these predefined classes, or it allows us to run the module directly in order to start up a streaming API server. The code that lets us both import the module and run it as a daemon can be seen in the next listing.

Before you put these two blocks of code into a file and run them, remember that we're still missing two functions that are called as part of the streaming API server, parse_identifier() and process_filters(), which we'll cover next.

Listing 8.10 The code to actually start and run the streaming HTTP server

Run the block of code below if this module is being run from the command line.

Print an informational line.

Create an instance of the streaming API server listening on localhost port 8080, and use the StreamingAPIRequestHandler to process requests.

```
if __name__ == '__main__':
    server = StreamingAPIServer(
        ('localhost', 8080), StreamingAPIRequestHandler)
    print 'Starting server, use <Ctrl-C> to stop'
    server.serve_forever()
```

Run the server until someone kills it.

IDENTIFYING THE CLIENT

The first of these two functions is a way of fetching identifying information about the client. This basic method extracts an identifier from the request query arguments. For a production scenario, we'd want to perform some amount of client validation of the identifier. Our simple method to parse an identifier from the request can be seen in the next listing.

Listing 8.11 An example function to parse and store the client identifier

If there were query arguments as part of the request, process them.

Extract the query portion from the path and update the path.

Fetch the list of query arguments with the name "identifier."

Set the identifier and query arguments to be placeholder values.

```
def parse_identifier(handler):
    handler.identifier = None
    handler.query = {}
    if '?' in handler.path:
        handler.path, _, query = handler.path.partition('?')
        handler.query = urlparse.parse_qs(query)
        identifier = handler.query.get('identifier') or [None]
        handler.identifier = identifier[0]
```

Parse the query.

Use the first identifier passed.

That function shouldn't do anything surprising; we set some initial values for the query arguments (if we want to use them later) and the identifier, parse the query arguments, and then store the identifier from the query if it was available.

HANDLING HTTP STREAMING

There's one final piece to the HTTP server portion of our request—actually sending the filtered responses. To prepare to send these filtered messages one by one, we first need to verify the requests are valid. Assuming that everything is okay, we must then send to the client the notification that we'll be entering an HTTP mode called *chunked transfer encoding*, which will allow us to send messages one at a time as they come in. The function that performs this validation and the actual transfer of streamed messages to the client is shown next.

Listing 8.12 A function that will verify the request and stream data to the client

Keep a listing of filters that need arguments.

Return an error if an identifier was not provided by the client.

```
FILTERS = ('track', 'filter', 'location')
def process_filters(handler):
    id = handler.identifier
    if not id:
        return handler.send_error(401, "identifier missing")
```

Fetch the method; should be one of "sample" or "filter".

```python
method = handler.path.rsplit('/')[-1].split('.')[0]
name = None
args = None
if method == 'filter':
    data = cgi.FieldStorage(
        fp=handler.rfile,
        headers=handler.headers,
        environ={'REQUEST_METHOD':'POST',
                 'CONTENT_TYPE':handler.headers['Content-Type'],
        })
```

If this is a filtering method, we need to fetch the arguments.

Parse the POST request to discover the type and arguments to the filter.

Fetch any of the filters provided by the client request.

```python
        for name in data:
            if name in FILTERS:
                args = data.getfirst(name).lower().split(',')
                break
```

If there were no filters specified, return an error.

```python
        if not args:
            return handler.send_error(401, "no filter provided")
        else:
            args = handler.query
```

Finally, return a response to the client, informing them that they will be receiving a streaming response.

For sample requests, pass the query arguments as the "args".

```python
handler.send_response(200)
handler.send_header('Transfer-Encoding', 'chunked')
handler.end_headers()
```

Use a Python list as a holder for a pass-by-reference variable, which will allow us to tell the content filter to stop receiving messages.

```python
quit = [False]
for item in filter_content(id, method, name, args, quit):
    try:
        handler.wfile.write('%X\r\n%s\r\n'%(len(item), item))
    except socket.error:
        quit[0] = True
if not quit[0]:
    handler.wfile.write('0\r\n\r\n')
```

Iterate over the results of the filter.

Send the pre-encoded response to the client using the chunked encoding.

Send the "end of chunks" message to the client if we haven't already disconnected.

If sending to the client caused an error, then we need to tell the subscriber to unsubscribe and shut down.

A few details in this function are tricky, but the basic idea is that we make sure that we have an identifier for the client and fetch the filtering arguments for the specific calls. If everything is okay, we then announce to the client that we'll be streaming responses and pass the actual filtering off to a generator, which will produce the sequence of messages that match the filter criteria.

And that's it for the streaming HTTP server. In the next section, we'll build the methods that will filter messages that pass through the system.

8.5.3   *Filtering streamed messages*

So far we've built a server to serve the streamed messages; now it's time to filter through the messages for streaming. We filter the messages so that a client making a request only sees the messages they're interested in. Though our social network may not have a lot of traffic, sites like Twitter, Facebook, or even Google+ will see tens to hundreds of thousands of events every second. And for both third parties and ourselves, the cost of bandwidth to send all of that information can be quite high, so only sending messages that match up is important.

In this section, we'll write functions and classes that will filter posted messages to be streamed to clients. These filters will plug into the streaming web server we wrote in section 8.5.2. As I mentioned at the beginning of section 8.5, we'll support random sampling of all messages and access to the full firehose, as well as filtering for specific users, words, and the location of messages.

As mentioned way back in chapter 3, we'll use Redis PUBLISH and SUBSCRIBE to implement at least part of the streaming functionality. More specifically, when users post messages, we'll PUBLISH the posted message information to a channel in Redis. Our filters will SUBSCRIBE to that same channel, receive the message, and yield messages that match the filters back to the web server for sending to the client.

UPDATING STATUS MESSAGE POSTING AND DELETION

Before we get ahead of ourselves, let's first update our message posting function from section 8.1.2 and message deletion function from section 8.4 to start producing messages to filter. We'll start with posting in the next listing, which shows that we've added a line to our function that sends messages out to be filtered.

Listing 8.13 Updated `create_status()` from listing 8.2 to support streaming filters

```
def create_status(conn, uid, message, **data):
    pipeline = conn.pipeline(True)
    pipeline.hget('user:%s'%uid, 'login')
    pipeline.incr('status:id:')
    login, id = pipeline.execute()

    if not login:
        return None

    data.update({
        'message': message,
        'posted': time.time(),
        'id': id,
        'uid': uid,
        'login': login,
    })
    pipeline.hmset('status:%s'%id, data)
    pipeline.hincrby('user:%s'%uid, 'posts')
    pipeline.publish('streaming:status:', json.dumps(data))    ⟵  The added line to
    pipeline.execute()                                              send a message to
    return id                                                       streaming filters
```

All it took was one more line to add streaming support on the posting side. But what about deletion? The update to status message deletion is shown in the following listing.

Listing 8.14 Updated `delete_status()` from listing 8.8 to support streaming filters

```
def delete_status(conn, uid, status_id):
    key = 'status:%s'%status_id
    lock = acquire_lock_with_timeout(conn, key, 1)
```

```
    if not lock:
        return None

    if conn.hget(key, 'uid') != str(uid):
        return None

    pipeline = conn.pipeline(True)
    status = conn.hgetall(key)
    status['deleted'] = True
    pipeline.publish('streaming:status:', json.dumps(status))
    pipeline.delete(key)
    pipeline.zrem('profile:%s'%uid, status_id)
    pipeline.zrem('home:%s'%uid, status_id)
    pipeline.hincrby('user:%s'%uid, 'posts', -1)
    pipeline.execute()

    release_lock(conn, key, lock)
    return True
```

Fetch the status message so that streaming filters can perform the same filters to determine whether the deletion should be passed to the client.

Mark the status message as deleted.

Publish the deleted status message to the stream.

At first glance, you're probably wondering why we'd want to send the entire status message that's to be deleted to the channel for filtering. Conceptually, we should only need to send message-deleted information to clients that received the status message when it was posted. If we perform the same filtering on deleted messages as we do on newly posted messages, then we can always send message-deleted notifications to those clients that would've received the original message. This ensures that we don't need to keep a record of the status IDs for messages sent to all clients, which simplifies our server and reduces memory use.

RECEIVING STREAMED MESSAGES FOR FILTERING

Now that we're sending information about status messages being posted and deleted to a channel in Redis, we only need to subscribe to that channel to start receiving messages to filter. As was the case in chapter 3, we'll need to construct a special pubsub object in order to subscribe to a channel. When we've subscribed to the channel, we'll perform our filtering, and produce one of two different messages depending on whether the message was posted or deleted. The code for handling these operations is next.

Listing 8.15   A function to receive and process streamed messages

Create the filter that will determine whether a message should be sent to the client.

Use our automatic connection decorator from chapter 5.

```
@redis_connection('social-network')
def filter_content(conn, id, method, name, args, quit):
    match = create_filters(id, method, name, args)

    pubsub = conn.pubsub()
    pubsub.subscribe(['streaming:status:'])

    for item in pubsub.listen():
        message = item['data']
        decoded = json.loads(message)

        if match(decoded):
```

Prepare the subscription.

Receive messages from the subscription.

Get the status message information from the subscription structure.

Check if the status message matched the filter.

For deleted messages, send a special "deleted" placeholder for the message.

For matched status messages that are not deleted, send the message itself.

```
        if decoded.get('deleted'):
            yield json.dumps({
                'id': decoded['id'], 'deleted': True})
        else:
            yield message
    if quit[0]:
        break

pubsub.reset()
```

If the web server no longer has a connection to the client, stop filtering messages.

Reset the Redis connection to ensure that the Redis server clears its outgoing buffers if this wasn't fast enough.

As I said before, this function needs to subscribe to a channel in Redis in order to receive posted/deleted notifications for status messages. But it also needs to handle cases where the streaming client has disconnected, and it needs to properly clean up the connection if Redis has been trying to send it too much data.

As we covered in chapter 3, there's a Redis server setting to determine the maximum outgoing buffer for subscriptions to support. To ensure that our Redis server stays up even under heavy load, we'll probably want to set `client-output-buffer-limit pubsub` to lower than the default 32 megabytes per connection. Where to set the limit will depend on how many clients we expect to support and how much other data is in Redis.

FILTERING MESSAGES

At this point we've built every other layer; it now remains to actually write filtering. I know, there was a lot of build-up, but you may be surprised to find out that actually filtering messages isn't difficult for any of our cases. To create filters, we'll first define our `create_filters()` function in listing 8.16, which will delegate off to one of a variety of filtering classes, depending on the filter that we want to build. We'll assume that clients are sending reasonable arguments, but if you're considering using any of this in a production scenario, you'll want to add validation and verification.

> **Listing 8.16 A factory function to dispatch to the actual filter creation**

```
def create_filters(id, method, name, args):
    if method == 'sample':
        return SampleFilter(id, args)
    elif name == 'track':
        return TrackFilter(args)
    elif name == 'follow':
        return FollowFilter(args)
    elif name == 'location':
        return LocationFilter(args)
    raise Exception("Unknown filter")
```

For the "sample" method, we don't need to worry about names, just the arguments.

For the "filter" method, we actually worry about which of the filters we want to apply, so return the specific filters for them.

If no filter matches, then raise an exception.

Nothing surprising there: we're distinguishing the different kinds of filters. The first filter we'll create will be the `sample` filter, which will actually implement the functionality of the Twitter-style `firehose`, `gardenhose`, and `spritzer` access levels, and anything in between. The implementation of the sampling filter is shown next.

Listing 8.17   The function to handle `firehose`, `gardenhose`, **and** `spritzer`

The "args" parameter is actually a dictionary based on the parameters passed as part of the GET request.

We're defining a filter class called "SampleFilter", which is created by passing "id" and "args" parameters.

We use the "id" parameter to randomly choose a subset of IDs, the count of which is determined by the "percent" argument passed.

We'll use a Python set to allow us to quickly determine whether a status message matches our criteria.

If we create a specially named method called "__call__" on an instance, it will be called if the instance is used like a function.

To filter status messages, we fetch the status ID, find its value modulo 100, and return whether it's in the status IDs that we want to accept.

```python
def SampleFilter(id, args):
    percent = int(args.get('percent', ['10'])[0], 10)
    ids = range(100)
    shuffler = random.Random(id)
    shuffler.shuffle(ids)
    keep = set(ids[:max(percent, 1)])

    def check(status):
        return (status['id'] % 100) in keep
    return check
```

As you can see, we started using classes again, primarily because we need to encapsulate data and behavior together. This first class that defines sampling does one interesting thing—it uses a random number generator seeded with the user-provided identifier to choose the IDs of status messages that it should accept. This allows the sampling filters to receive a `deleted` notification for a message, even if the client had disconnected (as long as the client reconnected before the delete notification came through). We use Python sets here to quickly determine whether the ID modulo 100 is in the group that we want to accept, as Python sets offer O(1) lookup time, compared to O(n) for a Python list.

Continuing on, we'll now build the `track` filter, which will allow users to track words or phrases in status messages. Similar to our sample filter in listing 8.17, we'll use a class to encapsulate the data and filtering functionality together. The filter class definition is shown in the following listing.

Listing 8.18   A filter that matches groups of words that are posted in status messages

We'll split words in the message on whitespace.

Then we'll iterate over all of the groups.

The filter has been provided with a list of word groups, and the filter matches if a message has all of the words in any of the groups.

We'll only keep groups that have at least 1 word.

If all of the words in any of the groups match, we'll accept the message with this filter.

```python
def TrackFilter(list_of_strings):
    groups = []
    for group in list_of_strings:
        group = set(group.lower().split())
        if group:
            groups.append(group)

    def check(status):
        message_words = set(status['message'].lower().split())
        for group in groups:
            if len(group & message_words) == len(group):
                return True
        return False
    return check
```

About the only interesting thing about the tracking filter is to make sure that if someone wants to match a group of words, the filter matches *all* of the words in the message and not just *some* of them. We again use Python sets, which, like Redis SETs, offer the ability to calculate intersections.

Moving on to the `follow` filter, we're trying to match status messages that were posted by one of a group of users, or where one of the users is mentioned in the message. The class that implements user matching is shown here.

Listing 8.19   Messages posted by or mentioning any one of a list of users

We'll match login names against posters and messages.

```
def FollowFilter(names):
    names = set()
    for name in names:
        names.add('@' + name.lower().lstrip('@'))

    def check(status):
        message_words = set(status['message'].lower().split())
        message_words.add('@' + status['login'].lower())

        return message_words & names
    return check
```

Store all names consistently as '@username'.

Construct a set of words from the message and the poster's name.

Consider the message a match if any of the usernames provided match any of the whitespace-separated words in the message.

As before, we continue to use Python sets as a fast way to check whether a name is in the set of names that we're looking for, or whether any of the names to match are also contained in a status message.

We finally get to the location filter. This filter is different from the others in that we didn't explicitly talk about adding location information to our status messages. But because of the way we wrote our `create_status()` and `post_status()` functions to take additional optional keyword arguments, we can add additional information without altering our status creation and posting functions. The location filter for this optional data is shown next.

Listing 8.20   Messages within boxes defined by ranges of latitudes and longitudes

We'll create a set of boxes that define the regions that should return messages.

```
def LocationFilter(list_of_boxes):
    boxes = []
    for start in xrange(0, len(list_of_boxes)-3, 4):
        boxes.append(map(float, list_of_boxes[start:start+4]))

    def check(self, status):
        location = status.get('location')
        if not location:
            return False

        lat, lon = map(float, location.split(','))
        for box in self.boxes:
```

Try to fetch "location" data from a status message.

If the message has no location information, then it can't be inside the boxes.

Otherwise, extract the latitude and longitude of the location.

To match one of the boxes, we need to iterate over all boxes.

```
                   if (box[1] <= lat <= box[3] and
                       box[0] <= lon <= box[2]):
                       return True
                   return False
               return check
```

If the message status location is within the required latitude and longitude range, then the status message matches the filter.

About the only thing that may surprise you about this particular filter is how we're preparing the boxes for filtering. We expect that requests will provide location boxes as comma-separated sequences of numbers, where each chunk of four numbers defines latitude and longitude ranges (minimum longitude, minimum latitude, maximum longitude, maximum latitude—the same order as Twitter's API).

With all of our filters built, a working web server, and the back-end API for everything else, it's now up to you to get traffic!

8.6   *Summary*

In this chapter, we've built the majority of functionality that makes a site like Twitter work. Though these structures won't scale to the extent that Twitter does, the methods used can be used to build a small social network easily. With a front end for users to interact with, you can start your own social network with your friends!

If there's one thing that you should take away from this chapter, it's that even immensely popular websites have functionality that can be built with the tools available inside of Redis.

In the upcoming chapters 9 through 11, we'll look into methods to help reduce memory use, methods to help scaling Redis read and write loads, and scripting Redis to simplify (and sometimes help scale) applications. These things will help to scale Redis applications, like our social network, beyond expected single-machine limits. Our first step down this path is chapter 9, where I'll show you how to reduce Redis's memory use.

Part 3

Next steps

In these final chapters, you'll learn about common pitfalls that many Redis users encounter (reducing memory use, scaling performance, and scripting with Lua), as well as how to solve those issues with standard techniques.

Reducing memory use

In this chapter, we'll cover three important methods to help reduce your memory use in Redis. By reducing the amount of memory you use in Redis, you can reduce the time it takes to create or load a snapshot, rewrite or load an append-only file, reduce slave synchronization time,[1] and store more data in Redis without additional hardware.

We'll begin this chapter by discussing how the use of short data structures in Redis can result in a more efficient representation of the data. We'll then discuss how to apply a concept called *sharding* to help make some larger structures small.[2] Finally, we'll talk about packing fixed-length data into STRINGs for even greater memory savings.

---

[1] Snapshots, append-only file rewriting, and slave synchronization are all discussed in chapter 4.

[2] Our use of sharding here is primarily driven to reduce memory use on a single server. In chapter 10, we'll apply similar techniques to allow for increased read throughput, write throughput, and memory partitioning across multiple Redis servers.

When used together, these methods helped me to reduce memory use from more than 70 gigabytes, split across three machines, down to under 3 gigabytes on a single machine. As we work through these methods, remember that some of our earlier problems would lend themselves well to these optimizations, which I'll point out when applicable. Let's get started with one of the first and easiest methods to reduce memory use: short structures.

9.1   Short structures

The first method of reducing memory use in Redis is simple: use short structures. For LISTs, SETs, HASHes, and ZSETs, Redis offers a group of configuration options that allows for Redis to store short structures in a more space-efficient manner. In this section, we'll discuss those configuration options, show how to verify that we're getting those optimizations, and discuss some drawbacks to using short structures.

When using short LISTs, HASHes, and ZSETs, Redis can optionally store them using a more compact storage method known as a *ziplist*. A ziplist is an unstructured representation of one of the three types of objects. Rather than storing the doubly linked list, the hash table, or the hash table plus the skiplist as would normally be the case for each of these structures, Redis stores a serialized version of the data, which must be decoded for every read, partially re-encoded for every write, and may require moving data around in memory.

9.1.1   The ziplist representation

To understand why ziplists may be more efficient, we only need to look at the simplest of our structures, the LIST. In a typical doubly linked list, we have structures called *nodes*, which represent each value in the list. Each of these nodes has pointers to the previous and next nodes in the list, as well as a pointer to the string in the node. Each string value is actually stored as three parts: an integer representing the length, an integer representing the number of remaining free bytes, and the string itself followed by a null character. An example of this in figure 9.1 shows the three string values "one", "two", and "ten" as part of a larger linked list.

Ignoring a few details (which only make linked lists look worse), each of these three strings that are each three characters long will actually take up space for three pointers, two integers (the length and remaining bytes in the value), plus the string and an extra byte. On a 32-bit platform, that's 21 bytes of overhead to store 3 actual bytes of data (remember, this is an underestimate of what's actually stored).

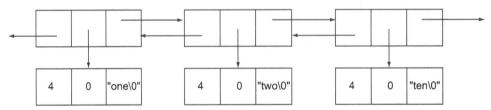

Figure 9.1   How long LISTs are stored in Redis

On the other hand, the ziplist representation will store a sequence of length, length, string elements. The first length is the size of the previous entry (for easy scanning in both directions), the second length is the size of the current entry, and the string is the stored data itself. There are some other details about what these lengths really mean in practice, but for these three example strings, the lengths will be 1 byte long, for 2 bytes of overhead per entry in this example. By not storing additional pointers and metadata, the ziplist can cut down overhead from 21 bytes each to roughly 2 bytes (in this example).

Let's see how we can ensure that we're using the compact ziplist encoding.

USING THE ZIPLIST ENCODING

In order to ensure that these structures are only used when necessary to reduce memory, Redis includes six configuration options, shown in the following listing, for determining when the ziplist representation will be used for LISTs, HASHes, and ZSETs.

Listing 9.1 Configuration options for the ziplist representation of different structures

```
list-max-ziplist-entries 512          Limits for ziplist
list-max-ziplist-value 64             use with LISTs.

hash-max-ziplist-entries 512
hash-max-ziplist-value 64

zset-max-ziplist-entries 128          Limits for ziplist
zset-max-ziplist-value 64             use with ZSETs.
```

Limits for ziplist use with HASHes (previous versions of Redis used a different name and encoding for this).

The basic configuration options for LISTs, HASHes, and ZSETs are all similar, composed of -max-ziplist-entries settings and -max-ziplist-value settings. Their semantics are essentially identical in all three cases. The entries settings tell us the maximum number of items that are allowed in the LIST, HASH, or ZSET for them to be encoded as a ziplist. The value settings tell us how large in bytes each individual entry can be. If either of these limits are exceeded, Redis will convert the LIST, HASH, or ZSET into the nonziplist structure (thus increasing memory).

If we're using an installation of Redis 2.6 with the default configuration, Redis should have default settings that are the same as what was provided in listing 9.1. Let's play around with ziplist representations of a simple LIST object by adding some items and checking its representation, as shown in the next listing.

Listing 9.2 How to determine whether a structure is stored as a ziplist

We can discover information about a particular object with the "debug object" command.

Let's start by pushing four items onto a LIST.

The information we're looking for is the "encoding" information, which tells us that this is a ziplist, which is using 24 bytes of memory.

```
>>> conn.rpush('test', 'a', 'b', 'c', 'd')
4
>>> conn.debug_object('test')
{'encoding': 'ziplist', 'refcount': 1, 'lru_seconds_idle': 20,
'lru': 274841, 'at': '0xb6c9f120', 'serializedlength': 24,
'type': 'Value'}
```

| Let's push four more items onto the LIST. | ```
>>> conn.rpush('test', 'e', 'f', 'g', 'h')
8
>>> conn.debug_object('test')
{'encoding': 'ziplist', 'refcount': 1, 'lru_seconds_idle': 0,
 'lru': 274846, 'at': '0xb6c9f120', 'serializedlength': 36,
 'type': 'Value'}
``` | |

We still have a ziplist, and its size grew to 36 bytes (which is exactly 2 bytes overhead, 1 byte data, for each of the 4 items we just pushed).

```
>>> conn.rpush('test', 65*'a')
9
```

While the serialized length went down, for nonziplist encodings (except for the special encoding for SETs), this number doesn't represent the amount of actual memory used by the structure.

```
>>> conn.debug_object('test')
{'encoding': 'linkedlist', 'refcount': 1, 'lru_seconds_idle': 10,
 'lru': 274851, 'at': '0xb6c9f120', 'serializedlength': 30,
 'type': 'Value'}
>>> conn.rpop('test')
'aaaaaaaaaaaaaaaaaaaaaaaaaaaaaaaaaaaaaaaaaaaaaaaaaaaaaaaaaaaaaaaaaaaaa'
>>> conn.debug_object('test')
{'encoding': 'linkedlist', 'refcount': 1, 'lru_seconds_idle': 0,
 'lru': 274853, 'at': '0xb6c9f120', 'serializedlength': 17,
 'type': 'Value'}
```

When we push an item bigger than what was allowed for the encoding, the LIST gets converted from the ziplist encoding to a standard linked list.

After a ziplist is converted to a regular structure, it doesn't get re-encoded as a ziplist if the structure later meets the criteria.

With the new DEBUG OBJECT command at our disposal, discovering whether an object is stored as a ziplist can be helpful to reduce memory use.

You'll notice that one structure is obviously missing from the special ziplist encoding, the SET. SETs also have a compact representation, but different semantics and limits, which we'll cover next.

9.1.2   *The intset encoding for SETs*

Like the ziplist for LISTs, HASHes, and ZSETs, there's also a compact representation for short SETs. If our SET members can all be interpreted as base-10 integers within the range of our platform's signed long integer, and our SET is short enough (we'll get to that in a moment), Redis will store our SET as a sorted array of integers, or *intset.*

By storing a SET as a sorted array, not only do we have low overhead, but all of the standard SET operations can be performed quickly. But how big is too big? The next listing shows the configuration option for defining an intset's maximum size.

> **Listing 9.3   Configuring the maximum size of the intset encoding for SETs**

```
set-max-intset-entries 512
```

Limits for intset use with SETs

As long as we keep our SETs of integers smaller than our configured size, Redis will use the intset representation to reduce data size. The following listing shows what happens when an intset grows to the point of being too large.
```

Listing 9.4   When an intset grows to be too large, it's represented as a hash table.

Let's add 500 items to the set and see that it's still encoded as an intset.

```
>>> conn.sadd('set-object', *range(500))
500
>>> conn.debug_object('set-object')
{'encoding': 'intset', 'refcount': 1, 'lru_seconds_idle': 0,
'lru': 283116, 'at': '0xb6d1a1c0', 'serializedlength': 1010,
'type': 'Value'}
>>> conn.sadd('set-object', *range(500, 1000))
500
>>> conn.debug_object('set-object')
{'encoding': 'hashtable', 'refcount': 1, 'lru_seconds_idle': 0,
'lru': 283118, 'at': '0xb6d1a1c0', 'serializedlength': 2874,
'type': 'Value'}
```

When we push it over our configured 512-item limit, the intset is translated into a hash table representation.

Earlier, in the introduction to section 9.1, I mentioned that to read or update part of an object that uses the compact ziplist representation, we may need to decode the entire ziplist, and may need to move in-memory data around. For these reasons, reading and writing large ziplist-encoded structures can reduce performance. Intset-encoded SETs also have similar issues, not so much due to encoding and decoding the data, but again because we need to move data around when performing insertions and deletions. Next, we'll examine some performance issues when operating with long ziplists.

9.1.3   *Performance issues for long ziplists and intsets*

As our structures grow beyond the ziplist and intset limits, they're automatically converted into their more typical underlying structure types. This is done primarily because manipulating the compact versions of these structures can become slow as they grow longer.

For a firsthand look at how this happens, let's start by updating our setting for list-max-ziplist-entries to 110,000. This setting is a lot larger than we'd ever use in practice, but it does help to highlight the issue. After that setting is updated and Redis is restarted, we'll benchmark Redis to discover performance issues that can happen when long ziplist-encoded LISTs are used.

To benchmark the behavior of long ziplist-encoded LISTs, we'll write a function that creates a LIST with a specified number of elements. After the LIST is created, we'll repeatedly call the RPOPLPUSH command to move an item from the right end of the LIST to the left end. This will give us a lower bound on how expensive commands can be on very long ziplist-encoded LISTs. This benchmarking function is shown in the next listing.

Listing 9.5   Our code to benchmark varying sizes of ziplist-encoded LISTs

We'll parameterize everything so that we can measure performance in a variety of ways. →

Start by deleting the named key to ensure that we only benchmark exactly what we intend to.

Initialize the LIST by pushing our desired count of numbers onto the right end.

Each call will result in popping the rightmost item from the LIST, pushing it to the left end of the same LIST.

```
def long_ziplist_performance(conn, key, length, passes, psize):
    conn.delete(key)
    conn.rpush(key, *range(length))
    pipeline = conn.pipeline(False)

    t = time.time()
    for p in xrange(passes):
        for pi in xrange(psize):
            pipeline.rpoplpush(key, key)
        pipeline.execute()

    return (passes * psize) / (time.time() - t or .001)
```

Prepare a pipeline so that we are less affected by network round-trip times.

Start the timer ←

We'll perform a number of pipeline executions provided by passes.

Each pipeline execution will include psize actual calls to RPOPLPUSH.

Execute the psize calls to RPOPLPUSH.

Calculate the number of calls per second that are performed.

As mentioned before, this code creates a LIST of a given size and then executes a number of RPOPLPUSH commands in pipelines. By computing the number of calls to RPOPL-PUSH divided by the amount of time it took, we can calculate a number of operations per second that can be executed on ziplist-encoded LISTs of a given size. Let's run this with steadily increasing list sizes to see how long ziplists can reduce performance.

Listing 9.6   As ziplist-encoded LISTs grow, we can see performance drop

```
>>> long_ziplist_performance(conn, 'list', 1, 1000, 100)
52093.558416505381
>>> long_ziplist_performance(conn, 'list', 100, 1000, 100)
51501.154762768667
>>> long_ziplist_performance(conn, 'list', 1000, 1000, 100)
49732.490843316067
>>> long_ziplist_performance(conn, 'list', 5000, 1000, 100)
43424.056529592635
>>> long_ziplist_performance(conn, 'list', 10000, 1000, 100)
36727.062573334966
>>> long_ziplist_performance(conn, 'list', 50000, 1000, 100)
16695.140684975777
>>> long_ziplist_performance(conn, 'list', 100000, 500, 100)
553.10821080054586
```

With lists encoded as ziplists at 1000 entries or smaller, Redis is still able to perform around 50,000 operations per second or better.

But as lists encoded as ziplists grow to 5000 or more, performance starts to drop off as memory copy costs start reducing performance.

When we hit 50,000 entries in a ziplist, performance has dropped significantly.

And when we hit 100,000 entries, ziplists are effectively unusable.

At first glance, you may be thinking that this isn't so bad even when you let a ziplist grow to a few thousand elements. But this shows only a single example operation, where all we're doing is taking items off of the right end and pushing them to the left end. The ziplist encoding can find the right or left end of a sequence quickly (though shifting all of the items over for the insert is what slows us down), and for this small example we can exploit our CPU caches. But when scanning through a list for a particular value, like our autocomplete example from section 6.1, or fetching/updating individual fields of a HASH, Redis will have to decode many individual entries, and CPU caches won't be as effective. As a point of data, replacing our RPOPLPUSH command with a call to LINDEX that gets an element in the middle of the LIST shows performance at roughly half the number of operations per second as our RPOPLPUSH call when LISTs are at least 5,000 items long. Feel free to try it for yourself.

If you keep your max ziplist sizes in the 500–2,000 item range, and you keep the max item size under 128 bytes or so, you should get reasonable performance. I personally try to keep max ziplist sizes to 1,024 elements with item sizes at 64 bytes or smaller. For many uses of HASHes that we've used so far, these limits should let you keep memory use down, and performance high.

As you develop solutions to problems outside of our examples, remember that if you can keep your LIST, SET, HASH, and ZSET sizes small, you can help keep your memory use low, which can let you use Redis for a wider variety of problems.

> **KEEPING KEY NAMES SHORT** One thing that I haven't mentioned before is the use of minimizing the length of keys, both in the key portion of all values, as well as keys in HASHes, members of SETs and ZSETs, and entries in LISTs. The longer all of your strings are, the more data needs to be stored. Generally speaking, whenever it's possible to store a relatively abbreviated piece of information like user:joe as a key or member, that's preferable to storing username:joe, or even joe if user or username is implied. Though in some cases it may not make a huge difference, if you're storing millions or billions of entries, those extra few megabytes or gigabytes may be useful later.

Now that you've seen that short structures in Redis can be used to reduce memory use, in the next section we'll talk about sharding large structures to let us gain the benefits of the ziplist and intset optimizations for more problems.

9.2   *Sharded structures*

Sharding is a well-known technique that has been used to help many different databases scale to larger data storage and processing loads. Basically, sharding takes your data, partitions it into smaller pieces based on some simple rules, and then sends the data to different locations depending on which partition the data had been assigned to.

In this section, we'll talk about applying the concept of sharding to HASHes, SETs, and ZSETs to support a subset of their standard functionality, while still letting us use the small structures from section 9.1 to reduce memory use. Generally, instead of storing value X in key Y, we'll store X in key Y:<shardid>.

> **SHARDING LISTS** Sharding LISTs without the use of Lua scripting is difficult, which is why we omit it here. When we introduce scripting with Lua in chapter 11, we'll build a sharded LIST implementation that supports blocking and nonblocking pushes and pops from both ends.

SHARDING ZSETS   Unlike sharded HASHes and SETs, where essentially all operations can be supported with a moderate amount of work (or even LISTs with Lua scripting), commands like ZRANGE, ZRANGEBYSCORE, ZRANK, ZCOUNT, ZREM-RANGE, ZREMRANGEBYSCORE, and more require operating on all of the shards of a ZSET to calculate their final result. Because these operations on sharded ZSETs violate almost all of the expectations about how quickly a ZSET should perform with those operations, sharding a ZSET isn't necessarily that useful, which is why we essentially omit it here.

If you need to keep full information for a large ZSET, but you only really perform queries against the top- or bottom-scoring X, you can shard your ZSET in the same way we shard HASHes in section 9.2.1: keeping auxiliary top/bottom scoring ZSETs, which you can update with ZADD/ZREMRANGEBYRANK to keep limited (as we've done previously in chapters 2 and 4–8).

You could also use sharded ZSETs as a way of reducing single-command latencies if you have large search indexes, though discovering the final highest- and lowest-scoring items would take a potentially long series of ZUNIONSTORE/ZREMRANGEBYRANK pairs.

When sharding structures, we can make a decision to either support all of the functionality of a single structure or only a subset of the standard functionality. For the sake of simplicity, when we shard structures in this book, we'll only implement a subset of the functionality offered by the standard structures, because to implement the full functionality can be overwhelming (from both computational and code-volume perspectives). Even though we only implement a subset of the functionality, we'll use these sharded structures to offer memory reductions to existing problems, or to solve new problems more efficiently than would otherwise be possible.

The first structure we'll talk about sharding is the HASH.

9.2.1 *HASHes*

One of the primary uses for HASHes is storing simple key/value pairs in a grouped fashion. Back in section 5.3, we developed a method of mapping IP addresses to locations around the world. In addition to a ZSET that mapped from IP addresses to city IDs, we used a single HASH that mapped from city IDs to information about the city itself. That HASH had more than 370,000 entries using the August 2012 version of the database, which we'll now shard.

To shard a HASH table, we need to choose a method of partitioning our data. Because HASHes themselves have keys, we can use those keys as a source of information to partition the keys. For partitioning our keys, we'll generally calculate a hash function on the key itself that will produce a number. Depending on how many keys we want to fit in a single shard and how many total keys we need to store, we'll calculate the number of shards we need, and use that along with our hash value to determine the shard ID that the data will be stored in.

For numeric keys, we'll assume that the keys will be more or less sequential and tightly packed, and will assign them to a shard ID based on their numeric key value (keeping numerically similar keys in the same shard). The next listing shows our function for calculating a new key for a sharded HASH, given the base key and the HASH key HASH.

> **Listing 9.7   A function to calculate a shard key from a base key and a secondary entry key**

We'll call the shard_key() function with a base HASH name, along with the key to be stored in the sharded HASH, the total number of expected elements, and the desired shard size.

If the value is an integer or a string that looks like an integer, we'll use it directly to calculate the shard ID.

For integers, we assume they are sequentially assigned IDs, so we can choose a shard ID based on the upper "bits" of the numeric ID itself. We also use an explicit base here (necessitating the str() call) so that a key of 010 turns into 10, and not 8.

```
def shard_key(base, key, total_elements, shard_size):
    if isinstance(key, (int, long)) or key.isdigit():
        shard_id = int(str(key), 10) // shard_size
    else:
        shards = 2 * total_elements // shard_size
        shard_id = binascii.crc32(key) % shards
    return "%s:%s"%(base, shard_id)
```

For non-integer keys, we first calculate the total number of shards desired, based on an expected total number of elements and desired shard size.

When we know the number of shards, we hash the key modulo the number of shards.

Finally, we combine the base key with the shard ID we calculated to determine the shard key.

In our function, you'll notice that for non-numeric keys we calculate a CRC32 checksum. We're using CRC32 in this case because it returns a simple integer without additional work, is fast to calculate (much faster than MD5 or SHA1 hashes), and because it'll work well enough for most situations.

> **BEING CONSISTENT ABOUT `total_elements` AND `shard_size`**   When using non-numeric keys to shard on, you'll notice that we use the `total_elements` value to calculate the total number of shards necessary, in addition to the `shard_size` that's used for both numeric and non-numeric keys. These two pieces of information are necessary to keep the total number of shards down. If you were to change either of these numbers, then the number of shards (and thus the shard that any piece of data goes to) will change. Whenever possible, you shouldn't change either of these values, or when you do change them, you should have a process for moving your data from the old data shards to the new data shards (this is generally known as *resharding*).

We'll now use our shard_key() to pick shards as part of two functions that will work like HSET and HGET on sharded hashes in the following listing.

> **Listing 9.8   Sharded HSET and HGET functions**

```
def shard_hset(conn, base, key, value, total_elements, shard_size):
    shard = shard_key(base, key, total_elements, shard_size)
    return conn.hset(shard, key, value)
```

Calculate the shard to store our value in.

Set the value in the shard.

```
def shard_hget(conn, base, key, total_elements, shard_size):
    shard = shard_key(base, key, total_elements, shard_size)       ← Calculate the
    return conn.hget(shard, key)                          ←          shard to fetch
                               Get the value in the shard.          our value from.
```

Nothing too complicated there; we're finding the proper location for the data to be stored or fetched from the HASH and either setting or getting the values. To update our earlier IP-address-to-city lookup calls, we only need to replace one call in each of two functions. The next listing shows just those parts of our earlier functions that need to be updated.

Listing 9.9   Sharded IP lookup functions

```
TOTAL_SIZE = 320000
SHARD_SIZE = 1024                              ⎤ We set the arguments for the sharded
                                               ⎟ calls as global constants to ensure that
def import_cities_to_redis(conn, filename):    ⎦ we always pass the same information.
    for row in csv.reader(open(filename)):
        ...
        shard_hset(conn, 'cityid2city:', city_id,          ⎤ To fetch the data,
            json.dumps([city, region, country]),           ⎟ we need to use the
            TOTAL_SIZE, SHARD_SIZE)                         ⎟ same information
                                                            ⎟ for TOTAL_SIZE
def find_city_by_ip(conn, ip_address):                     ⎟ and SHARD_SIZE
    ...                                                     ⎟ for general
    data = shard_hget(conn, 'cityid2city:', city_id,        ⎦ sharded keys.
        TOTAL_SIZE, SHARD_SIZE)
    return json.loads(data)
```

To set the data, we need to pass the TOTAL_SIZE and SHARD_SIZE information, though in this case TOTAL_SIZE is unused because our IDs are numeric.

On a 64-bit machine, storing the single HASH of all of our cities takes up roughly 44 megabytes. But with these few small changes to shard our data, setting hash-max-ziplist-entries to 1024 and hash-max-ziplist-value to 256 (the longest city/country name in the list is a bit over 150 characters), the sharded HASHes together take up roughly 12 megabytes. That's a 70% reduction in data size, which would allow us to store 3.5 times as much data as before. For shorter keys and values, you can potentially see even greater percentage savings (overhead is larger relative to actual data stored).

STORING STRINGS IN HASHES   If you find yourself storing a lot of relatively short strings or numbers as plain STRING values with consistently named keys like namespace:id, you can store those values in sharded HASHes for significant memory reduction in some cases.

Exercise: Adding other operations

As you saw, getting and setting values in a sharded HASH is easy. Can you add support for sharded HDEL, HINCRBY, and HINCRBYFLOAT operations?

We've just finished sharding large hashes to reduce their memory use. Next, you'll learn how to shard SETs.

9.2.2 *SETs*

One common use of an operation known as *map-reduce* (which I mentioned in chapters 1 and 6) is calculating unique visitors to a website. Rather than waiting until the end of the day to perform that calculation, we could instead keep a live updated count of unique visitors as the day goes on. One method to calculate unique visitors in Redis would use a SET, but a single SET storing many unique visitors would be very large. In this section, we'll shard SETs as a way of building a method to count unique visitors to a website.

To start, we'll assume that every visitor already has a unique identifier similar to the UUIDs that we generated in chapter 2 for our login session cookies. Though we could use these UUIDs directly in our SET as members and as keys to shard using our sharding function from section 9.2.1, we'd lose the benefit of the intset encoding. Assuming that we generated our UUIDs randomly (as we've done in previous chapters), we could instead use the first 15 hexadecimal digits from the UUID as a full key. This should bring up two questions: First, why would we want to do this? And second, why is this enough?

For the first question (why we'd want to do this), UUIDs are basically 128-bit numbers that have been formatted in an easy-to-read way. If we were to store them, we'd be storing roughly 16 bytes (or 36 if we stored them as-is) per unique visitor. But by only storing the first 15 hexadecimal digits[3] turned into a number, we'd only be storing 8 bytes per unique visitor. So we save space up front, which we may be able to use later for other problems. This also lets us use the intset optimization for keeping memory use down.

For the second question (why this is enough), it boils down to what are called *birthday collisions*. Put simply: What are the chances of two 128-bit random identifiers matching in the first 56 bits? Mathematically, we can calculate the chances exactly, and as long as we have fewer than 250 million unique visitors in a given time period (a day in our case), we'll have at most a 1% chance of a single match (so if every day we have 250 million visitors, about once every 100 days we'll have about 1 person not counted). If we have fewer than 25 million unique visitors, then the chance of not counting a user falls to the point where we'd need to run the site for roughly 2,739 years before we'd miss counting a single user.

Now that we've decided to use the first 56 bits from the UUID, we'll build a sharded SADD function, which we'll use as part of a larger bit of code to actually count unique visitors. This sharded SADD function in listing 9.10 will use the same shard key calculation that we used in section 9.2.1, modified to prefix our numeric ID with a non-numeric character for shard ID calculation, since our 56-bit IDs aren't densely packed (as is the assumption for numeric IDs).

---

[3] Another good question is why 56 and not 64 bits? That's because Redis will only use intsets for up to 64-bit signed integers, and the extra work of turning our 64-bit unsigned integer into a signed integer isn't worth it in most situations. If you need the extra precision, check out the Python `struct` module and look at the Q and q format codes.

Listing 9.10 A sharded `SADD` function we'll use as part of a unique visitor counter

```
def shard_sadd(conn, base, member, total_elements, shard_size):
    shard = shard_key(base,
        'x'+str(member), total_elements, shard_size)
    return conn.sadd(shard, member)
```

Shard the member into one of the sharded SETs; remember to turn it into a string because it isn't a sequential ID.

Actually add the member to the shard.

With a sharded `SADD` function, we can now keep unique visitor counts. When we want to count a visitor, we'll first calculate their shorter ID based on the first 56 bits of their session UUID. We'll then determine today's date and add the ID to the sharded unique visitor `SET` for today. If the ID wasn't already in the `SET`, we'll increment today's unique visitor count. Our code for keeping track of the unique visitor count can be seen in the following listing.

Listing 9.11 A function to keep track of the unique visitor count on a daily basis

```
SHARD_SIZE = 512

def count_visit(conn, session_id):
    today = date.today()
    key = 'unique:%s'%today.isoformat()
    expected = get_expected(conn, key, today)

    id = int(session_id.replace('-', '')[:15], 16)
    if shard_sadd(conn, key, id, expected, SHARD_SIZE):
        conn.incr(key)
```

Get today's date and generate the key for the unique count.

Fetch or calculate the expected number of unique views today.

Add the ID to the sharded SET.

We stick with a typical shard size for the intset encoding for SETs.

Calculate the 56-bit ID for this 128-bit UUID.

If the ID wasn't in the sharded SET, then we increment our unique view count.

That function works exactly as described, though you'll notice that we make a call to `get_expected()` to determine the number of expected daily visitors. We do this because web page visits will tend to change over time, and keeping the same number of shards every day wouldn't grow as we grow (or shrink if we have significantly fewer than a million unique visitors daily).

To address the daily change in expected viewers, we'll write a function that calculates a new expected number of unique visitors for each day, based on yesterday's count. We'll calculate this once for any given day, estimating that today will see at least 50% more visitors than yesterday, rounded up to the next power of 2. Our code for calculating this can be seen next.

Listing 9.12 Calculate today's expected unique visitor count based on yesterday's count

We start with an initial expected number of daily visits that may be a little high.

Keep a local copy of any calculated expected counts.

```
DAILY_EXPECTED = 1000000
EXPECTED = {}

def get_expected(conn, key, today):
```

If someone else has already calculated the expected number of views for today, use that number.

If we've already calculated or seen the expected number of views for today, use that number.

Add 50% to yesterday's count, and round up to the next even power of 2, under the assumption that view count today should be at least 50% better than yesterday.

Fetch the unique count for yesterday, or if not available, use our default 1 million.

Save our calculated expected number of views back to Redis for other calls if possible.

If someone else stored the expected count for today before us, use their count instead.

Keep a local copy of today's expected number of hits, and return it back to the caller.

```python
if key in EXPECTED:
    return EXPECTED[key]

exkey = key + ':expected'
expected = conn.get(exkey)

if not expected:
    yesterday = (today - timedelta(days=1)).isoformat()
    expected = conn.get('unique:%s'%yesterday)
    expected = int(expected or DAILY_EXPECTED)

    expected = 2**int(math.ceil(math.log(expected*1.5, 2)))
    if not conn.setnx(exkey, expected):
        expected = conn.get(exkey)
EXPECTED[key] = int(expected)
return EXPECTED[key]
```

Most of that function is reading and massaging data in one way or another, but the overall result is that we calculate an expected number of unique views for today by taking yesterday's view count, increasing it by 50%, and rounding up to the next power of 2. If the expected number of views for today has already been calculated, we'll use that.

Taking this exact code and adding 1 million unique visitors, Redis will use approximately 9.5 megabytes to store the unique visitor count. Without sharding, Redis would use 56 megabytes to store the same data (56-bit integer IDs in a single SET). That's an 83% reduction in storage with sharding, which would let us store 5.75 times as much data with the same hardware.

> ### Exercise: Filling out the sharded SET API
>
> For this example, we only needed a single SET command to determine the unique visitor count for a given day. Can you add sharded SREM and SISMEMBER calls? Bonus points: Assuming that you have two sharded SETs with the same expected total number of items, as well as the same shard size, you'll have the same number of shards, and identical IDs will be in the same shard IDs. Can you add sharded versions of SINTERSTORE, SUNIONSTORE, and SDIFFSTORE?

OTHER METHODS TO CALCULATE UNIQUE VISITOR COUNTS If you have numeric visitor IDs (instead of UUIDs), and the visitor IDs have relatively low maximum value, rather than storing your visitor information as sharded SETs, you can store them as bitmaps using techniques similar to what we describe in the next section. A Python library for calculating unique visitor counts and other interesting analytics based on bitmaps can be found at https://github.com/Doist/bitmapist.

After sharding large SETs of integers to reduce storage, it's now time to learn how to pack bits and bytes into STRINGs.

9.3   *Packing bits and bytes*

When we discussed sharding HASHes, I briefly mentioned that if we're storing short strings or counters as STRING values with keys like namespace:id, we could use sharded HASHes as a way of reducing memory use. But let's say that we wanted to store a short fixed amount of information for sequential IDs. Can we use even less memory than sharded HASHes?

In this section, we'll use sharded Redis STRINGs to store location information for large numbers of users with sequential IDs, and discuss how to perform aggregate counts over this stored data. This example shows how we can use sharded Redis STRINGs to store, for example, location information for users on Twitter.

Before we start storing our data, we need to revisit four commands that'll let us efficiently pack and update STRINGs in Redis: GETRANGE, SETRANGE, GETBIT, and SET-BIT. The GETRANGE command lets us read a substring from a stored STRING. SETRANGE will let us set the data stored at a substring of the larger STRING. Similarly, GETBIT will fetch the value of a single bit in a STRING, and SETBIT will set an individual bit. With these four commands, we can use Redis STRINGs to store counters, fixed-length strings, Booleans, and more in as compact a format as is possible without compression. With our brief review out of the way, let's talk about what information we'll store.

9.3.1   *What location information should we store?*

When I mentioned locations, you were probably wondering what I meant. Well, we could store a variety of different types of locations. With 1 byte, we could store country-level information for the world. With 2 bytes, we could store region/state-level information. With 3 bytes, we could store regional postal codes for almost every country. And with 4 bytes, we could store latitude/longitude information down to within about 2 meters or 6 feet.

Which level of precision to use will depend on our given use case. For the sake of simplicity, we'll start with just 2 bytes for region/state-level information for countries around the world. As a starter, listing 9.13 shows some base data for ISO3 country codes around the world, as well as state/province information for the United States and Canada.

Listing 9.13   Base location tables we can expand as necessary

```
COUNTRIES = '''
ABW AFG AGO AIA ALA ALB AND ARE ARG ARM ASM ATA ATF ATG AUS AUT AZE BDI
BEL BEN BES BFA BGD BGR BHR BHS BIH BLM BLR BLZ BMU BOL BRA BRB BRN BTN
BVT BWA CAF CAN CCK CHE CHL CHN CIV CMR COD COG COK COL COM CPV CRI CUB
CUW CXR CYM CYP CZE DEU DJI DMA DNK DOM DZA ECU EGY ERI ESH ESP EST ETH
FIN FJI FLK FRA FRO FSM GAB GBR GEO GGY GHA GIB GIN GLP GMB GNB GNQ GRC
GRD GRL GTM GUF GUM GUY HKG HMD HND HRV HTI HUN IDN IMN IND IOT IRL IRN
IRQ ISL ISR ITA JAM JEY JOR JPN KAZ KEN KGZ KHM KIR KNA KOR KWT LAO LBN
LBR LBY LCA LIE LKA LSO LTU LUX LVA MAC MAF MAR MCO MDA MDG MDV MEX MHL
MKD MLI MLT MMR MNE MNG MNP MOZ MRT MSR MTQ MUS MWI MYS MYT NAM NCL NER
NFK NGA NIC NIU NLD NOR NPL NRU NZL OMN PAK PAN PCN PER PHL PLW PNG POL
```

```
PRI PRK PRT PRY PSE PYF QAT REU ROU RUS RWA SAU SDN SEN SGP SGS SHN SJM
SLB SLE SLV SMR SOM SPM SRB SSD STP SUR SVK SVN SWE SWZ SXM SYC SYR TCA
TCD TGO THA TJK TKL TKM TLS TON TTO TUN TUR TUV TWN TZA UGA UKR UMI URY
USA UZB VAT VCT VEN VGB VIR VNM VUT WLF WSM YEM ZAF ZMB ZWE'''.split()
```

STATES = {   **Province/territory information for Canada.**
    'CAN':'''AB BC MB NB NL NS NT NU ON PE QC SK YT'''.split(),
    'USA':'''AA AE AK AL AP AR AS AZ CA CO CT DC DE FL FM GA GU HI IA ID
IL IN KS KY LA MA MD ME MH MI MN MO MP MS MT NC ND NE NH NJ NM NV NY OH
OK OR PA PR PW RI SC SD TN TX UT VA VI VT WA WI WV WY'''.split(),
}
                                                        **State information for
the United States.**

**A table of ISO3 country codes. Calling split() will split the string
on whitespace, turning the string into a list of country codes.**

I introduce these tables of data initially so that if/when we'd like to add additional state, region, territory, or province information for countries we're interested in, the format and method for doing so should be obvious. Looking at the data tables, we initially define them as strings. But these strings are converted into lists by being split on whitespace by our call to the `split()` method on strings without any arguments. Now that we have some initial data, how are we going to store this information on a per-user basis?

Let's say that we've determined that user 139960061 lives in California, U.S., and we want to store this information for that user. To store the information, we first need to pack the data into 2 bytes by first discovering the code for the United States, which we can calculate by finding the index of the United States' ISO3 country code in our COUNTRIES list. Similarly, if we have state information for a user, and we also have state information in our tables, we can calculate the code for the state by finding its index in the table. The next listing shows the function for turning country/state information into a 2-byte code.

Listing 9.14   ISO3 country codes

Because uninitialized data in Redis will return as nulls, we want "not found" to be 0 and the first country to be 1.

Pull the state information for the country, if it's available.

Handle not-found states like we did countries.

Find the offset for the country.

If the country isn't found, then set its index to be -1.

Find the offset for the state.

The chr() function will turn an integer value of 0..255 into the ASCII character with that same value.

Keep not-found states at 0 and found states > 0.

```
def get_code(country, state):
    cindex = bisect.bisect_left(COUNTRIES, country)
    if cindex > len(COUNTRIES) or COUNTRIES[cindex] != country:
        cindex = -1
    cindex += 1

    sindex = -1
    if state and country in STATES:
        states = STATES[country]
        sindex = bisect.bisect_left(states, state)
        if sindex > len(states) or states[sindex] != state:
            sindex = -1
    sindex += 1)

    return chr(cindex) + chr(sindex)
```

Location code calculation isn't that interesting or difficult; it's primarily a matter of finding offsets in lookup tables, and then dealing with "not found" data. Next, let's talk about actually storing our packed location data.

9.3.2 Storing packed data

After we have our packed location codes, we only need to store them in STRINGs with SETRANGE. But before we do so, we have to think for a moment about how many users we're going to be storing information about. For example, suppose that Twitter has 750 million users today (based on the observation that recently created users have IDs greater than 750 million); we'd need over 1.5 gigabytes of space to store location information for all Twitter users. Though most operating systems are able to reasonably allocate large regions of memory, Redis limits us to 512 megabyte STRINGs, and due to Redis's clearing out of data when setting a value beyond the end of an existing STRING, setting the first value at the end of a long STRING will take more time than would be expected for a simple SETBIT call. Instead, we can use a technique similar to what we used in section 9.2.1, and shard our data across a collection of STRINGs.

Unlike when we were sharding HASHes and SETs, we don't have to worry about being efficient by keeping our shards smaller than a few thousand elements, since we can access an element directly without decoding any others. Similarly, we can write to a given offset efficiently. Instead, our concern is more along the lines of being efficient at a larger scale—specifically what will balance potential memory fragmentation, as well as minimize the number of keys that are necessary. For this example, we'll store location information for 2^{20} users (just over 1 million entries) per STRING, which will use about 2 megabytes per STRING. In the next listing, we see the code for updating location information for a user.

Listing 9.15 A function for storing location data in sharded STRINGs

```
USERS_PER_SHARD = 2**20                                          Set the size of
                                                                 each shard.
def set_location(conn, user_id, country, state):
    code = get_code(country, state)

    shard_id, position = divmod(user_id, USERS_PER_SHARD)
    offset = position * 2                                        Calculate the
                                                                 offset of the
    pipe = conn.pipeline(False)                                  user's data.
    pipe.setrange('location:%s'%shard_id, offset, code)

    tkey = str(uuid.uuid4())
    pipe.zadd(tkey, 'max', user_id)
    pipe.zunionstore('location:max',                            Update a ZSET that
        [tkey, 'location:max'], aggregate='max')                stores the maximum
    pipe.delete(tkey)                                           user ID seen so far.

    pipe.execute()
```

Get the location code to store for the user.
Find the shard ID and position of the user in the specific shard.
Set the value in the proper sharded location table.

For the most part, there shouldn't be anything surprising there. We calculate the location code to store for a user, calculate the shard and the individual shard offset for the user, and then store the location code in the proper location for the user. The only thing that's strange and may not seem necessary is that we also update a ZSET that stores the highest-numbered user ID that has been seen. This is primarily important when calculating aggregates over everyone we have information about (so we know when to stop).

9.3.3 *Calculating aggregates over sharded STRINGs*

To calculate aggregates, we have two use cases. Either we'll calculate aggregates over all of the information we know about, or we'll calculate over a subset. We'll start by calculating aggregates over the entire population, and then we'll write code that calculates aggregates over a smaller group.

To calculate aggregates over everyone we have information for, we'll recycle some code that we wrote back in section 6.6.4, specifically the readblocks() function, which reads blocks of data from a given key. Using this function, we can perform a single command and round trip with Redis to fetch information about thousands of users at one time. Our function to calculate aggregates with this block-reading function is shown next.

Listing 9.16   A function to aggregate location information for everyone

```
def aggregate_location(conn):
    countries = defaultdict(int)
    states = defaultdict(lambda:defaultdict(int))

    max_id = int(conn.zscore('location:max', 'max'))
    max_block = max_id // USERS_PER_SHARD

    for shard_id in xrange(max_block + 1):
        for block in readblocks(conn, 'location:%s'%shard_id):
            for offset in xrange(0, len(block)-1, 2):
                code = block[offset:offset+2]
                update_aggregates(countries, states, [code])

    return countries, states
```

Annotations:
- **Initialize two special structures that will allow us to update existing and missing counters quickly.**
- **Fetch the maximum user ID known, and use that to calculate the maximum shard ID that we need to visit.**
- **Sequentially check every shard...**
- **... reading each block.**
- **Extract each code from the block and look up the original location information (like US, CA for someone who lives in California).**
- **Update our aggregates.**

This function to calculate aggregates over country- and state-level information for everyone uses a structure called a defaultdict, which we also first used in chapter 6 to calculate aggregates about location information before writing back to Redis. Inside this function, we refer to a helper function that actually updates the aggregates and decodes location codes back into their original ISO3 country codes and local state abbreviations, which can be seen in this next listing.

Listing 9.17   Convert location codes back to country/state information

```
def update_aggregates(countries, states, codes):
    for code in codes:
        if len(code) != 2:
            continue
```

Annotation:
- **Only look up codes that could be valid.**

```
country = ord(code[0]) - 1
state = ord(code[1]) - 1
```
Calculate the actual offset of the country and state in the lookup tables.

If the country is out of the range of valid countries, continue to the next code.
```
if country < 0 or country >= len(COUNTRIES):
    continue
```
Fetch the ISO3 country code.
```
country = COUNTRIES[country]
```
Count this user in the decoded country.
```
countries[country] += 1

if country not in STATES:
    continue
if state < 0 or state >= STATES[country]:
    continue
```
If we don't have state information or if the state is out of the range of valid states for the country, continue to the next code.

Fetch the state name from the code.
```
state = STATES[country][state]
```
Increment the count for the state.
```
states[country][state] += 1
```

With a function to convert location codes back into useful location information and update aggregate information, we have the building blocks to perform aggregates over a subset of users. As an example, say that we have location information for many Twitter users. And also say that we have follower information for each user. To discover information about where the followers of a given user are located, we'd only need to fetch location information for those users and compute aggregates similar to our global aggregates. The next listing shows a function that will aggregate location information over a provided list of user IDs.

Listing 9.18   A function to aggregate location information over provided user IDs

Set up our base aggregates as we did before.
```
def aggregate_location_list(conn, user_ids):
    pipe = conn.pipeline(False)
    countries = defaultdict(int)
    states = defaultdict(lambda: defaultdict(int))
```
Set up the pipeline so that we aren't making too many round trips to Redis.

Calculate the shard ID and offset into the shard for this user's location.
```
    for i, user_id in enumerate(user_ids):
        shard_id, position = divmod(user_id, USERS_PER_SHARD)
        offset = position * 2

        pipe.substr('location:%s'%shard_id, offset, offset+1)
```

Every 1000 requests, we'll actually update the aggregates using the helper function we defined before.
```
        if (i+1) % 1000 == 0:
            update_aggregates(countries, states, pipe.execute())

    update_aggregates(countries, states, pipe.execute())

    return countries, states
```
Send another pipelined command to fetch the location information for the user.

Handle the last hunk of users that we might have missed before.

Return the aggregates.

This technique of storing fixed-length data in sharded STRINGs can be useful. Though we stored multiple bytes of data per user, we can use GETBIT and SETBIT identically to store individual bits, or even groups of bits.

9.4 *Summary*

In this chapter, we've explored a number of ways to reduce memory use in Redis using short data structures, sharding large structures to make them small again, and by packing data directly into STRINGs.

If there's one thing that you should take away from this chapter, it's that by being careful about how you store your data, you can significantly reduce the amount of memory that Redis needs to support your applications.

In the next chapter, we'll revisit a variety of topics to help Redis scale to larger groups of machines, including read slaves, sharding data across multiple masters, and techniques for scaling a variety of different types of queries.

Scaling Redis

This chapter covers

- Scaling reads
- Scaling writes and memory capacity
- Scaling complex queries

As your use of Redis grows, there may come a time when you're no longer able to fit all of your data into a single Redis server, or when you need to perform more reads and/or writes than Redis can sustain. When this happens, you have a few options to help you scale Redis to your needs.

In this chapter, we'll cover techniques to help you to scale your read queries, write queries, total memory available, and techniques for scaling a selection of more complicated queries.

Our first task is addressing those problems where we can store all of the data we need, and we can handle writes without issue, but where we need to perform more read queries in a second than a single Redis server can handle.

10.1 Scaling reads

In chapter 8 we built a social network that offered many of the same features and functionalities of Twitter. One of these features was the ability for users to view their *home timeline* as well as their *profile timeline*. When viewing these timelines, we'll be fetching 30 posts at a time. For a small social network, this wouldn't be a serious issue, since we could still support anywhere from 3,000–10,000 users fetching timelines every second (if that was all that Redis was doing). But for a larger social network, it wouldn't be unexpected to need to serve many times that number of timeline fetches every second.

In this section, we'll discuss the use of read slaves to support scaling read queries beyond what a single Redis server can handle.

Before we get into scaling reads, let's first review a few opportunities for improving performance before we must resort to using additional servers with slaves to scale our queries:

- If we're using small structures (as we discussed in chapter 9), first make sure that our max ziplist size isn't too large to cause performance penalties.
- Remember to use structures that offer good performance for the types of queries we want to perform (don't treat LISTs like SETs; don't fetch an entire HASH just to sort on the client—use a ZSET; and so on).
- If we're sending large objects to Redis for caching, consider compressing the data to reduce network bandwidth for reads and writes (compare lz4, gzip, and bzip2 to determine which offers the best trade-offs for size/performance for our uses).
- Remember to use pipelining (with or without transactions, depending on our requirements) and connection pooling, as we discussed in chapter 4.

When we're doing everything that we can to ensure that reads and writes are fast, it's time to address the need to perform more read queries. The simplest method to increase total read throughput available to Redis is to add read-only slave servers. If you remember from chapter 4, we can run additional servers that connect to a master, receive a replica of the master's data, and be kept up to date in real time (more or less, depending on network bandwidth). By running our read queries against one of several slaves, we can gain additional read query capacity with every new slave.

> **REMEMBER: WRITE TO THE MASTER** When using read slaves, and generally when using slaves at all, you must remember to write to the master Redis server only. By default, attempting to write to a Redis server configured as a slave (even if it's also a master) will cause that server to reply with an error. We'll talk about using a configuration option to allow for writes to slave servers in section 10.3.1, but generally you should run with slave writes disabled; writing to slaves is usually an error.

Chapter 4 has all the details on configuring Redis for replication to slave servers, how it works, and some ideas for scaling to many read slaves. Briefly, we can update the Redis configuration file with a line that reads slaveof host port, replacing host and port with the host and port of the master server. We can also configure a slave by running the SLAVEOF host port command against an existing server. Remember: When a slave connects to a master, any data that previously existed on the slave will be discarded. To disconnect a slave from a master to stop it from slaving, we can run SLAVEOF no one.

One of the biggest issues that arises when using multiple Redis slaves to serve data is what happens when a master temporarily or permanently goes down. Remember that when a slave connects, the Redis master initiates a snapshot. If multiple slaves connect before the snapshot completes, they'll all receive the same snapshot. Though this is great from an efficiency perspective (no need to create multiple snapshots), sending multiple copies of a snapshot at the same time to multiple slaves can use up the majority of the network bandwidth available to the server. This could cause high latency to/from the master, and could cause previously connected slaves to become disconnected.

One method of addressing the slave resync issue is to reduce the total data volume that'll be sent between the master and its slaves. This can be done by setting up intermediate replication servers to form a type of tree, as can be seen in figure 10.1, which we borrow from chapter 4.

These slave trees will work, and can be necessary if we're looking to replicate to a different data center (resyncing across a slower WAN link will take resources, which should be pushed off to an intermediate slave instead of running against the root master). But slave trees suffer from having a complex network topology that makes manually or automatically handling failover situations difficult.

An alternative to building slave trees is to use compression across our network links to reduce the volume of data that needs to be transferred. Some users have found that using SSH to tunnel a connection with compression dropped bandwidth use significantly. One company went from using 21 megabits of network bandwidth for replicating to a single slave to about 1.8 megabits (http://mng.bz/2ivv). If you use this method, you'll want to use a mechanism that automatically reconnects a disconnected SSH connection, of which there are several options to choose from.

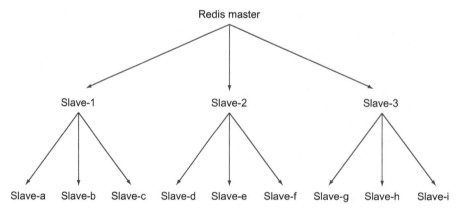

Figure 10.1   An example Redis master/slave replica tree with nine lowest-level slaves and three intermediate replication helper servers

ENCRYPTION AND COMPRESSION OVERHEAD   Generally, encryption overhead for SSH tunnels shouldn't be a huge burden on your server, since AES-128 can encrypt around 180 megabytes per second on a single core of a 2.6 GHz Intel Core 2 processor, and RC4 can encrypt about 350 megabytes per second on the same machine. Assuming that you have a gigabit network link, roughly one moderately powerful core can max out the connection with encryption. Compression is where you may run into issues, because SSH compression defaults to gzip. At compression level 1 (you can configure SSH to use a specific compression level; check the man pages for SSH), our trusty 2.6 GHz processor can compress roughly 24–52 megabytes per second of a few different types of Redis dumps (the initial sync), and 60–80 megabytes per second of a few different types of append-only files (streaming replication). Remember that, though higher compression levels may compress more, they'll also use more processor, which may be an issue for high-throughput low-processor machines. Generally, I'd recommend using compression levels below 5 if possible, since 5 still provides a 10–20% reduction in total data size over level 1, for roughly 2–3 times as much processing time. Compression level 9 typically takes 5–10 times the time for level 1, for compression only 1–5% better than level 5 (I stick to level 1 for any reasonably fast network connection).

USING COMPRESSION WITH OPENVPN   At first glance, OpenVPN's support for AES encryption and compression using lzo may seem like a great turnkey solution to offering transparent reconnections with compression and encryption (as opposed to using one of the third-party SSH reconnecting scripts). Unfortunately, most of the information that I've been able to find has suggested that performance improvements when enabling lzo compression in OpenVPN are limited to roughly 25–30% on 10 megabit connections, and effectively zero improvement on faster connections.

One recent addition to the list of Redis tools that can be used to help with replication and failover is known as *Redis Sentinel*. Redis Sentinel is a mode of the Redis server binary where it doesn't act as a typical Redis server. Instead, Sentinel watches the behavior and health of a number of masters and their slaves. By using PUBLISH/SUBSCRIBE against the masters combined with PING calls to slaves and masters, a collection of Sentinel processes independently discover information about available slaves and other Sentinels. Upon master failure, a single Sentinel will be chosen based on information that all Sentinels have and will choose a new master server from the existing slaves. After that slave is turned into a master, the Sentinel will move the slaves over to the new master (by default one at a time, but this can be configured to a higher number).

Generally, the Redis Sentinel service is intended to offer automated failover from a master to one of its slaves. It offers options for notification of failover, calling user-provided scripts to update configurations, and more.

Now that we've made an attempt to scale our read capacity, it's time to look at how we may be able to scale our write capacity as well.

10.2   *Scaling writes and memory capacity*

Back in chapter 2, we built a system that could automatically cache rendered web pages inside Redis. Fortunately for us, it helped reduce page load time and web page processing overhead. Unfortunately, we've come to a point where we've scaled our cache up to the largest single machine we can afford, and must now split our data among a group of smaller machines.

> **SCALING WRITE VOLUME**   Though we discuss sharding in the context of increasing our total available memory, these methods also work to increase write throughput if we've reached the limit of performance that a single machine can sustain.

In this section, we'll discuss a method to scale memory and write throughput with sharding, using techniques similar to those we used in chapter 9.

To ensure that we really need to scale our write capacity, we should first make sure we're doing what we can to reduce memory and how much data we're writing:

- Make sure that we've checked all of our methods to reduce read data volume first.
- Make sure that we've moved larger pieces of unrelated functionality to different servers (if we're using our connection decorators from chapter 5 already, this should be easy).
- If possible, try to aggregate writes in local memory before writing to Redis, as we discussed in chapter 6 (which applies to almost all analytics and statistics calculation methods).
- If we're running into limitations with WATCH/MULTI/EXEC, consider using locks as we discussed in chapter 6 (or consider using Lua, as we'll talk about in chapter 11).
- If we're using AOF persistence, remember that our disk needs to keep up with the volume of data we're writing (400,000 small commands may only be a few megabytes per second, but 100,000 x 1 KB writes is 100 megabytes per second).

Now that we've done everything we can to reduce memory use, maximize performance, and understand the limitations of what a single machine can do, it's time to actually shard our data to multiple machines. The methods that we use to shard our data to multiple machines rely on the number of Redis servers used being more or less fixed. If we can estimate that our write volume will, for example, increase 4 times every 6 months, we can preshard our data into 256 shards. By presharding into 256 shards, we'd have a plan that should be sufficient for the next 2 years of expected growth (how far out to plan ahead for is up to you).

> **PRESHARDING FOR GROWTH**   When presharding your system in order to prepare for growth, you may be in a situation where you have too little data to make it worth running as many machines as you could need later. To still be able to separate your data, you can run multiple Redis servers on a single

machine for each of your shards, or you can use multiple Redis databases inside a single Redis server. From this starting point, you can move to multiple machines through the use of replication and configuration management (see section 10.2.1). If you're running multiple Redis servers on a single machine, remember to have them listen on different ports, and make sure that all servers write to different snapshot files and/or append-only files.

The first thing that we need to do is to talk about how we'll define our shard configuration.

10.2.1 Handling shard configuration

As you may remember from chapter 5, we wrote a method to create and use named Redis configurations automatically. This method used a Python decorator to fetch configuration information, compare it with preexisting configuration information, and create or reuse an existing connection. We'll extend this idea to add support for sharded connections. With these changes, we can use much of our code developed in chapter 9 with minor changes.

To get started, first let's make a simple function that uses the same configuration layout that we used in our connection decorator from chapter 5. If you remember, we use JSON-encoded dictionaries to store connection information for Redis in keys of the format `config:redis:<component>`. Pulling out the connection management part of the decorator, we end up with a simple function to create or reuse a Redis connection, based on a named configuration, shown here.

> **Listing 10.1   A function to get a Redis connection based on a named configuration**

```
                       def get_redis_connection(component, wait=1):
                           key = 'config:redis:' + component
   Get the new              old_config = CONFIGS.get(key, object())
 configuration,             config = get_config(
       if any.                  config_connection, 'redis', component, wait)

                           if config != old_config:
If the new and old             REDIS_CONNECTIONS[key] = redis.Redis(**config)
configuration don't
match, create a new         return REDIS_CONNECTIONS.get(key)
    connection.
```

Fetch the old configuration, if any.

Return the desired connection object.

This simple function fetches the previously known as well as the current configuration. If they're different, it updates the known configuration, creates a new connection, and then stores and returns that new connection. If the configuration hasn't changed, it returns the previous connection.

When we have the ability to fetch connections easily, we should also add support for the creation of sharded Redis connections, so even if our later decorators aren't useful in every situation, we can still easily create and use sharded connections. To connect to a new sharded connection, we'll use the same configuration methods, though sharded configuration will be a little different. For example, shard 7 of component `logs` will be stored at a key named `config:redis:logs:7`. This naming scheme will let us reuse the existing connection and configuration code we already have. Our function to get a sharded connection is in the following listing.

Listing 10.2   Fetch a connection based on shard information

```
def get_sharded_connection(component, key, shard_count, wait=1):
    shard = shard_key(component, 'x'+str(key), shard_count, 2)
    return get_redis_connection(shard, wait)
```

Calculate the shard ID of the form
<component>:<shard>.

Return the connection.

Now that we have a simple method of fetching a connection to a Redis server that's sharded, we can create a decorator like we saw in chapter 5 that creates a sharded connection automatically.

10.2.2 *Creating a server-sharded connection decorator*

Now that we have a method to easily fetch a sharded connection, let's use it to build a decorator to automatically pass a sharded connection to underlying functions.

We'll perform the same three-level function decoration we used in chapter 5, which will let us use the same kind of "component" passing we used there. In addition to component information, we'll also pass the number of Redis servers we're going to shard to. The following listing shows the details of our shard-aware connection decorator.

Listing 10.3   A shard-aware connection decorator

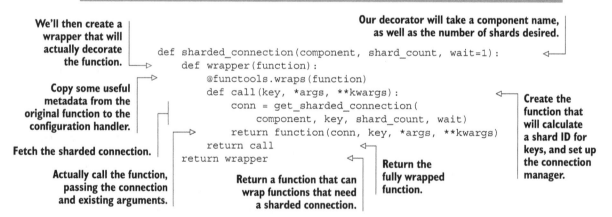

We'll then create a wrapper that will actually decorate the function.

Our decorator will take a component name, as well as the number of shards desired.

```
def sharded_connection(component, shard_count, wait=1):
    def wrapper(function):
        @functools.wraps(function)
        def call(key, *args, **kwargs):
            conn = get_sharded_connection(
                component, key, shard_count, wait)
            return function(conn, key, *args, **kwargs)
        return call
    return wrapper
```

Copy some useful metadata from the original function to the configuration handler.

Fetch the sharded connection.

Actually call the function, passing the connection and existing arguments.

Return a function that can wrap functions that need a sharded connection.

Return the fully wrapped function.

Create the function that will calculate a shard ID for keys, and set up the connection manager.

Because of the way we constructed our connection decorator, we can decorate our count_visit() function from chapter 9 almost completely unchanged. We need to be careful because we're keeping aggregate count information, which is fetched and/or updated by our get_expected() function. Because the information stored will be used and reused on different days for different users, we need to use a nonsharded connection for it. The updated and decorated count_visit() function as well as the decorated and slightly updated get_expected() function are shown next.

Listing 10.4   A machine and key-sharded `count_visit()` function

Our changed call to get_expected().

```
@sharded_connection('unique', 16)
def count_visit(conn, session_id):
    today = date.today()
    key = 'unique:%s'%today.isoformat()
    conn2, expected = get_expected(key, today)

    id = int(session_id.replace('-', '')[:15], 16)
    if shard_sadd(conn, key, id, expected, SHARD_SIZE):
        conn2.incr(key)
@redis_connection('unique')
def get_expected(conn, key, today):
    'all of the same function body as before, except the last line'
    return conn, EXPECTED[key]
```

We'll shard this to 16 different machines, which will automatically shard to multiple keys on each machine.

Use the returned nonsharded connection to increment our unique counts.

Use a nonsharded connection to get_expected().

Also return the nonsharded connection so that count_visit() can increment our unique count as necessary.

In our example, we're sharding our data out to 16 different machines for the unique visit SETs, whose configurations are stored as JSON-encoded strings at keys named `config:redis:unique:0` to `config:redis:unique:15`. For our daily count information, we're storing them in a nonsharded Redis server, whose configuration information is stored at key `config:redis:unique`.

> **MULTIPLE REDIS SERVERS ON A SINGLE MACHINE** This section discusses sharding writes to multiple machines in order to increase total memory available and total write capacity. But if you're feeling limited by Redis's single-threaded processing limit (maybe because you're performing expensive searches, sorts, or other queries), and you have more cores available for processing, more network available for communication, and more available disk I/O for snapshots/AOF, you can run multiple Redis servers on a single machine. You only need to configure them to listen on different ports and ensure that they have different snapshot/AOF configurations.

> **ALTERNATE METHODS OF HANDLING UNIQUE VISIT COUNTS OVER TIME** With the use of SETBIT, BITCOUNT, and BITOP, you can actually scale unique visitor counts without sharding by using an indexed lookup of bits, similar to what we did with locations in chapter 9. A library that implements this in Python can be found at https://github.com/Doist/bitmapist.

Now that we have functions to get regular and sharded connections, as well as decorators to automatically pass regular and sharded connections, using Redis connections of multiple types is significantly easier. Unfortunately, not all operations that we need to perform on sharded datasets are as easy as a unique visitor count. In the next section, we'll talk about scaling search in two different ways, as well as how to scale our social network example.

10.3   Scaling complex queries

As we scale out a variety of services with Redis, it's not uncommon to run into situations where sharding our data isn't enough, where the types of queries we need to execute require more work than just setting or fetching a value. In this section, we'll discuss one problem that's trivial to scale out, and two problems that take more work.

The first problem that we'll scale out is our search engine from chapter 7, where we have machines with enough memory to hold our index, but we need to execute more queries than our server can currently handle.

10.3.1   Scaling search query volume

As we expand our search engine from chapter 7 with SORT, using the ZSET-based scored search, our ad-targeting search engine (or even the job-search system), at some point we may come to a point where a single server isn't capable of handling the number of queries per second required. In this section, we'll talk about how to add query slaves to further increase our capability to serve more search requests.

In section 10.1, you saw how to scale read queries against Redis by adding read slaves. If you haven't already read section 10.1, you should do so before continuing. After you have a collection of read slaves to perform queries against, if you're running Redis 2.6 or later, you'll immediately notice that performing search queries will fail. This is because performing a search as discussed in chapter 7 requires performing SUNIONSTORE, SINTERSTORE, SDIFFSTORE, ZINTERSTORE, and/or ZUNIONSTORE queries, all of which write to Redis.

In order to perform writes against Redis 2.6 and later, we'll need to update our Redis slave configuration. In the Redis configuration file, there's an option to disable/enable writing to slaves. This option is called slave-read-only, and it defaults to yes. By changing slave-read-only to no and restarting our slaves, we should now be able to perform standard search queries against slave Redis servers. Remember that we cache the results of our queries, and these cached results are only available on the slave that the queries were run on. So if we intend to reuse cached results, we'll probably want to perform some level of session persistence (where repeated requests from a client go to the same web server, and that web server always makes requests against the same Redis server).

In the past, I've used this method to scale an ad-targeting engine quickly and easily. If you decide to go this route to scale search queries, remember to pay attention to the resync issues discussed in section 10.1.

When we have enough memory in one machine and our operations are read-only (or at least don't really change the underlying data to be used by other queries), adding slaves can help us to scale out. But sometimes data volumes can exceed memory capacity, and we still need to perform complex queries. How can we scale search when we have more data than available memory?

10.3.2   Scaling search index size

If there's one thing we can expect of a search engine, it's that the search index will grow over time. As search indexes grow, the memory used by those search indexes also grows. Depending on the speed of the growth, we may or may not be able to keep buying/renting larger computers to run our index on. But for many of us, getting bigger and bigger computers is just not possible.

In this section, we'll talk about how to structure our data to support sharded search queries, and will include code to execute sharded search queries against a collection of sharded Redis masters (or slaves of sharded masters, if you followed the instructions in section 10.3.1).

In order to shard our search queries, we must first shard our indexes so that for each document that we index, all of the data about that document is on the same shard. It turns out that our index_document() function from chapter 7 takes a connection object, which we can shard by hand with the docid that's passed. Or, because index_document() takes a connection followed by the docid, we can use our automatic sharding decorator from listing 10.3 to handle sharding for us.

When we have our documents indexed across shards, we only need to perform queries against the shards to get the results. The details of what we need to do will depend on our type of index—whether it's SORT-based or ZSET-based. Let's first update our SORT-based index for sharded searches.

SHARDING SORT-BASED SEARCH

As is the case with all sharded searches, we need a way to combine the results of the sharded searches. In our implementation of search_and_sort() from chapter 7, we received a total count of results and the document IDs that were the result of the required query. This is a great building block to start from, but overall we'll need to write functions to perform the following steps:

1 Perform the search and fetch the values to sort on for a query against a single shard.
2 Execute the search on all shards.
3 Merge the results of the queries, and choose the subset desired.

First, let's look at what it takes to perform the search and fetch the values from a single shard.

Because we already have search_and_sort() from chapter 7, we can start by using that to fetch the result of a search. After we have the results, we can then fetch the data associated with each search result. But we have to be careful about pagination, because we don't know which shard each result from a previous search came from. So, in order to always return the correct search results for items 91–100, we need to fetch the first 100 search results from every shard. Our code for fetching all of the necessary results and data can be seen in the next listing.

Listing 10.5 SORT-based search that fetches the values that were sorted

```
def search_get_values(conn, query, id=None, ttl=300, sort="-updated",
                      start=0, num=20):
```

> We need to take all of the same parameters to pass on to search_and_sort().

```
count, docids, id = search_and_sort(
    conn, query, id, ttl, sort, 0, start+num)

key = "kb:doc:%s"
sort = sort.lstrip('-')

pipe = conn.pipeline(False)
for docid in docids:
    pipe.hget(key%docid, sort)
sort_column = pipe.execute()

data_pairs = zip(docids, sort_column)
return count, data_pairs, id
```

First get the results of a search and sort.

Fetch the data that the results were sorted by.

Pair up the document IDs with the data that it was sorted by.

Return the count, data, and cache ID of the results.

This function fetches all of the information necessary from a single shard in preparation for the final merge. Our next step is to execute the query on all of the shards.

To execute a query on all of our shards, we have two options. We can either run each query on each shard one by one, or we can execute our queries across all of our shards simultaneously. To keep it simple, we'll execute our queries one by one on each shard, collecting the results together in the next listing.

Listing 10.6   A function to perform queries against all shards

Prepare structures to hold all of our fetched data.

Use cached results if we have any; otherwise, start over.

Get or create a connection to the desired shard.

Fetch the search results and their sort values.

```
def get_shard_results(component, shards, query, ids=None, ttl=300,
                      sort="-updated", start=0, num=20, wait=1):
    count = 0
    data = []
    ids = ids or shards * [None]
    for shard in xrange(shards):
        conn = get_redis_connection('%s:%s'%(component, shard), wait)
        c, d, i = search_get_values(
            conn, query, ids[shard], ttl, sort, start, num)
        count += c
        data.extend(d)
        ids[shard] = i
    return count, data, ids
```

In order to know what servers to connect to, we'll assume that all of our shard information is kept in the standard configuration location.

Combine this shard's results with all of the other results.

Return the raw results from all of the shards.

This function works as explained: we execute queries against each shard one at a time until we have results from all shards. Remember that in order to perform queries against all shards, we must pass the proper shard count to the get_shard_results() function.

> ### Exercise: Run queries in parallel
>
> Python includes a variety of methods to run calls against Redis servers in parallel. Because most of the work with performing a query is actually just waiting for Redis to respond, we can easily use Python's built-in threading and queue libraries to send requests to the sharded Redis servers and wait for a response. Can you write a version of get_shard_results() that uses threads to fetch results from all shards in parallel?

Now that we have all of the results from all of the queries, we only need to re-sort our results so that we can get an ordering on all of the results that we fetched. This isn't terribly complicated, but we have to be careful about numeric and non-numeric sorts, handling missing values, and handling non-numeric values during numeric sorts. Our function for merging results and returning only the requested results is shown in the next listing.

> **Listing 10.7 A function to merge sharded search results**

We need to take all of the sharding and searching arguments, mostly to pass on to lower-level functions, but we use the sort and search offsets.

We'll use the Decimal numeric type here because it transparently handles both integers and floats reasonably, defaulting to 0 if the value wasn't numeric or was missing.

Always return a string, even if there was no value stored.

Fetch the results of the unsorted sharded search.

Prepare all of our sorting options.

Actually sort our results based on the sort parameter.

Fetch just the page of results that we want.

Return the results, including the sequence of cache IDs for each shard.

```
def to_numeric_key(data):
    try:
        return Decimal(data[1] or '0')
    except:
        return Decimal('0')

def to_string_key(data):
    return data[1] or ''

def search_shards(component, shards, query, ids=None, ttl=300,
                  sort="-updated", start=0, num=20, wait=1):

    count, data, ids = get_shard_results(
        component, shards, query, ids, ttl, sort, start, num, wait)

    reversed = sort.startswith('-')
    sort = sort.strip('-')
    key = to_numeric_key
    if sort not in ('updated', 'id', 'created'):
        key = to_string_key

    data.sort(key=key, reverse=reversed)

    results = []
    for docid, score in data[start:start+num]:
        results.append(docid)

    return count, results, ids
```

In order to handle sorting properly, we needed to write two function to convert data returned by Redis into values that could be consistently sorted against each other. You'll notice that we chose to use Python `Decimal` values for sorting numerically. This is because we get the same sorted results with less code, and transparent support for handling infinity correctly. From there, all of our code does exactly what's expected: we fetch the results, prepare to sort the results, sort the results, and then return only those document IDs from the search that are in the requested range.

Now that we have a version of our SORT-based search that works across sharded Redis servers, it only remains to shard searching on ZSET-based sharded indexes.

SHARDING ZSET-BASED SEARCH

Like a SORT-based search, handling searching for ZSET-based search requires running our queries against all shards, fetching the scores to sort by, and merging the results properly. We'll go through the same steps that we did for SORT-based search in this section: search on one shard, search on all shards, and then merge the results.

To search on one shard, we'll wrap the chapter 7 search_and_zsort() function on ZSETs, fetching the results and scores from the cached ZSET in the next listing.

Listing 10.8   ZSET-based search that returns scores for each result

```
def search_get_zset_values(conn, query, id=None, ttl=300, update=1,
                            vote=0, start=0, num=20, desc=True):
    count, r, id = search_and_zsort(
        conn, query, id, ttl, update, vote, 0, 1, desc)
    if desc:
        data = conn.zrevrange(id, 0, start + num - 1, withscores=True)
    else:
        data = conn.zrange(id, 0, start + num - 1, withscores=True)
    return count, data, id
```

Annotations:
- **Call the underlying search_and_zsort() function to get the cached result ID and total number of results.**
- **We need to accept all of the standard arguments for search_and_zsort().**
- **Fetch all of the results we need, including their scores.**
- **Return the count, results with scores, and the cache ID.**

Compared to the SORT-based search that does similar work, this function tries to keep things simple by ignoring the returned results without scores, and just fetches the results with scores directly from the cached ZSET. Because we have our scores already as floating-point numbers for easy sorting, we'll combine the function to search on all shards with the function that merges and sorts the results.

As before, we'll perform searches for each shard one at a time, combining the results. When we have the results, we'll sort them based on the scores that were returned. After the sort, we'll return the results to the caller. The function that implements this is shown next.

Listing 10.9   Sharded search query over ZSETs that returns paginated results

```
def search_shards_zset(component, shards, query, ids=None, ttl=300,
                        update=1, vote=0, start=0, num=20, desc=True, wait=1):
    count = 0
    data = []
    ids = ids or shards * [None]
    for shard in xrange(shards):
        conn = get_redis_connection('%s:%s'%(component, shard), wait)
        c, d, i = search_get_zset_values(conn, query, ids[shard],
            ttl, update, vote, start, num, desc)
        count += c
        data.extend(d)
        ids[shard] = i
    def key(result):
        return result[1]
    data.sort(key=key, reversed=desc)
    results = []
```

Annotations:
- **Use cached results, if any; otherwise, start from scratch.**
- **Prepare structures for data to be returned.**
- **We need to take all of the sharding arguments along with all of the search arguments.**
- **Fetch or create a connection to each shard.**
- **Perform the search on a shard and fetch the scores.**
- **Merge the results together.**
- **Sort all of the results together.**
- **Prepare the simple sort helper to return only information about the score.**

```
for docid, score in data[start:start+num]:
    results.append(docid)
```
| **Extract the document IDs from the results, removing the scores.**

```
return count, results, ids
```
← **Return the search results to the caller.**

With this code, you should have a good idea of the kinds of things necessary for handling sharded search queries. Generally, when confronted with a situation like this, I find myself questioning whether it's worth attempting to scale these queries in this way. Given that we now have at least working sharded search code, the question is easier to answer. Note that as our number of shards increase, we'll need to fetch more and more data in order to satisfy our queries. At some point, we may even need to delegate fetching and merging to other processes, or even merging in a tree-like structure. At that point, we may want to consider other solutions that were purpose-built for search (like Lucene, Solr, Elastic Search, or even Amazon's Cloud Search).

Now that you know how to scale a second type of search, we really have only covered one other problem in other sections that might reach the point of needing to be scaled. Let's take a look at what it would take to scale our social network from chapter 8.

10.3.3 *Scaling a social network*

As we built our social network in chapter 8, I pointed out that it wasn't designed to scale to the size of a social network like Twitter, but that it was primarily meant to help you understand what structures and methods it takes to build a social network. In this section, I'll describe a few methods that can let us scale a social networking site with sharding, almost without bounds (mostly limited by our budget, which is always the case with large projects).

One of the first steps necessary to helping a social network scale is figuring out what data is read often, what data is written often, and whether it's possible to separate often-used data from rarely used data. To start, say that we've already pulled out our posted message data into a separate Redis server, which has read slaves to handle the moderately high volume of reads that occurs on that data. That really leaves two major types of data left to scale: timelines and follower/following lists.

SCALING POSTED MESSAGE DATABASE SIZE If you actually built this system out, and you had any sort of success, at some point you'd need to further scale the posted message database beyond just read slaves. Because each message is completely contained within a single HASH, these can be easily sharded onto a cluster of Redis servers based on the key where the HASH is stored. Because this data is easily sharded, and because we've already worked through how to fetch data from multiple shards as part of our search scaling in section 10.3.2, you shouldn't have any difficulty here. Alternatively, you can also use Redis as a cache, storing recently posted messages in Redis, and older (rarely read) messages in a primarily on-disk storage server (like PostgreSQL, MySQL, Riak, MongoDB, and so on). If you're finding yourself challenged, please feel free to post on the message board or on the Redis mailing list.

As you may remember, we had three primary types of timelines: home timelines, profile timelines, and list timelines. Timelines themselves are all similar, though both list timelines and home timelines are limited to 1,000 items. Similarly, followers, following, list followers, and list following are also essentially the same, so we'll also handle them the same. First, let's look at how we can scale timelines with sharding.

SHARDING TIMELINES

When we say that we're sharding timelines, it's a bit of a bait-and-switch. Because home and list timelines are short (1,000 entries max, which we may want to use to inform how large to set `zset-max-ziplist-size`),[1] there's really no need to shard the contents of the ZSETs; we merely need to place those timelines on different shards based on their key names.

On the other hand, the size that profile timelines can grow to is currently unlimited. Though the vast majority of users will probably only be posting a few times a day at most, there can be situations where someone is posting significantly more often. As an example of this, the top 1,000 posters on Twitter have all posted more than 150,000 status messages, with the top 15 all posting more than a million messages.

On a practical level, it wouldn't be unreasonable to cap the number of messages that are kept in the timeline for an individual user to 20,000 or so (the oldest being hidden or deleted), which would handle 99.999% of Twitter users generally. We'll assume that this is our plan for scaling profile timelines. If not, we can use the technique we cover for scaling follower/following lists later in this section for scaling profile timelines instead.

In order to shard our timelines based on key name, we could write a set of functions that handle sharded versions of ZADD, ZREM, and ZRANGE, along with others, all of which would be short three-line functions that would quickly get boring. Instead, let's write a class that uses Python dictionary lookups to automatically create connections to shards.

First, let's start with what we want our API to look like by updating our `follow_user()` function from chapter 8. We'll create a generic sharded connection object that will let us create a connection to a given shard, based on a key that we want to access in that shard. After we have that connection, we can call all of the standard Redis methods to do whatever we want on that shard. We can see what we want our API to look like, and how we need to update our function, in the next listing.

Listing 10.10   An example of how we want our API for accessing shards to work

```
sharded_timelines = KeyShardedConnection('timelines', 8)          ◁─┐

def follow_user(conn, uid, other_uid):                    Create a connection that knows about
    fkey1 = 'following:%s'%uid                             the sharding information for a given
                                                           component with a number of shards.
```

---

[1] Because of the way we add items to home and list timelines, they can actually grow to roughly 2,000 entries for a short time. And because Redis doesn't turn structures back into ziplist-encoded versions of themselves when they've gotten too large, setting `zset-max-ziplist-size` to be a little over 2,000 entries can keep these two timelines encoded efficiently.

```
                        fkey2 = 'followers:%s'%other_uid

                        if conn.zscore(fkey1, other_uid):
                            print "already followed", uid, other_uid
                            return None

                        now = time.time()

                        pipeline = conn.pipeline(True)
                        pipeline.zadd(fkey1, other_uid, now)
                        pipeline.zadd(fkey2, uid, now)
                        pipeline.zcard(fkey1)
                        pipeline.zcard(fkey2)
                        following, followers = pipeline.execute()[-2:]
                        pipeline.hset('user:%s'%uid, 'following', following)
                        pipeline.hset('user:%s'%other_uid, 'followers', followers)
                        pipeline.execute()
```

Fetch the recent status messages from the profile timeline of the now-followed user.

```
                        pkey = 'profile:%s'%other_uid
                        status_and_score = sharded_timelines[pkey].zrevrange(
                            pkey, 0, HOME_TIMELINE_SIZE-1, withscores=True)
```

Get a connection based on the shard key provided, and fetch a pipeline from that.

```
                        if status_and_score:
                            hkey = 'home:%s'%uid
                            pipe = sharded_timelines[hkey].pipeline(True)
                            pipe.zadd(hkey, **dict(status_and_score))
                            pipe.zremrangebyrank(hkey, 0, -HOME_TIMELINE_SIZE-1)
```

Execute the transaction.

```
                            pipe.execute()
```

Add the statuses to the home timeline ZSET on the shard, and then trim it.

```
                        return True
```

Now that we have an idea of what we want our API to look like, let's build it. We first need an object that takes the component and number of shards. When a key is referenced via dictionary lookup on the object, we need to return a connection to the shard that the provided key should be stored on. The class that implements this follows.

Listing 10.11   A class that implements sharded connection resolution based on key

When an item is fetched from the object, this method is called with the item that was requested.

```
class KeyShardedConnection(object):
    def __init__(self, component, shards):
        self.component = component
        self.shards = shards
    def __getitem__(self, key):
        return get_sharded_connection(
            self.component, key, self.shards)
```

The object is initialized with the component name and number of shards.

Use the passed key along with the previously known component and shards to fetch the sharded connection.

For simple key-based sharding, this is all that's necessary to support almost every call that we'd perform in Redis. All that remains is to update the remainder of unfollow_user(), refill_timeline(), and the rest of the functions that access home timelines and list timelines. If you intend to scale this social network, go ahead and update those functions yourself. For those of us who aren't scaling the social network, we'll continue on.

> ### Exercise: Syndicating posts to home and list timelines
>
> With the update to where data is stored for both home and list timelines, can you update your list timeline supporting syndication task from chapter 8 to support sharded profiles? Can you keep it almost as fast as the original version? Hint: If you're stuck, we include a fully updated version that supports sharded follower lists in listing 10.15.

Up next is scaling follower and following lists.

SCALING FOLLOWER AND FOLLOWING LISTS WITH SHARDING

Though our scaling of timelines is pretty straightforward, scaling followers, following, and the equivalent "list" ZSETs is more difficult. The vast majority of these ZSETs will be short (99.99% of users on Twitter have fewer than 1,000 followers), but there may be a few users who are following a large number of users, or who have a large number of followers. As a practical matter, it wouldn't be unreasonable to limit the number of users that a given user or list can follow to be somewhat small (perhaps up to 1,000, to match the limits on home and list timelines), forcing them to create lists if they really want to follow more people. But we still run into issues when the number of followers of a given user grows substantially.

To handle the situation where follower/following lists can grow to be very large, we'll shard these ZSETs across multiple shards. To be more specific, a user's followers will be broken up into as many pieces as we have shards. For reasons we'll get into in a moment, we only need to implement specific sharded versions of ZADD, ZREM, and ZRANGEBYSCORE.

I know what you're thinking: since we just built a method to handle sharding automatically, we could use that. We will (to some extent), but because we're sharding data and not just keys, we can't just use our earlier class directly. Also, in order to reduce the number of connections we need to create and call, it makes a lot of sense to have data for both sides of the follower/following link on the same shard, so we can't just shard by data like we did in chapter 9 and in section 10.2.

In order to shard our follower/following data such that both sides of the follower/following relationship are on the same shard, we'll use both IDs as part of the key to look up a shard. Like we did for sharding timelines, let's update `follow_user()` to show the API that we'd like to use, and then we'll create the class that's necessary to implement the functionality. The updated `follow_user()` with our desired API is next.

Listing 10.12   Access follower/following ZSET shards

```
sharded_timelines = KeyShardedConnection('timelines', 8)
sharded_followers = KeyDataShardedConnection('followers', 16)

def follow_user(conn, uid, other_uid):
    fkey1 = 'following:%s'%uid
    fkey2 = 'followers:%s'%other_uid
```

Create a connection that knows about the sharding information for a given component with a number of shards.

```
sconn = sharded_followers[uid, other_uid]
if sconn.zscore(fkey1, other_uid):
    return None

now = time.time()
spipe = sconn.pipeline(True)
spipe.zadd(fkey1, other_uid, now)
spipe.zadd(fkey2, uid, now)
following, followers = spipe.execute()

pipeline = conn.pipeline(True)
pipeline.hincrby('user:%s'%uid, 'following', int(following))
pipeline.hincrby('user:%s'%other_uid, 'followers', int(followers))
pipeline.execute()

pkey = 'profile:%s'%other_uid
status_and_score = sharded_timelines[pkey].zrevrange(
    pkey, 0, HOME_TIMELINE_SIZE-1, withscores=True)

if status_and_score:
    hkey = 'home:%s'%uid
    pipe = sharded_timelines[hkey].pipeline(True)
    pipe.zadd(hkey, **dict(status_and_score))
    pipe.zremrangebyrank(hkey, 0, -HOME_TIMELINE_SIZE-1)
    pipe.execute()

return True
```

Fetch the connection object for the uid, other_uid pair.

Check to see if the other_uid is already followed.

Add the follower/ following information to the ZSETs.

Update the follower and following information for both users.

Aside from a bit of rearrangement and code updating, the only difference between this change and the change we made earlier for sharding timelines is that instead of passing a specific key to look up the shard, we pass a pair of IDs. From these two IDs, we'll calculate the proper shard that data involving both IDs should be stored on. The class that implements this API appears next.

Listing 10.13 Sharded connection resolution based on ID pairs

When the pair of IDs is passed as part of the dictionary lookup, this method is called.

```
class KeyDataShardedConnection(object):
    def __init__(self, component, shards):
        self.component = component
        self.shards = shards
    def __getitem__(self, ids):
        id1, id2 = map(int, ids)
        if id2 < id1:
            id1, id2 = id2, id1
        key = "%s:%s"%(id1, id2)
        return get_sharded_connection(
            self.component, key, self.shards)
```

The object is initialized with the component name and number of shards.

Unpack the pair of IDs, and ensure that they are integers.

If the second is less than the first, swap them so that the first ID is less than or equal to the second.

Construct a key based on the two IDs.

Use the computed key along with the previously known component and shards to fetch the sharded connection.

The only thing different for this sharded connection generator, compared to listing 10.11, is that this sharded connection generator takes a pair of IDs instead of a key. From those two IDs, we generate a key where the lower of the two IDs is first, and the higher is second. By constructing the key in this way, we ensure that whenever we reference the same two IDs, regardless of initial order, we always end up on the same shard.

With this sharded connection generator, we can update almost all of the remaining follower/following ZSET operations. The one remaining operation that's left is to properly handle ZRANGEBYSCORE, which we use in a few places to fetch a "page" of followers. Usually this is done to syndicate messages out to home and list timelines when an update is posted. When syndicating to timelines, we could scan through all of one shard's ZSET, and then move to the next. But with a little extra work, we could instead pass through all ZSETs simultaneously, which would give us a useful sharded ZRANGE-BYSCORE operation that can be used in other situations.

As we saw in section 10.3.2, in order to fetch items 100–109 from sharded ZSETs, we needed to fetch items 0–109 from all ZSETs and merge them together. This is because we only knew the index that we wanted to start at. Because we have the opportunity to scan based on score instead, when we want to fetch the next 10 items with scores greater than X, we only need to fetch the next 10 items with scores greater than X from all shards, followed by a merge. A function that implements ZRANGEBYSCORE across multiple shards is shown in the following listing.

Listing 10.14   A function that implements a sharded ZRANGEBYSCORE

Fetch the sharded connection for the current shard.

We need to take arguments for the component and number of shards, and we'll limit the arguments to be passed on to only those that'll ensure correct behavior in sharded situations.

```
def sharded_zrangebyscore(component, shards, key, min, max, num):
    data = []
    for shard in xrange(shards):
        conn = get_redis_connection("%s:%s"%(component, shard))
        data.extend(conn.zrangebyscore(
            key, min, max, start=0, num=num, withscores=True))
    def key(pair):
        return pair[1], pair[0]
    data.sort(key=key)

    return data[:num]
```

Get the data from Redis for this shard.

Sort the data based on score, and then by member.

Return only the number of items requested.

This function works a lot like the query/merge that we did in section 10.3.2, only we can start in the middle of the ZSET because we have scores (and not indexes).

USING THIS METHOD FOR SHARDING PROFILE TIMELINES   You'll notice that we use timestamps for follower/following lists, which avoided some of the drawbacks to paginate over sharded ZSETs that we covered in section 10.3.2. If you'd planned on using this method for sharding profile timelines, you'll need to go back and update your code to use timestamps instead of offsets, and you'll need to implement a ZREVRANGEBYSCORE version of listing 10.14, which should be straightforward.

With this new sharded ZRANGEBYSCORE function, let's update our function that syndicates posts to home and list timelines in the next listing. While we're at it, we may as well add support for sharded home timelines.

Listing 10.15 Updated syndicate status function

```
def syndicate_status(uid, post, start=0, on_lists=False):
    root = 'followers'
    key = 'followers:%s'%uid
    base = 'home:%s'
    if on_lists:
        root = 'list:out'
        key = 'list:out:%s'%uid
        base = 'list:statuses:%s'

    followers = sharded_zrangebyscore(root,
        sharded_followers.shards, key, start, 'inf', POSTS_PER_PASS)

    to_send = defaultdict(list)
    for follower, start in followers:
        timeline = base % follower
        shard = shard_key('timelines',
            timeline, sharded_timelines.shards, 2)
        to_send[shard].append(timeline)

    for timelines in to_send.itervalues():
        pipe = sharded_timelines[timelines[0]].pipeline(False)
        for timeline in timelines:
            pipe.zadd(timeline, **post)
            pipe.zremrangebyrank(
                timeline, 0, -HOME_TIMELINE_SIZE-1)
        pipe.execute()

    conn = redis.Redis()
    if len(followers) >= POSTS_PER_PASS:
        execute_later(conn, 'default', 'syndicate_status',
            [uid, post, start, on_lists])

    elif not on_lists:
        execute_later(conn, 'default', 'syndicate_status',
            [uid, post, 0, True])
```

Annotations:
- **Prepare a structure that will group profile information on a per-shard basis.**
- **Fetch the next group of followers using the sharded ZRANGEBYSCORE call.**
- **Calculate the key for the timeline.**
- **Find the shard where this timeline would go.**
- **Get a connection to the server for the group of timelines, and create a pipeline.**
- **Add the timeline key to the rest of the timelines on the same shard.**
- **Add the post to the timeline, and remove any posts that are too old.**

As you can see from the code, we use the sharded ZRANGEBYSCORE function to fetch those users who are interested in this user's posts. Also, in order to keep the syndication process fast, we group requests that are to be sent to each home or list timeline shard server together. Later, after we've grouped all of the writes together, we add the post to all of the timelines on a given shard server with a pipeline. Though this may be slower than the nonsharded version, this does allow us to scale our social network much larger than before.

All that remains is to finish updating the rest of the functions to support all of the sharding that we've done in the rest of section 10.3.3. Again, if you're going to scale this social network, feel free to do so. But if you have some nonsharded code that you want to shard, you can compare the earlier version of `syndicate_status()` from section 8.4 with our new version to get an idea of how to update your code.

10.4 Summary

In this chapter, we revisited a variety of problems to look at what it'd take to scale them to higher read volume, higher write volume, and more memory. We've used read-only slaves, writable query slaves, and sharding combined with shard-aware classes and functions. Though these methods may not cover all potential use cases for scaling your particular problem, each of these examples was chosen to offer a set of techniques that can be used generally in other situations.

If there's one concept that you should take away from this chapter, it's that scaling any system can be a challenge. But with Redis, you can use a variety of methods to scale your platform (hopefully as far as you need it to scale).

Coming up in the next and final chapter, we'll cover Redis scripting with Lua. We'll revisit a few past problems to show how our solutions can be simplified and performance improved with features available in Redis 2.6 and later.

Scripting Redis with Lua

This chapter covers

- Adding functionality without writing C
- Rewriting locks and semaphores with Lua
- Doing away with WATCH/MULTI/EXEC
- Sharding LISTs with Lua

Over the last several chapters, you've built up a collection of tools that you can use in existing applications, while also encountering techniques you can use to solve a variety of problems. This chapter does much of the same, but will turn some of your expectations on their heads. As of Redis 2.6, Redis includes *server-side scripting* with the Lua programming language. This lets you perform a variety of operations inside Redis, which can both simplify your code and increase performance.

In this chapter, we'll start by discussing some of the advantages of Lua over performing operations on the client, showing an example from the social network in chapter 8. We'll then go through two problems from chapters 4 and 6 to show examples where using Lua can remove the need for WATCH/MULTI/EXEC transactions. Later, we'll revisit our locks and semaphores from chapter 6 to show how they can be implemented using Lua for fair multiple client access and higher performance. Finally, we'll build a sharded LIST using Lua that supports many (but not all) standard LIST command equivalents.

Let's get started by learning about some of the things that we can do with Lua scripting.

11.1   *Adding functionality without writing C*

Prior to Redis 2.6 (and the unsupported scripting branch of Redis 2.4), if we wanted higher-level functionality that didn't already exist in Redis, we'd either have to write client-side code (like we have through the last 10 chapters), or we'd have to edit the C source code of Redis itself. Though editing Redis's source code isn't too difficult, supporting such code in a business environment, or trying to convince management that running our own version of the Redis server is a good idea, could be challenging.

In this section, we'll introduce methods by which we can execute Lua inside the Redis server. By scripting Redis with Lua, we can avoid some common pitfalls that slow down development or reduce performance.

The first step in executing Lua code in Redis is loading the code into Redis.

11.1.1   *Loading Lua scripts into Redis*

Some older (and still used) Python Redis libraries for Redis 2.6 don't yet offer the capability to load or execute Lua scripts directly, so we'll spend a few moments to create a loader for the scripts. To load scripts into Redis, there's a two-part command called SCRIPT LOAD that, when provided with a string that's a Lua script, will store the script for later execution and return the SHA1 hash of the script. Later, when we want to execute that script, we run the Redis command EVALSHA with the hash that was returned by Redis, along with any arguments that the script needs.

Our code for doing these operations will be inspired by the current Python Redis code. (We use our method primarily because it allows for using any connection we want without having to explicitly create new scripting objects, which can be useful when dealing with server sharding.) When we pass a string to our script_load() function, it'll create a function that can later be called to execute the script in Redis. When calling the object to execute the script, we must provide a Redis connection, which will then call SCRIPT LOAD on its first call, followed by EVALSHA for all future calls. The script_load() function is shown in the following listing.

Listing 11.1   A function that loads scripts to be called later

Store the cached SHA1 hash of the result of SCRIPT LOAD in a list so we can change it later from within the call() function.

When calling the loaded script, we must provide a connection, a set of keys that the script will manipulate, and any other arguments to the function.

We'll only try loading the script if the SHA1 hash isn't cached.

```
def script_load(script):
    sha = [None]
    def call(conn, keys=[], args=[], force_eval=False):
        if not force_eval:
            if not sha[0]:
                sha[0] = conn.execute_command(
                    "SCRIPT", "LOAD", script, parse="LOAD")

            try:
```

Execute the command from the cached SHAI.

```
                         return conn.execute_command(
                             "EVALSHA", sha[0], len(keys), *(keys+args))

                     except redis.exceptions.ResponseError as msg:
                         if not msg.args[0].startswith("NOSCRIPT"):
                             raise

                 return conn.execute_command(
                     "EVAL", script, len(keys), *(keys+args))

         return call
```

If the error was unrelated to a missing script, raise the exception again.

Return the function that automatically loads and executes scripts when called.

If we received a script-related error, or if we need to force-execute the script, directly execute the script, which will automatically cache the script on the server (with the same SHAI that we've already cached) when done.

You'll notice that in addition to our SCRIPT LOAD and EVALSHA calls, we captured an exception that can happen if we've cached a script's SHA1 hash locally, but the server doesn't know about it. This can happen if the server were to be restarted, if someone had executed the SCRIPT FLUSH command to clean out the script cache, or if we provided connections to two different Redis servers to our function at different times. If we discover that the script is missing, we execute the script directly with EVAL, which caches the script in addition to executing it. Also, we allow clients to directly execute the script, which can be useful when executing a Lua script as part of a transaction or other pipelined sequence.

> **KEYS AND ARGUMENTS TO LUA SCRIPTS** Buried inside our script loader, you may have noticed that calling a script in Lua takes three arguments. The first is a Redis connection, which should be standard by now. The second argument is a list of keys. The third is a list of arguments to the function.
>
> The difference between keys and arguments is that you're supposed to pass all of the keys that the script will be reading or writing as part of the keys argument. This is to potentially let other layers verify that all of the keys are on the same shard if you were using multiserver sharding techniques like those described in chapter 10.
>
> When Redis cluster is released, which will offer automatic multiserver sharding, keys will be checked before a script is run, and will return an error if any keys that aren't on the same server are accessed.
>
> The second list of arguments has no such limitation and is meant to hold data to be used inside the Lua call.

Let's try it out in the console for a simple example to get started.

Results will be returned and converted into the appropriate Python types, when possible.

Most uses will load the script and store a reference to the returned function.

We can then call the function by passing the connection object and any desired arguments.

```
>>> ret_1 = script_load("return 1")
>>> ret_1(conn)
1L
```

As you can see in this example, we created a simple script whose only purpose is to return a value of 1. When we call it with the connection object, the script is loaded and then executed, resulting in the value 1 being returned.

RETURNING NON-STRING AND NON-INTEGER VALUES FROM LUA
Due to limitations in how Lua allows data to be passed in and out of it, some data types that are available in Lua aren't allowed to be passed out, or are altered before being returned. Table 11.1 shows how this data is altered upon return.

Table 11.1 Values returned from Lua and what they're translated into

Lua value	What happens during conversion to Python
`true`	Turns into 1
`false`	Turns into None
`nil`	Doesn't turn into anything, and stops remaining values in a table from being returned
`1.5` (or any other float)	Fractional part is discarded, turning it into an integer
`1e30` (or any other large float)	Is turned into the minimum integer for your version of Python
`"strings"`	Unchanged
`1` (or any other integer +/-2^{53}-1)	Integer is returned unchanged

Because of the ambiguity that results when returning a variety of data types, you should do your best to explicitly return strings whenever possible, and perform any parsing manually. We'll only be returning Booleans, strings, integers, and Lua tables (which are turned into Python lists) for our examples.

Now that we can load and execute scripts, let's get started with a simple example from chapter 8, creating a status message.

11.1.2 Creating a new status message

As we build Lua scripts to perform a set of operations, it's good to start with a short example that isn't terribly complicated or structure-intensive. In this case, we'll start by writing a Lua script combined with some wrapper code to post a status message.

> **LUA SCRIPTS—AS ATOMIC AS SINGLE COMMANDS OR MULTI/EXEC** As you already know, individual commands in Redis are *atomic* in that they're run one at a time. With MULTI/EXEC, you can prevent other commands from running while you're executing multiple commands. But to Redis, EVAL and EVALSHA are each considered to be a (very complicated) command, so they're executed without letting any other structure operations occur.

LUA SCRIPTS—CAN'T BE INTERRUPTED IF THEY HAVE MODIFIED STRUCTURES   When executing a Lua script with EVAL or EVALSHA, Redis doesn't allow any other read/ write commands to run. This can be convenient. But because Lua is a general-purpose programming language, you can write scripts that never return, which could stop other clients from executing commands. To address this, Redis offers two options for stopping a script in Redis, depending on whether you've performed a Redis call that writes.

If your script hasn't performed any calls that write (only reads), you can execute SCRIPT KILL if the script has been executing for longer than the configured lua-time-limit (check your Redis configuration file).

If your script has written to Redis, then killing the script could cause Redis to be in an inconsistent state. In that situation, the only way you can recover is to kill Redis with the SHUTDOWN NOSAVE command, which will cause Redis to lose any changes that have been made since the last snapshot, or since the last group of commands was written to the AOF.

Because of these limitations, you should always test your Lua scripts before running them in production.

As you may remember from chapter 8, listing 8.2 showed the creation of a status message. A copy of the original code we used for posting a status message appears next.

> **Listing 11.2   Our function from listing 8.2 that creates a status message HASH**

```
def create_status(conn, uid, message, **data):                    Get the user's login
    pipeline = conn.pipeline(True)                                name from their user ID.
    pipeline.hget('user:%s' % uid, 'login')        ←┘
    pipeline.incr('status:id:')                          ←┐ Create a new ID for
    login, id = pipeline.execute()                         │ the status message.

    if not login:                     │ Verify that we have a proper
        return None                   │ user account before posting.

    data.update({
        'message': message,
        'posted': time.time(),
        'id': id,                                            Prepare and set
        'uid': uid,                                          the data for the
        'login': login,                                      status message.
    })
    pipeline.hmset('status:%s' % id, data)
    pipeline.hincrby('user:%s' % uid, 'posts')
    pipeline.execute()                                    │ Return the ID of the newly
    return id                                   ←┘ created status message.
```

Record the fact that a status message has been posted. (annotation pointing to the hincrby line)

Generally speaking, the performance penalty for making two round trips to Redis in order to post a status message isn't very much—twice the latency of one round trip. But if we can reduce these two round trips to one, we may also be able to reduce the number of round trips for other examples where we make many round trips. Fewer round trips means lower latency for a given group of commands. Lower latency means less waiting, fewer required web servers, and higher performance for the entire system overall.

To review what happens when we post a new status message: we look up the user's name in a HASH, increment a counter (to get a new ID), add data to a Redis HASH, and increment a counter in the user's HASH. That doesn't sound so bad in Lua; let's give it a shot in the next listing, which shows the Lua script, with a Python wrapper that implements the same API as before.

Listing 11.3   Creating a status message with Lua

```
def create_status(conn, uid, message, **data):      ◁─┐  Take all of the arguments
    args = [                                              as before.
        'message', message,
        'posted', time.time(),
        'uid', uid,                                   Prepare the
    ]                                                 arguments/attributes
    for key, value in data.iteritems():              to be set on the status
        args.append(key)                             message.
        args.append(value)

    return create_status_lua(                         │  Call the
        conn, ['user:%s' % uid, 'status:id:'], args)  │  script.
create_status_lua = script_load('''
local login = redis.call('hget', KEYS[1], 'login')
if not login then                                      If there's no login,
    return false                                       return that no
end                                                    login was found.
local id = redis.call('incr', KEYS[2])
local key = string.format('status:%s', id)

redis.call('hmset', key,                              Set the data      Increment
    'login', login,                                   for the status   the post
    'id', id,                                         message.         count of
    unpack(ARGV))                                                      the user.
redis.call('hincrby', KEYS[1], 'posts', 1)        ◁─┘

return id                                             Return the ID of
''')                                                  the status message.
```

Fetch the user's login name from their ID; remember that tables in Lua are 1-indexed, not 0-indexed like Python and most other languages.

Get a new ID for the status message.

Prepare the destination key for the status message.

This function performs all of the same operations that the previous all-Python version performed, only instead of needing two round trips to Redis with every call, it should only need one (the first call will load the script into Redis and then call the loaded script, but subsequent calls will only require one). This isn't a big issue for posting status messages, but for many other problems that we've gone through in previous chapters, making multiple round trips can take more time than is necessary, or lend to WATCH/MULTI/EXEC contention.

WRITING KEYS THAT AREN'T A PART OF THE KEYS ARGUMENT TO THE SCRIPT In the note in section 11.1.1, I mentioned that we should pass all keys to be modified as part of the keys argument of the script, yet here we're writing a HASH based on a key that wasn't passed. Doing this makes this Lua script incompatible with the future Redis cluster. Whether this operation is still correct in a noncluster sharded server scenario will depend on your sharding methods. I did this to highlight that you may need to do this kind of thing, but doing so prevents you from being able to use Redis cluster.

SCRIPT LOADERS AND HELPERS You'll notice in this first example that we have two major pieces. We have a Python function that handles the translation of the earlier API into the Lua script call, and we have the Lua script that's loaded from our earlier `script_load()` function. We'll continue this pattern for the remainder of the chapter, since the native API for Lua scripting (KEYS and ARGV) can be difficult to call in multiple contexts.

Since Redis 2.6 has been completed and released, libraries that support Redis scripting with Lua in the major languages should get better and more complete. On the Python side of things, a script loader similar to what we've written is already available in the source code repository for the redis-py project, and is currently available from the Python Package Index. We use our script loader due to its flexibility and ease of use when confronted with sharded network connections.

As our volume of interactions with Redis increased over time, we switched to using locks and semaphores to help reduce contention issues surrounding WATCH/MULTI/EXEC transactions. Let's take a look at rewriting locks and semaphores to see if we might be able to further improve performance.

11.2 *Rewriting locks and semaphores with Lua*

When I introduced locks and semaphores in chapter 6, I showed how locks can reduce contention compared to WATCH/MULTI/EXEC transactions by being pessimistic in heavy traffic scenarios. But locks themselves require two to three round trips to acquire or release a lock in the best case, and can suffer from contention in some situations.

In this section, we'll revisit our lock from section 6.2 and rewrite it in Lua in order to further improve performance. We'll then revisit our semaphore example from section 6.3 to implement a completely fair lock while also improving performance there.

Let's first take a look at locks with Lua, and why we'd want to continue using locks at all.

11.2.1 *Why locks in Lua?*

Let's first deal with the question of *why* we would decide to build a lock with Lua. There are two major reasons.

Technically speaking, when executing a Lua script with EVAL or EVALSHA, the first group of arguments after the script or hash is the keys that will be read or written within Lua (I mentioned this in two notes in sections 11.1.1 and 11.1.2). This is primarily to allow for later Redis cluster servers to reject scripts that read or write keys that aren't available on a particular shard. If we don't know what keys will be read/written in advance, we shouldn't be using Lua (we should instead use WATCH/MULTI/EXEC or locks). As such, any time we're reading or writing keys that weren't provided as part of the KEYS argument to the script, we risk potential incompatibility or breakage if we transition to a Redis cluster later.

The second reason is because there are situations where manipulating data in Redis requires data that's not available at the time of the initial call. One example would be fetching some HASH values from Redis, and then using those values to access information from a relational database, which then results in a write back to Redis. We saw this first when we were scheduling the caching of rows in Redis back in section 2.4. We didn't bother locking in that situation because writing two copies of the same row twice wouldn't have been a serious issue. But in other caching scenarios, reading the data to be cached multiple times can be more overhead than is acceptable, or could even cause newer data to be overwritten by older data.

Given these two reasons, let's rewrite our lock to use Lua.

11.2.2 *Rewriting our lock*

As you may remember from section 6.2, locking involved generating an ID, conditionally setting a key with SETNX, and upon success setting the expiration time of the key. Though conceptually simple, we had to deal with failures and retries, which resulted in the original code shown in the next listing.

Listing 11.4   Our final `acquire_lock_with_timeout()` function from section 6.2.5

```
def acquire_lock_with_timeout(
    conn, lockname, acquire_timeout=10, lock_timeout=10):        A 128-bit random
    identifier = str(uuid.uuid4())                               identifier.
    lockname = 'lock:' + lockname
    lock_timeout = int(math.ceil(lock_timeout))                  Only pass integers
                                                                 to our EXPIRE calls.
    end = time.time() + acquire_timeout
    while time.time() < end:
        if conn.setnx(lockname, identifier):                    Get the lock and
            conn.expire(lockname, lock_timeout)                 set the expiration.
            return identifier
        elif not conn.ttl(lockname):                            Check and update the
            conn.expire(lockname, lock_timeout)                 expiration time as necessary.

        time.sleep(.001)

    return False
```

There's nothing too surprising here if you remember how we built up to this lock in section 6.2. Let's go ahead and offer the same functionality, but move the core locking into Lua.

Listing 11.5   A rewritten `acquire_lock_with_timeout()` that uses Lua

```
def acquire_lock_with_timeout(
    conn, lockname, acquire_timeout=10, lock_timeout=10):
    identifier = str(uuid.uuid4())
    lockname = 'lock:' + lockname
    lock_timeout = int(math.ceil(lock_timeout))
```

```
    acquired = False
    end = time.time() + acquire_timeout
    while time.time() < end and not acquired:
        acquired = acquire_lock_with_timeout_lua(
            conn, [lockname], [lock_timeout, identifier]) == 'OK'

        time.sleep(.001 * (not acquired))

    return acquired and identifier
acquire_lock_with_timeout_lua = script_load('''
if redis.call('exists', KEYS[1]) == 0 then
    return redis.call('setex', KEYS[1], unpack(ARGV))
end
''')
```

> **Actually acquire the lock, checking to verify that the Lua call completed successfully.**

> **If the lock doesn't already exist, again remembering that tables use I-based indexing.**

> **Set the key with the provided expiration and identifier.**

There aren't any significant changes in the code, except that we change the commands we use so that if a lock is acquired, it always has a timeout. Let's also go ahead and rewrite the release lock code to use Lua.

Previously, we watched the lock key, and then verified that the lock still had the same value. If it had the same value, we removed the lock; otherwise we'd say that the lock was lost. Our Lua version of release_lock() is shown next.

Listing 11.6   A rewritten `release_lock()` that uses Lua

```
def release_lock(conn, lockname, identifier):
    lockname = 'lock:' + lockname
    return release_lock_lua(conn, [lockname], [identifier])

release_lock_lua = script_load('''
if redis.call('get', KEYS[1]) == ARGV[1] then
    return redis.call('del', KEYS[1]) or true
end
''')
```

> **Call the Lua function that releases the lock.**

> **Make sure that the lock matches.**

> **Delete the lock and ensure that we return true.**

Unlike acquiring the lock, releasing the lock became shorter as we no longer needed to perform all of the typical WATCH/MULTI/EXEC steps.

Reducing the code is great, but we haven't gotten far if we haven't actually improved the performance of the lock itself. We've added some instrumentation to the locking code along with some benchmarking code that executes 1, 2, 5, and 10 parallel processes to acquire and release locks repeatedly. We count the number of attempts to acquire the lock and how many times the lock was acquired over 10 seconds, with both our original and Lua-based acquire and release lock functions. Table 11.2 shows the number of calls that were performed and succeeded.

Table 11.2   Performance of our original lock against a Lua-based lock over 10 seconds

Benchmark configuration	Tries in 10 seconds	Acquires in 10 seconds
Original lock, 1 client	31,359	31,359
Original lock, 2 clients	30,085	22,507

Table 11.2 Performance of our original lock against a Lua-based lock over 10 seconds *(continued)*

Benchmark configuration	Tries in 10 seconds	Acquires in 10 seconds
Original lock, 5 clients	47,694	19,695
Original lock, 10 clients	71,917	14,361
Lua lock, 1 client	44,494	44,494
Lua lock, 2 clients	50,404	42,199
Lua lock, 5 clients	70,807	40,826
Lua lock, 10 clients	96,871	33,990

Looking at the data from our benchmark (pay attention to the right column), one thing to note is that Lua-based locks succeed in acquiring and releasing the lock in cycles significantly more often than our previous lock—by more than 40% with a single client, 87% with 2 clients, and over 100% with 5 or 10 clients attempting to acquire and release the same locks. Comparing the middle and right columns, we can also see how much faster attempts at locking are made with Lua, primarily due to the reduced number of round trips.

But even better than performance improvements, our code to acquire and release the locks is significantly easier to understand and verify as correct.

Another example where we built a synchronization primitive is with semaphores; let's take a look at building them next.

11.2.3 *Counting semaphores in Lua*

As we worked through our counting semaphores in chapter 6, we spent a lot of time trying to ensure that our semaphores had some level of fairness. In the process, we used a counter to create a sort of numeric identifier for the client, which was then used to determine whether the client had been successful. But because we still had race conditions when acquiring the semaphore, we ultimately still needed to use a lock for the semaphore to function correctly.

Let's look at our earlier implementation of the counting semaphore and think about what it may take to improve it using Lua.

Listing 11.7 The `acquire_semaphore()` function from section 6.3.2

```
def acquire_semaphore(conn, semname, limit, timeout=10):
    identifier = str(uuid.uuid4())                                    A 128-bit
    now = time.time()                                                 random
                                                                      identifier.
    pipeline = conn.pipeline(True)
    pipeline.zremrangebyscore(semname, '-inf', now - timeout)
    pipeline.zadd(semname, identifier, now)
    pipeline.zrank(semname, identifier)                               Try to acquire
    if pipeline.execute()[-1] < limit:                               the semaphore.
        return identifier
```

Time out old semaphore holders. → *(annotation)*

Check to see if we have it. *(annotation)*

```
        conn.zrem(semname, identifier)
        return None
```
We failed to get the semaphore; discard our identifier.

In the process of translating this function into Lua, after cleaning out timed-out semaphores, it becomes possible to know whether a semaphore is available to acquire, so we can simplify our code in the case where a semaphore isn't available. Also, because everything is occurring inside Redis, we don't need the counter or the owner ZSET, since the first client to execute their Lua function should be the one to get the semaphore. The Lua version of `acquire_semaphore()` can be seen in the next listing.

Listing 11.8 The `acquire_semaphore()` function rewritten with Lua

Get the current timestamp for handling timeouts.

Pass all of the required arguments into the Lua function to actually acquire the semaphore.

```
def acquire_semaphore(conn, semname, limit, timeout=10):
    now = time.time()
    return acquire_semaphore_lua(conn, [semname],
        [now-timeout, limit, now, str(uuid.uuid4())])

acquire_semaphore_lua = script_load('''
redis.call('zremrangebyscore', KEYS[1], '-inf', ARGV[1])

if redis.call('zcard', KEYS[1]) < tonumber(ARGV[2]) then
    redis.call('zadd', KEYS[1], ARGV[3], ARGV[4])
    return ARGV[4]
end
''')
```

Clean out all of the expired semaphores.

If we haven't yet hit our semaphore limit, then acquire the semaphore.

Add the timestamp to the timeout ZSET.

This updated semaphore offers the same capabilities of the lock-wrapped `acquire_fair_semaphore_with_lock()`, including being completely fair. Further, because of the simplifications we've performed (no locks, no ZINTERSTORE, and no ZREMRANGEBYRANK), our new semaphore will operate significantly faster than the previous semaphore implementation, while at the same time reducing the complexity of the semaphore itself.

Due to our simplification, releasing the semaphore can be done using the original `release_semaphore()` code from section 6.3.1. We only need to create a Lua-based refresh semaphore function to replace the fair semaphore version from section 6.3.3, shown next.

Listing 11.9 A `refresh_semaphore()` function written with Lua

If the semaphore is still valid, then we update the semaphore's timestamp.

```
def refresh_semaphore(conn, semname, identifier):
    return refresh_semaphore_lua(conn, [semname],
        [identifier, time.time()]) != None

refresh_semaphore_lua = script_load('''
if redis.call('zscore', KEYS[1], ARGV[1]) then
    return redis.call('zadd', KEYS[1], ARGV[2], ARGV[1]) or true
end
''')
```

If Lua had returned nil from the call (the semaphore wasn't refreshed), Python will return None instead.

With acquire and refresh semaphore rewritten with Lua, we now have a completely fair semaphore that's faster and easier to understand.

Now that we've rewritten locks and semaphores in Lua and have seen a bit of what they can do to improve performance, let's try to remove WATCH/MULTI/EXEC transactions and locks from two of our previous examples to see how well we can make them perform.

11.3   Doing away with WATCH/MULTI/EXEC

In previous chapters, we used a combination of WATCH, MULTI, and EXEC in several cases to implement a form of transaction in Redis. Generally, when there are few writers modifying WATCHed data, these transactions complete without significant contention or retries. But if operations can take several round trips to execute, if contention is high, or if network latency is high, clients may need to perform many retries in order to complete operations.

In this section, we'll revisit our autocomplete example from chapter 6 along with our marketplace example originally covered in chapter 4 to show how we can simplify our code and improve performance at the same time.

First up, let's look at one of our autocomplete examples from chapter 6.

11.3.1   Revisiting group autocomplete

Back in chapter 6, we introduced an autocomplete procedure that used a ZSET to store user names to be autocompleted on.

As you may remember, we calculated a pair of strings that would surround all of the values that we wanted to autocomplete on. When we had those values, we'd insert our data into the ZSET, and then WATCH the ZSET for anyone else making similar changes. We'd then fetch 10 items between the two endpoints and remove them between a MULTI/EXEC pair. Let's take a quick look at the code that we used.

Listing 11.10   Our autocomplete code from section 6.1.2

```
def autocomplete_on_prefix(conn, guild, prefix):
    start, end = find_prefix_range(prefix)          Find the start/
    identifier = str(uuid.uuid4())                  end range for
    start += identifier                             the prefix.
    end += identifier
    zset_name = 'members:' + guild

    conn.zadd(zset_name, start, 0, end, 0)          Add the start/end
    pipeline = conn.pipeline(True)                  range items to the
    while 1:                                        ZSET.
        try:
            pipeline.watch(zset_name)
            sindex = pipeline.zrank(zset_name, start)     Find the ranks
            eindex = pipeline.zrank(zset_name, end)       of our end
            erange = min(sindex + 9, eindex - 2)          points.
            pipeline.multi()
```

```
                    pipeline.zrem(zset_name, start, end)              Get the values
                    pipeline.zrange(zset_name, sindex, erange)        inside our range,
                    items = pipeline.execute()[-1]                    and clean up.
                    break
            except redis.exceptions.WatchError:              Retry if someone modified
                continue                                     our autocomplete ZSET.

        return [item for item in items if '{' not in item]        Remove start/end entries
                                                                   if an autocomplete was
                                                                   in progress.
```

If few autocomplete operations are being performed at one time, this shouldn't cause many retries. But regardless of retries, we still have a lot of code related to handling hopefully rare retries—roughly 40%, depending on how we count lines. Let's get rid of all of that retry code, and move the core functionality of this function into a Lua script. The result of this change is shown in the next listing.

Listing 11.11   Autocomplete on prefix using Redis scripting

```
                       def autocomplete_on_prefix(conn, guild, prefix):
    Get the range          start, end = find_prefix_range(prefix)
    and identifier.        identifier = str(uuid.uuid4())

                           items = autocomplete_on_prefix_lua(conn,      Fetch the data
                               ['members:' + guild],                     from Redis with
                               [start+identifier, end+identifier])       the Lua script.

    Filter out any         return [item for item in items if '{' not in item]   Add our place-
    items that we                                                                holder endpoints
    don't want.        autocomplete_on_prefix_lua = script_load('''         to the ZSET.
                       redis.call('zadd', KEYS[1], 0, ARGV[1], 0, ARGV[2])
    Find the endpoint  local sindex = redis.call('zrank', KEYS[1], ARGV[1])
positions in the ZSET. local eindex = redis.call('zrank', KEYS[1], ARGV[2])
                       eindex = math.min(sindex + 9, eindex - 2)            Calculate the proper
    Remove the         redis.call('zrem', KEYS[1], unpack(ARGV))            range of values to fetch.
    placeholder        return redis.call('zrange', KEYS[1], sindex, eindex)
    endpoints.         ''')                                        Fetch and return
                                                                   our results.
```

The body of the Lua script should be somewhat familiar; it's a direct translation of the chapter 6 code. Not only is the resulting code significantly shorter, it also executes much faster. Using a similar benchmarking method to what we used in chapter 6, we ran 1, 2, 5, and 10 concurrent processes that performed autocomplete requests against the same guild as fast as possible. To keep our chart simple, we only calculated attempts to autocomplete and successful autocompletes, over the course of 10 seconds. Table 11.3 shows the results of this test.

Looking at our table, when executing the older autocomplete function that uses WATCH/MULTI/EXEC transactions, the probability of finishing a transaction is reduced as we add more clients, and the total attempts over 10 seconds hit a peak limit. On the other hand, our Lua autocomplete can attempt and finish far more times every second, primarily due to the reduced overhead of fewer network round trips, as well as

Table 11.3 Performance of our original autocomplete versus our Lua-based autocomplete over 10 seconds

Benchmark configuration	Tries in 10 seconds	Autocompletes in 10 seconds
Original autocomplete, 1 client	26,339	26,339
Original autocomplete, 2 clients	35,188	17,551
Original autocomplete, 5 clients	59,544	10,989
Original autocomplete, 10 clients	57,305	6,141
Lua autocomplete, 1 client	64,440	64,440
Lua autocomplete, 2 clients	89,140	89,140
Lua autocomplete, 5 clients	125,971	125,971
Lua autocomplete, 10 clients	128,217	128,217

not running into any WATCH errors due to contention. Looking at just the 10-client version of both, the 10-client Lua autocomplete is able to complete more than 20 times as many autocomplete operations as the original autocomplete.

Now that we've seen how well we can do on one of our simpler examples, let's look at how we can improve our marketplace.

11.3.2 Improving the marketplace, again

In section 6.2, we revisited the marketplace example we introduced in section 4.4, replacing our use of WATCH, MULTI, and EXEC with locks, and showed how using coarse-grained and fine-grained locks in Redis can help reduce contention and improve performance.

In this section, we'll again work on the marketplace, further improving performance by removing the locks completely and moving our code into a Lua script.

Let's first look at our marketplace code with a lock. As a review of what goes on, first the lock is acquired, and then we watch the buyer's user information HASH and let the buyer purchase the item if they have enough money. The original function from section 6.2 appears next.

Listing 11.12 The purchase item with lock function from section 6.2

```
def purchase_item_with_lock(conn, buyerid, itemid, sellerid):
    buyer = "users:%s" % buyerid
    seller = "users:%s" % sellerid
    item = "%s.%s" % (itemid, sellerid)
    inventory = "inventory:%s" % buyerid
    end = time.time() + 30

    locked = acquire_lock(conn, 'market:')        ◁── Get the lock
    if not locked:
        return False

    pipe = conn.pipeline(True)
```

```
try:
    while time.time() < end:
        try:
            pipe.watch(buyer)
            pipe.zscore("market:", item)
            pipe.hget(buyer, 'funds')
            price, funds = pipe.execute()
            if price is None or price > funds:
                pipe.unwatch()
                return None

            pipe.hincrby(seller, int(price))
            pipe.hincrby(buyerid, int(-price))
            pipe.sadd(inventory, itemid)
            pipe.zrem("market:", item)
            pipe.execute()
            return True
        except redis.exceptions.WatchError:
            pass
finally:
    release_lock(conn, 'market:', locked)
```

Check for a sold item or insufficient funds.

Transfer funds from the buyer to the seller, and transfer the item to the buyer.

⟵ **Release the lock.**

Despite using a lock, we still needed to watch the buyer's user information HASH to ensure that enough money was available at the time of purchase. And because of that, we have the worst of both worlds: chunks of code to handle locking, and other chunks of code to handle the potential WATCH errors. Of all of the solutions we've seen so far, this one is a prime candidate for rewriting in Lua.

When rewriting this function in Lua, we can do away with the locking, the WATCH/MULTI/EXEC transactions, and even timeouts. Our code becomes straightforward and simple: make sure the item is available, make sure the buyer has enough money, transfer the item to the buyer, and transfer the buyer's money to the seller. The following listing shows the rewritten item-purchasing function.

Listing 11.13   The purchase item function rewritten with Lua

```
def purchase_item(conn, buyerid, itemid, sellerid):
    buyer = "users:%s" % buyerid
    seller = "users:%s" % sellerid
    item = "%s.%s"%(itemid, sellerid)
    inventory = "inventory:%s" % buyerid

    return purchase_item_lua(conn,
        ['market:', buyer, seller, inventory], [item, itemid])

purchase_item_lua = script_load('''
local price = tonumber(redis.call('zscore', KEYS[1], ARGV[1]))
local funds = tonumber(redis.call('hget', KEYS[2], 'funds'))

if price and funds and funds >= price then
    redis.call('hincrby', KEYS[3], 'funds', price)
    redis.call('hincrby', KEYS[2], 'funds', -price)
    redis.call('sadd', KEYS[4], ARGV[2])
    redis.call('zrem', KEYS[1], ARGV[1])
```

Prepare all of the keys and arguments for the Lua script.

Get the item price and the buyer's available funds.

If the item is still available and the buyer has enough money, transfer the item.

```
            return true
    end
    ''')
```
⟵┐ **Signify that the purchase
     completed successfully.**

Just comparing the two code listings, the Lua-based item-purchase code is far easier to understand. And without the multiple round trips to complete a single purchase (locking, watching, fetching price and available money, then the purchase, and then the unlocking), it's obvious that purchasing an item will be even faster than the fine-grained locking that we used in chapter 6. But how much faster?

> ### Exercise: Rewrite item listing in Lua
>
> We rewrote the purchase-item function in Lua for our benchmarks, but can you rewrite the original item-listing function from section 4.4.2 into Lua? Hint: The source code for this chapter includes the answer to this exercise, just as the source code for each of the other chapters includes the solutions to almost all of the exercises.

We now have an item-purchase function rewritten in Lua, and if you perform the exercise, you'll also have an item-listing function written in Lua. If you read the hint to our exercise, you'll notice that we also rewrote the item-listing function in Lua. You may remember that at the end of section 6.2.4, we ran some benchmarks to compare the performance of WATCH/MULTI/EXEC transactions against coarse-grained and fine-grained locks. We reran the benchmark for five listing and five buying processes using our newly rewritten Lua versions, to produce the last row in table 11.4.

Table 11.4   Performance of Lua compared with no locking, coarse-grained locks, and fine-grained locks over 60 seconds

	Listed items	Bought items	Purchase retries	Average wait per purchase
5 listers, 5 buyers, no lock	206,000	<600	161,000	498ms
5 listers, 5 buyers, with lock	21,000	20,500	0	14ms
5 listers, 5 buyers, with fine-grained lock	116,000	111,000	0	<3ms
5 listers, 5 buyers, using Lua	505,000	480,000	0	<1ms

As in other cases where we've moved functionality into Lua, we see a substantial performance increase. Numerically, we see an improvement in listing and buying performance of more than 4.25 times compared with fine-grained locking, and see latencies of under 1 millisecond to execute a purchase (actual latencies were consistently around .61 milliseconds). From this table, we can see the performance advantages of coarse-grained locks over WATCH/MULTI/EXEC, fine-grained locks over coarse-grained locks, and Lua over fine-grained locks. That said, try to remember that while Lua can offer extraordinary performance advantages (and substantial code simplification in some cases), Lua scripting in Redis is limited to data we can access from within Lua and Redis, whereas there are no such limits when using locks or WATCH/MULTI/EXEC transactions.

Now that you've seen some of the amazing performance advantages that are available with Lua, let's look at an example where we can save memory with Lua.

11.4 Sharding LISTs with Lua

Back in sections 9.2 and 9.3, we sharded HASHes, SETs, and even STRINGs as a way of reducing memory. In section 10.3, we sharded ZSETs to allow for search indexes to grow beyond one machine's memory and to improve performance.

As promised in section 9.2, in this section we'll create a sharded LIST in order to reduce memory use for long LISTs. We'll support pushing to both ends of the LIST, and we'll support blocking and nonblocking pops from both ends of the list.

Before we get started on actually implementing these features, we'll look at how to structure the data itself.

11.4.1 Structuring a sharded LIST

In order to store a sharded LIST in a way that allows for pushing and popping from both ends, we need the IDs for the first and last shard, as well as the LIST shards themselves.

To store information about the first and last shards, we'll keep two numbers stored as standard Redis strings. These keys will be named <listname>:first and <listname>:last. Any time the sharded LIST is empty, both of these numbers will be the same. Figure 11.1 shows the first and last shard IDs.

Additionally, each shard will be named <listname>:<shardid>, and shards will be assigned sequentially. More specifically, if items are popped from the left, then as items are pushed onto the right, the last shard index will increase, and more shards with higher shard IDs will be used. Similarly, if items are popped from the right, then as items are pushed onto the left, the first shard index will decrease, and more shards with lower shard IDs will be used. Figure 11.2 shows some example shards as part of the same sharded LIST.

The structures that we'll use for sharded LISTs shouldn't seem strange. The only interesting thing that we're doing is splitting a single LIST into multiple pieces and keeping track of the IDs of the first and last shards. But actually implementing our operations? That's where things get interesting.

Figure 11.1   First and last shard IDs for sharded LISTs

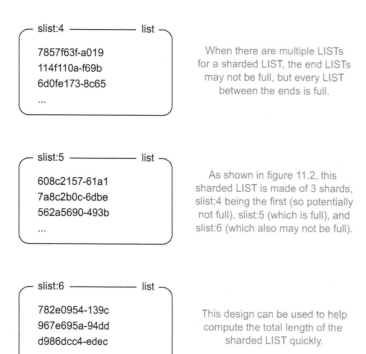

When there are multiple LISTs
for a sharded LIST, the end LISTs
may not be full, but every LIST
between the ends is full.

As shown in figure 11.2, this
sharded LIST is made of 3 shards,
slist:4 being the first (so potentially
not full), slist:5 (which is full), and
slist:6 (which also may not be full).

This design can be used to help
compute the total length of the
sharded LIST quickly.

Figure 11.2 LIST
shards with data

11.4.2 *Pushing items onto the sharded LIST*

It turns out that one of the simplest operations that we'll perform will be pushing items onto either end of the sharded LIST. Because of some small semantic changes to the way that blocking pop operations work in Redis 2.6, we have to do some work to ensure that we don't accidentally overflow a shard. I'll explain when we talk more about the code.

In order to push items onto either end of a sharded LIST, we must first prepare the data for sending by breaking it up into chunks. This is because if we're sending to a sharded LIST, we may know the total capacity, but we won't know if any clients are waiting on a blocking pop from that LIST,[1] so we may need to take multiple passes for large LIST pushes.

After we've prepared our data, we pass it on to the underlying Lua script. And in Lua, we only need to find the first/last shards, and then push the item(s) onto that LIST until it's full, returning the number of items that were pushed. The Python and Lua code to push items onto either end of a sharded LIST is shown in the following listing.

---

[1] In earlier versions of Redis, pushing to a LIST with blocking clients waiting on them would cause the item to be pushed immediately, and subsequent calls to LLEN would tell the length of the LIST after those items had been sent to the blocking clients. In Redis 2.6, this is no longer the case—the blocking pops are handled after the current command has completed. In this context, that means that blocking pops are handled after the current Lua call has finished.

Listing 11.14 Functions for pushing items onto a sharded `LIST`

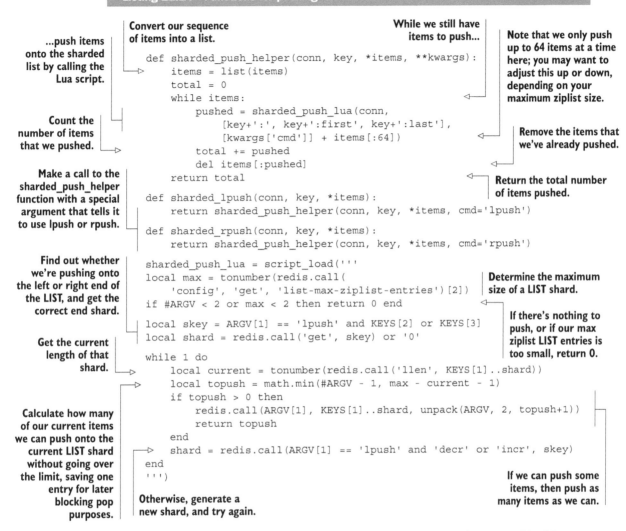

...push items onto the sharded list by calling the Lua script.

Convert our sequence of items into a list.

While we still have items to push...

Note that we only push up to 64 items at a time here; you may want to adjust this up or down, depending on your maximum ziplist size.

Count the number of items that we pushed.

Remove the items that we've already pushed.

Make a call to the sharded_push_helper function with a special argument that tells it to use lpush or rpush.

Return the total number of items pushed.

Find out whether we're pushing onto the left or right end of the LIST, and get the correct end shard.

Determine the maximum size of a LIST shard.

If there's nothing to push, or if our max ziplist LIST entries is too small, return 0.

Get the current length of that shard.

Calculate how many of our current items we can push onto the current LIST shard without going over the limit, saving one entry for later blocking pop purposes.

If we can push some items, then push as many items as we can.

Otherwise, generate a new shard, and try again.

```python
def sharded_push_helper(conn, key, *items, **kwargs):
    items = list(items)
    total = 0
    while items:
        pushed = sharded_push_lua(conn,
            [key+':', key+':first', key+':last'],
            [kwargs['cmd']] + items[:64])
        total += pushed
        del items[:pushed]
    return total
def sharded_lpush(conn, key, *items):
    return sharded_push_helper(conn, key, *items, cmd='lpush')

def sharded_rpush(conn, key, *items):
    return sharded_push_helper(conn, key, *items, cmd='rpush')

sharded_push_lua = script_load('''
local max = tonumber(redis.call(
    'config', 'get', 'list-max-ziplist-entries')[2])
if #ARGV < 2 or max < 2 then return 0 end

local skey = ARGV[1] == 'lpush' and KEYS[2] or KEYS[3]
local shard = redis.call('get', skey) or '0'

while 1 do
    local current = tonumber(redis.call('llen', KEYS[1]..shard))
    local topush = math.min(#ARGV - 1, max - current - 1)
    if topush > 0 then
        redis.call(ARGV[1], KEYS[1]..shard, unpack(ARGV, 2, topush+1))
        return topush
    end
    shard = redis.call(ARGV[1] == 'lpush' and 'decr' or 'incr', skey)
end
''')
```

As I mentioned before, because we don't know about whether clients are blocking on pops, we can't push all items in a single call, so we choose a modestly sized block of 64 at a time, though you should feel free to adjust it up or down depending on the size of your maximum ziplist-encoded LIST configuration.

LIMITATIONS TO THIS SHARDED LIST Earlier in this chapter, I mentioned that in order to properly check keys for sharded databases (like in the future Redis cluster), we're supposed to pass all of the keys that will be modified as part of the KEYS argument to the Redis script. But since the shards we're supposed to write to aren't necessarily known in advance, we can't do that here. As a result, this sharded LIST is only able to be contained on a single actual Redis server, not sharded onto multiple servers.

You'll notice that for our sharded push, we may loop in order to go to another shard when the first is full. Because no other commands can execute while the script is executing, the loop should take at most two passes: one to notice that the initial shard is full, the second to push items onto the empty shard.

Exercise: Finding the length of a sharded LIST

Now that you can create a sharded LIST, knowing how long your LIST has grown can be useful, especially if you're using sharded LISTs for very long task queues. Can you write a function (with or without Lua) that can return the size of a sharded LIST?

Let's work on popping items from the LIST next.

11.4.3 *Popping items from the sharded LIST*

When popping items from a sharded LIST, we technically don't need to use Lua. Redis already has everything we need to pop items: WATCH, MULTI, and EXEC. But like we've seen in other situations, when there's high contention (which could definitely be the case for a LIST that grows long enough to need sharding), WATCH/MULTI/EXEC transactions may be slow.

To pop items in a nonblocking manner from a sharded LIST in Lua, we only need to find the endmost shard, pop an item (if one is available), and if the resulting LIST shard is empty, adjust the end shard information, as demonstrated in the next listing.

Listing 11.15 The Lua script for pushing items onto a sharded LIST

```
def sharded_lpop(conn, key):
    return sharded_list_pop_lua(
        conn, [key+':', key+':first', key+':last'], ['lpop'])

def sharded_rpop(conn, key):
    return sharded_list_pop_lua(
        conn, [key+':', key+':first', key+':last'], ['rpop'])

sharded_list_pop_lua = script_load('''
local skey = ARGV[1] == 'lpop' and KEYS[2] or KEYS[3]
local okey = ARGV[1] ~= 'lpop' and KEYS[2] or KEYS[3]
local shard = redis.call('get', skey) or '0'
local ret = redis.call(ARGV[1], KEYS[1]..shard)
if not ret or redis.call('llen', KEYS[1]..shard) == '0' then
    local oshard = redis.call('get', okey) or '0'

    if shard == oshard then
        return ret
    end

    local cmd = ARGV[1] == 'lpop' and 'incr' or 'decr'
```

Get the key for the end we'll be popping from.

Get the key for the end we won't be popping from.

Pop from the shard.

Get the shard ID that we'll be popping from.

Get the shard ID for the end we didn't pop from.

If both ends of the sharded LIST are the same, then the list is now empty and we're done.

If we didn't get anything because the shard was empty, or we have just made the shard empty, we should clean up our shard endpoint.

Determine whether to increment or decrement the shard ID, based on whether we were popping off the left end or right end.

```
Adjust our shard  ┌─▷        shard = redis.call(cmd, skey)
      endpoint.   │          if not ret then
                  │              ret = redis.call(ARGV[1], KEYS[1]..shard)   ◁─┐
                  │          end                                               │
              end                              If we didn't get a value before,│
              return ret                       try again on the new shard.     │
              ''')
```

When popping items from a sharded LIST, we need to remember that if we pop from an empty shard, we don't know if it's because the whole sharded LIST is empty or just the shard itself. In this situation, we need to verify that we still have space between the endpoints, in order to know if we can adjust one end or the other. In the situation where just this one shard is empty, we have an opportunity to pop an item from the proper shard, which we do.

The only remaining piece for our promised API is blocking pop operations.

11.4.4 *Performing blocking pops from the sharded LIST*

We've stepped through pushing items onto both ends of a long LIST, popping items off both ends, and even written a function to get the total length of a sharded LIST. In this section, we'll build a method to perform blocking pops from both ends of the sharded LIST. In previous chapters, we've used blocking pops to implement messaging and task queues, though other uses are also possible.

Whenever possible, if we don't need to actually block and wait on a request, we should use the nonblocking versions of the sharded LIST pop methods. This is because, with the current semantics and commands available to Lua scripting and WATCH/MULTI/EXEC transactions, there are still some situations where we may receive incorrect data. These situations are rare, and we'll go through a few steps to try to prevent them from happening, but every system has limitations.

In order to perform a blocking pop, we'll cheat somewhat. First, we'll try to perform a nonblocking pop in a loop until we run out of time, or until we get an item. If that works, then we're done. If that doesn't get an item, then we'll loop over a few steps until we get an item, or until our timeout is up.

The specific sequence of operations we'll perform is to start by trying the nonblocking pop. If that fails, then we fetch information about the first and last shard IDs. If the IDs are the same, we then perform a blocking pop on that shard ID. Well, sort of.

Because the shard ID of the end we want to pop from could've changed since we fetched the endpoints (due to round-trip latencies), we insert a pipelined Lua script EVAL call just before the blocking pop. This script verifies whether we're trying to pop from the correct LIST. If we are, then it does nothing, and our blocking pop operation occurs without issue. But if it's the wrong LIST, then the script will push an extra "dummy" item onto the LIST, which will then be popped with the blocking pop operation immediately following.

There's a potential race between when the Lua script is executed and when the blocking pop operation is executed. If someone attempts to pop or push an item from that same shard between when the Lua script is executed and when the blocking pop operation is executed, then we could get bad data (the other popping client getting our dummy item), or we could end up blocking on the wrong shard.

> **WHY NOT USE A MULTI/EXEC TRANSACTION?** We've talked a lot about MULTI/ EXEC transactions as a way of preventing race conditions through the other chapters. So why don't we use WATCH/MULTI/EXEC to prepare information, and then use a BLPOP/BRPOP operation as the last command before EXEC? This is because if a BLPOP/BRPOP operation occurs on an empty LIST as part of a MULTI/EXEC transaction, it'd block forever because no other commands can be run in that time. To prevent such an error, BLPOP/BRPOP operations within a MULTI/EXEC block will execute as their nonblocking LPOP/RPOP versions (except allowing the client to pass multiple lists to attempt to pop from).

To address the issue with blocking on the wrong shard, we'll only ever block for one second at a time (even if we're supposed to block forever). And to address the issue with our blocking pop operations getting data that wasn't actually on the end shard, we'll operate under the assumption that if data came in between two non-transactional pipelined calls, it's close enough to being correct. Our functions for handling blocking pops can be seen in the next listing.

Listing 11.16   Our code to perform a blocking pop from a sharded LIST

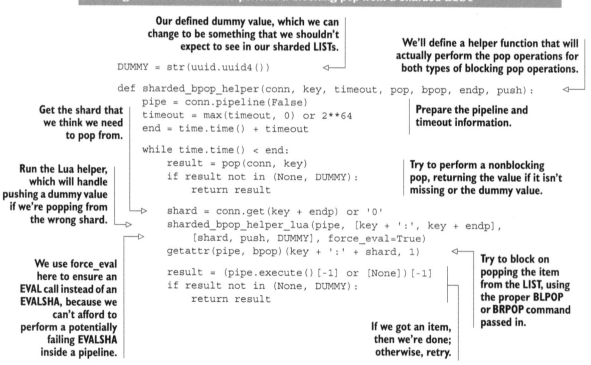

```
DUMMY = str(uuid.uuid4())
```
Our defined dummy value, which we can change to be something that we shouldn't expect to see in our sharded LISTs.

```
def sharded_bpop_helper(conn, key, timeout, pop, bpop, endp, push):
    pipe = conn.pipeline(False)
    timeout = max(timeout, 0) or 2**64
    end = time.time() + timeout

    while time.time() < end:
        result = pop(conn, key)
        if result not in (None, DUMMY):
            return result

        shard = conn.get(key + endp) or '0'
        sharded_bpop_helper_lua(pipe, [key + ':', key + endp],
            [shard, push, DUMMY], force_eval=True)
        getattr(pipe, bpop)(key + ':' + shard, 1)

        result = (pipe.execute()[-1] or [None])[-1]
        if result not in (None, DUMMY):
            return result
```

We'll define a helper function that will actually perform the pop operations for both types of blocking pop operations.

Prepare the pipeline and timeout information.

Get the shard that we think we need to pop from.

Run the Lua helper, which will handle pushing a dummy value if we're popping from the wrong shard.

We use force_eval here to ensure an EVAL call instead of an EVALSHA, because we can't afford to perform a potentially failing EVALSHA inside a pipeline.

Try to perform a nonblocking pop, returning the value if it isn't missing or the dummy value.

Try to block on popping the item from the LIST, using the proper BLPOP or BRPOP command passed in.

If we got an item, then we're done; otherwise, retry.

These functions prepare the actual call to the underlying blocking pop operations.

```
def sharded_blpop(conn, key, timeout=0):
    return sharded_bpop_helper(
        conn, key, timeout, sharded_lpop, 'blpop', ':first', 'lpush')

def sharded_brpop(conn, key, timeout=0):
    return sharded_bpop_helper(
        conn, key, timeout, sharded_rpop, 'brpop', ':last', 'rpush')
```

If we were going to try to pop from the wrong shard, push an extra value.

```
sharded_bpop_helper_lua = script_load('''
local shard = redis.call('get', KEYS[2]) or '0'
if shard ~= ARGV[1] then
    redis.call(ARGV[2], KEYS[1]..ARGV[1], ARGV[3])
end
''')
```

Get the actual shard for the end we want to pop from.

There are a lot of pieces that come together to make this actually work, but remember that there are three basic pieces. The first piece is a helper that handles the loop to actually fetch the item. Inside this loop, we call the second piece, which is the helper/blocking pop pair of functions, which handles the blocking portion of the calls. The third piece is the API that users will actually call, which handles passing all of the proper arguments to the helper.

For each of the commands operating on sharded LISTs, we could implement them with WATCH/MULTI/EXEC transactions. But a practical issue comes up when there's a modest amount of contention, because each of these operations manipulates multiple structures simultaneously, and will manipulate structures that are calculated as part of the transaction itself. Using a lock over the entire structure can help somewhat, but using Lua improves performance significantly.

11.5 *Summary*

If there's one idea that you should take away from this chapter, it's that scripting with Lua can greatly improve performance and can simplify the operations that you need to perform. Though there are some limitations with Redis scripting across shards that aren't limitations when using locks or WATCH/MULTI/EXEC transactions in some scenarios, Lua scripting is a significant win in the majority of situations.

Sadly, we've come to the end of our chapters. Up next you'll find appendixes that offer installation instructions for three major platforms; references to potentially useful software, libraries, and documentation; and an index to help you find relevant topics in this or other chapters.

appendix A
Quick and dirty setup

Depending on your platform, setting up Redis can range from easy to difficult. I've broken down installation instructions into sections for the three major platforms. Feel free to skip ahead to your platform, which will also include instructions for installing and configuring Python and the Redis client libraries for Python on your system.

A.1   *Installation on Debian or Ubuntu Linux*

If you're using a Debian-derived Linux, your first instinct will be to `apt-get install redis-server`, but this is probably the wrong thing to do. Depending on your version of Debian or Ubuntu, you could be installing an old version of Redis. As an example, if you're using Ubuntu 10.4, you'd be downloading Redis 1.2.6, which was released in March 2010 and doesn't support many of the commands that we use.

In this section, you'll first install the build tools because you'll compile Redis from scratch. Then you'll download, compile, and install Redis. After Redis is running, you'll download the Redis client libraries for Python.

To get started, make sure that you have all of the standard required build tools installed by fetching and downloading `make`, as can be seen in the following listing.

Listing A.1   Installing build tools on Debian Linux

```
~$ sudo apt-get update
~$ sudo apt-get install make gcc python-dev
```

When your build tools are installed (they were probably installed before; this was a verification step), you'll take these steps:

1   Download the most recent stable Redis source code from http://redis.io/download.
2   Extract, compile, install, and start Redis.
3   Download and install the necessary Redis client libraries for Python.

273

The first two steps in this process are shown next.

Listing A.2   Installing Redis on Linux

Download the most recent version of Redis 2.6 (or later): http://redis.io/download).

```
~:$ wget -q http://redis.googlecode.com/files/redis-2.6.9.tar.gz
~:$ tar -xzf redis-2.6.9.tar.gz
~:$ cd redis-2.6.9/
~/redis-2.6.9:$ make
cd src && make all
[trimmed]
make[1]: Leaving directory `~/redis-2.6.9/src'
~/redis-2.6.9:$ sudo make install
cd src && make install
[trimmed]
make[1]: Leaving directory `~/redis-2.6.9/src'
~/redis-2.6.9:$ redis-server redis.conf
[13792] 2 Feb 17:53:16.523 * Max number of open files set to 10032
[trimmed]
[13792] 2 Feb 17:53:16.529 * The server is now ready to accept
connections on port 6379
```

Compile Redis.

Install Redis.

Start Redis server.

Extract the source code.

Watch compilation messages go by; you shouldn't see any errors.

Watch installation messages go by; you shouldn't see any errors.

See the confirmation that Redis has started.

After you have Redis installed and running, you need to install the Redis client libraries for Python. You won't bother to install Python, because Python 2.6 or 2.7 should already be installed by default on Ubuntu or Debian releases in the last few years. But you'll download and install a simple helper package called setuptools, which will help you download and install the Redis client libraries.[1] This last step of installing the Redis client libraries for Python is shown next.

Listing A.3   Installing the Redis client libraries for Python on Linux

Download the setuptools ez_setup module.

```
~:$ wget -q http://peak.telecommunity.com/dist/ez_setup.py
~:$ sudo python ez_setup.py
Downloading http://pypi.python.org/packages/2.7/s/setuptools/...
[trimmed]
Finished processing dependencies for setuptools==0.6c11
~:$ sudo python -m easy_install redis hiredis
Searching for redis
[trimmed]
Finished processing dependencies for redis
```

Run the ez_setup module to download and install setuptools.

The redis package offers a somewhat standard interface to Redis from Python.

Run setuptools' easy_install package to install the redis and hiredis packages.

---

[1] Experienced Python users will ask "Why not pip?" which is another package for installing Python libraries. This is because virtualenv, which is necessary for the easy download of pip, is out of the scope of these instructions.

```
Searching for hiredis                            The hiredis package is a
[trimmed]                                        C accelerator library for
Finished processing dependencies for hiredis     the Python Redis library.
~:$
```

Now that you have the Python libraries installed, you can skip ahead to section A.4 to test Redis from Python, which should prepare you for all of the other chapters.

A.2 Installing on OS X

As is the case with other platforms, there are a few ways to download and install Redis and the Python Redis client library. In this section, we'll discuss the following:

1 Downloading, installing, and running Redis on OS X.
2 Installing the Redis client library for Python.

If you read the Linux section, you'll know that we made sure that the necessary tools for building Redis from scratch were available, because it was easy to do so. Though the installation of Xcode for OS X is a bit more difficult, the fact that the build tools download is 10 times larger makes following along without a long break much more difficult. As such, you'll use a method to install Redis that doesn't require a compiler.

To install Redis in OS X without using a compiler, you'll use a Python utility called *Rudix*, which installs precompiled binaries for a variety of software. Conveniently, as of this writing it includes an installer for the most recent version of Redis.

To download and install Rudix and Redis, you should open a Terminal. The Terminal application can be found in the Utilities group inside of Applications. After you've started the terminal, please follow along with the next listing to install Redis using Rudix.

Listing A.4   Installing Redis on OS X

Download the bootstrap script that installs Rudix.

```
~:$ curl -O http://rudix.googlecode.com/hg/Ports/rudix/rudix.py
[trimmed]
~:$ sudo python rudix.py install rudix
Downloading rudix.googlecode.com/files/rudix-12.10-0.pkg
[trimmed]
installer: The install was successful.
All done
~:$ sudo rudix install redis
Downloading rudix.googlecode.com/files/redis-2.6.9-0.pkg
[trimmed]
installer: The install was successful.
All done
~:$ redis-server
[699] 6 Feb 21:18:09 # Warning: no config file specified, using the
default config. In order to specify a config file use 'redis-server
/path/to/redis.conf'
[699] 6 Feb 21:18:09 * Server started, Redis version 2.6.9
```

Tell Rudix to install itself.

Tell Rudix to install Redis.

Start the Redis server.

Redis started and is running with the default configuration.

Rudix is downloading and installing itself.

Rudix is downloading and installing Redis.

Redis started and is running with the default configuration.

```
[699] 6 Feb 21:18:09 * The server is now ready to accept connections
on port 6379
[699] 6 Feb 21:18:09 - 0 clients connected (0 slaves), 922304 bytes
in use
```

Now that you've installed Redis, it's time to install the Redis client library for Python. You don't need to install Python, because OS X versions 10.6 and 10.7 come with either Python 2.6 or 2.7 preinstalled and available via python by default. While Redis is running in one terminal, open up a new tab (command + T), and follow along with the next listing to install the Python Redis library.

Listing A.5   Installing the Redis client library for Python on OS X

Because you have Rudix installed, you can install a Python package manager called pip.

```
~:$ sudo rudix install pip
Downloading rudix.googlecode.com/files/pip-1.1-1.pkg
[trimmed]
installer: The install was successful.
All done
~:$ sudo pip install redis
Downloading/unpacking redis
[trimmed]
Cleaning up...
~:$
```

Rudix is installing pip.

Pip is installing the Redis client library for Python.

You can now use pip to install the Python Redis client library.

If you read either of the Linux or Windows install instructions, you may have noticed that we used setuptools's easy_install method to install the Redis client library, but here you use pip. This is because Rudix offers a pip package, but doesn't have a setuptools package, so it was easier to install pip, and then use pip to install the Redis client library for Python instead of manually downloading and installing setuptools.

Also, if you read the installation instructions for Linux, you may have noticed that we installed the hiredis helper library there, but you don't install it on OS X. This is because, like before, you can't guarantee that users will have Xcode installed, so you'll use what you have available.

Now that you have the Redis Python library installed, you should skip ahead to section A.4 and follow along to use Redis from Python for the first time.

A.3   *Installing on Windows*

Before we get into how to install Redis on Windows, I'd like to point out that running Redis on Windows isn't recommended, for a variety of reasons. In this section we'll cover these points:

- Reasons why you shouldn't be running Redis on Windows.
- How to download, install, and run a precompiled Windows binary.
- How to download and install Python for Windows.
- How to install the Redis client library.

Our first step is to discuss why you shouldn't be running Redis on Windows.

A.3.1   *Drawbacks of Redis on Windows*

Windows doesn't support the `fork` system call, which Redis uses in a variety of situations to dump its database to disk. Without the ability to fork, Redis is unable to perform some of its necessary database-saving methods without blocking clients until the dump has completed.

Recently, Microsoft has contributed engineering time helping to address background saving issues, using threads to write to disk instead of a forked child process. As of this writing, Microsoft does have an alpha-stage branch of Redis 2.6, but it's only available as source, and Microsoft makes no guarantees as to its worthiness in production scenarios.

At least for the short term, there's an unofficial port of Redis by Dusan Majkic that offers precompiled binaries for Redis 2.4.5, but it has the previously mentioned issue that Redis blocks when dumping the database to disk.

> **COMPILING REDIS IN WINDOWS YOURSELF**   If you find yourself in the position of needing the most up-to-date version of Redis on Windows as possible, you'll need to compile Redis yourself. Your best option is to use Microsoft's official port (https://github.com/MSOpenTech/redis/), which requires Microsoft Visual Studio, though the free Express 2010 works just fine. If you choose to go this route, be warned that Microsoft makes no guarantees as to the fitness of their ports to Windows for anything except development and testing.

Now that you know the state of Redis on Windows, if you still want to run Redis on Windows, let's install it.

A.3.2   *Installing Redis on Windows*

You can download a moderately out-of-date precompiled version of Redis for 32-bit and 64-bit Windows thanks to Dusan Majkic from his GitHub page: https://github.com/dmajkic/redis/downloads. Go ahead and do that now.

After you download Redis, you'll need to extract the executables from the zip file. As long as you're using a version of Windows more recent than Windows XP, you should be able to extract Redis without any additional software. Do that now.

After you've extracted either the 32- or 64-bit version of Redis to a location of your choice (depending on your platform and preferences; remember that 64-bit Windows can run 32- or 64-bit Redis, but 32-bit Windows can only run 32-bit Redis), you can start Redis by double-clicking on the `redis-server` executable. After Redis has started, you should see a window similar to figure A.1.

Now that Redis is up and running, it's time to download and install Python.

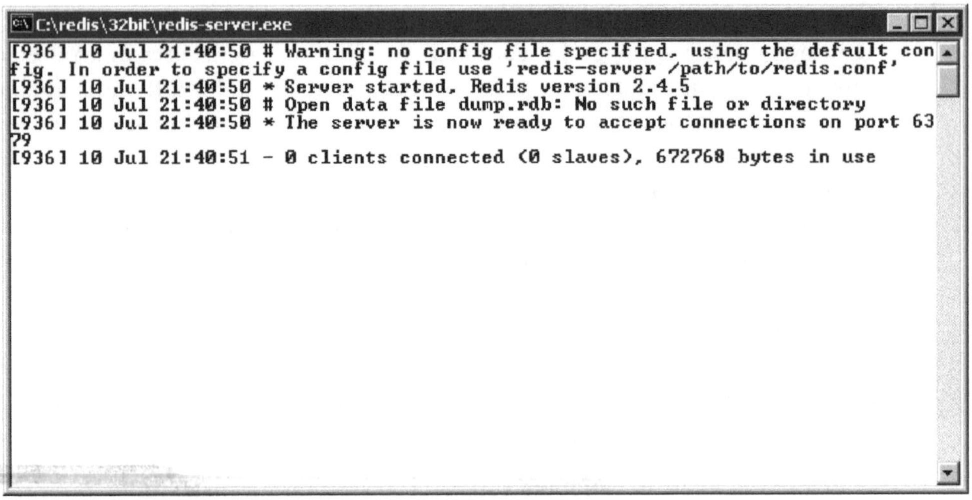

Figure A.1   Redis running in Windows

A.3.3   *Installing Python on Windows*

If you already have Python 2.6 or 2.7 installed, you're fine. If not, you'll want to download the latest version of Python 2.7, because that's the most recent version of Python that has support for the Redis library. Go to http://www.python.org/download/ and select the most recent version of the 2.7 series that's available for Windows in either the 32- or 64-bit version (again, depending on your platform). When Python is done downloading, you can install it by double-clicking on the downloaded .msi file.

Assuming that you accepted all of the default options for installing Python 2.7, Python should be installed in C:\Python27\. From here, you only need to install the Python Redis library to be ready to use Redis with Python. If you're using Python 2.6, any time the book refers to *Python27*, you can instead use *Python26*.

To help you to install the Redis client library, you'll use the easy_install utility from the setuptools package. This is because you can easily download setuptools from the command line. To get started, open a command prompt by going into the Accessories program group in the Start menu and clicking on Command Prompt. After you have a command prompt open, follow along with the next listing; it shows how to download and install setuptools and the Redis client library.

> **Listing A.6   Installing the Redis client library for Python on Windows**

Start Python
by itself in
interactive
mode.
```
C:\Users\josiah>c:\python27\python
Python 2.7.3 (default, Apr 10 2012, 23:31:26) [MSC v.1500 32 bit...
Type "help", "copyright", "credits" or "license" for more information.
>>> from urllib import urlopen
>>> data = urlopen('http://peak.telecommunity.com/dist/ez_setup.py')
```

Fetch a module that will help
you install other packages.

Import the urlopen factory
function from the urllib module.

```
>>> open('ez_setup.py', 'wb').write(data.read())
>>> exit()
```

Write the downloaded module to a file on disk.

Quit the Python interpreter by running the builtin exit() function.

```
C:\Users\josiah>c:\python27\python ez_setup.py
Downloading http://pypi.python.org/packages/2.7/s/setuptools/...
[trimmed]
Finished processing dependencies for setuptools==0.6c11
```

Run the ez_setup helper module.

```
C:\Users\josiah>c:\python27\python -m easy_install redis
Searching for redis
[trimmed]
Finished processing dependencies for redis
C:\Users\josiah>
```

The ez_setup helper downloads and installs setuptools, which will make it easy to download and install the Redis client library.

Use setuptools' easy_install module to download and install Redis.

Now that you have Python and the Redis client library installed, you should continue with section A.4 to use Redis from Python for the first time.

A.4   Hello Redis

After Redis itself is installed, you need to ensure that Python has the proper libraries for accessing Redis. If you followed the earlier instructions, you may still have a command prompt open. In this command prompt (you can open a new one if you closed the old one), you'll run Python. (Windows users can refer to how you ran Python during the setup procedure.) Inside of the Python console, you'll try connecting to Redis and issue a couple commands, as shown in the next listing.

Listing A.7   Testing Redis from Python

Import the redis library; it will automatically use the hiredis C accelerator library if it's available.

Start Python so that you can verify everything is up and running correctly.

```
~:$ python
Python 2.6.5 (r265:79063, Apr 16 2010, 13:09:56)
[GCC 4.4.3] on linux2
Type "help", "copyright", "credits" or "license" for more information.
>>> import redis
>>> conn = redis.Redis()                    Create a connection to Redis.
>>> conn.set('hello', 'world')
True
>>> conn.get('hello')
'world'
```

Set a value and see that it was set.

Get the value you just set.

RUNNING PYTHON IN OTHER WAYS   Though you can run Python in a standard terminal, there are a variety of other more "fully featured" ways to have a Python console available. A basic editor and console called Idle ships with Python on Windows and OS X; you can also install it on Linux (install the idle-python2.6 or idle-python2.7 package, as relevant). In a console, you can run python -m idlelib.idle from the command line, and Idle should load. Idle is a fairly basic editor and Python console itself, so if you're new to programming, it should be a gentle introduction. Many other people have found IPython to be the Python console of choice, offering a list of amazing features too long to mention here. Whether you go basic or fully featured, you can't go wrong.

REDIS ON OS X AND WINDOWS   Right now, precompiled versions of Redis for Windows and OS X are from the 2.4 series. In some chapters, we use features that are only available in the Redis 2.6 and later series. If you find that something we do doesn't work, and you're using Redis 2.4, it's probably because the feature or usage was added in Redis 2.6. See the notes in chapter 3 for specific examples.

CONFIGURING REDIS   By default, Redis should be configured to keep your data using either snapshots or append-only files, and as long as you execute shutdown on a client, Redis should keep your data around. Depending on how you started it, Redis may be keeping the on-disk version of data in the same path as the path you're running it from. To update that, you'll want to edit redis.conf and use system startup scripts appropriate for your platform (remember to move your data to the newly configured path). More information about configuring Redis is available in chapter 4.

IS HIREDIS AVAILABLE ON NON-LINUX PLATFORMS?   For those who are using Windows or OS X and peeked at the Debian/Ubuntu install instructions, you'll have noticed that we installed a library called hiredis to be used with Python. This library is an accelerator that passes protocol processing to a C library. Though this library can be compiled for OS X and Windows, binaries for them aren't readily downloadable on the internet. Also, because I didn't have you install a compiler, if you're interested in compiling and using hiredis on your platform, you're on your own.

Periodically in other chapters, we'll use the Python console to show interactions with Redis. In other cases, we'll show function definitions and executable statements outside of a console. In those cases where we're not using the console, it's assumed that those functions are defined in a Python module. If you haven't used Python before, you should read Python's tutorial on modules and running modules as programs in the first part of http://docs.python.org/tutorial/modules.html, up to and including the section "Executing modules as scripts."

If you're the kind of person who can read through language documentation and tutorials and just "get it," and you haven't spent a lot of time with Python in the past, you may want to consider going through the Python language tutorial at http://docs.python.org/tutorial/. If you're only interested in the important stuff where you'll learn the most about Python's syntax and semantics, read sections 3-7, and then 9.10 and 9.11 (which are about generators, which we use a couple of times).

By now you'll have Redis and a Python interpreter running. If you got here via a reference from chapter 1, go back to really start using Redis from Python.

If you're having difficulty installing Redis or Python, please post your questions or read others' answers on the *Redis in Action* Manning forum: http://mng.bz/vB6c.

appendix B
Other resources
and references

Over the last 11 chapters and appendix A, we've covered a variety of topics relating to Redis. As part of the problems that we solved, we introduced ideas that you may not have been familiar with and provided references for more information so that you can learn more.

This appendix gathers all of those references and more into a single location for easy access to other software, libraries, services, and/or documentation relating to the topics that we've covered, grouped by general topic.

B.1 Forums for help

These URLs will take you to forums where you can get help using Redis or with examples in other chapters:

- https://groups.google.com/forum/#!forum/redis-db—Redis forum
- http://www.manning-sandbox.com/forum.jspa?forumID=809—Manning forum for *Redis in Action*

B.2 Introductory topics

This list of introductory topics covers some of the basic information about Redis and its use:

- http://redis.io/—Main Redis web site
- http://redis.io/commands—Full Redis command listing
- http://redis.io/clients—Redis client listing
- http://redis.io/documentation—Main reference page for documentation about Lua, pub/sub, replication, persistence, and so on.

- http://github.com/dmajkic/redis/—Dusan Majkic's port of Redis to Windows
- http://github.com/MSOpenTech/redis/—Microsoft's official port of Redis to Windows

This list of introductory topics covers some of the basic information about Python and its use:

- http://www.python.org/—Main web page for the Python programming language
- http://docs.python.org/—Main Python documentation page
- http://docs.python.org/tutorial/—Python tutorial for new users
- http://docs.python.org/reference/—Python language reference for the full details on syntax and semantics
- http://mng.bz/TTKb—Generator expressions
- http://mng.bz/I31v—Python loadable Module tutorial
- http://mng.bz/9wXM—Defining functions
- http://mng.bz/q7eo—Variable argument lists
- http://mng.bz/1jLF—Variable arguments and keywords
- http://mng.bz/0rmB—List comprehensions
- http://mng.bz/uIdf—Python generators
- http://mng.bz/1XMr—Function and method decorators

B.3   *Queues and other libraries*

- http://celeryproject.org/—Python queue library that supports multiple back ends, including Redis
- https://github.com/josiahcarlson/rpqueue/—Python queue library for Redis only
- https://github.com/resque/resque—Standard Ruby + Redis queue
- http://www.rabbitmq.com/—Queue server for multiple languages
- http://activemq.apache.org/—Queue server for multiple languages
- https://github.com/Doist/bitmapist—Support for powerful bitmap-enabled analytics

B.4   *Data visualization and recording*

- http://www.jqplot.com/—Open source plotting library intended to be used with jQuery
- http://www.highcharts.com/—Free/commercial plotting library
- http://dygraphs.com/—Open source plotting library
- http://d3js.org/—General open source data visualization library
- http://graphite.wikidot.com/—Statistics gathering and visualization library

B.5   *Data sources*

In chapter 5, we used a database of IP-to-location information. This list includes a reference to that data, along with alternate data sources that may or may not be as up to date:

- http://dev.maxmind.com/geoip/geolite—IP address-to-geographic location information, first used in chapter 5
- http://www.hostip.info/dl/—Freely downloadable and usable IP-to-geographic location information database
- http://software77.net/geo-ip/—Another free IP-to-geographic location information database

B.6   *Redis experiences and articles*

- http://mng.bz/2ivv—An example architecture for cross-data-center Redis replication with compression
- http://mng.bz/LCgm—Real-time updates using Redis
- http://mng.bz/UgAD—Using Redis STRINGs to store some real-time metrics
- http://mng.bz/1OJ7—Instagram's experience storing many key-value pairs in Redis
- http://mng.bz/X564—A brief summary of some problems where Redis shines, some of which we covered in previous chapters
- http://mng.bz/oClc—Sharding data into Redis at Craigslist
- http://mng.bz/07kX—An example of Redis being used in multiple parts of a stack that syncs photos between phones and desktops
- http://mng.bz/4dgD—One way that Disqus uses Redis in production
- http://mng.bz/21iE—Using Redis to store RSS feed information
- http://mng.bz/L254—Early example using Redis LISTs as storage for recent filtered Twitter messages

index

F